Children of World War II

Children of World War II

The Hidden Enemy Legacy

Edited by
Kjersti Ericsson and Eva Simonsen

Oxford • New York

English edition
First published in 2005 by
Berg
Editorial offices:
First Floor, Angel Court, 81 St Clements Street, Oxford OX4 1AW, UK
175 Fifth Avenue, New York, NY 10010, USA

Berg is the imprint of Oxford International Publishers Ltd.

Library of Congress Cataloging-in-Publication Data
Children of World War II : the hidden enemy legacy / edited by Kjersti
Ericsson and Eva Simonsen.
    p. cm.
Includes bibliographical references and index.
ISBN 1-84520-207-4 (pbk.)—ISBN 1-84520-206-6 (cloth)
1. World War, 1939-1945--Children. 2. Children of Nazis. 3.
Lebensborn e.V. (Germany) 4. World War, 1939-1945—Occupied
territories. I. Title: Children of World War Two. II. Title: Children
of World War 2. III. Ericsson, Kjersti. IV. Simonsen, Eva, 1946-

    D810.C4C527 2005
    940.53'161—dc22   2005013802

British Library Cataloguing-in-Publication Data
A catalogue record for this book is available from the British Library.

ISBN-13 978 1 84520 206 4 (Cloth)
           978 1 84520 207 1 (Paper)

ISBN-10 1 84520 206 6 (Cloth)
           1 84520 207 4 (Paper)

Typeset by Avocet Typeset, Chilton, Aylesbury, Bucks
Printed in the United Kingdom by Biddles Ltd, King's Lynn.

www.bergpublishers.com

Contents

Preface   vii

Introduction   1
Kjersti Ericsson

Part I: North   13

1   Under the Care of Lebensborn: Norwegian War Children and
their Mothers   15
Kåre Olsen

2   War, Cultural Loyalty and Gender: Danish Women's Intimate
Fraternization   35
Anette Warring

3   Silences, Public and Private   53
Arne Øland

4   Meant to be Deported   71
Lars Borgersrud

5   Life Stories of Norwegian War Children   93
Kjersti Ericsson and Dag Ellingsen

Part II: West   113

6   Ideology and the Psychology of War Children in Franco's
Spain, 1936–1945   115
Michael Richards

7   Enfants de Boches: The War Children of France   138
Fabrice Virgili

8   Stigma and Silence: Dutch Women, German Soldiers and
their Children   151
Monika Diederichs

Part III: East   165

9   Between Extermination and Germanization: Children of
German Men in the 'Occupied Eastern Territories', 1942–1945   167
Regina Mühlhäuser

10   Race, Heredity and Nationality: Bohemia and Moravia,
1939–1945   190
Michal Šimůnek

Part IV: Germany   211

11   A Topic for Life: Children of German Lebensborn Homes   213
Dorothee Schmitz-Köster

12   *Besatzungskinder* and *Wehrmachtskinder*: Germany's War
Children   229
Ebba D. Drolshagen

13   Black German 'Occupation' Children: Objects of Study in
the Continuity of German Race Anthropology   249
Yara-Colette Lemke Muniz de Faria

Epilogue   267

14   Children in Danger: Dangerous Children   269
Eva Simonsen

Index   287

Preface

The prelude to this book is Norwegian: In the autumn of 2001 a research project was started on Norwegian 'war children', i.e. children born during World War II, with Norwegian mothers and fathers from the German occupying forces. The research was financed by the Ministry of Social Affairs and the Ministry of Children and Family Affairs, and implemented as a part of the Research Programme on Welfare Research by the Research Council of Norway. A group of four researchers, Lars Borgersrud, Dag Ellingsen, Kjersti Ericsson and Eva Simonsen, were commissioned to do the work.

The Norwegian authorities were not motivated by sheer historical interest to launch war children as a field of research. The war children themselves, through their organizations, had been active in raising the issue. They demanded that light should be thrown on dubious actions in the past on the part of government officials, professionals and others, and that injustices committed should be read-dressed. Without this impetus, the research would hardly have been initiated. We are grateful to the Norwegian children of war for being instrumental in making this book possible.

As part of the research, it was decided to initiate a European network of researchers working on related issues. If this had been attempted only five years earlier, the catch would probably have been quite meagre. In all of Europe, the topic of children of German soldiers and native women has been shrouded in silence. Now, however, the timing seemed just right. Sixty years after the end of World War II, some research is at last under way. The 'children' themselves have also started to tell their stories. The research and the autobiographical testimonies are clearly not independent occurrences.

We managed to make several valuable contacts, and the research network materialized. Two international workshops were arranged in Oslo, Norway; the first in November 2002, the second in November 2003. The discussions were lively and fruitful and produced a tangible result: this book.

We are grateful to the Norwegian Ministry of Social Affairs, the Ministry of Children and Family Affairs and the Research Council of Norway for financing the workshops that made this book possible. Dag Ellingsen has received additional financial support from the Norwegen Non-fiction Literature Fund. It should, however, be emphasized that not all the contributing researchers have had the financial support and conditions of work from which the Norwegian group has benefited. Funding is not easily available for this kind of research, and some have had to do their work partly or wholly without remuneration. This book is a result not only of scholarship but also of idealism and personal commitment. We would also like to thank Hege Wolleng, our very competent and efficient secretary, who has done an excellent job in organizing the last workshop and in helping us prepare the manuscript for publishing.

Kjersti Ericsson and Eva Simonsen

Introduction

Wars go on for a long time after armistices have been declared or peace treaties signed. Traumatic war experiences are not easily overcome, and the bitter divisions which wars create may be beyond conciliation. Wars have repercussions in the lives of the next generation as well. Children with no personal experience of war may nonetheless have to cope with the traumas of their parents. The wartime reputation of the parents may stick to the children, forcing upon them the identity of daughter of a hero or son of a traitor.

This book is about one group of people for whom the war seems to have lasted until this day. Sixty years have elapsed since the end of World War II. Only now, their stories are beginning to emerge in several European countries.

The war did not only take lives, it also created lives. But for the war, the people who are the subjects of this book would not exist. They were born during or shortly after the German occupation. The fathers belonged to the German forces, the mothers to the native population of the occupied countries. The life course and personal experience of these children have been deeply affected by this contingent constellation of parents, and the meaning given to this particular constellation by society. The children grew up enveloped in public and private silence. This silence, however, was not a void or a blank. It was filled with meaning: a silence of shame and guilt. Somehow, these children were simultaneously invisible and too visible. In many countries, silence still reigns. In others, the children's existence and fate is only now reaching public consciousness.

Children of German fathers and mothers from an occupied country are the main subjects of this book. However, we have also included chapters on the children of the prelude and the aftermath to World War II. The prelude was the Spanish civil war. The children of the losing side were regarded as dangerous and depraved by the Franco regime. The aftermath was the Allied occupation of Germany. This occupation also produced children. The most visible among them, who caused most concern, were the children of German mothers and US soldiers of African-American origin. In spite of differences, there are striking parallels between the ways all three groups of children were regarded and treated by authorities, professionals and lay people in their respective countries.

From the stories of the children unfold not only painful personal experience but also a series of issues only now coming under scholarly scrutiny as part of the history of World War II.

One such issue concerns the dark sides of the war against Nazism. In the name of anti-Nazism and liberation, not only acts of heroism but also acts of cruelty and vengeance were committed. The attitudes expressed toward those who were seen to belong to the enemy camp might in some instances have a chilling resemblance to the mentality of the Nazis. This is not at all surprising. The societies participating on the Allied side were by no means free from racism and oppression. Neither was the ideological climate in the Allied countries entirely untouched by ideas similar to those which gained hegemony in Nazi Germany. One should in no way minimize the difference between these societies and the extreme violence and inhumanity of the Nazi regime. To preserve the myth of an unblemished war against Nazism, however, one would have to exclude much painful experience from history, and silence many voices. Among them are the voices of the subjects of this book.

Another issue concerns the policies pursued, in Nazi Germany and in its opponents, to strengthen the population in numbers and quality. Mothers and the children they bear are the targets of such policies. Children may be conceived as the riches of a nation. However, they may also be seen as liabilities, if they are 'foreign' nationally or racially, or 'defective' in other ways. The Norwegian historian Kari Melby[1] has pointed out the need to reformulate the subject of political history: 'Not only 'wars and kings' but also body, sex – and women – have been the objects of political action.' To body, sex and women we could safely add children. Few topics are better suited to illustrate Melby's statement than the one treated in this book.

A third issue, related to the previous one, concerns gender, nation and war. In the first heated days of liberation, women who were known to have had sexual relations with enemy soldiers were subjected to humiliating reprisals by their compatriots. In several European countries, these women had to bear the brunt of the popular rage against the former occupant. Hate and resentment lingered on for years, and abusive names, like 'German sluts', stuck to the women. Their children could hardly escape being affected. The context of this treatment must be sought in the conception of female sexuality as a national resource, which should not be treacherously offered to the enemy.

A fourth issue concerns scientific and professional attitudes toward the children who are the subjects of this book, and their mothers. The sinister role played by members of the medical profession in Nazi Germany, weeding out 'inferior' lives, is well known. The role of medical doctors and other professional experts in post-war Europe was a far cry from that of their Nazi colleagues. There was, however, an important political aspect to the task they set out to solve: to safeguard democracy and social stability, they were to identify deviants and defective minds, applying measures of treatment, correction and/or institutionalization. In some countries, children of German soldiers and native women were seen as obvious targets for the professional gaze.

The last, but not least important issue concerns lived experience, as presented in the personal testimonies and narratives of the children. In a way, lived experience sums up all the other issues, from the people who had to bear the consequences, of the hate and vengeance inherent in a grand and just war, of being alternately constructed as assets and dangers, of the stigma impressed on their mothers, of the diagnostic zeal of the professionals. More often than not, the resulting experience was that of being 'other'.

If this book has an overarching topic, it is just the construction of 'the other'. The chapters are discussing various aspects of this construction, in different national contexts. They are ordered by geography: five chapters on Northern Europe, three chapters on Western Europe, two chapters on Eastern Europe and lastly three chapters on post-war Germany and the German perspective on the children who resulted from war and occupations. However, the central topics of the book cut across both chapters and geography, as outlined below.

Dark Stains

In the minds of most people, World War II was not only a war over territories, resources and narrow national interests. Central to the image of this war is the fight against Nazism and Fascism as ideologies and systems. World War II is represented as a war over ideas and values, good pitted against evil. This special quality gave an added impetus to a process by no means exclusive to World War II: that of demonizing the enemy. The diabolical Nazi image rubbed off on everybody seen as associated with the Germans, even small children. The (hopefully isolated) episodes related in the chapter on Netherlands by Diederichs, where babies of Dutch mothers and German fathers were battered to death, demonstrate extreme consequences of this mechanism. There is a painful paradox here: By demonizing the enemy and everybody with the slightest connection to the Nazis, one risked violating the ideals which were the motivating force behind the struggle against them. In her book on the Danish women who had liaisons with Germans during the occupation, the Danish historian Anette Warring states: 'In the retribution against the women, undemocratic, half racist, and especially sexist attitudes and methods were reproduced, methods that in many ways were more similar to the Nazism one opposed than to the ideals of freedom that were embodied in the struggle of resistance'.[2] As will be demonstrated in several chapters in this book, Warring's statement has some relevance also beyond the Danish context.

The enormous sufferings caused to millions and millions of people by the Nazi occupation, and the sacrifices to be made in order to crush the Nazi regime, makes the fierce hatred directed against everybody seen as connected to the Nazis under-standable, if not always excusable. However, the war experience of the peoples of Europe varied widely. The war took its toll also in a country like Norway. Jews were deported and murdered in concentration camps. Resistance members were tortured, imprisoned and executed. Civilians suffered many kinds of privations. The northern counties were burnt down and totally destroyed, the population evac-uated by force. Nevertheless, what Norway (and Denmark even more so) had to suffer is in no way comparable to the ravages of the war in countries like Poland, Yugoslavia or the Soviet Union.

Is it possible to spot a relation between the harshness of a country's war experi-ence and the post-war fate of its children of German fathers and their mothers? As yet, too little is known to answer such a question. Or should one be so bold as to interpret the extent to which silence reigns as a sign of the painfulness of the issue? If so, the countries of Eastern Europe which suffered most from the war still have problems, not only with coming to terms with, but even *speaking* of women who chose Germans as sexual partners, and of their offspring. To speak of them would perhaps introduce an intolerable false note in the grand theme of suffering, resist-ance and victory. The scantiness of material on the Eastern European situation in this book may be a reflection of this.

In the countries where we *do* know something about the fate of the women and their children, there is no easily visible link between the treatment they received and the amount of suffering the country endured from war and occupation. There seems to have been several uses to which the women could be put. In a 'non-heroic' nation like Denmark with a need to demonstrate patriotic zeal in the last part of the war, the resistance picked the women as suitable targets in an effort to mobilize the population into a broader uprising against the occupant, as shown in Warring's chapter in this book. In Diederichs' chapter on the Netherlands, it is described how the women had their hair shorn at liberation. The women were used as scapegoats to prevent a general day of reckoning, Diederichs states. These two examples demonstrate that the women could be put to opposite uses: In Denmark, the resentment against them was channelled to boost rebellion. In the Netherlands, the scissors were employed to stave off 'a night of long knives' – an uncontrollable popular justice against all kinds of collaborators.

Children as Riches and Liabilities

From the pre-war years on, most countries pursued some kind of population policy, distinguishing between the worthless and the valuable, between what was to be hindered and what was to be furthered. The extreme case is the double face of the Nazi racial policy: the extermination camp and the Lebensborn maternity home.

Mothers in occupied countries who bore children with German fathers were treated in accordance with Nazi racial policy. War and conquest created a need for new Germans. In his chapter, Kåre Olsen quotes the Nazi slogan stating that 'the victory in the battlefield must be succeeded by the victory of the cradle'. To be considered a victory, however, the child in the cradle had to be Aryan. In the occupied countries, the crucial question was whether the mothers were considered racially valuable or not. The policy varied in relation to different territories. The racial qualities of the populations of Norway, Denmark and the Netherlands were evaluated positively, while the populations of most of the occupied parts of Eastern Europe were seen as racially worthless. France was placed in an intermediate position.

In 'racially valuable' areas, it was important to supply maternity homes and financial support for mothers of children with German fathers. As Kåre Olsen describes, the SS organization Lebensborn took on this task in some parts of Europe, most successfully in Norway. In the Netherlands it was not the SS, but another Nazi organization, NSV, filling this role (see Diederichs in Chapter 8). The attitude toward rape, as reflected in court-martial decisions, was an inverted expression of the supposed 'value' of women from different nations: While rape of native women in the Eastern territories was treated leniently, soldiers who raped women in Northern occupied countries were severely punished.[3] The age-old dichotomy of Madonna and whore was here given a 'racial' interpretation: The 'Aryan' women of the North had the makings of a worthy mother in them. They must not be violated, and should be supported in bearing children. The 'Slav' women of the East, on the other hand, were both worthless as prospective mothers and with no sexual honour worth defending.

The need for new Germans, however, made the Nazis think twice. Mühlhäuser, demonstrates in Chapter 9 the ambiguous attitude of the Nazis to children born as the result of relations between German soldiers and native women in Eastern Europe. With partly 'Aryan' blood, such children were seen on the one hand as a possible population resource for Germany. On the other hand, it was feared that an influx of 'superior' blood would strengthen the enemy. Also, there existed ideas that 'half-breeds' were particularly noxious.

If children were seen as assets, it was important to make them national property. This is clearly demonstrated by Šimůnek in Chapter 10 on the Czech case. Ardent efforts were made to turn children of mixed Czech-German marriages into Germans through upbringing and education. Nationality clearly was not only a question of 'blood', but also of culture. Virgili, in Chapter 7 on France, relates how both France and Germany wanted to claim the children of German fathers and mothers from Normandy, whose population was deemed racially acceptable by Nazi standards. At liberation the issue of children as the property of the nation was again addressed. Their nationality was contested, and so was their status as assets or liabilities. Should one grab them or get rid of them? As Diederichs describes in

Chapter 8, the actions of the Dutch Government threatened to place the children in a limbo, making them stateless. In France, it was felt that the children belonged to France, and the authorities feared that a large number of French women with children by Germans had been transported into Germany during the war. The long-standing natalist preoccupation of the French authorities may have made them anxious not to lose any of 'their' children to other nations (see Virgili in Chapter 7). Also Spain, after the Civil War, wanted the refugee children of Republican parents back, and implemented a repatriation campaign which may also be described as a kidnapping campaign (see Richards in Chapter 6). In Norway, on the other hand, the question of whether the children ought to be deported to Germany 'where they did belong' was seriously raised and discussed (see Borgersrud in Chapter 4). Neither was Norway very eager to get back Norwegian children who had been moved to Germany during the war. Their German blood made them nationally 'foreign' and of dubious value to the Norwegian nation.

The quantity and quality of children was a question of political importance, both during the war and afterward. However, the children of German fathers and native mothers were not necessarily made a public issue on this account. After liberation, countries seem to have differed on this point. Norway was special, perceiving itself as burdened by a serious 'war-child problem' which merited a Government-appointed War Child Committee. The committee put forward its recommendations and proposed an act of law. Even if many of the Committee's recommendations were not acted on, and no war-child act was ever passed, this whole process con-tributed strongly to the construction of children of German fathers and Norwegian mothers as a separate category and a social problem.

In no other country did the 'war-child problem' get similar public attention. The Netherlands had its controversy on the question of fatherhood, which put the chil-dren on the public agenda for a while. In France, the children were mainly con-sidered a private issue. To Germany, the vast number of children by German soldiers and women from occupied countries was no issue at all. These children, who received such ample attention from the Nazi regime, now became invisible, and mostly still are. As Drolshagen points out in Chapter 12, no German name existed for the '*enfants de Boches*', '*tyskerunger*', '*moeffenkinder*' and others. In contrast to the '*Wehrmachtskinder*' (Drolshagen's suggested term), the children of German women and African-American Soldiers from the Allied occupying forces were sharply visible – and became the subject of intense debate and special meas-ures (see Muniz de Faria in Chapter 13).

When the quantity and quality of children and their nationality is at stake, the family institution is drawn into the political orbit. The quality of parents as breeders and educators has to be checked, whether quality is interpreted in racial, national or political terms. The fact that Hitler reserved for himself the privilege of sanctioning marriages between members of the German forces and women from some of the occupied countries attests to their political importance. The acute political significance which marriages may acquire in times of war is also demonstrated by Šimůnek in Chapter 10 on the ethnically mixed Czech territories. Choice of marriage partners became entangled in the conflict between German expansionism and Czech nationalism. After the war, Norwegian women who married their German partners and moved to Germany with them (their only option if they wanted to live with their husbands) were deprived of their Norwegian citizenship (see Borgersrud in Chapter 4).

State intervention in family life took many forms. Both the Nazi and the Vichy regime of France strongly prescribed traditional family roles in the face of circumstances hardly favouring such a model. After the Civil War, the Franco regime took steps to amend the 'crisis' of the Spanish family, seen as caused by the political ideas of the Republicans. In Norway after liberation, the maternal qualifications of mothers of children with German fathers were strongly questioned. A tightened control and intervention by the Child Welfare authorities was advocated. The political significance of the family points to important issues of gender and nation.

Gender, Nation and War

As Capdevila et al. have demonstrated in the case of France,[4] wars have contradictory effects on gender relations. On the one hand, wars may destabilize traditional practices and discourses. Women may, by choice or necessity, fill positions vacated by men, positions hitherto considered incompatible with their sex. The violent upheavals, the strain and insecurity of everyday life may make the social norms of 'normal' times seem less relevant and binding, with consequences also for sexual behaviour. Wars make new demands on and offer new opportunities to both sexes, with resultant disturbances in power relations.

On the other hand, a tightening of the norms of gender-appropriate behaviour and an obsession with the sexual morals of women often follows in the wake of wars. Men are called upon to exhibit the manly virtues which the role of soldier or resistance fighter demands. Women are expected to tend to the hearth and remain faithful to absent husbands and boyfriends. The sexuality of women takes on an urgent significance: sexuality become not only a question of decency and virtue, but also a question of national honour and survival. The reproductive capacity of women and traditional motherhood are regarded as national resources. As actual and prospective mothers, women play a decisive role in the biological and cultural reproduction of the nation. In this perspective, sexual relations between native women and enemy soldiers constitute a national threat. Women who enter into such relations are offenders against both sexual and national norms (see Warring in Chapter 2).

Writing on the Algerian war of liberation from France, Franz Fanon[5] attributes a sexualized imagery of imperialist conquest to the French: The hoped-for surrender of Algeria is imagined in terms such as 'the flesh of Algeria laid bare', 'accepting the rape of the colonizer'. Fanon is not alone in employing metaphors of this kind. War and sex are often used as metaphors for each other, a fact attesting to the important link between them: When women are 'conquered' sexually by the enemy, the whole nation is at stake. Women who voluntarily enter into sexual relations with enemy soldiers are not only morally 'loose', but also traitorous. Children born from such relations may be considered a threat, as bearers of a foreign national essence.

During and after World War II, women who had consorted with the occupant were made to feel the force of such conceptions. The widespread practice of hair-shearing served as a sexualized and shame-inducing punishment many women had to suffer. It is notable that this kind of punishment was also meted out to women who supported the Republican side in the Spanish Civil War. The shearing of hair as a sexualized form of punishment has been interpreted as signifying women as national territory. A male enemy is eliminated, through death or imprisonment. Victory over a female enemy, however, does not take the form of destruction but of re-conquest. One function of the shearing of hair is to symbolize this re-conquest.[6] The names given to women having liaisons with Germans – '*moeffenmeiden*', '*tyskertøser*' and others – marked them as territory traitorously surrendered to the enemy.

Their children risked being doubly stigmatized, not only as 'bastards' – sons and daughters of women of easy virtue – but also as '*German* bastards'. The reputation of the mother sometimes 'rubbed off' on her daughter, who from an early age might be regarded as morally dubious and sexually available, at worst an easily targeted victim of sexual abuse (see Ericsson and Ellingsen in Chapter 5).

Scientific and Professional Attitudes

To the professional and scientific eye, the losers of the war were not simply losers of the war. Discourses were produced translating political and social contradictions into individual pathology. Psychiatrists and other professionals took on the task of diagnosis and remedy. The mothers of children with German fathers might be suspected of being depraved, mentally disturbed and/or feeble-minded, and in danger of passing on their deficiencies to their offspring by biological and social inheritance. The children were seen as both in danger and dangerous, in need of the double intervention of care and control. The Norwegian War Child Committee saw the need for a thorough psychiatric examination of both mothers and children, so that their treatment would rest on a solid scientific base. The objectives of the planned treatment – installing the correct national and political attitudes and abating psychological pathology – were viewed as integrated, two sides of a coin.

In Norway, the grand plans were never carried out. However, the ideas behind them were not home-made. They were part of international currents of thought, which spread through conferences attended by experts from many parts of the world. The millions and millions of war-damaged children in Europe were on the agenda. If not handled properly, according to correct principles of education and mental hygiene, the psychological development of these children might become stunted, with delinquency or proneness to support undemocratic ideologies as the result. An associated concern was to spot and weed out, by institutionalization or other means of control, children who, because of congenital defects, were seen as a threat to the reconstruction of society and democratic institutions. It was a question of 'making the mind safe for democracy' as a contemporary slogan put it (see the Epilogue by Simonsen).

In Franco's Spain a similar juxtaposition of political attitudes and mental pathology was motivating the programmes directed at women who had supported the Republican side during the Civil War, and children of Republican parents. In the Spanish case, however, *anti-Fascist* attitudes were diagnosed as manifestations of delinquent, depraved or deficient minds, in need of education, control and correction. While UNESCO was anxious to 'make the mind safe for democracy', one could perhaps say that the Franco regime directed similar efforts at 'making the mind safe for dictatorship'.

After its brutal implementation by the Nazi regime, it is easy to forget that eugenics was never an exclusively Nazi doctrine or practice. Before World War II, light or heavy versions of eugenics were scientifically respectable on both sides of the Atlantic, informing social policy, legislation on sterilization and immigration regulations. What is striking is the continuity in pre- and post-war ideas in this field. How may the tenacity of eugenic ideas, in the face of shocking exposures of Nazi practices, be explained?

Persons may be one reason: The most influential and prestigious experts in the post-war years had usually been trained, and had formed their professional convictions, before the war. Their habits of thought were not easily changed. An illuminating example is a famous Norwegian psychiatrist, Johan Scharffenberg, who was an ardent spokesman for strong eugenic measures both before and after the war. Scharffenberg could by no means be labelled a Nazi. On the contrary, he was something of a war hero. Scharffenberg was one of the first to rally the Norwegian population to resist the occupant regime. With great personal courage, he launched this appeal in a public speech. To Scharffenberg, his anti-Nazism and his professional opinions seem to have been locked in separate compartments.

It should also be remembered that the Nazi brand of eugenics were widely discredited in scientific circles, even before the war. Few scientific experts rejected eugenic ideas and measures in principle. However, many repudiated the Nazi brand and other extreme versions as resting on scientifically invalid claims. If eugenic measures were carried out in accordance with what they considered to be scientifically valid, these experts had no objections. After the war, they may have felt that the disclosure of the Nazi atrocities was in no way relevant to their own beliefs.

A last point may be the general attraction of biological explanations to human behaviour and social problems. After the war, eugenic ideas were successively contested by other paradigms, stressing nurture more than nature. However, biological explanations of one kind or another have repeatedly made comebacks. Today's fascination with genes causing everything from suicide to infidelity is a case in point.

An informative example of the pre- and post-war continuity of ideas is given by Muniz de Faria in Chapter 13 on children of German women and African-American soldiers, the so-called '*Mischlinge*', who became objects of much attention and concern. Muniz de Faria demonstrates how conceptions of race from early German anthropology were reproduced in examinations and scientific studies of these children. In Spain, a special brand of Catholic eugenics influenced the treatment of women and children from the Republican side. In Norway there were popular fears that the 'German' biological heritage of the children would make them inclined to marching and commandeering. In scientific and professional circles, however, 'the chromosomes of the mother of easy virtue', to quote a medical expert, caused more worry. After the war, as a painful irony of history, children who by Nazi racial doctrines were exalted as exceptionally valuable had their value inverted because of related eugenic ideas.

Lived Experience

What happened after the first heated period of liberation resembles a conspiracy of silence. More than a conspiracy, however, it was a convergence of interests, private and public (see Øland in Chapter 3). The mothers had their reasons for trying to hide the shameful relation which had resulted in a child. Whether they kept the child or gave it up for adoption or institutional care, the paternity was more often than not tabooed. The authorities also had their reasons for the maintenance of silence: stability of family life, preventing continued contacts between native women and former enemies, protecting the children from harassment, covering up the national shame. In wartime France, the Vichy authorities granted women the right to give birth and give the child away in total anonymity. Children born under such circumstances would never learn the identity of their parents. After the war, an appeal was issued to former prisoners of war to legitimize children conceived and born in their absence, and to forgive their unfaithful wives. In Norway, after the first exposure and discussion on deportation of the children, a policy of invisibility was adopted. Among other measures, it was recommended that German-sounding names be changed into unambiguously Norwegian ones. In Denmark, the identity of a considerable number of German fathers was lost through sheer sloppiness, when only part of the German paternity records were secured by the Danish authorities. Later even these incomplete records seem to have vanished.

Many children of native women and German soldiers are probably still ignorant of their origins. Many learn the truth only upon the death of their adoptive parents. Legislation preventing the children from access to relevant archives and their own histories was in several instances not amended until the children were well into middle age.

However, the silence surrounding the origin of the children was not impenetrable. Hints and innuendo often slipped through, creating doubts and uneasy questions in the minds of the children, questions the family often refused to answer, even if the children dared to pose them. One reason for keeping the facts of the paternity of the children a secret was to protect the children from harassment. Frequently, however, silence proved an ineffective strategy in this respect. Many children experienced abuse, stigmatization and rejection. Confusion and problems of identity might follow in the wake of secrecy. The silence also deprived the children of the chance to learn to know their fathers and other relatives in Germany. In Franco's Spain a similar strategy of silence was adopted, keeping Republican children from learning what had happened to their parents.

Personal testimonies from Denmark, France, the Netherlands and Norway focus on the topics of silence, shame and guilt. For many of these children, shame came before knowledge. The family did not always prove to be a haven in a heartless world. As living tokens of the guilt of their mothers, destroying her life by being born, the children sensed their precarious position. The traumas of the mothers frequently affected the relationship between mother and child, making it strained and filled with conflicting emotions.

Learning about the Nazi atrocities at school, many children experienced strong feelings of guilt, as if their birth implicated them in the brutal actions of the Nazi regime. 'Such children carried the weight of the German guilt on their tiny shoulders', to quote Virgili in Chapter 7 of this book. With the political sign reversed, children of Spanish Republicans were made to feel guilty on behalf of *their* parents. The parallels to the feelings and experiences of the German Lebensborn children (see Schmitz-Koester in Chapter 11) are also striking. Born in a Lebensborn institution, under the sign of the SS, they feel forever tainted by the crimes of the Nazi regime.

Sixty years after the end of the war, the process of breaking the silence and coming to terms with often painful experiences is under way in several countries. This should not be a process exclusively on a personal level. The societies where the children grew up and are now approaching old age should use this opportunity to examine and reflect on certain aspects of their wartime and post-war history: how did it happen that in the wake of a grand and heroic war, fought for humanistic ideals, small children were made into enemies and constructed as 'others' in ways marking them for life? An examination and reflection of this kind will not in the least of ways detract from the gratitude and reverence which the struggle against Nazism merits. On the contrary, such a process of reflection will be in tune with the finest legacy of that struggle. We hope that this book may serve as a contribution.

Notes

1. Kari Melby, 'Husmorens epoke. 1900–1950', in I. Blom and S. Sogner (eds), *Med kjønnsperspektiv på norsk historie: Fra vikingtid til 2000–årsskiftet* (Cappelen Akademisk Forlag, 1999), p. 257.
2. Anette Warring, *Tyskerpiger under besættelse og retsopgør* (Gyldendal Forlag, 1994), p. 203.
3. Birgit Beck, 'Rape: The Military Trials of Sexual Crimes Committed by Soldiers in the Wehrmacht, 1939–1944', in K. Hagemann and S. Schüler-Springorum (eds), *Home/Front: The Military, War and Gender in Twentieth-Century Germany* (Berg, 2002), pp. 255–73.
4. Luc Capdevila, François Rouquet, Fabrice Virgili and Danièle Voldman, *Hommes et femmes dans la France en Guerre (1914–1945)* (Éditions Payot & Rivages, 2003).
5. Franz Fanon, 'Algeria Unveiled', in F. Fanon, *Studies in a Dying Colonialism* (Earthscan Publications, 1989, English edn), p. 42.
6. Fabrice Virgili, *La France 'virile': Des femmes tondues à la libération* (Payot, 2000), p. 279.

References

Beck, B., 'Rape: The Military Trials of Sexual Crimes Committed by Soldiers in the Wehrmacht, 1939–1944', in K. Hagemann and S. Schüler-Springorum (eds), *Home/Front: The Military, War and Gender in Twentieth-Century Germany*, Oxford, New York: Berg, 2002.

Capdevila, L., Rouquet, F., Virgili, F. and Voldman, D., *Hommes et femmes dans la France en Guerre (1914–1945)*, Paris: Éditions Payot & Rivages, 2003.

Fanon, F., 'Algeria Unveiled', in F. Fanon, *Studies in a Dying Colonialism*, London: Earthscan Publications, 1989, English edn.

Melby, K., 'Husmorens epoke: 1900–1950', in I. Blom and S. Sogner (eds), *Med kjønnsperspektiv på norsk historie: Fra vikingtid til 2000–årsskiftet*, Oslo: Cappelen Akademisk Forlag, 1999.

Virgili, F., *La France 'virile'. Des femmes tondues à la libération*, Paris: Payot, 2000.

Warring, A., *Tyskerpiger: under besættelse og retsopgør*, Copenhagen: Gyldendal, 1994.

Part I

North

–1–

Under the Care of Lebensborn:
Norwegian War Children and their Mothers

Kåre Olsen

The SS organization Lebensborn was established before the war as an instrument in the Nazi racial policy, for furthering the birth of 'Aryan' children. During the war, the organization tried to get a foothold in several occupied countries. Their only success story was Norway, with a population considered to be of special value according to Nazi standards. This chapter presents the Lebensborn organization and its activities in a number of European countries. Encounters between the racial ideology of Lebensborn and the political and social realities in places where the organization sought to implement its ideas are explored.

The Lebensborn in Norway developed extensive activities with solid organizations, numerous institutions and employees. The Norwegian case is being examined in more depth in order to bring out the character and tragic consequences of racial and political elitism of this kind.

The Norwegian case may throw some light on more general aspects of the fate of war children and their mothers during the war and its aftermath. After liberation, these women and children were also singled out for attention, but with the nature of that attention reversed: formerly highly valued, they were now suspected of being deficient, both intellectually and morally. Included in this chapter is the story of how the women and children were treated by Norwegian authorities and the public at large when the war was over and their former protectors out of power.

The Lebensborn Organization

The SS organization Lebensborn e.V. was established in 1935.[1] The term 'Lebensborn' means 'well of life', implying that the main objective of the organization was to strengthen the Aryan race. The primary Lebensborn strategy was to raise the racial standard of the German population. The intention was to make the organization a powerful agent in the realization of the Nazi racial policy in the Third Reich by helping to increase the number of births of 'racially valuable' children in the German population. The Lebensborn part of the racial policy of the SS was the inverse of the other side of that policy: genocide against other groups in the population. The objective, however, was quite similar: the improvement of the quality of the population by strengthening the 'Aryan' and the 'Nordic' component in the nation. 'Nordic' was used in a racial, not geographical, sense.

In order to increase the birth rate of Germany in the 1930s, the Lebensborn organization advocated the birth of children born out of wedlock. Heinrich Himmler and the SS envisioned the Lebensborn as the saviour of at least 100,000 children from abortion every year. Unwed mothers were offered protection and the opportunity of anonymous delivery. Lebensborn maternity homes were launched in Germany. Here pregnant women could stay until the babies had been born. Births might be registered in secret, and the Lebensborn gave some economic support for mothers and arranged adoptions.

With the outbreak of World War II, it became imperative to German authorities to compensate for loss of 'Nordic blood'. After the war on the USSR had been declared in 1941, followed by great losses on the German side, the pressure to increase the birth rate became urgent. Abortion had been forbidden up till then, but from 1943 it became a capital crime. The SS-organization did register all members who were the only and last sons in their families. Such members were encouraged to have their own children before they eventually were killed in the war. Another way to compensate for the loss on the battlefield was kidnapping of Aryan children from occupied countries. The children were brought to Germany for adoption in German families. The Lebensborn engaged in such activities in Poland and in other occupied areas in eastern Europe. In Germany the children were seldom placed in families. Instead they were gathered in huge institutions, suffering as victims of maltreatment, abuse and hunger.[2]

There have been speculations from authors, journalists, the public and war children themselves, as to the character of the Lebensborn homes, whether they functioned as 'stud-farms' destined for procreation of the Aryan 'race'. When two French journalists in 1975 published a book on the Lebensborn, these ideas came to the attention of the Norwegian audience as well.[3] There is, however, no evidence for such assumptions either in Germany nor in Norway or in any other country where the Lebensborn was active. The Lebensborn organization was an instrument in the Nazi racial policy and a supplier of mother- and childcare for racially selected persons

The first Lebensborn maternity home opened its doors in Bavaria in 1936.
Austria had its first Lebensborn maternity home in 1938. A key concept of the Lebensborn was racial selection or 'Auslese'.[4] Mothers and children were classified according to a four-level standard. Only those of the first and second level qualified as receivers of economic and social support from the Lebensborn e.V. Children of lesser 'quality' were dismissed from the Lebensborn and sent off to the

competing organization, the Nationalsozialistische Volkswohlfahrt (NSV), the welfare organization of the German Nazi party. The NSV programme on mother and child welfare was less racially directed than that of the Lebensborn. A number of disabled children, and those labelled as 'lebensunwerten Lebens' were victims of the Nazi euthanasia programme.[5] The 'top-class' children were meant to be brought up in superior SS families, either their own or in an adoptive family. But as children of mostly unwed mothers the children were rejected by SS families as the progeny of loose and immoral women whose character was further disputed by the fact that they were willing to give up their child for adoption. In principle the children were not in the custody of their mothers. In many cases full guardianship was taken over by the Lebensborn organization, clearly contradictory to German legislation, but nonetheless a fact. Consequently children were placed in private care and foster homes, beyond control by official authorities. Poor planning and lack of funding soon resulted in homes which were overcrowded. Hygiene and care decayed rapidly, followed by a rise in mortality rate. Statistics were faked in order to make things look better. When war broke out, the importance of the organization was more readily acknowledged on the top political level and financial support increased accordingly.

The German Concern for War Children in Occupied Countries

The Nazis had an ambiguous attitude to children born as the result of relations between German soldiers and native civilian women in the occupied countries in the western part of Europe.[6] Theoretically the populations in various countries could be ranged according to a racial scale established by German scientists and Nazi ideologists. At a closer look, however, some of these nations in western Europe turned out to be less pure and more 'racially' mixed than anticipated by the Germans. On the other hand, in eastern Europe for instance, there might be racially valuable elements also worth acquiring. In these countries, however, the majority of the population was not deemed to be especially valuable according to the German Nazi race theory. On the one hand, with partly 'Aryan' blood, they were seen as a potential population resource for Germany; on the other hand, it was feared that an influx of 'superior' blood would strengthen the enemy.

In the occupied countries in western Europe, however, the situation was different. A differentiated system of racial value was applied, separating the racially 'valuable' nations from nations whose populations were of less precious quality. The populations of the Netherlands, Denmark and Norway were ranked as superior to those in the rest of Europe, while the French were mostly considered as below standards. This system for categorization was decisive as to how the steadily increasing numbers of children of German soldiers were to be classified, controlled and cared for.

The implementation of the Lebensborn organization in occupied countries depended on a range of circumstances. Among these were the estimated racial quality of its population, the political character of the occupation, political preferences of leaders of the occupational regime and the influence and power of the competing Nazi organization Nationalsozialistische Volkswohlfahrt (NSV).

In the Netherlands, although considered as racially valuable, it was not Lebensborn, but the organization NSV which started up the engagement for war children. The NSV had established maternity homes, and up to the summer of 1943 about 1,000 war children were born in the NSV homes. The NSV and the Lebensborn were competitors in this field, a situation reflecting certain clashes of interests between the Nazi party and the SS inside the German Nazi regime. In that rivalry the NSV was the stronger. Lebensborn had difficulties establishing its organization in the country. From the end of 1942 Lebensborn tried to open a home in the Netherlands, but the liberation put an end to their efforts.

The Danish population was highly ranked in the Nazi racial hierarchy. Still, Lebensborn never succeeded in Denmark, for a number of reasons. Up to 1943 the country was not formally occupied by Germany. In reality the German Nazis had been in control since the military invasion in April 1940, but formally the Danish authorities still governed the country. As a consequence the war-child issue was handled by Danish authorities. From 1943 when Denmark was occupied by the Wehrmacht, children of German soldiers and Danish women were no longer dealt with by Danish but by German authorities. Due to internal relations between the German Nazi party and the SS organization, the Lebensborn never got a hold on the Danish war-child issue. During the last two years of the war, the Lebensborn sought to establish itself in the country. These efforts met with obstacles. The first home was not opened until May 1945 when the German Nazi regime surrendered.

In Belgium the Lebensborn organization faced other problems than those in the Netherlands and in Denmark. The Belgian population consists of two groups, Flemings and Walloons. According to German Nazi ideology the French-speaking Walloons were inferior to the Flemings in the racial hierarchy. For political reasons, however, it was in the interest of the German occupational regime to deal with the two population groups on the same level. The war children presented the Germans with a dilemma. The situation was further complicated by the fact that the German military leader in Belgium aspired to take a part in the treatment of the children of Belgian women and the foreign soldiers. Finally, in spring 1943 a maternity home run by the Lebensborn was opened in Belgium. Only one year later the Allied invasion started.

The French population as such was not highly esteemed racially by the German Nazis. From the German point of view there were, however, some Aryan components within the population worth caring for. Plans were made for kidnapping of children of 'Germanic' families in France in the same manner as in eastern Europe. Himmler considered the populations of Normandy, Alsace-Lorraine and Brittany to be 'Germanic', of more or less 'Aryan' origins.[7] The children were to be placed in German institutions, freed of their arbitrary French nationality and made 'German'.[8] Untill May 1942 there were reports of 50,000 births of children with a French mother and a German father. In the following years, numbers increased. The German Nazis took little interest in the majority of these children. But the assumption that some of the children might be racially valuable led to the establishment of the Lebensborn organization in France in 1942. In the winter of 1943 a Lebensborn maternity home near Paris opened its doors. After close examination of the racial quality of the mothers and thorough scrutiny of their pedigree, children who might be of future use to the Third Reich were separated out to be taken care of by the Lebensborn.

The Lebensborn and partly NSV were established in several of the occupied countries in western Europe, but for a variety of reasons in most places they did not succeed very well. Norway was the main exception to this rule. Why the Lebensborn was an achievement and how its policies and welfare programme were implemented in this country will be dealt with in the succeeding paragraphs.[9]

The Lebensborn Organization in Norway

Only a few weeks after the invasion of Norway on 9 April 1940, the German occupational forces anticipated that a lot of German-Norwegian children might subsequently be born. In accordance with the racial policy of the German Nazis, most of the Norwegian population was regarded as belonging to the so-called Nordic race and consequently genuine Aryans. Thus the SS organization headed by Heinrich Himmler, which was in charge of the Lebensborn, logically favoured relations between Norwegian women and German soldiers.

As stated above, the primary Lebensborn strategy was to raise the racial standard of the German population. This could be done in different ways, for instance by importing 'fresh' Nordic blood. Marriage between German soldiers and Norwegian women was one way of doing so. In accordance with the slogan '*After the victory on the battlefield comes the victory in the cradle*' it was imperative to help and support unmarried Norwegian women who became pregnant by German soldiers. During the autumn of 1940 the Germans started planning a mother-and-child welfare programme by establishing the Lebensborn organization in Norway.

Taking care of the newborn German-Norwegian children became a main concern for the German Nazis in Norway. In February 1941, there was a meeting of such high-ranking officials as Reicshführer-SS Heinrich Himmler, Reichskommissar Josef Terboven (the chief of the German civil administration in Norway), the German SS leader in Norway Wilhelm Rediess and the leader for

Lebensborn in Germany Max Sollmann. The outcome of the meeting was the decision to launch the Lebensborn in Norway.

One month later the Lebensborn came into effect, with the care of German-Norwegian children and their mothers as its core concern. As described above, the majority of the Norwegian population as well as the Danish and the Dutch were seen as racially precious; while the people of countries such as Belgium and France were judged to be below standard. There were, however, obstacles both in Denmark and in the Netherlands preventing the success of the Lebensborn, hindrances which did not exist in Norway. Favourable personal relations also made things easier in Norway because Reichskommissar Josef Terboven showed great sympathy with the idea of Lebensborn's activities in Norway, since its work there would set an excellent example of how the Lebensborn should be organized outside Germany.

During the winter of 1941 the number of war children increased. At the end of the year about 730 babies were registered in the Lebensborn records. A year later the number had grown to more than 2,200. By the end of the war in May 1945, about 8,000 children of German fathers and Norwegian mothers were registered in the Lebensborn files in Norway.

Being pregnant and giving birth to a baby with a German soldier as the father created stigma: the women were condemned often both by society as a whole and by their close family.[10] German soldiers, members of an occupant force, were the enemy. Neither family nor friends would accept a girl with a German boyfriend. If the girl became pregnant, rejection by both family and friends might follow. The mother in many cases had nowhere to turn but to the German authorities. The Lebensborn organization could support the mother economically, pay for clothes and pram for the baby and give her shelter and support both before and after the delivery. The women were offered a place in a maternity home with all medical expenses paid by the Germans. According to Norwegian legislature, fathers of children born out of wedlock were held responsible for the economical support of the child until the child reached the age of 16. In a case with a German soldier as father, the Lebensborn organization would take on the economic responsibility for the baby '*until the end of the war*', as it was stated.

Up to 1940 most Norwegian children were born in private homes with little or no medical support. Only hospitals in the largest cities had maternity units with sufficient capacity to care for a great number of births. The Lebensborn arranged for many of the mothers in their care to give birth in the existing maternity units in Trondheim, Bergen and Oslo. In spring 1941 Lebensborn started planning its own maternity institutions. By August 1941 the first Lebensborn home in Norway with a maternity unit, 'Hurdal Verk' near Oslo, was opened. This home was the first of about 10 Lebensborn homes in Norway, and the first Lebensborn institution established outside Germany and Austria. During 1942 two more maternity homes were opened: Klekken near Hønefoss and Dr Holm's Hotel at Geilo, and in 1945 Høsbjør by Hamar. These homes might cater for about 230 women altogether. During the war about 1,200 of the 8,000 'Lebensborn children' were born at these Lebensborn homes in Norway. The rest were born partly in Norwegian hospitals and partly in private homes.

The Germans soon experienced that some of the mothers left the Lebensborn home a while after the child was born without taking their child. Rejected by family, scorned by society and without money or housing, leaving the child behind was the only option for many of these women. The Lebensborn organization, however, could not accommodate all these children in its maternity homes. To solve the problem three orphanages were established during 1942 and 1943; Godthaab near Oslo, Stalheim at Voss and Moldegaard near Bergen. These homes could receive about 340 children at a time. In addition to these institutions, the Lebensborn organization also established three 'urban homes' in the cities of Trondheim, Bergen and Oslo. These homes were in fact small hostels. Here mothers could stay overnight when they were on their way to one of Lebensborns maternity homes to give birth, or they could stay there when they were waiting for transfer to a Norwegian hospital with a maternity unit in one of these three cities.

In order to handle all these institutions, staff, mothers and children a large administration was needed. The monthly economical support for mothers had to be administered, new cases were to be registered, the living conditions for mothers and children outside the Lebensborn institutions had to be inspected, and so on. At the end of the war a staff of about 300 was engaged in running the Lebensborn organization in Norway.

Racial Evaluations

After it was decided to establish the Lebensborn in Norway, the organization was determined to take responsibility for all children born with Norwegian mothers and German fathers. Even if some of the Norwegian mothers might turn out not to match their racial standard, the Lebensborn administrators regarded the Norwegian population as a whole to be valuable. The only elements of the Norwegian population not included by Lebensborn were women and children from the Sami ethnic minority – and of course Jews, Gypsies and a few others.

This meant that the Lebensborn accepted practically every mother and child if the father was likely to be a German. On the other hand the racial quality of the mother and child was still a vital matter. The policies of the Lebensborn had to remain a secret if the organization was to gain confidence and not create confusion among the Norwegian population. Revealing the true eugenic and racial scheme behind the Lebensborn activities was not in the interest of the occupational forces. They feared that a lot of pregnant women would avoid contact with the

Lebensborn if they were uncertain whether the Germans would help them or not.

In order to single out children of inferior heritage from those of good biological quality, each mother was closely examined and classified by German race experts. These evaluations were done secretly. The mothers were to be kept in the dark. According to German plans, the most valuable mothers should be given the opportunity of having their children born at the first-class Lebensborn home, Klekken. Mothers who were not that highly esteemed would stay at one of the other homes run by Lebensborn. Mothers who were not seen as valuable at all were to be offered a place in Norwegian institutions, at the very bottom of the Lebensborn hierarchy. These intentions were unambiguous, but in practice the plan did not work. The sorting and classification system appeared too complicated to handle in real life.

The children were also supposed to be examined and accommodated along the same eugenic scales. According to the Lebensborn system, mothers were to report to the organization once a year conveying exact information about the children. In addition Lebensborn inspectors visited mothers in their homes to check under what conditions their 'German' children were growing up.

Adoptions and Marriage in a Racial Perspective

Right from the beginning of the war, all children of German fathers and Norwegian mothers were considered German citizens by the German occupational forces. When the decision was made to establish the Lebensborn organization in Norway, it was still not quite clear what was to happen to the children and their mothers 'after the war', when Germany presumably had vanquished all its enemies. Officially it was said that until then they should be regarded as '*German outposts* (Vorposte) *in the Norwegian People*'.[11]

Cases where the mothers gave the Lebensborn organization the right to arrange adoptions give us some clues as to what might have been the fates of these children if the outcome of the war had been a different one. The children were closely examined by medical staff and, in accordance with the result of the evaluation, the Lebensborn organization tried to have them adopted, again within a hierarchic system. The less valuable children should be given away to Norwegian families, and the children who were regarded as more racially valuable were to be sent to Germany for adoption. Norwegian families adopted about 100 children during the war, and about 200 war children were sent to Germany for adoption.[12] The adoption process took a long time. It seems as if Lebensborn administrators were preparing adoptions for at least 600–700 war children before the end of the war.

During wartime no clear policy emerged on the status or future lives of the war children and their mothers after the war. From a German point of view, the best outcome or solution would be that the children grew up within a family. The optimal solution would be marriage between the Norwegian mother and the German father, settling in Germany and carrying on their lives with the child as an ordinary German family. If the couple did marry, they might produce even more children of superior quality in regard to the SS standards.

Many German-Norwegian couples were eager to marry. At the end of 1942 Lebensborn had registered 2,514 Norwegian women who already had babies with or were pregnant by German men. Of these women 139 had already married the German fathers, and another 890 women wanted to marry the father of their child. That means that 40 per cent of the Norwegian mothers at that time either had married or wanted to marry. 294 of the 2,514 women (more than 10 per cent) had also gone to Germany to live with the family of their husbands/boyfriends.

The main obstacle to marriages seems to have been the fact that the men were already married or engaged to be married in Germany. One investigation indicates that this was the situation in 30 per cent of all cases. In other cases the man tried to run away from his responsibility as a father. Neither did all mothers want to marry the fathers. In some cases the relationship between the parents was just a brief episode where the mother was unable to identify or name the German father.

Acceptance of paternity by the father is an indication of the stability of the relationship between the man and the woman. According to the files in approximately 50 per cent of all the Lebensborn cases, fatherhood was settled before the end of the war. In 38 per cent of the cases the paternity had been established as a fact by a German court – in most of these cases the verdict was based on a document signed by the father. In 11 per cent the German stated in writing that he was the father, but these cases were not treated in court until the end of the war. In 4 per cent of all cases the German court decided that it was not possible to identify the father. And in 47 per cent paternity was not decided, mainly because the father could not be found or because the case could not be dealt with before the end of the war.

Although many couples wanted to marry, most of them did not succeed until the end of the war. The Wehrmacht did not approve of their soldiers marrying abroad, and at the beginning of the war such marriages were legally forbidden. But in February 1942 Hitler decided that German soldiers could marry racially valuable women in Holland, Norway, Denmark and Sweden. Such marriages did, however, mean that foreign women should become a part of the German people. That was a serious matter and could only be allowed on strict conditions. In every case, thorough investigation of her family pedigree was needed. Parents and grandparents had to be presented by photographs and their racial certificates. The medical situation of her family had to be documented to the full extent. In addition, the German man had to guarantee that the bride could live with his family in Germany. After this scrutiny of family quality, each case would be sent to Germany and be decided by Hitler.

The SS and Lebensborn organizations tried to simplify the procedure, but without any success: in fact, during the war conditions became stricter, and the formal procedure might last for two or three years. Many couples did not succeed in getting married before the German soldier was killed or went missing at the front, or before the German capitulation in May 1945.

The exact number is unknown, but probably only 400–500 pairings of Norwegian women and German men were married during the war. That number also includes couples who did not have children until after the wedding. A fair estimate is that only about 200–300 of the war children's parents got married during the war.

A Substantial Problem?

The Lebensborn organization did register about 8,000 Norwegian war children during the war. In addition, many children with German fathers were born after the end of the war. When the Germans capitulated in May 1945, there were more than 350,000 Germans in Norway. The last soldier did not leave the country until 1947, and during these years several children with German fathers were born. We also know that some war children born during the war were not registered by the Germans. For a number of reasons their mothers avoided contact with the Lebensborn organization, or preferred to acknowledge unknown Norwegian men as fathers. Thus the exact number of children cannot be produced, but there are good reasons to estimate the number of Norwegian war children to be between 10,000 and 12,000.

Estimating the number of Norwegian women who had liaisons with German soldiers is not an easy task. In the 1940s the Norwegian population was only about three million. In such a small population a group of 10,000–12,000 children and their mothers were quite visible in society. If one of three German-Norwegian relations resulted in the birth of a child, it indicates that at least 30,000 women dated German soldiers. If the proportion was 1:5, the number of such women rises to at least 50,000. The correct number is probable within these numbers. This would mean that about 10 per cent of all Norwegian women aged between 15 and 30 years (about 400,000) had a German boyfriend during the war. Such figures are important for understanding why the war children, their mothers and other women with German boyfriends became a central topic in a heated public debate in Norway after the end of the war.

Preparing for Peace

Already during the war, exiled Norwegian authorities discussed the fate of German-Norwegian war children after the liberation. In 1944 a governmental committee in London was established with its main task to discuss whether the war children and their mothers were to leave Norway after the war. Intelligence from Norway reflected that public opinion favoured this line of action. Also inside Norway the same problem had been discussed during the war. Clerical authorities argued that the children and their mothers should be allowed to stay in Norway, but the children ought to be removed from their mothers. Women with German boyfriends should be punished in one way or another.

Norwegian exile authorities in Sweden discussed the war-child issue too. Their daily duties were to examine refugees from Norway in order to spot Nazi spies, criminals, etc. Every refugee who was accepted by the Norwegian authorities in Sweden got a Norwegian refugee passport and economical support. They were also offered education. About 2,100 refugees were not accepted and were handed over to the Swedish authorities who placed them in special camps. Among those were about 400 women who were denied status as Norwegian refugees because they had had relations with German soldiers during the war. In some of these cases the women brought their children with them to Sweden. The children were not accepted as refugees by the Norwegian authorities. As was concluded in one case, *'the child has a German father'*. Such conclusions were not in accordance with Norwegian law however: both child and mother were Norwegian citizens.

Norwegian Women: German Citizens

After five years of occupation the Norwegian population was very hostile toward the Germans and everything associated with them. In such an atmosphere of hatred and revenge, war children, their mothers and all women who during the war had had German boyfriends were exposed to hostile attitudes. Even if not all of them were exposed to physical punishment, many suffered traumatically, not knowing what was going to happen to them and their children. In one way or another, growing up in such a situation also influenced the children.

Many of the women were punished on the street and in their neighbourhood. We do not know how many had their hair cut off or were badly treated in other ways. Some women went to the police for protection, demanding that the persons who did the haircutting were to be punished. Investigation into some such cases indicates that very few of the perpetrators were brought to court and sentenced. As a policeman wrote about two such men: *'they are two good young men who during the occupation have shown a good national attitude'*.[13]
During the summer of 1945 the Ministry of Social Affairs made a nationwide enquiry about local attitudes toward women who had relations with German men.[14] The inquiry forms were filled out by one-third of the local municipalities in Norway. The answers indicated an aggressive attitude toward the women among the population. Letters to the editor and other newspaper articles also reflected

quite hostile feelings among the population, although not unanimously. Many families and friends rejected any contact with the women. Many of them lost their jobs or had problems finding a job or a place to live.

According to Norwegian law, the women having liaisons with Germans during the war had not violated any law. Such relationships were not illegal. But investigations into different aspects of reactions against the women indicate that the Norwegian authorities still tried to punish them. One example of such punishment is that several women who were employed by the state or in municipal administration lost their jobs if somebody reported that they had been seen with German soldiers during the war. On all levels of public administration, staff were scrutinized in order to find Nazis and collaborators. In this process also women with relations to Germans were registered and in many cases lost their jobs. These processes went on for more than a year after the end of the war: for instance, a woman employed in the municipality of Oslo lost her job in April 1946 because of her relationship with a German soldier over a period in 1940, more than five years earlier. It seems obvious that the loss of jobs was regarded as a form of punishment. In February 1947, local authorities in Oslo allowed 27 women to apply for jobs again, on the condition that they had been suspended without wages or had been without a job for at least one year.

All around the country many women who had been seen with Germans or had German boyfriends were arrested and placed in prison or special camps for shorter or longer periods. By the end of May 1945, about 1,000 women had been arrested in Oslo. During spring and summer the same year more than 300 women were arrested in the small town of Halden, 320 in Fredrikstad, about 200 in Sarpsborg and at least 55 in Moss. Thus, in the county of Østfold alone, a small region of Norway, at least 800 women were arrested during the first months after the end of the war. Comparing this number of arrested women to the number of inhabitants in this area might indicate that many thousands of women in the country at large were arrested and stayed in jail or camps for shorter or longer periods because of their relations with German soldiers. We do not know how many women were treated like this, but we do know that the Norwegian authorities punished many of these women in an irregular way.

As shown earlier, it was very difficult for Norwegian women to get married to their German boyfriends during the war. As soon as the war was over that situation changed. At the end of the war there were about 350,000 German soldiers in Norway. Some of the soldiers had Norwegian girlfriends, and now perhaps as many as 3,000 of these couples married.[15] Those marriages had dramatic consequences for many of these women and their children with German fathers. In August 1945 the Norwegian Government approved a provisional law of citizenship. Every Norwegian woman who had married a German soldier during the war or after immediately lost her Norwegian citizenship. She was to be regarded as a

German citizen and sent to Germany. While they were waiting for an opportunity to go to Germany, many of the women were interned in camps with their children.

These women were the only Norwegians who lost their citizenship as a consequence of their connection to the Germans. Even if the government used juridical arguments for changing the law, some of their statements indicate that their intention was to get rid of as many women as possible who had had affairs with German men. It was said for instance that the new law should be used until the authorities 'had sent out of the country all the persons whom it was not desirable to keep'.[16]

Thousands of women were interned in camps or sent to prison without legal justification. Many lost their jobs in state or municipal institutions. Several thousands who married their German boyfriends lost their Norwegian citizenship and were sent off to Germany.

War Children: A National Political Problem

As soon as the legal Norwegian government returned to Oslo in the summer of 1945, they were to decide how to handle the war-child problem. The government registered strong hostile attitudes among people toward the war children. Some warned the Norwegian society that in 20 years time the children could become a dangerous German fifth column. Others voiced different opinions. The children were Norwegian citizens and should be treated as such. They were innocent victims of the war and should be treated accordingly.

Two months after the end of the war, the government appointed a committee to discuss the war-child problem and put forward suggestions as to how the problem should be solved. The committee was to consider whether the war children and their mothers should be sent to Germany or not. The conclusion was unanimous. Such a 'solution' would be unacceptable. It was a Norwegian responsibility to take care of these children. The proposal was never followed up in Norway, but it reveals some of the attitudes and ideas held by Norwegian authorities at that time. The committee's unanimous conclusion, however, did not prevent its chairperson from suggesting that the whole group of war children might be sent to Australia, when an Australian delegation visited Norway in the hope of recruiting new immigrants to their country. (See Borgersrud in Chapter 4 of this volume for more details.)

While lay people were inclined to fear the 'German blood' of the war children, professionals were more concerned with possible mental retardation. One of the first actions of the war-children committee was to ask one of Norway's leading psychiatrics, Ørnulf Ødegård, to give a statement about the mental condition of the war children. In his statement Ødegård based his arguments on his clinical experiences during the war. Among his patients were 35 women who had relations with German soldiers. From his opinion on these women, Ødegård generalized his diagnosis to discuss the whole group of women who had children with German soldiers.

Ødegård estimated that half of all the 9,000 mothers (which was the number used at that time) were probably mentally retarded. According to theories of inheritance, 50–60 per cent of children with mentally retarded mothers would probably become retarded themselves. Ødegård concluded that about 2,500 of the war children probably were retarded because of their mothers. In addition, there were the German fathers. If both the parents were mentally retarded, the percentage of retarded children would increase to about 85–90 per cent. In Ødegård's opinion, the mental quality of Germans who had been satisfied with subnormal girlfriends could reasonably be questioned. This line of reasoning led him to indicate that about 4,000 of the 9,000 war children (85–90 per cent of the approximately 4,500 children with retarded mothers) might be mentally retarded and hereditarily inferior.

Neither the War Child Committee nor the Ministry of Social Affairs fully accepted this statement by the psychiatrist. But one of the members of the committee, also a doctor, wrote in a newspaper that many of the mothers were deficient. Therefore it was to be expected that many of their children would also be retarded. In this way the impression that there was something mentally wrong with war children was spread among the population.

Dealing with Specific Groups of War Children

When the German occupation came to an end in May 1945, most of the Norwegian war children lived with their mothers. Some hundreds were placed in Norwegian orphanages, and still others lived in Norwegian families who wanted to adopt them. Several hundreds lived in Germany, either with their parents who had married, in German orphanages or with German foster families.

At least 500 war children were still living in the earlier Lebensborn homes in Norway. At two of the orphanages, Stalheim and Moldegaard, the children were left on their own with a few mothers who were to take care of them. Local representatives from the Red Cross became aware of the situation and took over the responsibility for the institutions. The Red Cross did contact the Ministry of Social Affairs several times, asking for money to take care of the children at the homes. The authorities, however, did not react and the local Red Cross representatives had to pay for food supplies themselves and wait for months before the state authorities did something. It seems obvious that if the local Red Cross had not interfered, the situation at these two orphanages could have become critical for the children.

At the orphanage Godthaab, German Lebensborn personnel were not removed at the end of the war. In fact, 30 German nurses led by a former SS officer ran the home until October 1945. The SS officer requested that the Norwegian authorities to take over Godthaab, without success. For months the German officer was in charge of food and supplies for the home, retrieving them from Wehrmacht stocks and other sources.

The owners of the buildings used by the Lebensborn organization wanted to recover their property as soon as possible. During the summer and autumn of 1945 most of the children at the homes were removed. Many mothers took their children out of the institutions, other children were adopted, and some were handed over to Norwegian orphanages around the country. In spring 1946 most of the children had been removed. However there were still 27 war children left at Godthaab, and these children were considered to be mentally retarded. The Ministry of Social affairs had great problems getting them adopted, and no orphanage would take them. One suggestion was to place them in one of the camps for women who had had German boyfriends, and let these women nurse them. There were about 1,000 women in this camp. During the winter they had been IQ-tested by a doctor working for the authorities, with the convenient conclusion that most of them were mentally retarded. The camp was closed and the women released before anything could be done.

The solution of the problem was to place most of these children from Godthaab in a state institution for mentally retarded persons, and the rest of them in other institutions. Despite being treated as if they were mentally retarded, were these children in fact all retarded? They were not tested by Norwegian doctors before being sent from Godthaab: the diagnosis of mental retardation was based on state-ments by the German staff. A Norwegian doctor who visited Godthaab said that she did not believe that all of them could be characterized as imbecile, but many of these children have spent their lives in institutions. In 1990 one of the leading doctors at the state institution where most of them were placed stated that if the children had been offered a new start and a good life in 1945, they probably would have grown up as quite normal.

Norwegian authorities seemed to have forgotten the group of about 200 war children who had been sent to Germany for adoption by the Lebensborn organiza-tion during the war. These children were still Norwegian citizens, but until two years after the war Norwegian authorities did nothing to trace them and bring them back to Norway. The authorities did not do anything before they were contacted by an international relief organization working in Germany who wondered if Norway really did not want to have this group of Norwegian citizens returned from Germany.

The question of whether the Norwegian authorities wanted the children brought home or not is particularly relevant. In June 1945, only a month after the end of the war, Norwegian authorities had been informed about a group of 30 war chil-dren who had been found in a former Lebensborn home near Bremen. These chil-dren eventually ended up in Sweden, with the tacit consent of Norwegian authorities. Probably most of the children had their identity changed by the Swedish authorities before families in Sweden, where most of them probably are still living, adopted them. After the story about these children was told in Norwegian papers 55 years later, Norwegian authorities in the year 2,000 decided that these 'children' could get Norwegian passports if they wanted to.[17]

In 1947, when the question of what was to become of the war children who were still in Germany resurfaced, the government immediately started a project to trace the children and have them returned. During the next couple of years Norwegian authorities in cooperation with the Norwegian Red Cross tried to trace as many of the children as possible in Germany and bring them back to Norway. The project was not a success. Of more than 230 children, only about 50 were brought back to Norway before the early 1950s. Another 24 were reported to be dead, 50 were not found and 83 stayed in Germany either because the authorities found that the children were living under good conditions in the German families, or because they lived in the Russian Zone.

The mission only succeeded in bringing home about 50 of the children from Germany. Many of the children who were returned, however, seem to have been victims of a cynical and brutal treatment by those who were sent to bring them back to Norway. Especially in the first part of the process many of the children seem to have been taken from their new German families in unnecessarily brutal ways. In some cases Norwegian representatives suddenly visited the family and picked up the child on the pretext that the child was to se a doctor for medical examination. For many of the children it was a deeply traumatic experience to be separated from 'their families' in Germany.

Back in Norway only a few of the children were reunited with their mothers. The authorities established an orphanage where the children would stay for a short time before they were adopted. The Ministry of Social Affairs organized the operation in a careless and half-hearted way. The children were between 5 and 9 years old when they came to Norway and could speak only German. The Ministry seems not to have taken such facts into consideration when starting the operation. Most of the children were adopted, but it was not easy to find families who were willing to adopt war children who were only able to speak the German language. Many of them probably ended up in orphanages, and some of them lived for years in different institutions during their childhood and youth.

In addition to the children who had been sent to Germany by the Lebensborn organization during the war, there were more than 400 children who, in the postwar period, stayed in Germany with their mothers. Some of these children had gone to Germany with their mothers who married German soldiers during the war or just after the end of the war. Some of the children had been born after their mothers had settled in Germany. The situation for many of these women and children was very problematic both at the end of the war and in the following years. Living conditions were especially bad for those who lived in the cities which had been bombed, where there were problems with the supply of food and other commodities. Many of these women and children died in Germany at that time. Many of the women could not speak or understand German, and others had become widows when their German husbands were killed or were missing in battle. If their husband's family was unable to take care of them, their situation could become drastic.

In October 1945 a Norwegian Military officer reported from Germany that the Norwegian-born persons living in Germany were in danger. He was afraid that *'90% of them will die during the winter if they were not given efficient help very soon'*.[18] The Norwegian Red Cross tried to get support from Norwegian authorities to help the Norwegians in Germany, but due to the hostile attitude toward Germany among the Norwegian population, the Ministry of Social Affairs refused to initiate a relief action.

However, later on in winter 1946 the authorities accepted that the Norwegian Red Cross could start a relief project. From March 1946 the Norwegian Red Cross started sending monthly packages with food to Norwegians and Norwegian-born persons in Germany. At the end of the 1940s, the situation was particularly bad in the Russian Zone of Germany. In October 1946 Norwegian authorities registered about 430 Norwegian-born women in this zone who could have the right to get aid from Norway. From 1947 it was possible to send private packages from Norway to Germany. But during the following years the Cold War created new problems for the Norwegians in the Russian Zone. In January 1948 there were 250 Norwegians in Berlin. Most of them were Norwegian women married to German men and it was stated that *'Many of them are starving young women with small children. There are about 100 such children.'*[19] Until the autumn of 1948, food was also distributed to women and children in other parts of the Russian Zone. From that time, however, Russian authorities confiscated all packages from Norway.

Lives and destinies of war children of Norway and their mothers add in an illuminating way to our picture of what it means to be victims of war. From being among the chosen and selected during the war, the irony of their fate is to be degraded accordingly. Treated almost as untouchables, they served as objects of national shame, rejected by scientists and public scorn.

Notes

1. The following information on the Nazi Lebensborn policy is based on Georg Lilienthal, *Der 'Lebensborn e.V., Ein Instrument nationalsozialistischer Rassenpolitik* (Fischer Taschenbuch Verlag, 1993). The term 'e.V.' short for 'eintragener Verein', which means 'registered organization'.

2. G. Lilienthal and M. Pohl, 'Das "Lebensborn"-Heim "Taunus" in Wiesbaden (1949–1945)', *Nassauische Annalen: Jahrbuch des Vereins für Nassauische*

Altertumskunde und Geschichtforschung, Band 103 (1992), pp. 295–310; G. Lilienthal, 'Wissenschaft und Fürsorge als Rassenpolitik: Die Eindeutschung "fremdvölkischer" Kinder – oder: Der Historiker als Psychoterapeut', in Christoph Meinel and Peter Voswinkel (Hrsg /eds), *Medizin, Natur-wissenschaft, Teknik und Nationalsozialismus: Kontinuitäten und Diskon-kontinuitäten* (Verlag für Geschichte der Naturwissenschaft und der Teknik, 1994), pp. 236–45.

3. Marc Hillel and Clarissa Henry, *Lebensborn e.V. Im Namen der Rasse* (Zsolnay, 1975).

4. Lilienthal, *Der 'Lebensborn e.V.'.*

5. The term 'Vernichtung lebensunwerten Lebens' as a way of phrasing euthanasia appeared in a book by Karl Binding, professor of law, Leipzig and Alfred Hoche, professor of medicine, Freiburg; *Die Freigabe der Vernichtung lebensunwerten Lebens* (Leipzig, 1920). See also G. Lilienthal, 'Der Lebensborn e.V. Förderung "wertvollen" Lebens als Kontrast zur Vernichtung "lebensunwerten" Lebens', *Psychiatrie im Nationalsozialismus: Ein Tagungs-bericht des Landeswohlfahrtsvernbandes* (Hessen, 1989), pp. 45–55; G. Lilienthal and S. Hahn, 'Totentanz und Lebensborn. Zur Geschichte des Altes- und Phlegeheimes in Kohren Sahlis bei Leipzig', *Medizinhistorische Journal,* Heft 3/4, 1992, pp. 340–58. E. Klee, *'Euthanasie im NS- Staat'. Die 'Vernichtung lebensunwertens Lebens'* (S. Fischer Verlag, 1983), pp. 379–80.

6. The following presentation of strategy of the Lebensborn in occupied coun-tries is based on Lilienthal, *Der 'Lebensborn e.V.'.*

7. Jean-Paul Picaper and Ludwig Norz, *Enfants maudits* (Éditions des Syrtes, 2004), pp. 327–9.

8. Lilienthal, *Der 'Lebensborn e.V.'.*

9. The presentation of the Lebensborn organization in Norway is mainly based on Kåre Olsen, *Krigens barn: De norske krigsbarna og deres mødre* (Forum Aschehoug, 1998). German translation – Hardback: *Vater: Deutscher. Das Schicksal der Norwegischen Lebensbornkinder und ihrer Mütter von 1940 bis heute* (CampusVerlag, 2002). Paperback version: *Schicksal Lebensborn: Die Kinder der Schande und ihrer Mütter* (Knaur Taschenbuch, 2004).

10. See Ericsson and Ellingsen in Chapter 5 of this volume, 'Life stories of Norwegian war children'.

11. SsuPG, 7 (P/3/), letter to Himmler 5.12.1940 (cf. Lilienthal, *Der 'Lebensborn e.V.',* p. 169; H-D. Loock, *Quisling, Rosenberg und Terboven* (Deutsche Verlagsanstalt, 1970), p. 457; Hillel and Henry, *Lebensborn e.V. Im Namen Der Rasse,* p. 173).

12. Other researchers have suggested that Lebensborn during the war sent either 250 or 300 war children to Germany for adoption. I use the number 200, but there is no definite information concerning this.

13. Statsarkivet Stavanger, Haugesund Politikammer, sak 557/45.
14. See Borgersrud in Chapter 4 of this volume 'Meant to be deported'.
15. The exact number is not known by any official authority.
16. Ot.prp.nr 136. (1945–1946) 'Om lov om tillegg til statsborgerlovgivningen', p. 2.
17. See Lars Borgersrud, *Overlatt til svenske myndigheter: De norske krigsbarna som ble sendt til Sverige i 1945* (Televågkonferansen 2002: Born og krig).
18. Riksarkivet, Militærmisjonen i Berlin, boks 24, legg: '27.10.2 bind 2'. Brev 5.1., 22.1. og 26.5.1948.
19. Riksarkivet, Privatarkiv 250, Norges Røde Kors, lp. Nr 175, juni–juli.

References

Borgersrud, L., *Overlatt til svenske myndigheter: De norske krigsbarna som ble sendt til Sverige i 1945*, Televågkonferansen 2002: Born og krig.

Hillel, M. and Henry, C., *Lebensborn e.V. Im Namen der Rasse*, Vienna: Zsolnay, 1975.

Klee, E., *'Euthanasie im NS-Staat': Die 'Vernichtung lebensunwerten Lebens'*, Frankfurt am Main: Fischer Verlag, 1983.

Lilienthal, G., 'Der Lebensborn e.V. Förderung "wertvollen" Lebens als Kontrast zur Vernichtung "lebensunwerten" Lebens', *Psychiatrie im National-sozialismus: Ein Tagungsbericht des Landeswohlfahrtsvernbandes* (Hessen, 1989).

Lilienthal, G., *Der 'Lebensborn e.V.': Ein Instrument nationalsozialistischer Rassenpolitik*, Frankfurt am Main: Fischer Verlag, 1993.

Lilienthal, G., 'Wissenschaft und Fürsorge als Rassenpolitik: Die Eindeutschung "fremdvölkischer" Kinder – oder: Der Historiker als Psychoterapeut', in C. Meinel and P. Voswinkel (Hrsg /eds), *Medizin, Naturwissenschaft, Teknik und Nationalsozialismus: Kontinuitäten und Diskonkontinuitäten*, Stuttgart: Verlag für Geschichte der Naturwissenschaftund der Teknik, 1994.

Lilienthal, G. and Hahn, S., 'Totentanz und Lebensborn: Zur Geschichte des Altes-und Phlegeheimes in Kohren Sahlis bei Leipzig', *Medizinhistorische Journal*, 3/4 (1992).

Lilienthal, G. and Pohl, M., 'Das "Lebensborn"-Heim "Taunus" in Wiesbaden (1949–1945)', *Nassauische Annalen: Jahrbuch des Vereins Für Nassauische Altertumskunde und Geschichtforschung* 103 (1992).

Loock, H-D., *Quisling, Rosenberg und Terboven*, Stuttgart: Deutsche Verlags-anstalt, 1970.

Olsen, K., *Krigens barn: De norske krigsbarna og deres mødre*, Oslo: Aschehoug, 1998. German translation – Hardback: *Vater: Deutscher. Das Schicksal der norwegischen Lebensbornkinder und ihrer Mütter von 1940 bis heute*,

Frankfurt/New York: Campus, 2002. Paperback edn: *Schicksal Lebensborn: Die Kinder der Schande und ihrer Mütter*, Munich: Knaur Taschenbuch, 2004.

Picaper, J.-P. and Norz, L., *Enfants maudits*, Paris: Éditions des Syrtes, 2004

–2–

War, Cultural Loyalty and Gender: Danish Women's Intimate Fraternization

Anette Warring

All over occupied Europe local women had intimate relations with soldiers of the German occupying forces. Some of the liaisons bore fruit in a child. Most of the war children were illegitimate in both a national and a moral sense, and this mixture characterized the derogatory names given to the women who dated German soldiers. In Holland they were called 'moffenhoer', in France 'femme à boche', in Norway and Denmark 'tyskertøse' ('Germans' sluts').[1] These names branded them simultaneously as loose and as traitors.

The history of these mothers is highly relevant when examining the history of the war children. Their lives, and the treatment they suffered at the hands of society, had an impact on the life of their children and on their identity formation. In addition, the history of the mothers can be used to shed light on some important sociocultural mechanisms and historical conditions which later influenced the fate of their children.

Fraternization occurred in all occupied countries, but differed in scope, character and regulation depending on the German race policy and occupying policy, various occupation arrangements and the responses of the national and local communities. It was also influenced by the degree to which the war changed people's daily life. But everywhere the female body represented a combat zone between the occupiers and the occupied, and between collaboration and resistance. The intimate fraternization reflected both the national conflict between the German occupying power and the occupied countries and the internal conflict between the collaboration and resistance. After the war the exclusion of those who had fraternized with the enemy was an integral part of the formation of the national-patriotic interpretations of the occupation period. Gender and sexuality played an active part in these conflicts and collective identity processes. It will be the main theme in this chapter, which will concentrate on the Danish situation.[2]

The Female Body as a Combat Zone

'In all circumstances it was a catastrophe that I became pregnant as a seventeen-year-old girl. That the father was a German soldier made it doubly shameful', recounts Karin nearly 50 years after the war.[3] After an unsuccessful attempt at abortion and an attempted suicide she gave birth to a boy at a so-called 'discreet stay' and after ten days she had it adopted. She did not tell anyone about the child because she feared the reactions. This was not without reason. Women who dated the occupying soldiers were condemned and persecuted both during and after the occupation period. And even in politically neutral or pro-German milieus it could be difficult for the women to escape a reputation as being promiscuous.

Denmark took up a separate status among the occupied countries. Denmark stopped every military resistance in return for a formal maintenance of the sovereignty and political independence of the country. The political institutions remained intact, the administration of justice did not slip from Danish hands until the end of 1942, and the material losses were modest compared to those of other countries. The price paid was undemocratic attacks against the opposition and economical, political and moral support of Germany's war. In spite of this arrangement Denmark was able to be considered an Allied nation at the end of the war because of Allied interests, because of the Danish government being compelled to resign in August 1943, and because of the increasing, although relatively weak, Danish resistance movement.

The German occupation of Denmark had not lasted long before it became obvious that a significant number of Danish women fraternized intimately with the foreign soldiers. It is impossible to say precisely how widespread the fraternization was, but the women numbered tens of thousands.[4] It was a large number out of a population of about four million and on the whole corresponded to the size of the resistance movement after the considerable enrolment during the last months of the war. The extent of the fraternization was a result both of German racial and occupation politics and of the collaboration of the Danish state and Danish society. The occupation arrangement lent a sense of normality to daily life during the first years of the war and allowed German soldiers to have private and intimate relations with the civilian population.

Even if the political conflict between the collaboration and the resistance did not seriously mark daily life until the last two years of the occupation, the fraternization of Danish women frequently caused conflicts between Danes and German soldiers in the streets and in bars and restaurants.[5] During the very first days of the occupation the Danish police had to interfere in fights between Danes and German soldiers over Danish women or when the fraternizing women were denied service, shouted or spit at, physically molested, or had their hair cut off. But it was to a great extent for the same reasons that the German soldiers and the Danes got into conflict about the women. The soldiers considered it as defamatory and an insult to their personal honour when their Danish sweethearts were harassed and called names, usually with the symbolic content being an attack on the women's morality. As a German soldier explained after a violent quarrel with a Dane who had insulted his Danish girlfriend by calling her a 'German whore', he felt it was an attack on his honour and his 'duties as a gentleman'.[6] Danes on their part could be provoked by the fact that Danish women preferred German soldiers. They also considered it a question of honour, as will be elaborated more in the following.

The female body and sexuality were not only a question of honour and a combat zone between the individual German soldier and the Danish man, but also between the German and Danish nations. The German occupying power considered it an insult to the Wehrmacht itself when the Danish fraternizing women were insulted and harassed, and demanded that offenders should be severely punished. The Danish and German authorities had some common interests in cooperating on policies concerning marriage, paternity suits and prevention of venereal diseases and immorality. This was, however, a cooperation full of conflicts, intensified by the Wehrmacht's suspicion that there were anti-German motives behind certain practices. These included the Danish police checking the age of Danish girls who were in streets, parks or restaurants in the company of German soldiers, tracking down and questioning fraternizing women as part of the fight against venereal diseases, and the social authorities' monitoring and placing of the women in community homes and reformatories. This led to numerous clashes between the Danish police and Wehrmacht soldiers because of German distrust of the loyalty of the Danish police. Such cases often resulted in crises between Danish local chief constables and German commanders, just as it was a subject for negotiation at the highest political level several times during the occupation, the first time as early as at the beginning of May 1940.[7]

Especially at a local level Danish authorities often tried to obstruct the intimate Danish-German connections, and as far as possible they followed a judiciary practice which either acquitted those who molested the women or at least considered the molestations as the women's own fault. To avoid these conflicts in the regulation of the intimate fraternization the Danish authorities appealed to the Wehrmacht, trying to make them understand that the fight against immorality also was in Germany's interest, and that women's morality was of importance to every nation.[8] National conflicts ought to give way to a common effort in that field. The conflicts and the way they were treated were based on a gender discourse common to both countries' culture, where female sexuality was a constitutive part of the national and male honour.

Popular Reactions

Even if the family and parts of the local community accepted or even approved of the Danish women's love affairs with the occupying soldiers, the fraternizing women could not avoid being aware of the fact that a growing part of the society had a hostile and condemning attitude toward them and their actions. The most common and legally irreproachable way of showing contempt was social isolation, or 'the cold-shoulder policy' as it was called. It could be very effective and unpleasant as one woman, Lilly, recollects: 'Gradually I became more and more isolated from the people in my town, and the atmosphere became more and more tense and unpleasant. In my school the rumour quickly spread that my girlfriend and I were going out with German soldiers. No one would sit next to me in class, no one would talk to me or have anything to do with me at all.'[9]

Other ways in which the community showed its condemnation were by shouting profanities or spitting at the women, pushing them, refusing to serve them in tea-rooms and restaurants, sending lampoons or threatening letters, instigating rumours and making lists of their names which were made public. Demands to sack the women from places of work or ban them from public places were not unusual. Most incidents took place in public places, when people saw women accompanied by soldiers, or ran into women they knew to be dating soldiers. But systematic persecutions also occurred in schools and workplaces.

Physical molestation and cutting off of the women's hair was the most violent and apparent sign of people's dissatisfaction with the intimate fraternization. The police registered the first cropping incident as early as in August 1940, and this form of punishment was used during the whole occupation period.[10] The scale and brutality of the cropping incidents reached a peak during the August revolt in 1943 and in the days of the Liberation. The August revolt was also a domestic political confrontation, and strikes and street fights were not only aimed at the German occupiers, but also at the general policy of cooperation and at the collaborators. Among the collaborators being targeted were the 'tyskertøse', and the attacks could be very violent. In Odense for example, a woman who was known for dating a German soldier was persecuted and molested while on her way home. When the crowd threw stones at her windows and forced their way into her home, she took refuge on the roof. Some young men climbed after her and threw her down, leaving her badly hurt and unconscious. While she was unconscious her hair was cut off, her clothes were torn to pieces and she was again physically abused.[11]

As in the Odense case the cropping incidents during the revolt and at the time of the Liberation usually took place in daylight and were carried out by a large crowd of people. A few people used the scissors but most were eager onlookers. The haircutters were often young men but they acted in a general atmosphere of acceptance. Sometimes the attacks were well planned, but mostly they were a mixture of spontaneity and organization. The resistance movement was split over the issue of the persecution of the women. Local underground news-sheets brought campaigns against the fraternizing women and called for their punishment, and members of the resistance movement were among the hair cutters. Some believed that the anger and rebelliousness should be used more constructively, but at the same time they were not blind to the mobilizing effect of this explosive cocktail of sentiments and motives, national as well as personal, partly fuelled by specific notions of gender and sexual morality.

In the Days of Liberation

The cropping incidents and the mob justice were pervasive in the days of Liberation. All over the country women who had dated German soldiers were attacked, and at the end of May the Liberation Council of the Resistance Movement called for an end to the practice.[12] The incidents became fewer but continued until the end of the summer. It was in order to avoid mob justice and ambush that the resistance movement put more than 20,000 Danes into internment during the first days of Liberation. The taking of prisoners continued over the summer, and altogether 40,000 Danes were imprisoned because of their actions during the occupation.[13]

Intimate fraternization was not formally criminalized, nor was 'rendering the enemy sexual favours' included in the special and ex post facto legislation against the collaborationism, which was formed after Liberation. Nevertheless about 5,000 of the fraternizing women were interned for varying periods of time.[14] Even if it could not formally be a reason for detainment, most of them were interned because of their sexual fraternization. Some of them were under suspicion of and charged with other forms of collaboration, most often informing. In some cases the women were interned in order to protect them from mob justice, but this turned out to be a case of setting the fox to keep the geese, as the women often faced similar acts of retribution, during either their arrest or their imprisonment. It was common that the arrests had an inflammatory rather than calming effect on public sentiment, accelerating the violence.[15]

It was, however, commonly held that the women who had intimate relations to German soldiers should pay for making life comfortable for the occupiers. An opinion poll from mid-June 1945 concluded that approximately 75 per cent of the Danish population thought that the fraternizing women ought to be punished in one way or another.[16] Very few women reported the molestations, and it was not uncommon that the resistance movement tried to prevent legal proceedings, especially in the cases in which resistance fighters were charged. If it actually came to a trial against the offenders, it was nevertheless the woman who ended up being on trial because the police and the defence argued that her behaviour justified the violent attacks on her. She was to blame, and only in very few cases were the offenders convicted.[17]

A few critics thought that it was quite central for the re-establishment of Denmark as a community founded on the rule of law that such actions of mob justice should be punished. According to the political forces attempting to bring discredit to the resistance movement and to limit its influence, the resisters' actions were examples of the illegality of the movement and therefore ought to be punished. On the other hand, many people found that it was extremely unjust that those who had sacrificed themselves in the struggle for liberating Denmark should be punished because they had overstepped the mark a little in the hot summer of the Liberation. From this perspective it seemed unfair that those who had made life comfortable for the occupying power, and with their shamelessly exposed sexuality had offended the national honour, should be let off.

Motives and the Symbolic Content of the Persecutions

When Danish women went about in public with German soldiers, they became political actors. Regardless of their self-perception, the women signalled acceptance of the Wehrmacht and its presence in the country by socializing with the German occupying soldiers. The intimate and sexual character of the fraternization seems to have had an aggravating rather than a mitigating effect on the reactions of the community. The 'tyskertøse' were punished not only for not adopting a national attitude but also for not living up to their moral and virtuous obligations. While by far the greatest part of the population in the first years of the occupation dissociated itself from sabotage and any other violent resistance to the Germans, there was an extensive sympathy for the harassment of the fraternizing women. By reading the symbolic contents in the hair-cutting punishment, the illegal propaganda and the motives of the molestations, we can get an impression of what codes of behaviour were being breached by the fraternizing women.

The many illegal news-sheets in Denmark were distributed all over the country and had a major impact on public opinion through discussion of the intimate fraternization of Danish women, among other topics. The important and well-reputed *Frit Danmark* (A Free Denmark) carried an article in June 1942 which encouraged cutting off the women's hair and portrayed the 'tyskertøse' as stupid and miserable creatures of low moral standards. They and their 'brood of serpents' were considered a source of both physical and moral infection in society, and were identified with bestial and shameless creatures. Descriptions of a similar character are found in the manifold illegal agitations in form of leaflets, posters, flyers and series of photos of cropping incidents.

In local underground news-sheets it was a common practice to publish lists of the collaborators living in the area. In special lists with headlines such as 'The

Pillory', 'Blacklisted' and 'Camp Beds' (slang for soldiers' whores) the frater-nizing women's names and addresses were exposed.[18] In articles it was suggested that the women be isolated socially, have their hair cut off, and be subjected to other forms of punishment. After the war these lists were justified by referring to the potential security risk the women's intimate fraternization would have consti-tuted for the resistance movement, and therefore it is a surprising fact that the papers were much more preoccupied with commenting on the women's sexual behaviour than by warning against them.

This mixture of wounded national pride, moral outrage at the women's sexual escapades, and jealousy characterized also the statements given by the assailants who had harassed, assaulted and cut off the hair of fraternizing women during the Occupation and after the Liberation.[19] Some explained that 'their national pride had been hurt' by the fraternization of the women, but mostly it was what they saw as the women's amoral and indecent behaviour which had provoked them. That 'The way the girls were clinging to the soldiers was suggestive', that 'she had behaved in a sexually provocative manner', and that 'her behaviour had been impudent and provocative' were common explanations. A large group of men explained that they attacked two young women from their home town, because 'it was sad that several of the young girls went out with the German soldiers and there weren't that many girls in town'. So jealousy and anger at being 'rejected in favour of a German soldier' were also among the reasons given for harassing the women.[20]

The poem 'Hetærer' (Hetaerae), which was distributed in printed, duplicated and handwritten copies all over the country, sums up the symbolic content of the 'showdown'. It claimed that the intimate fraternization of the women constituted a shameless open exhibition of sexuality, which offended the national pride: 'Women, you who give your favours to a stranger betray your country with no shame. You who shamelessly display your heat, you are a threat to our honour'.[21] The women, and the female body and sexuality, were regarded as a masculine and national property, and a symbolic alliance between female respectability and the fate of the national community was constructed.

Cutting off the fraternizing women's hair was a form of punishment used all over occupied Europe. It is remarkable how quickly it became a common practice when considering the censorship which banned mentioning such anti-German actions, and the fact that the cropping incidents occurred long before the illegal propaganda had achieved any significance. Why hair-cutting became the chosen method of pun-ishment was not explicitly stated. It seems to have been self-evident that it should be the penalty for socializing intimately with a soldier of the enemy. It is possible to interpret the cutting off of hair as a symbolic act, as a cultural sign in the semi-otic sense, which refers to an underlying cultural system, but it is worth mentioning that even if the method had not been invented for the occasion in occupied Europe, it did not stem from a deep-rooted cultural tradition either. Over the centuries there have been various examples of women who, facing charges of infidelity or of fraternizing with strangers, had their hair cut off. But other forms of punishment have also been deployed in such cases, just as the cutting off of hair can have other symbolic and cultural implications.

As a ritual of punishment, the cutting off of hair can be seen as a social strategy, which was deployed to alter the appearance of the woman and her relations to the society. The punishment was visible, and for a certain duration of time, and it bore witness to her treason. It was a punishment of the body which had been given to the enemy, and as such it was a sexualized retribution for a sexual act. It was an attempt to make the women look less attractive by robbing them of an important feminine asset. Sometimes only a few tufts of hair were cut off, while in other cases the women had their heads completely shaven. Cutting off the women's hair was often combined with other kinds of sexualized punishments such as stripping and painting of the body.

Punishment by cutting of hair served as a de-sexualization, a symbolic castration of the female, and was a demonstration of masculine domination. The sexual natures of the punishments allowed the assailants to play down its seriousness and its implications. 'The hair will grow back', as it was commonly put. But to the women the same punishment and the sexualized violation of the body was an additional source of humiliation and shame and could be very traumatic. It concerned the individual as a whole and could not be expiated. A woman who had her hair cut off in the days of Liberation describes how the character of the punishment made it difficult to work through. 'It didn't ruin my life, but it has followed me and marked me for life. If it had been something that was finished either with a sentence or something else, there would have been put an end to it. But it is something that still is stirring up in a kind of No Man's Land. Was it something I couldn't help, or was it? One can never really defend oneself when there is nothing to defend oneself against.'[22]

Gendered National Identity Processes

The intimate fraternization between female occupied and male occupiers was a threat to the gender system, and challenged the accepted norms and morals surrounding gender and sexuality. But it seems more to have strengthened a traditional gender discourse than to have expanded the limits of women's freedom of actions. During the occupation of Denmark, specialists and authorities in the public debate were very concerned about the moral standard of the population. Attention was especially paid to youth and to the sexual moral of the female population. It would not be an overstatement to describe this as a moral panic. Different factors contributed to creating this moral panic: the expanded entertainment industry and the growth of eroticism as a theme in mass culture, the women's overt fraternization with German soldiers, and the dramatic rise in recorded cases of venereal diseases.[23]

As part of the process of national reconstruction during the German occupation of Denmark the demands on women's cultural and national loyalty were intensified, and they were strongly connected to a traditional understanding of femininity. This traditionalizing of the sexual moral and of the gender discourse becomes understandable when we relate it to the ways in which gender and sexuality are integrated in the national identity processes. As shown above, the female body and sexuality was a question of honour and a combat zone between the occupier and the occupied. National and individual honour was related to sexuality, but in different ways according to the gender in question. Gender and sexuality played a distinct role in the identity processes of inclusion and exclusion, both as cultural discourse and as social practice.

During the war, defending the national identity was a vital part of the symbolic dimension of the resistance. The national revival was a mass phenomenon, and its strongly gender-differentiated language and symbolism was taken from the national romantic period. In figurative language a mother represented the country itself: Mother Denmark. The woman and the female body were dominating iconographic representations of the Danish landscape, the Danish language and the Danish history. In spite of some national variation, the woman was everywhere in the European national symbolism, as a virtuous mother who embodied the nation and its continuity. The contrasting figure was the loose, sexually uncontrollable woman, who gave her body to the enemy and thus betrayed the nation itself and deprived it of its future. Complementary to this the man represented protection, heroism and vitality, and defended the nation and its women by virtue of the identity of these qualities. Men and women were relegated to different arenas of political and national activity, and appeared as metaphors for each part of the nation.[24] While a woman's honour was sexually defined in terms of chastity, a man's honour was considered identical with his gender as such. Honour was gender-differentiated attached to sexuality, and also gender-related. Female sexuality and respectability had a constitutive function in the masculine and national honour, which was demonstrated very clearly by the way the fraternizing women and their bodies became combat zones.

As imaginary communities national identities are dependent on practices giving sensuous reality. Because gender identities stand out as especially strong by virtue of being deeply rooted in a reference to the body, the systematic representation of nationality in terms of family and metaphorical references to the body and gender are ways of substantiating national identities.[25] In national-identity processes all bodies are transformed into bodies which belong to the nation, but according to the gender in question the transformation takes different directions.

During war the female body becomes a distinct marker for the nation's internal coherence and identity as well as for its external boundaries by virtue of the women's importance for the biological and cultural reproduction of the nation. As biological producers of children women are carriers of the collective as well as of the boundaries of nations. The more that biological genealogy and origin is considered as the major organizing principle of the nation, the more control of marriage, procreation and sexuality will tend to be high on the political agenda. The women then become not just the bearers of their own children but also the bearers of the children belonging to a specific nation.[26] Therefore the inclusion and exclusion of children in a nation is to a great extent structured by the same mechanisms as was the case for the women. The Nazi racial policy of population was an extreme result of such thinking, but different forms of eugenic construction of national reproduction was widespread in the inter-war period and was strengthened during the war and in the first post-war years. When born out of wedlock the Danish-German war children were automatically included as Danish citizens. But we know that the practices of different authorities to some extent discriminated against the war children because of their mixed parenthood. Also, more extreme opinions could be heard, for instance that the war children polluted the genetic pool of the nation.[27]

Common national culture and tradition is another way of imagining nations, and the cultural reproduction of the nation is closely linked to a whole system of so-called 'symbolic border guards', which identify people as members or non-members of the nation. As demonstrated, women and the female body play a significant role in this, and are constructed as the cultural symbols of the nation itself, of its boundaries, and as carriers of the national honour and intergenerational reproducers of culture. In a national crisis, such as a national defeat by a foreign occupying force, this burden of representation – or in other words the cultural loyalty – grows heavier, and the line between acceptable and unacceptable behaviour is drawn more sharply. The women who happen not to fulfil the national expectations and ideals of respectability and virtuousness and fail to respect the appropriate traditions, institutions and practices of sexuality, reproduction and marriage become a threat to the nation's survival and to the very order they are supposed to maintain and continue. The fraternizing women represented such a threat to the nation and its gender system, and consequently they were excluded from the national community.[28]

The Motives and Strategies of the Fraternizing Women

Contrary to the branding of the 'tyskertøse' as being of easy virtue and often also unintelligent, ugly and socially disadvantaged, the women were in reality a very heterogeneous group.[29] The stereotypical portrayal of the women was evoked in order to explain how the women could bring themselves to socialize intimately with soldiers of the enemy. But the women who dated German soldiers represented all social strata of society. The relations with the German soldiers ranged from work relationships, through casual flirtation and short affairs, to marriage and life-long love. And the women's appearance, intellectual ability, political conviction, age, matrimonial status, family relations and so on were very varied. So were the motives and different impulses and situations which could be conducive for engaging in an intimate relationship with a German soldier.

To some women it was of importance that they found the German soldiers to be handsome, well-groomed, dressed in uniform, and conducting themselves as true gentlemen. Others did not find the soldiers particularly attractive, but had rela-tionships with them because they represented an easy opportunity for gaining experience with men. Some women used the German soldiers to spice up the dreary everyday life in a provincial town, and went out with the soldiers as a revolt against the stifling bonds imposed by parents and a provincial environment. Some dated the soldiers because it tied in with the pro-German or Nazi convictions of their own or of their family. There were also women who, because they worked for the Germans or had German origins themselves, found it natural to socialize with the soldiers, and also to find a boyfriend among them. The prostitutes got German clients in order to make money, and for some it was important that a relationship with a German soldier meant getting easier access to goods and amusements. Getting a glimpse of the outside world and an opportunity to practice the German learned in school were other reasons for dating the soldiers. Others found that the anonymity of contact with a foreigner enabled them to feel free and to live out their erotic desires. Many intimate relationships with a German soldier grew out of a chance meeting at a bar or a dance restaurant, in a shop, in the park, on the train, at work, or in the home where he were stationed. Last, but not least, some of the women simply fell in love.

Faced with the condemnation by their community, and witnessing the destiny of other persecuted women, some women tried to stop socializing with the German soldiers. Others continued their relations because they were having fun, for political reasons or because they loved their German boyfriend. Some were convinced that it was wrong to consort with the enemy because they were con-fronted with the consequences of the presence of the German occupation power in the country. Many women, especially after the war, tried to start all over by moving to another, often bigger, town. But it could prove very difficult to get rid of their reputation and to be integrated in new circles of Danish friends. For most, the past caught up with them one way or another. The risk of this was much bigger if she had a child with a German soldier, even if she tried to hide this. As a single mother and a new arrival she attracted suspicion during the occupation and in the first post-war years.

In order to cope with the exclusion, it was a common strategy for the fraternizing women to excuse their actions by referring to its intimate and sexual nature.
They did not interpret their fraternization as being an unpatriotic and political act.
A general feature was that they thought they could deny responsibility for their
fraternization in the name of love. They sought legitimacy in an understanding of
emotions as a kind of a war-free zone and in the popular saying 'love is blind'.
They tried to separate the man from the soldier. It is a tragic fact that this was a
way of giving meaning to their actions and experiences which to a great extent corresponded with the traditional gender discourse structuring the identity processes
excluding them from the national community. If the woman managed to maintain
the interpretation that she did not do anything wrong, but was just in love, it could
help create a better foundation for her and her child's life. But this interpretation
was in strong opposition to that of the national community of memory and therefore it often did not succeed. Consequently, an ambivalent attitude to one's fraternization during the occupation was the common way of coming to terms with the
past.

Anna puts it this way: 'I never thought I was doing anything wrong. I always
believed that it depends on what you feel yourself … But I can understand if
someone who had suffered personally by acts of the German occupying power can
feel bitterness and think that what I did was a kind of treachery'. Nearly 50 years
after, the women who dated German soldiers during the Occupation period per-
ceive that the experiences marked them – with varying intensity, but nevertheless
– for life. Karin recounts that her silence about the German fatherhood of her child
makes her feel like a cheater. 'But I fear their reaction and I cannot bear not to have
their respect even if I have it on a false basis.' Lilly puts it this way when telling
how she perceived her fraternization and its consequences for her life: 'I never
spoke with anyone about what I did during the war. Except with a friend, who is
dead now, and with my psychoanalyst. Nor with my husband. Maybe he knows,
but we never speak about it. I have used 25–30 years to build up my life, and actually I am feeling good now. I have worked hard psychically, intellectually and culturally to catch up with all the years which were lost. I have worked to improve my
marriage. But if the war had not come, I think I would have found my balance
earlier. The experiences have always been in my system and still are. It has marked
me for life. Such things can be diluted, but you can never get rid of it. It is the fear
of being kept out. The fact that I was labelled, and then the incredible feeling of
guilt, which caused me for years to feel that I was no one at all. Feeling that I
should be grateful because my husband wanted me. For many years I had a terrible
feeling of guilt toward my parents, for of course it had hurt them. Maybe I felt
more guilt toward my parents than toward society. I have labelled myself as a very
bad human being, who could do something like that. At that time I probably
thought that I was a bad girl because I had sexual relations at such an early age.

Not only because it was with the Germans but no matter with whom. But I have never found that it was wrong. And it has not been so simple to explain to the "world" that I didn't mean it in a bad way.'[30]

The National Community of Memory

The exclusion of the collaborators, such as the 'tyskertøse', was an integral part of constructing the collective memory of the occupation period. It continued during the immediate post-war years and beyond, and seems to have had a decisive impact on the life of the former 'German girls'. Even more so because the collective memory of the occupation had and still has a constituting function for the national identity.

The fact that Denmark won a war she had not participated in meant that in 1945 the 'need for patriotic memories', as Pieter Lagrou puts it, was desperate.[31] From the end of the 1940s, this need became interwoven with the need of the Cold War period to demonstrate a willingness to undertake military defence in cooperation with the defence efforts of other democratic nations. Based on a political compromise between the Resistance and the collaborative politicians at the Liberation, it became possible to create a national patriotic narrative which portrayed Denmark as a nation of resistance. It was an image which included both so-called passive and active forms of resistance, and one which embraced all members of the population as having exhibited one of these two forms of resistance with exception of those few who could be clearly labelled traitors, and who were excluded from this nearly all-embracing national community of memory.[32]

This national-patriotic interpretation of the occupation period was called for in order to reconcile issues which otherwise threatened to split and dissolve the nation. This is the reason why this community of memory became nationalized, so to speak. It unified the story of everyday life, the politics of collaboration, the symbolic resistance and the military-organized resistance into a coherent whole. It put a pleasant shroud of oblivion over the period of collaboration and placed the origins of the resistance backward in time. It provided legitimacy for the activities of the resistance movement against the democratically elected government, by interpreting the resistance as being expressive of the real will and general attitude of the people. And it illuminated the memory of everyday life of occupation by the brilliance of the main theme of the narrative: the history of resistance. Resistance became the coordinating element in a national community of memory.

The reproduction of this community of memory was closely linked to identity processes of exclusion and inclusion based on a clear distinction between collaborators and those of the resistance. Consequently the resistance and the actors who were the bearers of this memory obtained a privileged status in deciding what was to be remembered and what was to be forgotten. Conversely it excluded the memories of those who had been 'on the wrong side' during the war, as it was called. The exclusion was transmitted to the descendants of these groups, and often caused serious problems for their welfare. This was the case for the women who had fraternized with German soldiers during the war, and for their children. Apparently the exclusion seldom took the form of direct persecution. But the omnipresent collective memory of the occupation reminded the women constantly about their experiences and often caused a sense of guilt and shame. As one woman puts it: 'I can't get myself to say: It was really terrible when the Germans were here. Because I think that they think that I was one of the girls who dated Germans. Every time we celebrate an anniversary for the Occupation or the Liberation or there is something on television about the occupation period I feel very bad. I am ashamed, although I would like to participate.'.[33]

The increasingly international outlook of the 1990s and the concomitant focus on human rights as a global standard for political and moral assessments have challenged the Danish community of memory of the occupation period. In this way the Danish community of memory has come to reflect an international departure from the scheme of interpretation which emerged in the wake of the Cold War. Historically, this scheme of interpretation is ideologically conditioned by the alliance formed during World War II between the Western Powers and the Soviet Union, with mutual acceptance of all actions on both sides. It is now gradually being acknowledged that the Soviet dictatorship played an active part in the war and the ensuing peace, which has affected our way of viewing World War II. Not all of the actions committed in the partisan warfare and resistance against the Nazi occupying power can be legitimized by referring to the war as just a battle waged by the democracies against a dictatorship. But even though a critical light has been shed on examples of this, for instance the – in many respects brutal – purging which the resistance movement performed, there has never been a general debate about whether the resistance was justified or worth the price. The main reason for this is probably that in Denmark, German reprisals did not occur to the same extent, or with the same brutality, as was seen in some of the other occupied countries. The material losses as well as the number of deaths were relatively low, and in retrospect this made it easier to adopt the views of resistance of the community of memory. But national interests are no longer the only evaluation criteria of the occupation past. Democracy and human rights are pushing forward as dominating standards. This has marked the present community of memory with ambivalence, which has an impact on the way of viewing the fraternizing women and their children.

The war children were illegitimate in a double sense, by being born out of wedlock and by having German fathers. As has been demonstrated here, the sexual and national questions were inseparable, and it is therefore not possible to say which was the worst. Today, I think it is possible. Many children are born out of wedlock and grow up without a father, and the concept of illegitimacy has disappeared. Seen in retrospect the women's fraternization is not problematic in a sexual moral sense. But what about the collaborative acts? On the one hand the resistance against the Germany which carried out the Holocaust is seen as the only morally acceptable act and – what is a real problem – also as the only understandable attitude toward the occupation power. The cooperation policy is, as are other kinds of collaboration, recognized as unacceptable and dishonourable. But on the other hand the treatment of people such as the fraternizing women, the German civilian refugees, the young men who worked voluntarily for Germany – all those who were excluded from the national community – is seen as cruel, unforgivable and not in accordance with the principles of Human Rights and of a constitutional state.[34] Constructing the fraternizing women and their children and other members of similar groups as victims of other's actions is a very common way of trying to solve this ambivalent memory. Perhaps these groups and their descendants find this victimhood a useful strategy for being integrated in the community of memory. But I have some doubts. First, it ignores the possibility that dating Germans could have been a deliberate choice. And, as a strategy for both individual memory and the national community of memory, it prevents us from asking painful but useful questions about the past and present, which might provide the basis for more reflecting politics of memory and identity.[35]

Notes

1. See in this volume Diederichs in Chapter 8 and Virgili in Chapter 7.
2. The chapter is based on my book, Anette Warring, *Tyskerpiger: under besættelse og retsopgør* (Gyldendal, 1994). The comparative perspective is elaborated in Anette Warring, 'Intimate Relations', in Robert Gildea et al. (eds), *Surviving Hitler and Mussolini: Daily Life in Occupied Europe* (Berg, 2006).
3. The women's names are used anonymously. Warring, *Tyskerpiger*, p. 53.
4. Warring, *Tyskerpiger*, p. 24 and Warring, 'Intimate Relations'.
5. All kinds of German-Danish episodes including harassment of the fraternizing women were to be reported or intercepted by the German or the local Danish authorities to a special department of the Public Prosecutor. These reports give a good impression of the conflicts but only show the tip of the iceberg.
6. Statsadvokaten for Særlige Anliggender, j.nr. AS 34–435.
7. Udenrigsministeriet, j. nr. 84.C.2.b.
8. Statsadvokaten for Særlige Anliggender, månedlige indberetninger, j. nr. AS, 0–1705, 0–1874, 3–403, 11–162, 36–276, 36–376, 53–277, 3–85, 41–381, 48–513, 48–1498. Socialministeriet, 3. kontor, 313/1941, 49/7/1943, 262/1944, 429/1944, 436(1944, 510/1944, 511/1944. Udenrigsministeriet, 84.C.2.b.

9. Warring, *Tyskerpiger*, pp. 44–7.
10. Statsadvokaten for Særlige Anliggender, j. nr. AS 0–2176, 0–2197, diverse sager, nr. 159.
11. Statsadvokaten for Særlige Anliggender, j. nr. AS, 27–408 og 27–340a.
12. Frode Jakobsens Ministerium, E 11–9/45.
13. Det statistiske Departement, 1958. Ditlev Tamm, *Retsopgøret efter besættelsen* (1984).
14. Warring, *Tyskerpiger*, pp. 163–77.
15. Ibid., pp. 177–87.
16. Gallup, 15.6.1945.
17. See e.g. Modstandsbevægelsen på Bornholm, Komiteens arkiv, II, læg1. Københavns Byret, afdeling 10 A, sag nr. 170/45. Østre Landsret, I. afdeling, sag nr. 304/45. Justitsministeriet, 3. kontor, 4268/45.
18. 'Gabestokken', 'Den sorte Liste' and 'Feltmadrasser'.
19. Based on a comprehensive sample of police reports during the occupation and after the Liberation.
20. Statsadvokaten for Særlige Anliggender, j. nr., AS 7–34, 12–106, 13–17, 48–159, 48–833, 48–483, 48–431, 36–376, 36–112, 27–79, 46–151, 48–1756.
21. 'Du kvinde, der giver en fremmed din gunst, forråder dit land uden blusel, du viser for alle så skamløst din brunst, du er for vor ære en trussel'. Printed in *De Frie Danske*, nr. 8, June 1942, among others.
22. Warring, *Tyskerpiger*, p. 194.
23. Kate Fleron, *Afsporet ungdom* (Fremad, 1942) and Fleron, *Vi er ungdommen* (Fremad, 1943). Hans Sode-Madsen, *Farlig ungdom* (Aarhus Universitetsforlag, 2003), pp. 83–93. Hans Hertel, 'Kulturlivet 1940–45', in H. Kirchhoff, et al. (eds), *Gads leksikon om dansk besættelsestid 1940–1945* (Gads Forlags, 2002), pp. 295–9. Erik Kjersgaard, *Danmark under besættelsen: Danskernes dagligliv 1940–45* (Politiken, 1995), Vol. 1, pp. 240–79 and Vol. 2, pp. 199–229. During the occupation the number of people with gonorrhoea nearly quadrupled and the cases of syphilis were eight times higher than normal. Anette Warring, 'Demokratische Erinnerungspolitik zwischen stabilen Werten und Reflexivität', in C. Lenz et al. (ed.), *Erinnerungskulturen im Dialog: Europäische Perspektiven auf die NS-Vergangeheit* (Unrast, 2002), pp. 304–6. Grethe Hartmann, *The Girls They Left Behind* (Munksgaard, 1946), pp. 1–41.
24. George Mosse, *Nationalism and Sexuality* (University of Wisconsin Press, 1985).
25. Anne Knudsen, 'Forvandlede kroppe: Nationalitet som identitet', *Kvinder, køn & forskning*, Vol. 2 (1994), pp. 9–20.
26. Nira Yuval-Davis, *Gender & Nation* (Sage, 1997).

27. Arne Øland, *Horeunger og helligdage* (Det Schønbergske Forlag, 2001). Warring, *Tyskerpiger*, pp. 146–54. See e.g. the illegal news-sheets *De Frie Danske*, April 1945 and *Frit Danmark*, June 1942.
28. Anette Warring, 'Køn og seksualitet i nationale identitetsprocesser', *Historisk Tidsskrift*, bd. 94, hft. 2 (1994), pp. 292–314.
29. The following is based on interviews with former fraternizing women, police reports and judicial material, reports from the resistance movement's internments of the women, female informer cases. See Warring, *Tyskerpiger*.
30. Warring, *Tyskerpiger*, p. 49, p. 66, p. 53, pp. 44–7.
31. Pieter Lagrou, 'Victims of Genocide and National Memory: Belgium, France and the Netherlands 1945–1965', *Past and Present*, 154 (1997), pp. 200–21.
32. Claus Bryld and Anette Warring, *Besættelsestiden som kollektiv erindring: Historie- og traditionsforvaltning af krig og besættelse 1945–97* (Roskilde Universitetsforlag, 1998).
33. Warring, *Tyskerpiger*, p. 194.
34. Claus Bryld, *Kampen om historien* (Roskilde Universitetsforlag, 2001), pp. 39–67.
35. Warring, 'Demokratische Erinnerungspolitik'.

References

Bryld, C., *Kampen om historien,* Frederiksberg: Roskilde Universitetsforlag, 2001.
Bryld, C. and Warring, A., *Besættelsestiden som kollektiv erindring: Historie- og traditionsforvaltning af krig og besættelse 1945–97,* Frederiksberg: Roskilde Universitetsforlag, 1998.
Fleron, K., *Afsporet ungdom,* Copenhagen: Fremad, 1942.
Fleron, K., *Vi er ungdommen,* Copenhagen: Fremad, 1943.
Hartmann, G., *The Girls They Left Behind,* Copenhagen: Munksgaard, 1946.
Hertel, H., 'Kulturlivet 1940–45', in H. Kirchhoff, J. Lauridsen and A. Trommer (eds), *Gads leksikon om dansk besættelsestid 1940–1945,* Copenhagen: Gads Forlags, 2002.
Kjersgaard, E., *Danmark under besættelsen: Danskernes dagligliv 1940–45,* Vols 1 and 2, Copenhagen: Politiken, 1995.
Knudsen, A., 'Forvandlede kroppe: Nationalitet som identitet', *Kvinder, køn & forskning,* Vol. 2 (1994).
Lagrou, P., 'Victims of Genocide and National Memory: Belgium, France and the Netherlands 1945–1965', *Past and Present,* 154 (1997).
Mosse, G., *Nationalism and Sexuality,* Madison, WI: University of Wisconsin Press, 1985.
Øland, A., *Horeunger og helligdage: tyskerbørns beretninger* Aarhus: Det Schønbergske Forlag, 2001.

Sode-Madsen, H., *Farlig ungdom*, Aarhus Universitetsforlag, 2003.

Det statistiske Departement (1958), *Retsopgøret med landssvigerne.*

Tamm, D., *Retsopgøret efter besættelsen,* Copenhagen: Jurist-og Økonom-forbundets forlag, 1984.

Warring, A., *Tyskerpiger: under besættelse og retsopgør,* Copenhagen: Gyldendal, 1994.

Warring, A., 'Køn og seksualitet i nationale identitetsprocesser', *Historisk Tidsskrift* 94(2) (1994).

Warring, A., 'Demokratische Erinnerungspolitik zwischen stabilen Werten und Reflexivität', in C. Lenz et al. (eds): *Erinnerungskulturen im Dialog: Europäische Perspektiven auf die NS-Vergangeheit*, Hamburg: Unrast, 2002.

Warring, A., 'Intimate Relations', in R. Gildea et al. (eds); *Surviving Hitler and Mussolini, Daily Life in Occupied Europe*, Oxford: Berg, 2006.

Yuval-Davis, N., *Gender & Nation,* London: Sage, 1997.

–3–

Silences, Public and Private

Arne Øland

Invisible Fathers

The importance of knowing the facts about one's biological origin is disputable. But to many Danish war children, including myself, who grew up without knowledge of their biological identity, and with years of secrecy, deception and lies about their background, the urge to know became a forceful drive and lead to the formation of the Danish War Child Association (DKBF) in 1996. Enquiries and searches for the biological fathers opened up a field of Danish war and post-war history which until recently had been effectively blocked off to the public.

The main purpose here is to reveal the motives and means by which the Danish government succeeded in concealing the German paternities of more than 5,500 children born during and shortly after World War II. What effects these policies had on the children is dealt with through the personal testimonies of some of them.

A national shame like the birth of children with fathers belonging to the German occupation forces could be kept a secret by concealing the names of the fathers. Thus silence and secrecy are key concepts in order to grasp both how and why paternity cases involving enemy soldiers were registered the way they were. Thus silence, both public and private, is the very essence of the war-child issue in Denmark. Mechanisms of silence and concealment, staged by the government, by mothers, by fathers and even by the war children themselves, can be examined by tracing the way the paternity of the children was handled by the Danish authorities. The ways in which the number of war children was assessed represent another opportunity for revealing how private, personal and psychological circumstances along with official, interpersonal and social conditions served to deny the very existence of Danish war children during and after World War II.

Legal and Biological Parenthood

In order to assess to what extent official policies and practices toward German-Danish war children differed from the general tendency it is necessary to consider prevailing ideas of motherhood and fatherhood in pre-war Denmark. The Child Laws of 1937 focused on the legal rights of illegitimate children, and relied heavily on the growing use and success of forensic medicine, especially blood tests. While biological origin did not play any legal role with regard to children born in wedlock, biology was crucial with regard to illegitimate children. Consequently we need to make a distinction between legal and biological parenthood, fatherhood in particular. This distinction is also relevant and useful with regard to children stemming from parents of differing nationality or ethnicity. While the legal constructs diverge, the biological ones do not. Nationality or ethnicity could be decisive for the handling of the paternity case during the occupation – and after, as the case of German-Danish war children demonstrates. The notorious ideas of Heinrich Himmler about '*Aryan blood*', '*Ausmertzung*' (classification for rejection) and '*Aufnorden*' (strengthening the Nordic element) set a ruthless scene in Germany. In Denmark the stage shifted perceptibly. From 1938 to 1941 any Danish or German male citizen summoned in a paternity case would be treated according to Danish law – on the assumption that the decisive sexual intercourse took place in Denmark and that the woman in question lived there. From 1941 to 1945 any male summoned in a paternity case would be treated as a German citizen[1] – on the assumption that he was a German soldier in the Wehrmacht or the SS.

Unquestionable Motherhood: Disputed Fatherhood

A Danish woman who gave birth to a baby was considered the mother of that specific child, regardless of her civil status as married or not. A midwife or sometimes an obstetrician attested the delivery just as other witnesses eventually could tell about the accouchement of the woman. The latter circumstance could be relevant if the pregnancy was not followed by the birth of a child, and doctors had to investigate the possibility of miscarriage, spontaneous or provoked abortion – or worse, infanticide. After the delivery the unmarried mother decided whether she would keep the child herself, temporarily place it in custody, or give it up for adoption. The last alternative meant giving away the title of mother for the rest of her life. Only by her death she might recover her former designation as mother, because the child in theory was entitled to inherit the biological mother in spite of an adoption.[2]

In times of turmoil there were ways in which the recognition of motherhood could, of course, be endangered. While the mixing up of babies was a realistic possibility at the more busy hospitals, it is a rather rarely reported incident. More likely, a long-time separation of mother and child could threaten or delay mutual recognition, and thereby jeopardize motherhood. This could be the case among refugees in the maelstrom of war or catastrophes, or by theft of children by criminals. While mistreatment of the child – whether caused by insanity, addiction, neglect or violence – could force the authorities to remove the child from its mother, the title of mother normally could not be taken away. Motherhood was, in other words, a well established social construct. Normally the midwife was perceived as someone who *separated* the mother from her baby by cutting the umbilical cord, but just as important was her function of *connecting* mother and child since the testimony of the midwife consolidated the construct of motherhood.

Because motherhood and biological maternity for the most part overlapped, motherhood was seldom questioned. It was conceived as a fact.

As opposed to the construction of motherhood by the word of a midwife upon having cut the umbilical cord, fatherhood had no firm witness testifying to its validity. The *Pater-est-principle* appointed the father by a mutual agreement, officially recorded. The title of fatherhood was fundamentally based upon confidence and therefore in its very nature more frail than the title of motherhood. Legal history documents many instances of disputed fatherhood, but exhibits very few of undecided motherhood. As a rule the person questioning the title of fatherhood would be the man. In most recorded cases it was the cuckolded 'father' who requested divorce on the grounds of infidelity.[3] If another man was proven to be the biological father of the child, the obligation to pay for 18 years was transferred to the secret lover. However, the mother could also be the one raising the case. Even the child could do so, if an adequate amount of evidence became available as time went by and the child could voice his or her own opinion.

Pre-war Policies and Practices

In 1937, legislation concerning children was intended, through a plethora of administrative provisions, to settle the questions of paternity and of alimony for those born out of wedlock.[4] Each delivery was to be officially reported with a form pertaining to the physical development of the newborn written by the midwife. The county medical officer was to interrogate the mother in order to estimate the time of conception. All relevant witnesses and the summoned man/men were examined. Blood samples from mother, child and putative father were taken by the county medical officer. Blood tests were also performed by the medico-legal institute. Years later the same institute might have to evaluate some cases by means of anthropological investigations. A guardian was appointed to question the mother closely to obtain information about the putative father(s). Punitive measures were to be taken against the mother if she lied or kept silent about the putative father(s). Alleged endorsement of the half-year governmental contribution was settled. Non-paying fathers were dealt with by the police.

The mother, the putative father(s) and witnesses were to be heard, but it was up to the court to decide in the paternity case. A paternity case was a civil affair behind closed doors. In principle neither the mother nor the supposed father had any influence upon the final outcome, except as witnesses. A paternity case in principle could have three potential outcomes:

1. Fatherhood (legal) and obligation to contribute to the upkeep of a child for 18 years (*Faderskab*)
2. Obligation to contribute for 18 years, but no legal fatherhood (*Bidragspligt*)
3. Acquittal (*Frifindelse*)

The first – legal fatherhood – could be achieved either by authorized agreement or by judgment in court. The second – obligation to pay – could be achieved only by judgement in court if more than one man could not be excluded, or if evidence of a specific single fatherhood was too weak. The third – acquittal – could be achieved if the suspected father was excluded by evidence (e.g. blood test or impotence).

It was an official duty to establish the paternity of children of unmarried mothers.[5] According to the Child Laws of 1937 the midwife was obliged to inform the county authorities – including the police – of all births. Then it was the duty of the police to interrogate the mother about the putative father(s).[6] The midwife was not supposed to get involved in the matter, but when the mother voluntarily informed the midwife about the father, she might pass on the information. Some police districts made their own Protocol of Paternities where the names of the mothers were listed side by side with those of the putative father(s). After the preliminary interrogation the police were supposed to pass on the case to the court, unless the putative father in the interim had voluntarily acknowledged his paternity. If he did so, the case was closed and the police had only to inform the county authorities. The church cleric was to enter the name and the occupation of the father into the church book (Ministerialbog). If nobody acknowledged paternity the case was taken to court.

Wartime Policies and Practices

The German occupation of Denmark and a new manner of handling paternity cases took place simultaneously. Between 1937 and 1940 the Child Laws were carried out, improved and defended against criticism by the Ministry of Justice. During wartime the Child Laws were implemented in new ways – because of the increasing number of children born to a Danish mother and a German father.

In 1940 the Ministry of Justice began changing the general practice. In a speech on 10 February 1941, secretary of the Ministry of Justice Hans Topsøe-Jensen announced how the Child Laws were to be applied from then on.[7] The Ministry of Justice had taken the law into their own hands.

One important step taken was to make it easier to remove the Danish-German paternity cases from the local courts. On 23 November 1944, former Minister of Justice and instigator of the legislature concerning children, K.K. Steincke, wrote an indignant article in a newspaper accusing the ministry of breaking the law.[8] His was a lonely voice that was largely ignored. Not until August 1945 were the cases – or at least 50 per cent of them – given back to the local courts where they belonged according to Danish and international law.

One year into the war a German-Danish Compromise Commission was set up as an agreement between Danish and German authorities settling the guidelines for handling payments toward maintenance of the Danish illegitimate 'children of German soldiers'.[9] Each Danish-German paternity case – in which the father could be a German soldier – was treated in a special way. The mother was preliminarily interrogated by a Danish police officer or judge, and the documentation furthered to the Danish part of the Compromise Commission, i.e. to the Danish Ministry of Justice, then translated and handed over to the German part of the Commission. The Compromise Commission or later on the German Court in Copenhagen eventually settled the case, either by rejection or by granting alimony. Danish civil servants were instructed not to record the German fathers in the so-called *Ministerialbog* ('The Book of the Church' where the names and dates of births and deaths are recorded along with the identities of the parents) unless the particular German soldier had acknowledged his paternity before a Danish district attorney. Information about the mother and child was, of course, fully recorded in the Ministerialbog, but information about the German fathers was only reliably documented in the German part of the Compromise Commission.

The mothers and fathers knew their own love story as a personal experience, but were, maybe, only vaguely aware of the legislation from 1937 concerning illegitimate children. They would hardly recognize their love affair transformed into a legal case story. The mothers sometimes obtained documentation from the authorities, Danish or German, stating the legal outcome, which for the mothers was tantamount to receiving or not receiving money and for the fathers to paying or not paying toward the maintenance of their illegitimate children.

In 1941 police officers and judges were informed by their superiors to pass on a paternity case to the Ministry of Justice if the putative father was a German soldier. In cases where the mother had confessed to having had sexual intercourse with a Danish citizen as well, only the Dane was to be summoned to the Ministry of Justice.[10] Thus a number of cases never reached The Ministry of Justice, either because the German soldier went to the police office and acknowledged his paternity right away – which some did – or a German soldier and a Danish citizen were putative fathers in the same paternity case.

The Child Laws of 1937 required an unwed mother to reveal the identity/identities of the putative father(s). The law could, however, give dispensation, if the mother was wealthy enough to care for her illegitimate child without public sub-vention. The number of dispensations is unknown. There seems to have been only a few in the first years after the implementation of the Child Laws in 1938, but they became more frequent toward the capitulation, and especially after. This practice served to disguise the identities of German paternities, and adds more problems to the complex task of assessing the number of war children in Denmark.

Although the authorities were determined to establish paternity, it was obviously impossible to be sure of the 'real' paternity of children of married women cohab-iting with their husbands: '... *when it is known to the police (or Overpræsidium) that the husband cannot be the father to the child of the married woman, infor-mation is furthered to the church book ...*'.[11] Many married Danes lived apart from their wives during the German occupation: as Allied sailors, foreign workers in Germany or Norway, soldiers at the east front, refugees in Sweden or German pris-oners. The wife might have had a secret lover – or several – to the extent that she herself could not tell who the father was. Or the married couple could agree to find a suited donor if the husband proved infertile.[12] It is a general impression that many 'good Danish men' – out of love, pity or naivety – undertook the paternity from German soldiers. Together authorities and the family might force the deserted mother to find 'a good Dane' instead of the missing German soldier who, as time went by, became more of a problem to the mother than a support. The number of such cases may be fairly high.

Concealing German Paternity: Collecting the Alimony

The Child Laws of 1937 were never generally implemented, either before, during or after the war. Some conservative judges continued with their 'business as usual' even after the war had ended. One of them was Otto Harpøth, a judge in the vicinity of Odense, Funen, during the occupation and after the German capitula-tion. In a pamphlet in 1946 he advocated dispensation of the Danish-German paternity cases using male and national chauvinism – or sheer sexism – against the vulnerable Danish mothers and their children:

> The liaisons with members of the German forces made by Danish women during the occupation did not have any deeper character generally speaking; normally they had one purpose only, intercourse, to state it clearly.

Harpøth wrote, and continued:

> The result of my considerations ... has been that I quite often annulled the cases to the effect that they were put away in the archive of the chief constable where nobody has asked for them.[13]

It is not known to what extent the judicial authorities complied with Harpøth to the effect that a large part of paternity cases were put away (*the Harpøth factor*). Complaints after the capitulation from judge deputies about low salaries and the heavy burden of the many (extra) German paternity cases indicate that this may have happened in a number of cases.[14] The willingness of judges to deal with these matters seems to have been low or totally lacking.

Some war children may also have been born outside Danish jurisdiction, thus leaving no traces of paternity in Danish records. There are indications that at least three (maybe four) Lebensborn maternity homes were established in Denmark toward the end of 1944.[15] There is, however, no evidence of any war children born in these homes. According to available documentation the women went to Danish hospitals for the birth, but stayed at the Lebensborn institutions afterward. Quite a number of Danish women moved to Germany as foreign workers without ever telling anybody. Many war children have been baffled when they later found out that their mothers had lived for some time in Germany during the war, either as workers or as part of the families of their German fiancés.[16]

Many of the 'Danish' women who had a child with a German soldier were not Danish in a strict sense, but originated for example from The Faeroe Islands, Greenland, Iceland, Norway or Sweden – and some went back home after the capitulation without any registration in Denmark. Even some of the Danish pregnant women emigrated shortly after the capitulation. The number is unknown. Danish authorities, however, knew the actual German and Danish figures and the particular cases they represented during the war, but the names of the fathers were not officially recorded.[17] Danish authorities were faced with the challenge of collecting the alimony while at the same time avoiding the official acceptance of German paternity of each war child.

Only by the end of the German occupation of Denmark did Hans Topsøe-Jensen, now principal in the Danish Ministry of Justice, realize that it could be a problem not to be in possession of accurate information about the German fathers. The former soldiers and civil servants in the German army – now individual civilians – were not necessarily prepared to pay for their illegitimate children. The lack of information could furthermore expose the perhaps too liberal cooperation (or collaboration) by the Danish authorities. Attention might be directed toward the obvious violation of the legal rights of illegitimate children according to the Child Laws of 1937. It was the responsibility of the State to make inquiries into the fatherhood of illegitimate children and eventually confirm it legally. How was that to be done when no authority in Denmark was in possession of reliable information about the fathers?

On 1 May 1945 Topsøe-Jensen persuaded the German staff judge, Dr Nadler, to procure information about the German fathers, which meant thousands of names, birthdates and addresses. Dr Nadler instructed five German secretaries to do the search. The Ministry made it look as if the children of the German soldiers had been taken care of. The 3,200 German names, birthdates and addresses Dr Nadler managed in the end to secure for the Ministry of Justice seem, however, to have disappeared, and have still not been located.

From August 1945 and in following years thousands of summonses were publicized in the daily paper *Statstidende*, with identification of the Danish mothers and their German lovers, alleged fathers of the illegitimate children. The stage was apparently set for thousands of delayed paternity cases. But no Germans were actually summoned by a Danish judge.[18] The many Danish-German paternity cases at Danish courts in the years after the capitulation were shams. The function of the entire set-up can be interpreted in different ways: e.g. as a method of legitimising the illegal administration of the Danish Ministry of Justice during the occupation, or as a way to secure money for the maintenance of the illegitimate children. Even though all three kinds of judgment mentioned above are represented in the fraud paternity cases after the capitulation, the vast majority of judgments are to *Bidragspligt*, i.e. the obligation to pay but without legal fatherhood. Whatever the judgments were they do not have much credibility, because none – or almost none – of the German fathers were ever heard.

The children themselves naturally knew nothing; at least in the conventional sense of the word *know*. In 1947 The Ministry of Justice was asked about the right of the children to obtain information about their 'real' fathers. '*The name of the father is to be found in the Ministerialbog if the paternity has been established either by acknowledgement or by judgment*', was the formal and somewhat condescending answer from the head of Ministry, ignoring the fact that the Ministry itself had banned the names of most German soldiers from being officially registered.

The Unknown Number of War Children in Denmark

Obviously national pride, religion and morality take their toll in history. The question is whether any national registration of illegitimate children whose fathers were foreign soldiers can be trusted. An answer to a request for information about the number of children of war in a Catholic country such as Poland is that the official number is zero, but really of a magnitude of 80,000–100,000 according to the German historian Michael Foedrowitz.[19] Perhaps the same observation pertains to almost any nation in the twentieth century, e.g. atheistic nations such as the USSR and nations with more mixed ideologies such as East and West Germany and the USA, since information – public as well as private – concerning foreign military paternities is very scarce. Seemingly all nations endeavoured to hide the enemy's invasion of the national body.

Although the precise number of Danish war children will obviously never be known, it can be taken for granted that the actual number exceeds the official numbers. There may be more than 8,000 Danish war children, though it is possible that illegal abortion, secret adoption (without investigation of paternity), the 'Harpøth factor', emigration, dispensation to silence and 'good male Danes' camouflage an even higher number.

In the period from 1940 to 1945 approximately half a million children were born in Denmark according to *Statistical Yearbook*.[20] Around 45,000 were illegitimate, born out of wedlock. According to official statistics approximately 5,500 were war children with Danish mothers and German fathers. By comparing the practice of registration of German soldiers as fathers in two Danish police districts, no patterns are revealed and little direction is given as to the number of children with German fathers, except that their number is higher than that of the official statistics. Unfortunately, registration of paternity cases was cancelled in both districts in the period from mid-September 1944 until August 1945. The seizure of the Danish police by the Wehrmacht on 19 September 1944 caused this irregularity. On this date German forces attacked police stations all over Denmark. Approximately 2,000 police inspectors were arrested. Apart from the chiefs, everyone under the age of sixty was sent to prison camps in Germany. German officials issued a declaration to the effect that they no longer trusted the Danish police in the combat against murder, sabotage and crime, and that for that reason the entire Danish police force was being stripped of its authority. The context of these measures was an intensification of the Danish resistance, acts of sabotage and liquidations of collaborationists. The police force remained out of action for the rest of the war. From then on the national council for unmarried mothers and their children (*Mødrehjælpen*) took on this field of work formerly under police supervision. The competence of this organization in these matters can be highly disputed when compared to the efficiency of the police.

The Danish-German Compromise Commission (see earlier) was formally established in Copenhagen on 1 May 1941 and started its work by the end of 1941. The figures from 1940 and 1941 indicate a much higher number of Danish-German war children than the later figures produced by the Danish-German Compromise Commission. The Commission tended to reduce the numbers. The Danish historian Anette Warring regards the number 5,579 of Danish-German offspring as an absolute minimum. According to Warring the actual number of Danish war children was higher.

During the occupation 5,579 children were born whose fathers were German soldiers, according to their Danish mothers. The German fathers acknowledged or were declared responsible for paternity in 1,417 of the cases. In all probability more [children of soldiers] were born than the 5,579 children registered, because the mothers generally speaking preferred a Dane as a putative father if at all possible (author's translation).[21]

Warring refers to numbers given by the Ministry of Justice.[22] Supplementing these data with information from the *Statstidende 1940–48*, the number of war children is about 6,200.[23] Since 1996 about 500 Danish war children have approached the Danish War Child Association. Many of them were not registered either by the Ministry of Justice or in the *Statstidende 1940–48*. This in itself is qualitative proof for Warring's contention.

National Disparities: Some Tentative Suggestions

Comparing the Danish numbers with those of Norway may reveal something about the character of relations between the Germans and the civil society in both countries. Apparently the number of war children was still higher in Norway than in Denmark – almost double, according to the Norwegian historian Kåre Olsen.[24] Bearing in mind the size of the Norwegian and the Danish populations, 3 million versus 4 million at that time, this discrepancy calls for further analysis. It is a fact that many Wehrmacht soldiers, especially in the Northern part of the country, lived close to Norwegian families, even under the same roof, and naturally intimate relations were bound to emerge. The number of German troops was also higher in Norway than in Denmark, although the difference may be minor if we count fertile German males only – the Germans in Denmark comprised many civilians in addition to the troops.[25] The situation in Denmark differed from that of Norway in several other respects. The offer of care, protection and financial support of mothers from the Lebensborn organization in Norway may have been more attractive than the similar offer in Denmark from the Danish legislation and 'Mødrehjælpen'. Seeking refuge in one of the Lebensborn homes in Norway meant anonymity but also naming a German as the father of your baby, a step that must have been quite drastic at the time, given that Norway was under German occupation. In Denmark, however, the German father could be concealed since the Danish authorities were in charge during a major part of the war.

The geographical closeness between Denmark and Germany may also have made it more of an option to the Danish than to the Norwegian women to move to Germany to give birth. Thus the number of war children registered in Denmark was diminished and made less comparable to Norwegian figures. Nazi policy favoured and coerced Aryan women engaged to German soldiers to move to Germany and settle there. It is also known that many Danish women did so, although the number is unknown. A great many of these women returned to Denmark either pregnant or with a child (born in Germany) – we know about it because their paternity cases were handled in the Compromise Commission in Copenhagen – unless their return was postponed considerably.[26] But it is not known how many women were to remain in Germany and how many of them put their child up for adoption in Germany.

Private Silence: Testimonies of War Children
Through a plethora of strategies and mechanisms, the public national shame of several thousand children with German fathers was diminished. The shame, as well as the wish to obliterate German paternities through silence, had their parallels in the private lives of many families.

Most war children describe the taboo of speaking about their real father in the same way as talking about sexual matters, a typical characteristic of the epoch.[27] Few of the children dared discuss the issue of fatherhood with their mothers – at least while they were still young and dependent. The latent memories from an early infancy in custody prevented many children from highlighting their latent social identity by asking impertinent questions and thereby jeopardizing the fragile relation with the parents. Even later on in life very few children used the power of independence to obtain information.[28] Most often the children succumbed to the whims of their parents in those rather authoritarian days.

Other members of the family, or friends, could disclose information, even if they were bound and silenced by loyalty, but could seldom yield the certain facts of which only the mother or unknown father was in possession. We should not forget that the Danish authorities failed to secure the legal German fatherhoods after the capitulation and thereby exposed the women as mere prostitutes or 'soldiers' whores'.

The accounts of the war children themselves bring us closer to the experience of living in an atmosphere of silence and taboo.[29] Let us listen to the stories of Bjarne S., Bente A. and Inge K.

Bjarne S.

While Bjarne was growing up, the subject of his father was always taboo. He did not know for sure that his father was a German soldier, but he guessed as much. The fact that he was born in 1944, and no father was ever mentioned, made him intuit the probable explanation. As a child he never asked his mother directly about his father. A small child is loyal to his family, Bjarne comments. The years of which Bjarne himself had no memory were never a topic of conversation in the family – nothing was ever said about the war and the occupation. This silence made Bjarne feel as if his family had fled from some unknown danger or situation, and had experienced circumstances and events that one preferred not to remember.

He harboured a deep sensation that there was some sort of secret about him. When he started school, he had to confront the problem of not having a father. The other small boys naturally asked questions about this, as small boys do. Bjarne's spontaneous reaction was: 'My father is dead!' He knew nothing about his father, not even if he was dead or still living. His answer indicates, however, that he was well aware that the question from his young schoolmates touched on a forbidden subject.

Bjarne was not the frank kind of child who simply asked direct questions and demanded to know the facts. Instead, he rummaged through drawers and other likely hiding places when he was alone in the house. On one such occasion, he found a photo that confirmed his suspicions: The photo represented a man in uniform with a swastika on his cap. Bjarne did not for a second doubt that this man was his father, the father who was never mentioned. Silently, he put the photo back where he had found it. He was ten years old.

At that time, Bjarne frequently went to the library, also to read about World War II and the occupation. There he looked at the terrible photos from the concentration camps. When he found the picture of his father, he did definitely not feel good about being the son of a German soldier.[30]

It was not until the late 1980s that Bjarne started his search for his father. In this search, he did not get much help from his mother, who died in 1996. Bjarne's relation to her was difficult: his conscience troubled him, as he did not want to hurt her. Bjarne did not tell his mother that he was searching for his father. 'Silence begot silence', he observes. On just one occasion he asked her direct questions about his father. The experience was very unsettling for both mother and son. His mother was clearly pained by his questions, and he resolved not to torment her any further. By asking her he learned nothing that he did not already know. However, his intuitions were confirmed when she exclaimed that he ought not to ask questions like that ever again, as this would make her fall ill and die.

In addition to the private silence, Bjarne has also come up against the public one. To this day, his search for his father has not resulted in a conclusive answer. He comments on this as follows:

> When I look at all the volumes on my shelf, with correspondence from the late Eighties and onwards – letters from ministry officials, judges, archivists and others, I cannot help pondering the costs to society of having a hurt little human being like me, sitting here complaining of the illegal and unjust treatment that I have received through fifty years.[31]

Bente A.

Bente's mother and father married in 1931. Their first child, a boy, was born the year they married. Bente's elder sister was born in 1941, Bente herself in 1944 and her younger brother late in 1945.

The siblings grew up in a quite unexceptional family, four children, mother and father. As a child, Bente did not know that there was anything out of the ordinary about her parents' marriage, except that it was not a happy one. At times her father drank heavily, and her mother had to fend for herself and the children. She was very particular about keeping up appearances; to outsiders, everything had to seem perfect.

In 1989, Bente's mother on several occasions treated her in a very unpleasant and rejecting way. Bente confided in a cousin, who explained the behaviour of Bente's mother by alluding to 'a very deep secret' that now ought to be revealed. In the cousin's view, Bente was entitled to know what her mother had kept from her. She went on: 'The three of you born during the occupation do not have the same father as your oldest brother. Your true father was a German officer.'

Bente did not believe her cousin. All the same, she decided to ask some other members of the family who were close to her mother. They confirmed what Bente had been told. In hindsight, she reflects that the person she ought to have asked was her older brother, who was living in England. He might have told her the truth in a more considerate manner. Bente remembers an occasion in the mid-1980s when her brother visited their parents. He was accompanied by his wife. On this occasion, Bente accidentally overheard a remark addressed to his wife: 'He's not her father', the brother said. Bente asked no questions. She did not know whom the remark concerned, but sensed, by her brother's sudden silence and startled face that this had something to do with her. She was, however, the product of an age with many taboos, so she did not pursue the matter.

When these innuendos were later confirmed by the family, Bente felt her identity crumbling. The father with whom she had a very close relationship, and who had defended her against her mother, was not her true father! He had also been deceived. She transferred the bitter feeling of having been kept in the dark onto her father. 'I did not know better at the time', Bente comments.

Some months later, Bente decided to ask her mother, who got furious and rejected her. Her mother clearly could not take it. It was all a lie, she answered. Her anger frightened Bente. She feared having triggered an avalanche which would cause a rupture in family relationships.

Bente now turned to her sister – partly hoping that she was wrong after all. Her sister, however, told her that she had known for a long time. She had refrained from digging further into the matter, and felt that Bente as well ought to let things rest as they were. To Bente, this was impossible. Her little brother would not have anything to do with the story of their supposed German father, nor did he believe in it. By removing the lid, Bente felt that she had set in motion something very sensitive and troublesome.

Three years before her death in 1995, Bente's mother softened and was able to tell her daughter about her loving relationship to Bente's father, a relationship that resulted in three children. Bente also succeeded in finding her relatives in Germany, and was well received by them. After long years of silence and deception, Bente experienced a 'happy ending'.

Inge K.

Inge was born in Denmark, but spent her childhood in Poland. Her mother was Polish, and died in a Danish refugee camp in 1947. Inge was sent to her grandparents in Poland, where she grew up. Her grandparents got divorced, and Inge spent her first years with her grandmother, her two uncles and her grandmother's lover. She addressed her grandmother as 'mother' and her grandmother's lover as 'father'. Her grandmother never told her the true facts. When Inge was five years old, her aunt tried to enlighten her, but Inge did not understand. In Inge's mind, her 'mother' was simply her mother.

Inge lost her grandmother when she was only six years old. The grandmother's sister now told her that the woman who had just died was not her true mother. She showed her a photo of a young woman, explaining: 'This is your mother.' Inge looked at the picture and immediately asked: 'Where is my father?' She received no answer.

Later Inge learned that she was born and baptized in Denmark. When she grew older, some relatives told her that her mother had worked as a waitress in a German soldiers' mess in the Polish city of Pelplin. There she got acquainted with Inge's father. Her grandmother did not approve of the relationship, and complained to the German authorities, who immediately transferred Inge's mother to a different place of work. Her father was sent to the front. 'His fate is uncertain,' Inge comments, 'as uncertain as is his paternity according to my birth certificate, which states: father unknown.'

Inge would not accept having a German for a father. As a child, she had repeatedly been told of the atrocities committed by the Nazis. She was fifty years old before she could bring herself to accept the facts. At that time she lived in Denmark after having left Poland in 1985 as a political refugee.

In Denmark she learned the dramatic story of her first years. Late in April 1945 her mother was on board a German ship with Polish and German refugees. The ship was bombed, and many refugees drowned. Inge's mother was among the survivors, who were taken ashore on one of the Danish islands. Later she was placed in a refugee camp for Poles on the Danish mainland.

The hatred against the Germans was strong, and Inge's mother presumably tried to hide the fact that she had had a German lover, and was now bearing his child. When Inge was born, her mother gave a Polish name for the child's father to both the Red Cross and to the church where Inge was baptized. In fact, it was the name of Inge's grandfather. By naming a man with her own surname, her mother could pose as married, and to a Pole. Through this manoeuvre, she escaped being despised by respectable Danish and Polish patriots, both for being an unwed mother and for her relation to a hated German, Inge explains. Later, however, her mother had second thoughts, and the registered fatherhood was changed to 'father unknown'.

Before Christmas in 1945, a local newspaper in the area where the refugee camp was located, wrote the following about the camp conditions:

Shortly after 5 May, the Danish Red Cross initiated work to create orderly conditions for the category of refugees who are registered as allied refugees. Naturally, the conditions in these camps are vastly different from these in the camps for German refugees. While the Germans are living under strict control, the allied refugees are granted freedom of movement, even if some control has to be kept of their activities. In this country there are now 12,000 allied refugees in 30 different camps, mostly Latvians and Poles, but also from other countries.[32]

'There was every reason to keep my German father a secret,' Inge comments. 'If not, my mother and I might have ended up in a refugee camp for Germans, where conditions were said to be far worse. Even if my mother, according to her Danish friends, was simply lying there, quietly dying, without receiving any medical treatment for her jaundice, the conditions were supposedly "vastly different" from those in camps for Germans.'

The refugees who surged into Denmark in the last months of the war were mostly Germans from the eastern parts of Germany, fleeing the advancing Red Army.

The estimated number of civilian German refugees to Denmark is about 250,000. Many were children, among them orphans. In 1945, 13,000 Germans died in Denmark. The children were especially vulnerable, and several thousand died from intestinal infections, dehydration, malnutrition and common children's diseases like measles and scarlet fever. Danish physicians were reluctant to treat German refugees, especially in the period before liberation, since such treatment could be regarded as assistance to the German side – the enemy.[33] Inge's comment that there was every reason to keep her German father a secret seems well founded.

Under the headline 'Those who postponed their return' the same local newspaper in August 1946 once again treated the topic of Polish refugees. The refugees who had not yet returned to Poland were scrutinized with suspicion. The head of the camp, Lieutenant Nordentoft, is quoted as saying:

Earlier, the Poles had only to report when they wanted to return home. However, the Polish Government is now reasoning as follows: Our compatriots have twice had the opportunity to return to their homeland. Those who have not wished to come home earlier must have had very specific reasons. They must be considered suspect, and their circumstances have to be closely examined before permit of entry is granted. Therefore, refugees who now want to go home will have to explain why they have chosen to postpone their return until now.[34]

Inge comments: 'My mother escaped having to explain why she had not already returned to Poland. She died half a year later, while I, two years old and unable to account for my patriotism, was granted permit of entry.'

Inge has now learned the name of her father. For the time being, his name has not brought her any further in her search. However, she is still hoping.

The price of silence, both public and private, was paid by the war children. It was paid in the painful currency of confusion, identity problems and vague feelings of guilt. At the age of grandparenthood, many are still searching for their fathers. The epithet of 'war children' pinned on people who are nearing or have passed their sixtieth birthday, may carry some psychological truth: questions which are still unresolved may constantly pull them back to a childhood of silence and taboo.

The efforts by the Danish government to conceal the paternities of the German fathers after the war obviously converged with existing ideas in Danish society of national pride and the importance of social and legal rather than biological parenthood.

Notes

1. He was not treated according to German law, but according to the compromise in The Compromise Commission (Vergleichskommission) in Copenhagen.
2. Lov om Ændring i Forordning af 21. Maj 1845 indeholdende nogle Forandringer i Lovgivningen om Arv. (Nr. 134 af 7. Maj 1937) samt Lov Nr. 87 af 26. Marts 1923 om Adoption.
3. Several cases from the period are described in *Ugeskrift for Retsvæsen* (1938–1961).
4. The seven laws were coined by the social-democratic politician and Minister of Justice, K.K. Steincke, also instigator of the so-called *Social Reform Programme* (1933).
5. Lov Nr. 131 af 7. Maj 1937. The Child Laws.
6. After 19 September 1944 when the Danish police force was interned by the Wehrmacht, the governmental institution 'Mødrehjælpen' took up this work.
7. 'Børnelovene i Praksis' by secretary in The Ministry of Justice, Hans Topsøe-Jensen (*Ugeskrift for Retsvæsen* 1941, 22 March), pp. 81–93.
8. K.K. Steincke, 'Faderskab eller Bidragspligt', *Social-Demokraten*, 23 November 1944.
9. If the German father was a civil citizen the paternity case was handled the ordinary way between the legal institutions of the countries.
10. Arne Øland, *Horeunger og helligdage: tyskerbørns beretninger* (Schønberg, 2001).

11. See e.g. '*Circular to all Bishops concerning notification in the church books about paternity to children of married women in special cases*', The Church Ministry, 7 April 1942 (Signed V. Holbøll).
12. It was probably the case of Bente Asaa and her sister and brother, all three children of a German officer who was introduced and paid frequent visits to the home of the barren Danish husband. See Øland, *Horeunger og helligdage*.
13. Otto Harpøth, 'De tyske faderskabssager', *Juristen* (The Lawyer) (January 1946).
14. See e.g. H.H. Wimmerslev, 'Om Dommeruddannelse og Dommer-fuldmægtige', *Fuldmægtigen* 12, 1 December 1945.
15. The homes were located in Højer, at Løgumkloster, at Møn and in Copenhagen. I am indebted to Kirsten Lylloff and Anette Warring for references to 'Det tyske mindretals arkiver 1920–1945', Landsarkivet for Sønderjylland, Aabenraa.
16. Personal information from several of the members of DKBF and from corresponding archival documentation.
17. Principal Danish legal officials were Permanent Under Secretary Aage Svendsen, Assistant Secretary Otto Bilfeldt and Principal (former secretary) Hans Topsøe-Jensen, all in the Ministry of Justice.
18. Up till now I have found only one case conducted according to the law, from 1949 (postponed from 1942). The German fatherhood was established by judgment. See Øland, *Horeunger og helligdage*, pp. 115–30.
19. Michael Foedrowitz, *Deutsch-Polnische Kriegskinder* (Paper delivered at '7. Historikertreffen' (Fantom e.V.) Berlin, 28 October 2002).
20. Some of the statistics are also given by Anette Warring in *Tyskerpiger: under besættelse og retsopgør* (Gyldendal, 1994), p. 224.
21. Warring, *Tyskerpiger*, p. 146.
22. *Justitsministeriets 1. Ekspeditionskontor* (Rigsarkivet). The references are given in Warring, *Tyskerpiger*, p. 224, note 75.
23. *Statstidende* is a Danish governmental newspaper publishing official juridical information and other public information according to Danish law.
24. Kåre Olsen, *Krigens barn: de norske krigsbarna og deres mødre* (Aschehoug, 1998). I am indebted to Kåre Olsen, Oslo, for the Norwegian figures. No reliable statistics are made due to the fact that both Norwegian and Danish figures are preliminary. At the moment there is exact documentation of about 6,500 cases – the number continues to grow.
25. About 'Wehrmachtsgefolge' and the phenomenon *JEIKO* (Jeder einmal in Kopenhagen), see Henrik Havrehed, *De tyske flygtninge i Denmark 1945–1949* (Odense Universitetsforlag, 1987).
26. See e.g. death notice 18 June and obituary 24 June 2003 in Aalborg Stiftstidende concerning the Danish citizen Ydun Hillner who in 1945

followed her future husband Helmuth Hillner, previously a German soldier in Denmark, to Berlin. They both returned to Denmark in the 1950s with two of their three children – the firstborn had died only seven months old in 1946 from malnutrition and starvation in Berlin.

27. See e.g. Stephanie Coontz, *The Way We Never Were* (Basic, 1992).
28. There are cases where the grown-up son used the threat of 'goodbye forever' if the mother refused to yield the desired information about the unknown father. See *Rødder*, nr. 3, 1999.
29. For more comprehensive accounts, see Øland, *Horeunger og helligdage*.
30. It should be noted that the Austrian father spent all the war years in Aalborg in Denmark.
31. See Øland, *Horeunger og helligdage*, pp. 141–58.
32. *Viborg Stiftstidende*, December 1945, quoted from Øland, *Horeunger og helligdage*.
33. Kirsten Lylloff, 'Kan lægeløftet gradbøjes? Dødsfald blant og lægehjelp til de tyske flygtninge i Danmark 1945', *Historisk tidsskrift* 1, 1999, pp. 33–68.
34. *Viborg Stiftstidende*, August 1946, quoted from Øland, *Horeunger og helligdage*.

References

Coontz, S., *The Way We Never Were*, New York: Basic, 1992.

Foedrowitz, M., *Deutsch-Polnische Kriegskinder* (Paper delivered at '7. Historikertreffen' (Fantom e.V.) Berlin 28 October 2002).

Harpøth, O., 'De tyske faderskabssager', *Juristen* (The Lawyer) (January 1946).

Havrehed, H., *De tyske flygtninge i Denmark 1945–1949*, Odense Universitetsforlag, 1987.

Lylloff, K., 'Kan lægeløftet gradbøjes? Dødsfald blant og lægehjelp til de tyske flygtninge i Danmark 1945', *Historisk tidsskrift* 1 (1999).

Øland, A., *Horeunger og helligdage: tyskerbørns beretninger*, Aarhus: Schønberg, 2001.

Olsen, K., *Krigens barn: de norske krigsbarna og deres mødre*, Oslo: Aschehoug, 1998.

Steincke, K., 'Faderskab eller Bidragspligt', *Social-Demokraten*, 23 November 1944.

Topsøe-Jensen, H., 'Børnelovene i Praksis', *Ugeskrift for Retsvæsen*, 22 March 1941.

Warring, A., *Tyskerpiger: under besættelse og retsopgør*, Copenhagen: Gyldendal, 1994.

Wimmerslev, H., 'Om Dommeruddannelse og Dommerfuldmægtige', *Fuldmægtigen* 12, 1 December 1945.

-4-

Meant to be Deported

Lars Borgersrud

In Norway, World War II resulted in 10,000–12,000 children of German fathers and Norwegian mothers. During the first months after the end of the war, Norwegian political authorities took on what they saw as an urgent task: to develop a judicial framework to regulate the national status and citizenship of these children, officially labelled 'war children'. This chapter aims to describe the process through which their national status and citizenship was established and to outline some important effects of that process on the condition of war children's upbringing. The process started with a proposal to deport the children, a proposal which influenced events in significant ways, even if it was not carried out.

The social-affairs authorities were faced with acute problems when thousands of single mothers and their children were left without any means of support once the German administration was dismantled after the armistice. However, when the topic of war children and their mothers was raised in the press and in public opinion, concerns for their maintenance were seldom voiced. Rather, the discussion was characterized by massive demands that the children and their mothers be deported to Germany, *their real fatherland*. Many senior civil servants and politicians held similar opinions. However, several practical and moral problems made such a plan difficult to implement. To present proposals as to what should be done, the Norwegian government appointed a fast-track committee, the War Child Committee. The authorities wanted answers as soon as possible, and before the autumn at the latest, as they stated.

Participants in the discussions on the 'war-child problem' took differing approaches to the question in 1945. It is, however, remarkable that so many concurred on one decisive point: Whether they referred to eugenics, culture, psychiatry, occupation history or fear of the future, they contended that the children of war were not genuine Norwegians. It was felt that the children had only limited or simply no right to continue to live in this country. Thus, taking away their citizenship and deporting them was a logical solution.

One of the main ideas underlying the national War Criminal and High Treason process in Norway following World War II was that the loss of citizenship should not at all be applied as punishment. Furthermore, from the judicial point of view, it was clear that the so-called 'tyskertøser' – i.e. women who had intimate relations with Germans during the war, had – not violated any law in the legal sense.[1] It was not feasible, without extensive legislative amendments, to define these women as legally German. Deporting them in an orderly fashion would call for a combination of new acts of legislation relating to both civil rights and child welfare. All the same, many confident individuals in positions of authority supported this idea. The impact of their views together with the bare existence of legislative amendments lent extra credence to the notion that there was something inferior about the children of war. In popular sense, their national status was defined as German, since they fell outside the systems which otherwise applied. The notion of their being 'German' and of a somehow inferior brand created an enduring image which 'everyone' agreed on. This image was broadly shared, and influenced regional and local authorities, not without consequences for the children of war in their formative years.

Agreement on deporting the children did not solve the problem of where to send them. We shall have a closer look at the solutions which were discussed. First, however, let us take a short glance at some relevant elements of the history of the phenomenon of deportation, in order to grasp what made such a solution thinkable in a country like Norway.

Some Aspects of Deportation History

Deportation must be seen in relation to the concept of citizenship and civil rights. Nothing of this nature was found in Scandinavia in feudal times or earlier. From early times, free people could settle wherever they wanted, within the law. During feudal times, the right to free movement disappeared. To be protected, everyone had to take an oath of allegiance to the king or to those he had authorized in the feudal construction. It was not until late in the age of Danish rule in Norway (1397–1814) that the first civil citizen legislation was adopted, as the oath of allegiance was supplemented by a birthright intended to keep Germans from holding Danish office. Thus, the first act introduced in this field aimed to restrict civil rights rather than enlarging them.

In the 1800s, most states in Europe introduced similar exclusion mechanisms, supplemented by persecution against the unaccepted. The Eidsvold Constitution of 1814 was an exception, even though it maintained exclusion of Jews, Jesuits and monasticism: exceptions of no practical significance. The oath of allegiance applied to the king and the Constitution for those who sought naturalization papers or to hold office. Otherwise, there were no rules or regulations of citizenship in Norway prior to 1888, when the first Citizenship Act was introduced, limiting citizenship to those whose parents were native-born in Norway. Whereas the electorate included people of the Sapmi ('Lapp') minority, people of Finnish decent (Kven) in Northern Norway were initially excluded, a fact which demonstrates that the concept of citizenship was not entirely based on cultural and political ideas, but also had some racial undertones. The Constitution's notion of free citizens as 'members of the State' was replaced by the notion of 'Norwegian nationals' used in the Citizenship Act.

According to the Act of 1888, the citizenship of women and children was defined indirectly through the citizenship of their husbands and fathers, as in most European countries. When a Swede working in Norway married a Norwegian and had children, they all became Swedish by law, even if they never left their place of birth. If the father died, the family risked being deported to Sweden. In 1924, the women's movement managed to revoke this discriminating provision. But as we shall see it was reintroduced in order to deport women who married Germans and their children, in August 1945. The changes in 1924 had been induced not only by relations between Norway and Sweden, but also with the US, since the US authorities deported Norwegian emigrants to Norway if their papers were not in order. Consequently, in the law of 1924, an automatic right to reacquire citizenship through a simplified procedure had been installed. This policy was to be changed in 1945.

Although the US pursued a deportation policy in the inter-war years, this did not involve relatively more people than those deported by Norway to Sweden each year, many of whose papers were deficient. The authorities, and in particular the police, therefore had plenty of experience in dealing with deportations. It concerned only poor people, among them some who rode on a deportation merry-go-round.

An aspect of the authorities' attitude to such groups of poor people who were not considered genuine 'Norwegians' is related to the development of the attitude to minorities and groups of 'losers' held by people involved in eugenic research, psychiatry and other related scientific activities. This trend paved the way for a change of mentality during the Occupation, as German racial prejudices influenced the bureaucracy and administration.

The occupation authorities of Norway from 1940 to 1945 introduced deportations in abundance. Roughly 9,000 Norwegians were deported to camps and prisons in the German-Polish area, of whom 1,400 died. Some were sent to be exterminated, such as more than half of the country's Jews, while others were deported as war prisoners or political prisoners, or as preventive measures, or to set an example, for instance the people of Telavåg and other places.[2] In 1944–45, there were 40,000–45,000 residents of Finnmark forced to evacuate. These measures involved not only centralized Nazi Norwegian government agencies in the police and justice system, but also regional and local authorities.

Among Norwegian officials who had fled to England after the defeat in the campaign in Norway 1940, some with special interests in social affairs came into contact with British ecclesiastical NGOs with pre-war experience in sending children overseas from the British isles, and probably was informed of their experiences. Since the early colonization, Britain had sent hundreds of thousands of children overseas from the British Isles. From 1880 to 1967 alone, interrupted only by World War II, the number is estimated at 150,000.[3] These were often homeless children, orphans or children without parental attention, or children devoted to adoption or child-welfare provisions. Recent surveys have documented that many of these children grew up in institutions under trying conditions, without knowledge of their real identity or background. Many were subject to assaults quite similar to those recounted by the Norwegian war children.[4]

The British deportations of children share factors relevant to the Norwegian children of war in a specific way. At the end of 1945, the Australian authorities sent a delegation to Europe to speed up emigration, in particular to attract children of war, refugee and stray children to Australia. The delegation also visited Norway, and was offered 9,000 children of war by the Ministry of Social Affairs, as will be dealt with later in this chapter.

Those Behind the Deportation Proposal

The first influential group discussing the idea of deporting war children during the war was an assembly of Norwegian politicians in exile in Stockholm in the autumn of 1943. Here the Labour Party had appointed a party Committee to suggest what should be done.[5] The reason for their action was the acquaintance with the book *Schwert und Wiege* ('Sword and Cradle'), which the head of the SS and police in Norway, Wilhelm Rediess, published early in the autumn of 1943. While the Wehrmacht had previously been reluctant to accept marriages or permanent personal relationships between Norwegian women and German soldiers, the book made it clear that the offspring of such liaisons could further Nazi Germany's racial objectives if the SS Lebensborn Maternity Home Programme were expanded and generous financial support provided for the mothers.

Early in December 1943, the party Committee completed its general recommendation, explicitly limiting the group of children and mothers to those who formally could be lawfully and unresistingly deported, which meant that those who were protected as Norwegian citizens should not be included. But the committee also proposed a separate supervision agency for the children of war with the power to separate mother and child in the event of failure of parental care of a specific national nature, which was to be in addition to the Child Welfare Act of 1896 giving the welfare councils the right to intervene on normal social grounds. The proposal left the future of such children uncertain. The recommendation, which also contained other proposals, was discussed by the Norwegian Labour Party in Sweden, without consensus being reached. In the end of March 1944, it was sent to the Minister of Justice in London, where it was followed up by active Labour Party officials in exile.

In London, the Norwegian Directorate of Health also received reports on Rediess' book and on the alarming number of war children born in Norway, indicating that many Norwegian women had entered into liaisons with Germans. However, the recommendation aroused scepticism, not because of the proposal for deportation, but because of the proposal to establish a separate child-supervision agency. Some civil servants disliked the proposal because it allowed public opinion to weigh more heavily than the children's needs, and because the proposal was based on a completely new perception of what constituted a failure of parental care, as it introduced a concept of 'national failure' of parental care. The issue was becoming a hot potato volleyed between ministries. Following many discussions, a provisional regulation was drafted, but never submitted. Prime Minister Nygaardsvold's private secretary, who had long experience of child-welfare cases, held a particularly negative view. She was one of the few women in the exile community in London, as well as one of the few Norwegians there, who took interest in the British child-welfare system and engaged in such issues and, ironically, even made donations to the largest NGO in charge of deporting children to Australia.

The Clergy

Rediess' book *Schwert und Wiege* also became familiar to a group of anti-Nazi clergymen, interned in the so-called 'clergy colony' in the Norwegian town of Lillehammer in 1943. There, the wife of one of the country's most prominent and imprisoned bishops, after reading Rediess' book, initiated the appointment of a committee of clergymen to study her information and discuss what to do.

She felt that the war children represented a serious threat to the future Norwegian society, even if Germany were to lose the war. She envisaged a scenario in which, thirsty for revenge, a German Nazi movement would locate the children of war some 20 years later, using secret records and underground efforts, then use them to form a fifth column during a new war. She referred to German children from World War I, supposedly used in Belgium in 1940. In her opinion, the mothers were trained Nazis who would inexorably pass their Nazi sympathies on to their children. There was no point in taking the children from their mothers, according to her, so all of them had be deported immediately after the war.

The bishop's wife had a second agenda. She expressed that it was necessary that the Christian Church be strict in respect to the 'tyskertøser' for preventive reasons, since Norway might be occupied by Allied troops once the war was over. At that point, it would be necessary to set an example and not demonstrate laxity, in order to protect 'our young girls', as she wrote. She warned against relationships between Norwegian girls and Allied soldiers.

Her opinions received some limited support, but the majority of the Committee opposed the key proposal to deport the children. On the other hand, they did agree that the children should systematically 'be guided away from their past', and be given Norwegian names, and that other initiatives should be implemented to obliterate their extraction, registered secretly and adopted confidentially. However, the draft recommendation was never completed, and was never made known in Stockholm or in London. The explanation was probably that the clergy lost interest in taking any action as the war neared its end and the colony was dispersed. One of the committee members preserved the unfinished document and made an abortive attempt to obtain final comments from the others, before filing the papers away.

The recommendation subsequently became known in the summer of 1945, because another minister, Ingvald Carlsen, who was appointed a member of the War Child Committee, took interest in it. Even though he did not agree on the views on deportation to Germany, he shared the other opinions. As head of the Norwegian reform programme for settling and housing of travelling people; or 'tatere', Carlsen was experienced in taking children away from their mothers. He was preoccupied with sterilization and interested in German eugenics.[6] Somehow, he obtained the document and finished writing it before turning it over to the War Child Committee, where it supported the motions forwarded by him.

British Military Rejects Deportation

Following the Stockholm Committee's proposal regarding a child- welfare agency and deportation had been rejected in London, other preparations for dealing with post-war problems relating to war children were put on the back burner. No further planning was made in general or with a view to the Lebensborn Maternity Homes. On that account, the Resistance and the Ministry of Social Affairs in Oslo were unprepared for how to keep those children alive once the German personnel were interned at liberation. While many of the Maternity Homes were left in a state of chaos and only the efforts of volunteer organizations at local level ensured food, fuel and other supplies, the matter became an issue to the British military, who forwarded a query to the Ministry of Social Affairs, which eventually sent representatives to alleviate the situation.

Pursuant to agreements concluded between the Norwegian government in London and the Allies, the German-occupied sector of Norway was to become a British occupation zone following German capitulation. Accordingly, British troops had arrived in Norway in the days following 8 May 1945. Under British supervision, the Allied headquarters established that the war children and their mothers in Norway were to be treated according to general British occupation policy. The British supreme commander convened representatives of the

Norwegian ministries for a conference on 13 June 1945 and presented a proposal for classifying them, among different types of civilian problem groups. The plan was generally accepted. Here it was ascertained that Norwegian women who had married Germans were entitled to double citizenship as long as they lived in Norway and that they could not be sent out of the country, unless they wanted to go. The same applied if their German husbands were dead. The offspring of such marriages were German citizens, but they should be allowed to stay in Norway or leave, depending on their mothers' wishes. Single women with or without children or who were pregnant were to be treated as ordinary Norwegian citizens and should not be forced to leave. The same applied to their children. Although reservations were raised regarding future negotiations with Germany, it was entirely clear that no war children or their mothers should be forced out of the country against their will.

These guidelines, to which Norwegian representatives had no objections, would have precluded every discussion regarding deportation, had they been respected. Three weeks later, however, the Norwegian government appointed the War Child Committee to determine how this question could be resolved.

The War Child Committee

The War Child Committee was appointed on 3 July 1945. On 9 July, the terms of reference were established, the members were appointed and the first meeting was held. The Committee was to recommend whether it was desirable to deport mothers and children to Germany, what legal adjustments would be needed and also what initiatives should be implemented if they were to remain in Norway. The Committee enjoyed considerable authority. Besides the chairperson Inge Debes – city court judge and head of the pre-war Social Legislation Committee as well as editor of the Ministry of Social Affairs' professional journal *Social Work* – the Committee consisted of Alf Frydenberg, deputy secretary of State at the Ministry of Social Affairs; Else Vogt Thingstad, chief physician at Ullevål Hospital; the already-mentioned Resident Vicar Carlsen, who was the head of Norway's Child Welfare Council; an assistant secretary of State at the Ministry of Justice; and former Prime Minister Johan Nygaardsvold's private London secretary, who had been a journalist before the war. A lawyer with the Ministry of Social Affairs acted as secretary.

The Committee was instructed to finish its proposals before autumn. Things did not turn out that way. As the Ministry began sending cases over to the Committee, it became necessary for Debes and others to take a number of initiatives. The Committee thus became the Ministry of Social Affairs' unofficial office for children-of-war cases, with its own premises and administration. After a number of meetings until November 1945, the Committee submitted a *proposal*, a *recommendation* to the Ministry of Social Affairs and a *draft legislation* for publication. In other words, the work was far more extensive than originally envisaged.

At its first three meetings, the Committee discussed the main questions and the secretary kept ordinary minutes of the meetings. The other meetings were devoted to detailed discussions of the wording of the documents and no minutes were kept. In terms of time, the work can be divided into two periods, before and after 12 October, when the Norwegian government adopted a resolution which put an end to the question of deportation to Germany.

Already at its first meeting, the Committee had voted against sending the children of war to Germany, and although they notified this in the minutes on grounds of principle, they emphasized the state of living conditions there as their practical concern throughout later documents. Shortly afterward, they were informed by the Parliament President, the Conservative Party leader C.J. Hambro, that the children could be sent to Sweden. They therefore decided to examine whether that was feasible, or whether it was feasible to send them to other countries, such as the US. Debes reported on the Lebensborn archives, where around 8,000 births had been recorded. Thingstad pointed out that a number were unaccounted for and likewise their whereabouts. Accordingly, this clarified the need to forward a motion from the Committee to the Ministry to ask the municipalities to get accurate information.

At its third meeting, based on new information, the Committee discussed whether from practical reasons it was possible to send the children to Germany. Further, they detailed how the authorities could intervene and take the children from their mothers if need be, not merely owing to failure of parental care from normal social reasons, but if the mother was nationally undeserving, or if local opinion so required. This was the same justification based on national failure of parental care that the Stockholm Committee had proposed. They also touched on the children's relations to their fathers, stating the undesirability of having future contact with Germany. Disregarding deportation or not, they asked the Ministry to perform psychiatric tests on the mothers and children. Debes made reference to a letter to the Ministry, probably written by Thingstad, which proposed that the children, with reference to their mental health, should be taken from their mothers and given an assumed name, place of birth and date of birth and be equipped with new identities before being put up for adoption or relocated by other means, at home or abroad. In another query to the Ministry, Debes asked that the establishment of a special War Child Office be officially formalized by the Ministry to deal with these important tasks. All in all, though it was not clearly stated, these elements most likely must be interpreted as preparations for a large-scale operation.

On 23 July, Social Minister Sven Oftedal travelled to Stockholm, where he had talks with Swedish politicians and senior civil servants about refugee issues and the question of sending the war children to Sweden. This is evident from interviews he gave to Swedish newspapers.[7] Although we have no detailed proof of it, he probably also made arrangements to organize the movement of the first group of children of war to Sweden, which actually occurred two days later. It consisted of 30 Norwegian children found at a Lebensborn home in Bremen, originally destined to be shipped to Norway.[8] Not long after, the children were announced for adoption in Swedish newspapers, labelled as children found in concentration camps in Germany, whose parents, place of birth and date of birth were unknown.[9] With falsified personal histories, most of them later were adopted through Swedish courts and subsequently granted Swedish nationality. The adoptions were at variance with Swedish and Norwegian adoption legislation and the Nordic Family Rights Convention of 1931, all of which require the permission of the children's parents, guardians or other responsible home authority. By and large, the similarity of these arrangements when compared to the plans of the Committee strongly indicates that the operation was considered to be the first project of a large-scale deportation to Sweden.

The Norwegian authorities were later presented with these cases, the first already in 1947, when they decided against allowing the mother to be informed or told the fate of her child. Another mother was pressured into accepting the adoption through the direct intervention in Norway of the Swedish adoptive parents' attorney, who had discovered her identity.[10] None of the other mothers was notified. Later, in the 1960s, many of the grown children contacted the Ministry of Social Affairs for assistance in locating their mothers.

Questionnaire to Poor-relief Councils

On 19 July, the Ministry of Social Affairs distributed the required questionnaire to the poor-relief county councils all over the country, with instructions to report the number of war children, where they currently were located, and whether they were with the mothers, at orphanages or elsewhere. It also included a question of how local opinion was disposed toward mother and child. Chair of the Committee Debes had proposed a rather imprecise text, which the Ministry had tightened up. Addresses were needed because the Lebensborn archives were not organized by residence addresses. If the Ministry was to utilize the archive in any practical sense, such as to collect the children or simply to contact them, it was imperative to know where the children were living and how many they were in each and every district.

Reporting practices were uneven. A total of 558 poor-relief agencies responded, or roughly 75 per cent of those who received the circular. They listed a total of 3,128 war children, of whom 1,492 had specific names and addresses. Other information[11] estimates the aggregate number at the end of the 1945 to be 7,853, which translates into an identification rate of only 19 per cent. Those who provided the most useful information were those with the largest numbers while, with some exceptions, the lowest scores were found where there were low numbers. As far as local opinion was concerned, a total of 360 responded; of that number only 38 reported that opinion was favourable while 116 reported that it was indifferent. The rest were negative to varying degrees. It did appear, however, that the atmosphere in distinctly rural communities was more conciliatory than in the most urban communities, but there were no sharply pronounced geographical patterns. Municipalities with condemning or conciliatory public opinion could be found side by side throughout the country, in the largest districts with children of war being along the coast from Rogaland to Finnmark, and in eastern Norway which, with the exception of Oslo, had the smallest number.

The low reporting rate for addresses weakened any implementing of large-scale projects in the immediate future, and in the longer term a new registration would be required. It is hard to tell whether or to what extent ideas of disobedience played a part in the poor-relief councils' failing reports. Conditions were difficult in the northern counties, even chaotic. Finnmark hardly had any poor-relief services at all. Several poor-relief councils responded that they would not provide names or addresses, stating only that the children living in their area were doing well, and that there was no need to do anything about them. Such motivation might be perceived as a reflection of a local protection mechanism against central authorities, a long-standing tradition in Norway. It was not unnatural to conclude that the children could be better cared for by regional or local authorities. As it was, the central authorities had little choice. Operating through normal manners and means, they simply could not reach the majority of the children.

Another element must also be mentioned. The reports showed that a mere 142 children received support from the poor-relief services. That figure must be far too low. Nonetheless, it does indicate that the children of war had not yet become a financial liability for the municipalities. Lebensborn had paid support to the mothers until the end of the war.[12] Many poor-relief councils wrote that if the municipalities were to bear such costs in future, public opinion would become more negative. That could be understood as a demand that the State should cover the costs.

The War Child Committee made special mention of the reports in its recommendation, but made no remarks to the fact that its main objective was to find out where the children were. Nor did it mention that so few respondents had specified names and addresses. Otherwise, it painted a far more favourable picture of public opinion throughout the country than the reports actually described. This was probably linked to an attempt to orchestrate a change in public opinion in the autumn of 1945. The Committee appeared to be paving the way for that. Actually, it is difficult to substantiate that type of statement so early.

The Government makes its Decision

Parallel to the deliberations of the War Child Committee, the Ministry of Justice explored the legal basis for deportation. No legislation contained any provision against being the sweetheart of or married to a citizen of an enemy state. Nor had any attempt ever been made to make it punishable, not even in the time of the London government, which had otherwise initiated a system of provisional laws on a large scale. To implement the deportation legally, it was important to make rules of law which were not at odds with the public's sense of justice.

As a judicial step, in mid-August 1945 a provisional law was adopted, reintroducing the provision from the Citizenship Act from before 1924, which had deprived married women of their own citizenship. The amendment stated that women who married a citizen of an enemy state, i.e. a German, would lose their Norwegian citizenship, even if they never left Norway. The provision applied to everyone who married after 9 April 1940. Although it was not mentioned directly, the Ministry of Justice contended that the regulation also abolished the right to re-acquire citizenship in the Citizenship Act of 1924. The regulation contravened two basic principles of Norwegian law: that no act of legislation shall have retroactive effect and that no act shall establish collective punishment. The women's movement protested, but to no avail.[13]

The provisional law can be seen as the first judicial step of the strategic policy of deportation, but this seems to be contradicted by the circumstances which gave birth to it; it was adopted owing to a near-panic reaction on the part of the authorities when, at the end of July 1945, it was reported that a Swedish ship with 'tyskertøser' and children of war was en route from Germany to Norway. This happened shortly before the first election after the war, and the government feared the effects on public opinion. The national chief of police was allowed to organize a press conference where he reassured people by telling them that the police were in full control of the situation. They had registered the 'tyskertøser' throughout the entire war, he contended, which was quite a stretch of the reality. However, the need of a provisional act had prior to this incident been signalled in the Ministry; eventually it would have found an appropriate occasion.

Thus, with immediate effect, it was possible to convey these married women and their children to Germany on the German military transports which were returning German prisoners. The authorities took care not to use the term 'deportation', which had negative connotations, opting for the term 'denationalization' instead. We have no idea how many women and children were denationalized in this way. Moreover, augmented by a number of women who *wanted* to leave along with their sweethearts, the numbers were considerable.

Following the capitulation, a corps of Norwegian repatriation officers worked in Germany to bring home prisoners and 'displaced persons', organized under the auspices of the Ministry of Social Affairs. In the field in Germany, they served under the British military occupation authorities, and their leader, the former bomber pilot Johan K. Christie and his subordinates, mostly officers or former civilian prisoners, had received British military commissions to execute this special work. They soon saw the need to bring home also human beings in distress in Germany other than former prisoners, among them war children and their mothers. This brought Christie and his men into conflict with the authorities at home, who were shipping off to Germany as many as possible more or less willing women and children. The repatriation corps' attitude was partly in response to its subordinate position under the British Army of the Rhine under whose auspices the repatriation corps found itself.[14] The BAOR feared that the children would become a burden on the occupation authorities. The British felt conditions were better off in Norway. Secondly, based on their own experience, the repatriation officers, who knew how to trawl for refugees in the countryside where the destitution was palpable, feared that the winter of 1945/46 would turn into a huge disaster, and felt it was advisable to get as many people as possible home, regardless of their background. These were the officers who found the 30 Norwegian children of war in Bremen in June 1945, sending them homeward on 25 July. The fact that they ended up in Sweden was the responsibility of the Norwegian Ministry of Social Affairs.[15]

Women with or without a child, who had either been in Germany during the war or arrived there immediately afterward, reported to the repatriation corps in growing numbers in autumn 1945, begging for help to get home. The British also sent such individuals to the repatriation corps. Meanwhile, the central passport office in Oslo did everything it could to prevent this by refusing to grant entry permits. The office tried to get those who were already under way interned in Denmark, before returning them to Germany. In early August, the rules were tightened up further on the part of Oslo, requiring strict documentation and demanding that those who made it through the eye of the needle had to pay their own very high travel expenses. In connection with the ship mentioned earlier, i.e. the one bound for Oslo and filled with women and children, the repatriation corps received a reprimand.

The criticism from the police in Oslo was followed by a proposal to dismantle the repatriation corps in Germany from October 1945, and to let the diplomats take over. Until then, the repatriation officers were prohibited from trying to repatriate anyone other than former prisoners. Christie protested, as did his British superiors. In a personal appeal to Prime Minister Einar Gerhardsen, Christie referred to Norway's humanitarian traditions and asked whether the Norwegian government realized what a disaster the German winter could inflict on Norwegian-born women and children who were leading miserable lives because they were not accepted and were barely able to make themselves understood. He demanded that all of them should be allowed to come home if they wanted to, and that if any of them had done anything illegal during the occupation, they should be judged individually, rather than making all of them suffer. Following meetings with Secretary of the Ministry of Refugee Affairs Kirsten Hansteen and the Ministry of Justice, Christie wrote a memo to the Norwegian government, urgently requesting that the rules for a so-called repatriation visa be made more lenient, after having been made more stringent four weeks earlier. To rally support, Christie made an exception for women who had been in the Nazi movement or who would not declare their willingness to divorce their German husbands.

In the middle of October 1945, the Government adopted a motion which leaned in the direction Christie wanted, but opened the door to a number of exceptions. The Ministry of Social Affairs presented the decision as a humanitarian relief operation, pointing out that it did not cover those who had married after 9 April 1940 or childless widows, and furthermore that everyone had to be politically acceptable. One condition had to be that they were in mortal danger. Everyone had to sign a personal declaration which would be controlled by the police.

In a new clarification late in October, the Ministry of Social Affairs had to admit that the decision could be interpreted as covering all children in distress, even if they preferred not to repatriate children born in wedlock and other specific groups. Meanwhile, the Ministry was aware of the problems involved in limiting the number of children and therefore began using the term 'children of Norwegian extraction or partially Norwegian extraction' instead of the more straightforward terms Norwegian or German citizen.

The formula of the personal declaration dictated by the Ministry stated that the person who signed it was aware that the public opinion against them was far from friendly, that she was prepared to face difficulties and unpleasantness for herself and her children, that she could be interned if need be, that their stay was temporary and that she had to be prepared to be sent back to Germany. Furthermore, she had to declare that she had not been a member of any Nazi organization. It was a quasi-legal and humiliating document, depriving them of their legal rights.

On the other hand, even though the declaration marked a defeat for humanism in the spirit of Fridtjof Nansen, as Christie wrote to the Prime Minister, the reality behind the Government's resolution was to put a stop to all further deportation plans to Germany and, as the police later stated in a report, probably also individual deportations. The authorities now found that it was not possible to dismantle the repatriation corps in Germany. The British would not allow Norway to establish diplomatic stations. The whole thing ended with the repatriation corps continuing, although in a slightly reorganized form. Following the government resolution, the corps could also seek out women and children in distress and bring them home. By mid-1946, they had repatriated 400–500 women and their children.

A Change in Attitude in Sweden

The Government resolution in October entailed that the Norwegian government supported the War Child Committee's resistance against deporting the children to Germany. It seems as if Sweden as a consequence appeared to be the only feasible option for relocation. During and after his visit to Stockholm late in July 1945, Secretary of the Ministry of Social Affairs Oftedal was in contact with the central social-democratic politician and educator Alva Myrdal, who had a major impact on relief organizations such as Save the Children and the Red Cross. Oftedal also met with the head of the Swedish Labour Market Board, Nils Hagelin, who took on the responsibility for the matter on behalf of the Swedish authorities. A few days later, Secretary of the Ministry of Refugee Affairs, Kirsten Hansteen visited Stockholm, where she continued talks with Myrdal and Hagelin about the placement of the children. The contact with Hagelin was subsequently handled through Debes, head of the War Child Committee, who dealt with the correspondence from his home address, probably owing to the delicate nature of the project. On 11 August, Hagelin wrote to Debes that the process was in progress and that the war children could soon be relocated to Sweden.

A month later, Oftedal and Director General Frydenberg met Swedish Minister of Social Affairs Gustav Möller and Minister of Culture, later Prime Minister Tage Erlander, at a conference in Copenhagen, where they were hoping to get a green light from Sweden. This issue was not the topic of the conference; it was discreetly dealt with off the record. Unexpectedly, however, Erlander signalled a new Swedish attitude. They were concerned about the project and Oftedal had to assure them that Norway would go no further in materializing it. Although we have no clear explanation, the reason for Sweden's change of heart was presumably that the adoption process for the 30 children who had already arrived was proving to be more controversial than expected and that the Swedish government feared the problems which could arise with thousands of children.

A new initiative was taken during Christmas week 1945, when a liaison from the Ministry of Trade and Industry was told at a conference in Sweden by his Swedish counterpart, the Minister of Trade Gunnar Myrdal, that Sweden was willing to take 1,000 war children. Oftedal subsequently wrote to Alva Myrdal, the wife of Gunnar Myrdal, telling her that Norway had not taken any new initiative after the conference in Copenhagen. A new initiative would have to come from Sweden, he wrote, adding that he would be pleased to send some of the children to Sweden. In mid-January 1946, the secretary general of the Norwegian Red Cross wrote to the Ministry of Social Affairs, recounting a query from the Swedish Save the Children. The Red Cross wanted to know if the project was still feasible and how far the inquiries had come. It does not appear that the Ministry followed up the query.

Since going to Sweden was no longer seen as an option, the war children were to remain in Norway. The War Child Committee had to re-write its documents and concentrate completely on proposals toward this end. The most important thing was to safeguard the children financially. Demanding individual child maintenance from the fathers was not an option for reasons of principle. Based on a similar Danish compensation to Finland for children fathered by fascist Danish soldiers during World War II, the Committee secretary concluded that any lump-sum payment from Germany had to be roughly 50 million Norwegian kroner. (That was $7 million or £2.5 million in the currencies of the day. A very rough estimate could be based on a cost-of-living increase from 1945 to 2005 of 1546 per cent: with today's £ sterling equivalent to about NOK 11.9, this sum would total £65 million.) The sum was totally unrealistic, in his opinion. Instead, the State should settle a sum on the mothers corresponding to the father's child-maintenance liability. Moreover, the State should provide education for the mothers.

On 18 October, the Committee finished its *Draft of an Act relating to War Children* and *Draft of the Special Circumstances Motivating the Act relating to the War Children*. Apart from the Act's definition of 'a war child' as being the child of a German father and Norwegian mother, the explanation in the special circumstances gave a more detailed definition by stating that one expected allied children of war in the near future. Although Norwegian law should apply to the determination of paternity, the same law's regulation for public announcement of paternity was not desirable. The Ministry should have the right to change the child's first name, even if the mother was not amenable to this. Registrars should have an obligation to give notification to the Ministry. Interventions in the family home in the event of national failure of parental care should be allowed. The State should have a broader right to take a child away from its mother based on living conditions, explained in the special circumstances as a hostile atmosphere on the part of the local population in respect of the foster home or the child. As far as deportation was concerned, the draft bill stated that the Ministry, based on a proposal from the Child Welfare Board, in compliance with international agreements, could relocate children of war to another country, even without the consent of the mother or guardian, if the child was in danger of being exposed to lasting damage if it stayed in Norway. Nevertheless the special circumstances emphasized that 'the case' primarily had to be dealt with here at home. The draft bill finally stipulated that child maintenance was not to be claimed from the German fathers, as links between the German father and the child in Norway was undesirable. The bill assumed that the State would provide child maintenance in advance.

The Committee accordingly wrote *A recommendation regarding measures for the war children* to the Ministry, which emphasized that children in distress in Germany should be brought home, that Norway's child-welfare system had to be expanded, that the Child Welfare Board had to be given higher priority, and that training of the mothers was crucial. Last but not least, it proposed a public campaign to shape opinion in respect of the children in a favorable direction. The Ministry had to ensure that the authorities and general public used the term children of war rather than derogatory characterizations. Points relating to the organization of deportation were also included as well as comments to the proposal that the State advance the payment of child maintenance to the war children. As a whole, the three documents contained everything from brutal suggestions about taking the children away from their mothers based on the wishes of the local community and sending them abroad or relocating them at home, to well-intentioned integrating proposals to advance child-maintenance payments and a campaign in the public and private sectors to get society-at-large to accept the children. Some of the motions, like the suggestion that the German fathers should not be requested to pay child maintenance, represented a violation of a main principle in the Child Act of 1915, which secured children born out of wedlock legal assistance from the State to enforce the fathers' contribution to their upbringing.

In mid-November, the secretary sent the material to be printed. It consisted of the general *Recommendation to the Ministry of Social Affairs from the War Child Committee* as well as the three above-mentioned documents, with an abundance of documentation, including quotations from the Clergy Committee, and a memo from a psychiatrist, Chief Physician at Gaustad Hospital in Oslo, contending that many of the children were mentally handicapped, as well as a report from a children's conference in Switzerland. Before it was printed, however, all the material was returned to the Ministry. New objections had been raised. They referred to doubts about whether the description of the situation was completely adequate, in particular in the light of reports which could indicate that more of the children than anticipated were with their mothers, doubts about establishing of numerous orphanages which would be needed according to the motions and whether it would be possible to fund their operation. Then there were doubts about the need for the psychiatrist's plans for psychiatric evaluations and how urgent the matter really was, now that deportation was no longer an option. A new motion to make it easier for those who really wanted to move to Germany with their children needed further clarification, since the Directorate of Refugee Affairs specifically advised against it.

In addition to these elements, the most decisive argument against publishing was probably that the Ministry had been notified that an Australian immigration delegation would be coming to Oslo in the next few days, for the purpose of speeding up immigration to Australia in general and in particular in taking 50,000 'war orphans' overseas.

Australian Solution?

The news reached the headlines, not solely as a solution to the war- children problem, but more so as it triggered the expectations to emigrate orchestrated by an association known as the 'Australia Club'. The newspapers wrote that Australia was also interested in taking in orphans. To make it clear that Norway was not in favour of emigration, the Ministry of Foreign Affairs wished to ignore the delegation, but felt obligated to arrange a meeting on a senior-civil-servant level. At the meetings which took place on 22 and 23 November 1945, Frydenberg invited himself and Debes to participate. While the Ministry of Foreign Affairs clarified to the point of a ban that it did not favour emigration from Norway, according to both Norwegian and Australian sources, Frydenberg and Debes offered 9,000 children of war to the Australians. The mothers were never mentioned. The delegation was taken on a tour to the former Lebensborn home Godthaab in Bærum, where they could see for themselves how some hundred children of war were living. At the closing lunch, the Ministry of Social Affairs added prestige and support to the motions to the delegation by seating two Ministers of Government at the table.

The Australians' report mentioned the possibility of mass emigration from Norway.[16] They referred to the offer of 9,000 children as one of the two largest, and most promising results of their trip. However, in March 1946, the Australian prime minister stated in a parliamentary debate that the lack of transportation made it hard to tell when the emigration of children could begin.[17] It had become clear to them during the trip that neither Norway nor any other country could transport that many emigrants. By the time the report was put before the parliament in November 1946, an Australian MP had visited Oslo and reported home that 7,000 of the 9,000 children had already been adopted and that the remaining 2,000 were to be 'absorbed'.[18] The immigration of children had become controversial. The head of the delegation to Oslo in 1945, Social Democrat Leslie Haylen, challenged the opposition to accept the Norwegian offer of 9,000 war children, ostracized from their own country, as he put it, although he himself opposed such a scheme. Notwithstanding, even the political opposition did not want the war children, since they considered them German children. They wanted white Europeans to stem the tide of Asians and to strengthen ties to the British Empire, but not the children of the empire's adversaries because that would strengthen ties to Germany.

Excluding Mechanism of Citizenship

Frydenberg probably postponed publication of the recommendations from the War Child Committee when the unexpected possibility of an Australian solution had popped up, because the latest wording of the War Child Act primarily was based on the idea that the children would be staying in Norway. Now some changes might have to be made. Three days after the Australians left Norway, another unexpected event took place when the chair of the War Child Committee Debes unexpectedly died, and with him the driving force behind the work.

Although work on the Act was shoved to the back burner pending an answer from Canberra, Frydenberg had many urgent questions linked to the children of war which had to be resolved. Later in 1946, the legislative work resumed. At that point, the objections within the Ministry led to a less comprehensive draft aimed at regulating paternity issues. The efforts continued in 1947, but no proposition was put forward. In other words, the temporary stop on publication in 1945 became permanent. Although the Committee's recommendation was made available to scientists and the war-children organizations in the beginning of the 1990s, it was not made public until 1999, 44 years after the fact.[19]

In the years subsequent to 1945, various problems of a legal and practical nature raised by the children-of-war issue were dealt with in other ways, through circulars, regulations and communications from the Ministry of Social Affairs. Neither the War Child Act nor the separate suggestions made by the War Child Committee were instituted. Proposals such as allowing the authorities to take children away from their mothers based on public opinion in the community and for specific political reasons were also put on ice. However, falsifying the children's identities, as proposed by the psychiatrists and psychologists, was instituted to some extent through a circular which gave the authorities the right to change their first names. The Ministry lost its motivation for funding the undertaking of the large-scale psychiatric investigation required for the deportation project, and as it was not claimed for other purposes, it was set aside, along with the proposal for separate orphanages. But the very important motion of not requesting child support from the German fathers was carried through, as we shall see.

What can be described as the legislative project begun in the summer of 1945 to legalize mass deportations and to be completed by the War Child Act was given an important sequel. The provisional regulation which had transformed married 'tyskertøser' and their children into 'Germans' and deprived them of important rights enjoyed by all Norwegians became regular law in December 1946. This took place despite the fact that the government resolution of October 1945 had caused more than 500 women with children to stay in the country without the police being able to deport them. The provisional regulation and the Act, as the Ministry of Justice interpreted them, also deprived the women of the right to reacquire Norwegian citizenship. Not even in 1949, when the ordinary rules for the acquisition and loss of citizenship in the Citizenship Act from 1924 were reintroduced in their entirety, also in relation to Germany, was this applied to the mothers of the children of war and to the children themselves. The Cold War was emerging in full, Germany was Norway's new ally, military collaboration was being initiated between the two countries under the new alliance, and the legal purge against treason had run its course.

This collective punishment had been sharply criticized as early as in 1945. The criticism swelled over the years, not least from the perspective of gender equality. A new Citizenship Act in 1950 brought the discussion to a close. The mothers could reacquire their citizenship by providing notification within five years. However, their children had to wait until they turned 18 to obtain the same right. That meant that a child born in 1943, whose mother had married a German, who had spent his or her whole life in the same village and never been in Germany or abroad at all, was not able to be 'Norwegian' until he or she gave notification in 1961. Once each year, by a particular date, these children or their guardians had to apply for a residence permit at their local police office. The signal effect of such a scheme can hardly be overstated, not merely for the local community, but also for the individuals involved. Even though it was only these children, remaining in Norway, who by law became German, and the vast majority of the others were by law Norwegians as offspring of single mothers, the German stamp rubbed off on everyone. The authorities might easily have reversed the regulation of August 1945 and established that these children should follow the nationality of their mothers, and thus be treated as any other citizen.

On the contrary, the concept of the war children as basically German and not entitled to *full* support and legal protection from society as Norwegian children, spread onto another field of legislature, with grave effects to them in the years to come. In the period 1946–1957 new laws on children and child care were introduced in Norway. But war children gained little from these.[20] In 1946 a law on child benefit from the State was put forward, without covering the first child. This proposal would exclude nearly all war children from benefiting. Protests from the women's movement resulted in a new draft, which included the first child out of wedlock. In order to receive the allowance at least one of the parents had to support the child and had to be *a* Norwegian citizen. As a consequence, the children of women who were dead, who had temporarily left their children to others, had left the country or had been Germanized inside Norway, received no support. The law came in to force in October 1946.

As indicated, more serious and extensive effects followed Ministry of Social Affairs' application of the Child Act from 1915 (*barnelovene*). It was the obligation of the State to enforce paternity order and maintenance from the father on behalf of all children born out of wedlock. As the Ministry of Social Affairs opposed all contact between the children, mothers and the German fathers, it suspended efforts by the local courts to fulfil the Act, and directed them to forward all paternity cases on war children to the Ministry. More than 6,000 cases were left there and never dealt with. Following a notion from the Ministry of Justice in 1950, the Ministry was instructed to return the cases to the local courts. The cases were returned, followed by strong appeal from the Ministry of Social Affairs that all cases ought to be closed without decisions. Along with other obstacles in the process of collecting of child maintenance from fathers in foreign countries, these policies reduced the number of cases to fewer than 500, and the number of children who were to receive paternity support from the German fathers likewise. Even as late as in the 1970s, the authorities did not want to forward claims against East German fathers.

A longtime claim for all children born out of wedlock was eventually met in 1956, as the Ministry forwarded a motion for a law on State prepayment of child maintenance from the fathers (*lov om forskuttering av barnebidrag*). This provision had been postponed for many years. But when it appeared, it demanded that the father had to live in Norway or in a country with which Norway had a formal agreement. Not so with Germany. As documents show, the Ministry had made this exception to exclude the war children; their vast number could halt the process in Parliament, a Deputy Secretary of State in the Ministry wrote. The motion came under heavy protest from social councils of many counties, and the Ministry was eventually pressed to supply the motion with a new law of supporter insurance (*lov om forsørgertrygd*) to meet the needs of these children. The two laws were put in motion from April 1958. Due to the many years' delay of the laws, combined with the fixed 18 years' age-limit regulations in them, few war children benefited much from them, as the youngest was 12 years of age and the oldest 17 at the time.

In these, as in other public regulations of importance for their lives to come, war children were faced with a general attitude from society which originated from the characteristics fixed in 1945 and the previous years. Individually, many of them were to experience both marginalizing and stigmatizing within private, public and local life, which clearly bore the hallmark of that category.

Notes

1. The term 'tyskertøs' (Jerry hussy, tart, whore) is not easily translated, as it mixes the concept of national deceit with female sexuality and girlish immaturity. Literally 'tøs' in dialect and old Norwegian refers to a young girl.

2. Of the country's approximately 1,800 Jews, 767 were sent to extermination camps in Poland. Only 32 survived. From Telavåg, on the west coast of Norway, 72 men were sent to Germany after a shooting incident, and 31 died.

3. Barry Coldrey, 'A Charity which has Outlived its Usefulness: The Last Phase of Catholic Child Migration, 1947–56', *History of Education* 25(4), 1996, p. 377.

4. M. Parsons, *Precious Commodities. Overseas Evacuation: England's Future* (Paper at Europeiske krigsbarndager, Uleåborg 13–15 June 2003, Riksförbundet Finska Krigsbarn, 2003).

5. Because of the Swedish ban on party politics for refugees, they acted under the cover of being a TUC study circle. This is the reason why most writers

incorrectly refer to the committee as the TUC committee in Stockholm ('AFL-komiteen i Stockholm').

6. Carlsson shared an interest in the application of eugenics toward minority groups such as Gypsies and travellers/tinkers or 'tatere' with the German eugenicist Robert Ritter. See Per Haave, *Sterilization of travellers* (Research Council of Norway, 2000), pp. 67–9.

7. Including *Dagens Nyheter* on 24 July 1945.

8. The story of these children, known in Sweden as 'the Fiskeboda children', is first described in detail in Lars Borgersrud, *Overlatt til svenske myndigheter* (Televågkonferansen 2002: Born og krig). See also Lars Borgersrud, *Staten og krigsbarna: En historisk undersøkelse av statsmyndighetenes behandling av krigsbarna i de første etterkrigsårene* (University of Oslo, 2004), pp. 85–137.

9. *Södermanlands Nyheter*, 4 September 1945, and *Dagens Nyheter* 4 September 1945.

10. Borgersrud, *Overlatt til svenske myndigheter*, pp 72–73.

11. *Statistisk sentralbyrå*: Folke- og boligtellingen i 1946.

12. In fact, all the expenses incurred by the Reichs Commissariat for Occupied Norway, including the cost of the Lebensborn programme, were charged to an account in Norges Bank and thus paid by the Norwegian state.

13. Henvendelse fra Norske Kvinners Nasjonalråd v/ Sigrid Stray 12.12.45, Justisdepartementet, Lovavdelingen, Dc- Statsrett og forvaltningsrett, 78, *Legg 43–44. Ny statborgerlov. Diverse 1923–1946, Justis-og-politideparte-mentet.*

14. 'British Army of the Rhine', i.e. the military authority in the sector of Germany occupied by the British.

15. Borgersrud, *Staten og krigsbarna*, pp. 133–5.

16. *Report 1946*, p. 30, A 436/1, 45/5/563 1, Australian Archives.

17. *International Affairs* 1946, p. 533 (22 March 1946), Parliamentary Debates, Commonwealth of Australia.

18. T. Dunbabine to Director-General, Dept. of Inf., Canberra, att. Mr Aub. Williams, 13 November 1946, A 436/1, 45/5/563 1.

19. In *A White Paper: Selected Public Documents Regarding the Children of War Issue* (Research Council Norway, 1999).

20. Borgersrud, *Staten og krigsbarna*, pp. 333–71.

References

Borgersrud, L., *Overlatt til svenske myndigheter: De norske krigsbarna som ble sendt til Sverige i 1945*, Televågkonferansen 2002, Born og krig.

Borgersrud, L., *Staten og krigsbarna: En historisk undersøkelse av statsmyn-*

dighetenes behandling av krigsbarna i de første etterkrigsårene, Oslo: University of Oslo, Department of Culture Studies, 2004.

Coldrey, B., 'A Charity which has Outlived its Usefulness: The Last Phase of Catholic Child Migration, 1947–56', *History of Education* 25(4) (1996).

Haave, P., *Sterilization of Travellers,* Oslo: Research Council Norway, 2000.

Parsons, M., *Precious Commodities. Overseas Evacuation: England's Future* (Paper at Europeiske krigsbarndager, Uleåborg 13.–15. juni 2003), Riksförbundet Finska Krigsbarn, 2003.

Statistisk sentralbyrå, Folke-og boligtellingen i 1946.

A White Paper: Selected Public Documents Regarding the Children of War Issue, Oslo: Research Council Norway, 1999.

–5–

Life Stories of Norwegian War Children

Kjersti Ericsson and Dag Ellingsen

The Creation of a Problem Category

During World War II and the first years of peace, the children of German soldiers and Norwegian women, born during the occupation or just afterward, were constituted as a new problem category, calling for special measures of control from society. At the time when these children were conceptually separated from other children born during the war, and defined as a social problem, the youngest of them were infants, and none had reached school age. The official name given to them was 'war children' ('German brats' in the vernacular). Authorities, media, professionals and laymen participated in the process of constructing war children as a problem category. The process had many aspects and several interacting levels. In 1945 the War Child Committee was appointed by the government to suggest solutions to the war-child problem.

The problem category 'war children', or 'German brats', was influenced by concept and ways of thinking stemming from several different discourses. The most important ones were the following: A national discourse, viewing children as the property of the nation, in which these children raised a difficult problem: should they be considered Norwegian or German? The question was posed as either/or. Both/and was no option. A social-policy discourse considered the war children and their mothers to be potential child- welfare and social-security clients, and as such a burden on public finances. A discourse of gender and sexuality stereotyped the mothers of war children as indecent and 'loose' women. And finally there was a medical discourse, concerned with feeblemindedness and defective heredity.

The perception of war children – who they were and what kind of problem they presented, was nourished by all the discourses mentioned. The extensive web of connotations surrounding the category of 'German child' made it extremely powerful. Denotatively, the term 'German child' pointed to the child's natural father. In this way, the category was naturalized, as if having a German father naturally made the child all the things implied by the web of connotations.

The national discourse is of special significance if we are to understand the plight of the war children in post-war Norway. The biological, cultural and national threats they were seen to constitute were tightly interwoven. An example is an editorial in the daily paper *Lofotposten*, from May 1945:[1]

> All these German children are bound to grow up and develop into an extensive bastard minority in the Norwegian people. By their descent they are doomed in advance to take a combative stance. They have no nation, they have no father, they just have hate, and this is their only heritage. They are unable to become Norwegians. Their fathers were Germans, their mothers were Germans in thought and action. To allow them to stay in this country is tantamount to legalizing the raising of a fifth column. They will forever constitute an element of irritation and unrest among the pure Norwegian population. It is best, for Norway as well as for the children themselves, that they continue their lives under the heavens where they naturally belong.

The concern that the children would develop into a fifth column loyal to Germany, the Trojan horse of Nazism in Norway, was widespread. Concerns of this kind were partly associated with ideas of a 'German' biological heritage which would find expression in marching and commandeering; partly they were associated with fears that the children would embrace Nazi ideology through influence from their mothers if they were to be raised by them. There is, however, no evidence indicating that there were large numbers of Nazis among the mothers.

The mothers of the war children were 'German in thought and action', the quoted editorial says. More than thought and action, it was a question of sexuality and body. The same editorial also makes this quite clear:[2]

> In our view, they ought to follow their children and leave the country. They have made their choice ... To them, sexual shamelessness was more important than the freedom and independence of Norway. They should be able to settle comfortably in the country and with the people which have led their urges and instincts.

One source of the rage against the war children and their mothers was the concept of the sexuality of women as national property. Anette Warring[3] in her book on Danish girls having sexual relations with German soldiers emphasizes the idea of the reproductive capacity of women and traditional motherhood as a 'national resource': Women have a key role in the biological and cultural survival of the nation. In this perspective, sexual relations between native women and enemy soldiers constitute a national threat. With a slightly different angle, Fabrice Virgili,[4] in his book on the shorn women of France, conceptualizes the bodies of women as national territory. As such, they may be conquered. A woman who voluntarily has sexual relations with an enemy soldier has treacherously surrendered part of the national territory to the enemy.

The sexuality of the mothers of the war children had been appropriated and contaminated by the Germans. What about the children they gave birth to? With Norwegian fathers, these children would have belonged to the Norwegian nation, the guarantee of its future survival and prosperity. But with German fathers? The author of the quoted editorial was clear in his opinion: The children were German and ought to be sent to Germany. This was not an eccentric and extremist position shortly after the war. The government-appointed War Child Committee, in its terms of reference, was asked to consider wholesale deportation of the war children to Germany as one option. The committee came down unanimously against this 'solution'. However, if the children were to stay in Norway, they had to become unambiguously Norwegian. All contacts with Germany had to be severed, all signs of German heritage had to be deleted.

Two Basic Questions

Two questions were central to the debate on the 'war-child problem', explicitly or implicitly: 1) Do the war children belong together with 'us' or not? 2) Are the war children a special kind of problematic, bad and/or dangerous people? The first question recalls the concept of children as national property. It was posed in the sharpest possible manner in the discussion on whether or not the war children ought to be deported to Germany. The second question sprang from a variety of concerns: it was feared that the biological and cultural heritage of the fathers, as well as the suspected congenital 'inferiority' of the mothers, would prove to have damaging effects on the children. Concerns of this kind motivated a recommendation by the War Child Committee to have all war children examined by psychiatrists (which was never done). However, the various discourses which influenced the war-child category all implied the relevance of both questions.

The debate on the 'war-child problem' petered out after a while. The report from the War Child Committee was placed in a drawer, there to gather dust. The war child was no longer an urgent point on the public agenda. However, this does not necessarily mean that the questions discussed in the first period after the liberation had lost their meaning. The two questions mentioned still framed the way war children were perceived, both centrally and locally. How was this situation experienced by the war children themselves, and in what way did it influence their life course?

To answer these questions, both a qualitative and quantitative approach has been used.

Based on life-history interviews with 100 war children[5] who have now passed or are nearing their sixtieth birthday, we will discuss some salient topics which emerge when war children in retrospect narrate, interpret and reflect upon their childhood and later life. Our interviewees have mostly been recruited through organizations for war children. Consequently, our sample is dominated by people who feel that being a 'war child' has been a considerable liability in their lives. In addition, a representative sample of war children (as representative as possible, given the methodological difficulties) has been selected. A picture of the living conditions of war children, based on data from modern electronic registers located at Statistics Norway, will be presented.

It should be noted that the life experiences of Norwegian war children varies considerably. Some have had reasonably happy childhoods. Others look back on a highly traumatic past. Even within our skewed qualitative sample, the variance is great. However, a sense of loss and lack of fulfilment may be experienced by war children whose early years seem quite normal from the vantage point of an outsider, as well as by those who have fared less well.

The two basic questions (mentioned above) framing the way war children were perceived lead directly into the two main preoccupations of the war children when they tell their life stories: 1) to belong or not to belong, to be socially included or excluded, and 2) to live with an imposed identity. The same two points are also the main focus of this chapter.

To Belong or not to Belong

School, Neighbourhood and Institutions

We had expected, and we also found, that being a 'German brat' in many instances was consonant with having a precarious and marginal position in school, among the children, and often also in the neighbourhood in general. The stories vary from accounts of very brutal treatment at the hands of both teachers and co-pupils, to a more vague feeling of being an outsider. A more subtle form of exclusion was experienced by some children who felt that their teachers simply ignored them. These children just sat in the classroom; they were never asked questions and they never received any help with their school work. Perhaps the teacher considered it a wasted effort to try to teach anything to 'stupid German brats', some interviewees reflect.

For some children, the question of inclusion or exclusion was also actualized in relation to the neighbouring community. One man says: 'I can still walk down the streets in my home town with my wife, and point out to her the houses where I was not allowed to enter.' Many parents rejected this boy as a playmate for their children.

It should be noted, however, that the picture is not altogether gloomy. We are also told about teachers who were both fair and helpful and about comradeship and happy play with other children in and out of school.

One group of war children was excluded from society in the full sense of the word by being placed in total institutions: orphanages, so-called 'special schools' or institutions for the feeble-minded. They were positioned as 'not us' – different from the 'normal' population. One man had never been outside the fenced enclosure surrounding the orphanage before he started school at the age of seven. The same man had not seen the inside of an ordinary private home until he was twelve. To see how 'normal' people lived made a deep impression on him. The extent of exclusion from society varied with the length of stay and the type of institution. War children placed in institutions for the feeble-minded fared the worst. Besides growing up in the institution, they often stayed on far into adult life. Nearly all war children with experience from total institutions speak of harsh regimes, lack of care and love, and more or less frequent episodes of maltreatment.

War children placed in total institutions constitute a minority. Their destiny may be regarded as the extreme end of a continuum of social exclusion and marginality.

The Family: A Safe Haven?

As mentioned, we had expected social exclusion and marginality to be an important issue. What we had *not* expected, however, was the salience of this issue within the *family*. Many mothers were confronted with the question of exclusion or inclusion in ways which profoundly influenced the life course of their children. Hate and contempt of women who had sexual relations with occupant soldiers was strong and widespread during and after the war. A large number of women suffered humiliating punishments such as having their hair hacked off publicly and/or being interned in special camps. Women who managed to escape this kind of punishment might nevertheless experience social ostracism in their local neighbourhoods.

In this situation, the mother's family of origin was not always a safe haven. The way the family reacted when a member became pregnant by a German soldier had repercussions through the life of the child. If mother and child were accepted by the family (or at least by the child's grandparents), they often stayed with the grandparents, enjoying some support and protection. For many war children, the grandmother was the main caregiver in their childhood. Some mothers left the child entirely in the care of relatives, most frequently the grandmother, hoping for a new chance in life unhampered by a 'German brat'.

If the mother was excluded from her own family during pregnancy or after childbirth, the situation of mother and child could be desperate. Some women did not dare to confront their parents with a 'German child', and tried to keep the birth secret. Others were turned away, or were met with such hostility that they decided to leave. To be an unwed mother in the 1940s, with the added label of 'German tart', and without support from their next of kin, was very difficult. Many mothers found it impossible to keep the child, who was given up for adoption or placed in an orphanage. If the mother managed to keep the child with her, she tended to struggle on the margins of economic survival: moving from place to place as a domestic servant or in other low-paid jobs, living in one room at the employer's mercy.

For some war children, the consequences of their mothers' inability to keep them were dramatic indeed. Long careers in total institutions could be the result. Others were lucky enough to be adopted by parents who loved them and treated them well. However, even the happy stories sometimes have a tragic streak. One interviewee, a woman, was given up for adoption because her mother did not dare to return to her family with a 'German brat': one of her brothers had been killed by the Germans, another brother was injured. This woman's childhood with her adopted parents was happy. The great sorrow in her life, however, is being rejected by her biological mother whom, as an adult, she managed to trace. The mother was still afraid that her family should learn of her daughter's existence.

Children who stayed with mothers who had been rejected by their own family, more often than not had a difficult start in life. Since the mother had to work hard to support the two of them, she was not in a position to look after her child properly. If the mother had to move from place to place in search for work, the child experienced ruptured friendships, fragmented schooling and a general instability in life.

Only Partly Belonging?

Whether or not the mother was included in her family of origin had dramatic consequences for the child. This was not the only critical point where inclusion or exclusion became an issue in family relationships, however. After some time, many mothers found Norwegian husbands. In some cases, the child was allowed to live with the mother and her new husband and children, in others not. Some men, when marrying the mother, clearly stated that 'the German brat' was not part of the bargain. In several instances, the mother was so eager for the social protection offered by marriage that she consented to not bring the child with her into her new family. War children with this experience often express feelings of betrayal and rejection by the mother.

Being allowed to live with the mother was not, however, a guarantee of security and happiness. Children who were physically included in their mother's new family risked being constantly reminded of only partly belonging. Some suffered at the hands of abusive stepfathers, as the mothers' deflated value as prospective marriage partners sometimes forced them to settle for what they could get in the way of spouses.

It should be mentioned that several war children have fond recollections of their caring grandmothers, and some also of their mothers and stepfathers. For many of our interviewees, however, what happened in intimate relationships is the crucial issue in the stories they tell: belonging or being excluded, being betrayed and rejected, having feelings of bitterness and loss. In the interviews, anecdotes highlighting the issues of inclusion and exclusion abound. Some of the episodes related are very dramatic, while others are trivial, at least superficially. A dramatic example is the story of a woman who, as a young mother with a newly born child, stands on the doorstep of the house where she grew up, begging her aunt to let her in, as she has nowhere else to stay with her little boy. The aunt turns her away. A more trivial story is told by a woman who is hurt because her mother presented her half-siblings with more precious wedding gifts than she herself received. However, for the woman telling it, this little episode is part of the larger story of rejection by the mother, to which it owes its impact. In some instances, the death of the mother brings to light new evidence of not really belonging: the 'German brat' is not allowed to sit with the rest of the family in church during the funeral, or does not receive his/her share of the inheritance.

The question of belonging or not belonging was highly relevant, both on the public and the private level. There is a connection between the two: the uncertainty of whether 'German brats' ought to be part of Norwegian society or not lingered on into the post-war years. Hostile attitudes toward the war children might find expression, even within the circle of family and kin. The options open to the mothers of the war children were limited, to the detriment of their children. Social conditions infused even the most intimate relationships, and were enacted as conflicts *within* the family, especially between mother and child. The public interpretation imposed on the behaviour of the mother during the war had deep and lasting effects in the private lives of the war children. Not only were the 'sins' of the mothers visited upon their children: so also were the sins *against* the mothers.

To Live with an Imposed Identity

Symbolic Violence

The war children have lived long lives with the definition of 'German brats' imposed on them by society. What do the life-history interviews tell us about the experience of living with an imposed identity? We find the concept of symbolic violence, as defined by Pierre Bourdieu, helpful in this context.

In the childhood of some of our interviewees, very real physical violence has been abundant. Could the war children also be said to have been subjected to symbolic violence, in Bourdieu's sense? According to Bourdieu,[6] symbolic violence implies that … 'the dominated apply categories constructed from the point of view of the dominant to the relations of domination, thus making them appear as natural'.

Have the war children been subjected to symbolic violence in the sense of having accepted the category ('German brat') constructed by the dominant as given, understanding themselves through it? If so, the imposed identity was (at least partly) internalized.

Reading Bourdieu on symbolic violence, one easily gets the impression that the dominated are totally imprisoned in the categories constructed from the point of view of the dominant. As this point of view appears to be natural, no other perspective is available.

> Because the foundation of symbolic violence lies not in mystified consciousnesses that only need to be enlightened but in dispositions attuned to the structure of domination of which they are the product, the relation of complicity that the victims of symbolic domination grant to the dominant can only be broken through a radical transformation of the social conditions of production of the dispositions that lead the dominated to take the point of view of the dominant on the dominant and on themselves.[7]

It should be noted that this comment relates to one of the oldest and most ingrained relations of dominance in most societies: the relations of the sexes. Even the dominated in *this* relation of dominance, however, have proved able to muster considerable resistance to the definitions of the dominant. In our view, being a victim of symbolic violence may not necessarily be a total experience. Some resistance may be possible without wholesale liberation, and contradictions may exist in the way people understand themselves. Structures of domination which produce certain dispositions in the dominated may change somewhat without being completely overthrown.

What relations of domination were at play in the case of the war children? Perhaps we could speak of a whole network of relations, in which multiple threads combine to anchor the war children into the dominated position. First, they were associated with the losers of the war. Secondly, they were the children of unwed mothers, which was in itself sufficient grounds to brand the children as bastards and the mothers as loose women. Thirdly, the majority of war children, at least in our sample, came from families which in no way belonged to the local elite. Combined with the damage done to the family's reputation by the mother's conduct during the war, their humble social position made the child very vulnerable. And finally, relations of knowledge and power in Foucault's sense were created when the state authorities produced a body of knowledge about the war children in the course of the process of handling the problem. Not least significant in this body of knowledge was the notion of suspected feeblemindedness in the war children.

Aligned with Evil

In post-war Norway, there was soon developed a strong and partly mythical collective tradition about the occupation and the resistance against it. Anne Eriksen notes that the collective tradition has helped national construction and integration and has created a national consensus and a base of values for the reconstruction after the war. The tradition also embodies the universal story of the struggle between good and evil.[8]

The war children have had to live with being associated with 'evil' in this tradition. One woman tells us that as a schoolchild she 'closed her ears' when they were taught about World War II. She felt guilty, as if the atrocities which had happened were in some way her fault. This woman was not harassed as a child: nobody knew that she had a German father. This did not prevent her from positioning herself among the unworthy. In our view, this exemplifies symbolic violence. The woman mentioned is not the only war child who felt responsible for the deeds of the German occupants. Several relate how they felt guilt and shame when the subject in school was World War II. One man constantly feared being exposed as the off-spring of 'war criminals'.

Some interviewees were expelled from the festivities of 17 May, the day when Norway celebrates its birth as a free nation. The classmates of one woman repeatedly painted the swastika on her books and school bag. Words and deeds of this kind left their marks. Some war children still grapple with feelings of guilt in relation to historical events which were far beyond their influence. One man feels 'a destructive darkness' inside him, which he sees as inherited from a father whom he has never met and knows nothing about. Others tell us, rather vehemently, that they neither *are* guilty nor *feel* so.

A Heavy Symbolic Burden

The medical discourse had very dramatic consequences in the lives of a small minority of war children: the minority who was placed in institutions for the 'feeble-minded'. They were deprived of opportunities to live and to learn. What was lost or destroyed can never be restored and repaired. That these war children have been able to provide some meaning and dignity to their lives in spite of such adversity is a tribute to their resilience.

In addition, the label of 'feebleminded' was an immense *symbolic* burden. This becomes evident through the ardent efforts of several war children to prove that they were erroneously and unjustly diagnosed and institutionalized. These efforts are central to their struggle for dignity. In adult age, some of our interviewees have managed to conquer the label of 'war child' or 'German brat' and give it a positive meaning, parallel to 'black is beautiful'. The label of 'feeble-minded' seems impossible to vanquish in a similar way. It has to be fought. To some interviewees, the struggle for dignity is identical with the struggle to disprove the diagnosis they once received.

Feelings of worthlessness and inferiority have been long-standing companions of many war children diagnosed as feeble-minded. Such feelings are not completely overcome even if one manages to redefine oneself. The importance of gaining public acknowledgement for this redefinition attests to the continued impact of the label of feeble-mindedness as a symbolic burden. Some of our interviewees have received economic compensation from the Parliament for reasons of equity. Others have taken their cases to court. The monetary value of the compensation received or hoped for may be less important than the symbolic one: the compensation granted equals a public authorization to shed the despised identity of 'feeble-minded'. The receivers of compensation are now worthy citizens, also in the eyes of the world.

The impact of the label of feeblemindedness was not only felt by children placed in institutions, however. As mentioned above, some experienced being ignored by their schoolteachers. These children received no diagnosis. They were just given the impression that they were intellectually substandard, and that this probably had something to do with their parentage. Some in this group have also spent their subsequent lives struggling to overcome deep-seated feelings of inferiority. It makes an impression on you as an interviewer when the interviewee suddenly pauses and asks: 'Do I strike you as feeble-minded?' In this case, the interviewer was called upon to do, in a small way, what monetary compensation from the Parliament has done to others: to serve as a means by which old definitions and labels publicly may be declared null and void.

Gendered Aspects of Symbolic Violence

There seem to be gendered aspects to the symbolic violence in the lives of the war children. Women who had given birth to a child out of wedlock had their value on the marriage market seriously impaired. Even more serious was the impairment if the child was a 'German child'. Because of this some of the mothers who married ended up with husbands who reflected their own diminished status as prospective marriage partners. Others seemed to feel that they had to put up with a lot from their husbands in exchange for the social protection marriage offered them. In several instances, the mothers of the war children were not only devalued in the eyes of the world: in all probability they considered themselves (and perhaps sometimes their children) as unworthy, and therefore easily became victimized by abusive men. The symbolic violence to which they were susceptible undermined their ability to avoid becoming victims of physical violence as well.

Many children, both boys and girls, also suffered at the hands of bad stepfathers. The symbolic violence to which their mothers were being subjected and which made them regard themselves as tainted women, not worthy of a man's respect, cast a dark shadow on the childhood of numerous war children.

Several of the female war children seem to have 'inherited' some of the problems of their mothers. The mother's reputation as a 'loose' woman rubbed off on the daughter. Some of the interviewees quote the saying 'like mother, like daughter' to explain the attitudes they were met with. They might be subjected to sexualized rumours of their allegedly 'loose' behaviour; they might be closely watched by the local community for any signs of being pregnant with a 'bastard' child of their own; or they might be regarded as sexually available to men in the neighbourhood. Some experienced sexual abuse by grown men. There are signs in the interviews that experiences of this kind have had consequences for the self-respect of the women *as* women. Some have become involved with violent and/or hard-drinking men themselves. One woman, reflecting on her own tendency to get involved with alcoholic partners, attributes her choices to her sense of inferiority: She is able to feel more on equal terms with a drunkard – 'it is like relating to a child,' she says. A sober and steady man, however, makes her feel unworthy. Statements of this kind point to gendered aspects of symbolic violence infusing the lives of many female war children.

It should, however, be added that there are good as well as bad stepfathers in the stories of war children. And there are good as well as bad husbands. Several female war children have found security, warmth and acceptance in their marriages to husbands who have helped them work through their difficult childhood experiences.

Silences

The stories of the war children abound with silences. In our view, symbolic violence may reside in this silence.

One form of silence is the silence of mothers (or other care-giving relatives) toward their children. Many speak of how their mothers refuse to answer questions they have about who their father was, where he is now and what happened during the war. Children are scolded for asking and dare not touch the subject again. Or they are made to feel that they have hurt their mother by asking. This may continue well into the mother's old age, and some mothers die without having disclosed their secrets.

There are exceptions to this story of maternal silence. Some mothers have been open toward their children, showing pictures of the father and speaking about him frequently. The dominant picture, however, is one of silence, more or less persistent. An almost impenetrable silence surrounds the contempt and abuse the *mothers* may have experienced during the war, the liberation and the first years afterward.

In many instances, this strategy of silence kept the child ignorant of the true identity of his or her father, while the rest of the community knew. Often, the moment of truth arrived when the child started school and the schoolmates heaped abuse on him/her, calling out 'German brat' and other hurtful names. But even then, the mothers would often refuse to speak. The child was left with a deep feeling of shame, but with no clear idea of what there was to be ashamed of. This situation made the child defenceless against feelings of worthlessness and inferiority.

In the case of children who *did* know that they had a German father, silence was often imposed on them by their mother or other relatives. One woman whose mother married her father during the war went with her mother to Germany when the war ended. When the girl was about six years old, her parents were divorced, and the mother moved back to Norway with the child. The girl bore the family name of her German father. When she arrived in Norway, she was adopted by her maternal grandparents in order to get rid of her German surname in favour of an unambiguously Norwegian one. The little girl had to repress and conceal most of her former life in Germany. She was not allowed to disclose that her father was German and lived in Germany; instead she had to tell others that he was dead. On arrival in Norway, the girl spoke German. Now she had to learn Norwegian in a hurry. This girl was never harassed as 'German brat', since nobody knew. However, she feels that she has been robbed of her childhood because of this enforced silence. She had to live with a constant lie.

Many more children than this girl became implicated in an extensive system of lies and concealment, making their childhood insecure and stressful. The shame associated with their origin was deeply ingrained, as denial and silence became second nature to them.

Sometimes children who knew the facts of their parentage kept silent for fear of detection and harassment. For children who had experienced harassment at school, finishing elementary school was a relief, and many took the opportunity to leave their home community to work or to further their education elsewhere. However, they could not feel safe: the rumour of their background might always reach the new place.

These children developed an expectation of ill treatment and harassment, and had to find strategies of avoidance and concealment. The expectation of being ill-treated simply because of who you are is bound to foster self-depreciation and a sense of worthlessness.

Silence and taboo are central themes in the majority of stories told by war children. Perhaps this silence brings us closest to symbolic violence. The effect of silence is to make shame stick to the victim, not to the offender. The victim is made to feel that there is something so shameful about his or her person that it cannot even be mentioned. For many war children, shame came before knowledge. Shame is a powerful emotion, signalling that your place among the dominated is caused by your own inferiority.

The stories of silence and taboo also highlight the tragic battle in which mother and child are mutually experiencing each other as the cause of suffering: the child is the living token of the false step that ruined the life of the mother. The mother's choice of the 'wrong' father has doomed the child to a life as a 'German brat'. Conversely, the child who wants to know the identity of its father is tormenting the mother: all that is shameful and painful, almost unbearable, is brought to the surface. To the child, the mother is the person who is denying him or her the opportunity to find the answer to a question of fundamental importance: who is my father? Several interviewees relate how this struggle develops into a painful stalemate that may last a lifetime.

The war children had many reasons for wanting to know the identity of their father: most felt an easily understandable curiosity regarding their own descent. Many were constantly confronted with their parentage, through remarks from schoolmates and neighbours, through knowing glances and hostile attitudes. Reactions of this kind were often their only sources of knowledge about their father. Several also needed and longed for a protector and caregiver, and had dreams of their missing father in this role. That their own mother stood in the way of finding him and made them feel guilty for hurting her if they searched is the cause of much bitterness. It is not unusual that mother and child, both vulnerable, both condemned by society, are locked in a destructive battle. In retrospect, most interviewees understand the difficult position of their mother. Even so, feelings of hurt and bitterness may still be very vivid.

The Tale Told by the Figures

In the tale emerging from the qualitative interviews, hurt and sorrow has a prominent place. What about the tale told by the figures?

The quantitative research also gives evidence of heavy social burdens laid on the war children. The sample of war children (approx. 1,150 persons born 1941–1945) has been compared to all other persons born during the same years, and to a sample of children born in 1940 and 1946/1947 who lived alone with their mother in 1960. For a comprehensive and far more detailed presentation of the methodology of this project, see Ellingsen 2004.[9]

To present the negative picture first, the pattern of high mortality during the post-war decades is striking. Those who probably have suffered the most have not survived to give their presentations of their tough lives as war children. The mortality is especially high among those born 1941 and 1942 when compared to that of others born in these two years. This is partially due to our methodological design, but probably also because they were the first to experience the lives as outcasts in families and the school system at a time when the post-war sentiments were still at the strongest. We have also analysed the reasons why they have died, and the rate of suicide among war children is significantly higher than that found among their peers.

The rate of people receiving disability pension is higher among war children than among the groups we compare them with, indicating greater health problems. What is the most significant finding, however, is that the war children on average received their pension at an earlier age than their peers. This again indicates an early social exclusion from the important area of employment, and early health problems.

The war children also have a lower level of education than those their age. The most significant differences are found at the extreme ends of the axis of education. We have not yet found a war child with a PhD, and also very few have higher education. On the other hand, a significant proportion of the war children have not fulfilled even the obligatory seven years of education which all children should have attended in the 1940s and 1950s.

The war children have a lower level of income. This is most typical among men, while the women are closer to the average of their sisters of the same age. A higher percentage of the war children have low income and, even more salient, few war children can be said to have high earnings or fortunes.

Finally, more war children have experienced divorces.

Judged by the results from the quantitative study, it has been a liability to grow up as a war child in post-war Norway. Their living conditions differ from those of their contemporaries on important dimensions. The stories told in the life-history interviews have some resonance in the figures.

On the other hand, the picture is not wholly bleak. Despite the negative findings, there are other tendencies as well. The figures speak of liabilities, but not exclusively.

To take a starting point in demography: very few war children have not, as adults, been living in a traditional family setting. One should perhaps have expected that the war children would have had extraordinary problems in getting included in ordinary family life, given the problems underlined in the qualitative interviews. The higher rate of divorce is of course an indicator of such problems, but close to 90 per cent of the war children are or have been living in a marriage.

Overall, the total impression is that a large group of the war children, seen from the outside, seem to live quite ordinary lives. They are married, have two or three children, have an ordinary income and live in well-equipped houses with good Norwegian standard. Few of them have had higher education, as is the case with these cohorts.

The underlying diagnosis causing the need for disability pension is to some extent different from those of their peers: a higher proportion of the war children are pensioned due to mental health problems, but the difference is not striking.

But should we be surprised by this picture of normality? Isn't it rather as might be expected? The literature on the concept and phenomenon of resilience points toward high rates of social survival among people who have suffered childhoods with a combination of very severe burdens; mentally ill parents, poverty, violence, etc.[10]

The tale told by the figures is partly one of resilience. Does this tale have a counterpart in the qualitative interviews? It has.

Strategies of Resistance

In their lives the war children have had to grapple with both the threat of social exclusion and the burden of an imposed identity. This chapter has concentrated on the sufferings our interviewees have experienced on this account. In the interviews, however, we are also told how the war children have struggled to overcome obstacles and lead productive and meaningful lives. The strengths, the dignity and the achievements of the interviewees are part of a story worth telling. To make visible and give significance to the strategies of resistance of the war children is important in making the interviews a contribution to the liberation from, not the reproduction of, symbolic violence.

The interviews mostly give information about individual strategies of resistance. We now briefly discuss four such strategies which may be glimpsed in the interviews:

'German is Beautiful'

We have named this strategy after 'Black is beautiful'. Another similar label is 'Proud to be gay'. The point is to turn the stigma into its opposite – a mark of distinction. This strategy has been used by many oppressed groups, but mainly in the context of a collective movement of resistance. For war children, a collective resistance based on a strategy of this kind would be very difficult, as it would easily risk being interpreted in political terms.

As an individual strategy, 'German is beautiful' is more available. Some war children relate how they changed from being ashamed to being proud of their German ancestry. They feel a warm connectedness to things German, the German language, German music and their German family if they manage to find them. This strategy offers relief not only from shame, but also from alienation and loneliness: the child who was not accepted in Norwegian society finally belongs.

The Multicultural Identity

One woman seems to have escaped being caught in the shameful category of 'war child' by assuming the identity of 'exotic foreigner'. She spent the first seven years of her life in Germany before moving to Norway with her mother. When she started school, she did not speak one word of Norwegian. However, she was not harassed. She was regarded as a foreigner who had moved into the community, which was something entirely different from being a 'German brat' born on the spot. The other children found her interesting because of her exotic appearance: She had pierced ears, a muff, an elaborate hairdo; she wore a coat, dress and slip while the other children wore ski pants in winter.

This woman has a mixed ancestry also on her mother's side. In the interview, she describes herself as 'fifty per cent German, twelve and a half per cent Finnish, twelve and a half per cent Sami and 25 per cent Norwegian'. She values multiculturality, and sees herself as a person of multicultural background, of which she is very proud.

This woman may have been luckier than most. However, she is not the only one who is now emphasising the value of having a mixed background. The multicultural category was not available in Norway of the 1950s and 1960s. Social changes may, at this late stage of their life, open some new opportunities for the war children to recast their identity in a more positive way.

'I Am a Survivor'

This is the most common strategy of resistance found in the interviews. Many point to their personal resilience, strength, stamina and willpower as explanations for their survival. References to their own strength and will-power are often made by interviewees who also recount feelings of inferiority and insecurity. The positive image of the survivor is not wholly able to oust the image of the despised 'German child'. However, it offers invaluable resistance to self-depreciation and despair. To be able to look back, not only on traumas and losses but also on accomplishments, is essential in coming to terms with one's life. A very moving experience was an interview with a woman who painstakingly pointed out her own upward social mobility through steps and distinctions hardly discernible to the eye of a securely positioned and reasonably well-to-do academic like the interviewer.

The passing of time and changing popular attitudes may also make it easier to emphasize the good which may come from evil: in retrospect, many war children regard valuable personal traits not only as explanations for their own psychological survival but also as lasting results of the harsh lessons of their childhood. Traits often mentioned are resilience, stamina, tolerance, generosity, capacity for caring and loving. In spite of this positive angle one should not forget or minimize the bouts of depression, anxiety, pain and despondence from which several still suffer.

Openness

For war children, leaving the closet may also be a decisive step in the resistance against symbolic violence. The connection between silence and shame is clearly expressed in the interview with a woman who has recently gone public. She waited until her mother was dead, and then she appeared, both on the radio and in the local newspaper. The responses she received were mixed. Some were positive. Others had trouble understanding why she had to make public facts of her origin now only known to the older generation in the community. The woman answered: 'I am sixty years old! How long do you want me to go on feeling ashamed?'

To go public in this way is a powerful statement. For most interviewees, the openness is more restricted. This restricted openness may have different reasons: To some, their origin is not so important and they see no point in making it a public issue. To others, there is still too much pain associated with being a 'German brat'.

Most of our interviewees are open in relation to their nearest family. Children are told of their German grandfather when they are old enough to understand. However, some parents hesitate, and children may be well into their teens when they finally learn the facts.

In many instances, the untroubled reaction of children when told of their German grandfather reflects positively on the parents: What is there to be ashamed of? Frequently, the children are also instrumental in making their parents search for and contact their German relatives. As members of a new generation, they demonstrate to their parents that times have changed, and the stigma of 'war child' may be about to lose its meaning.

The Changing Public Significance of the 'War Child' Label

The war children whom we have been interviewing have now come to think of the suffering they were subjected to as children as deeply unjust an undeserved. This does not necessarily free the war children from shame and anxiety. Long-standing feelings of shame are not easily ousted by rational arguments. All the same, it *is* important which public meaning the category of 'war child' has acquired in contemporary Norway. Is the hard-won recognition that society, not the war children themselves, is to blame for their misfortunes backed by a change in the way war children are perceived in society in general?

The war years and the first years after liberation saw the creation of the 'war-child' category, shaped and influenced by popular, professional and political attitudes and actors. The creation of this category had very real consequences in the lives of many war children. Then the long period of silence followed. Official policy dictated that the war children should no longer be singled out as a distinct group. The signs of their German descent should be erased and the whole issue suppressed. This silence may have been well intended, and it *may* also have had some beneficial effects. However, the silence did not protect the majority of children in our sample from being taunted and despised, and it added the vulnerability inherent in growing up knowing next to nothing about their descent, other than that it was too shameful to be mentioned. The silent period largely lasted until the 1980s, when the process of redefining and of breaking the silence began. The category of war child was successively redefined into a category of innocently victimized and wronged people. This process was initiated and driven by activists among the war children themselves. Little by little, they managed to get media coverage.

In the course of this process, an image has been created of the prototypical war child. Media have been instrumental to its creation. It is a gloomy image of a victimized and abandoned child, abused, maltreated, despised and rejected. In our sample, there are some who fit this prototype, and we have no doubt that many war children whom we have not interviewed do also. However, the prototypical war child seems to function as a point of reference for most war children, regardless of how their childhood was, influencing the way being a war child is experienced today. Some tell us that they are unable to identify with this image, or they claim not to be 'a typical war child'. 'Many have suffered much worse than I have' is a common statement, also from interviewees who have dark histories indeed to recount. The image of the prototypical war child may open up both positive and negative prospects. To some, it may pose a threat in that they do not want to be absorbed into this image of misery, pain and defeat simply because of the fact that their father was German. To others, it may represent an opportunity: by being associated with this icon of innocent suffering and persecution, their own sufferings are granted significance and dignity, even if they do not measure up to those of the prototypical war child. Contrary to this, some are afraid that their own misfortunes will mean nothing in comparison: 'I have not been locked up in a pigsty and declared an imbecile, but all the same I have suffered' one woman says.

The image of the prototypical war child implies acknowledging war children as more sinned against than sinning. Even so, some of our interviewees seem to fear a new kind of imposed identity as a consequence of this image. One challenge still faces Norwegian society: To acknowledge that the war children as a group have been wronged, without compelling them to take on what many experience as an ill-fitting and constraining identity, in order to be recognized as worthy victims.

Notes

1. *Lofotposten* 19 May 1945.
2. Ibid.
3. Anette Warring, *Tyskerpiger under besættelse og rettsopgør* (Gyldendal, 1994).
4. Fabrice Virgili, *La France 'virile': Des femmes tondues à la libération* (Payot, 2000).
5. The interviews are part of a research project on war children, funded by Research Council Norway. Interviewers were Eva Simonsen and Kjersti

Ericsson. Lars Borgersrud and Dag Ellingsen are also members of the project's group of researchers. Dag Ellingsen has carried out the quantitative work presented here.

6. Pierre Bourdieu, *Masculine Domination* (Polity, 2001), p. 35.
7. Ibid, p. 41.
8. Anne Eriksen, *Det var noe annet under krigen: 2. Verdenskrig i norsk kollektivtradisjon* (Pax, 1995), p. 173.
9. Dag Ellingsen, *Krigsbarns levekår.* Rapport 19 (Statistisk sentralbyrå, 2004).
10. See for instance Emmy Werner and Ruth Smith, *Journeys from Childhood to Midlife: Risk, Resilience and Recovery* (Cornell University Press, 2001).

References

Bourdieu, P., *Masculine Domination*, Cambridge: Polity, 2001.

Ellingsen, D., *Krigsbarns levekår.* Rapport 19, Oslo–Kongsvinger: Statistisk sentralbyrå, 2004.

Eriksen, A., *Det var noe annet under krigen: 2. Verdenskrig i norsk kollektivtradisjon,* Oslo: Pax Forlag, 1995.

En hvitbok: Utvalgte offentlige dokumenter om krigsbarnsaken, Oslo: Norges forskningsråd, 1999.

Lofotposten, 19 May 1945.

Virgili, F., *La France 'virile': Des femmes tondues à la libération,* Paris: Payot, 2000.

Warring, A. *Tyskerpiger: under besættelse og rettsopgør,* Copenhagen: Gyldendal, 1994.

Werner, E. and Smith, R., *Journeys from Childhood to Midlife: Risk, Resilience and Recovery,* Ithaca/London: Cornell University Press, 2001.

Part II

West

–6–

Ideology and the Psychology of War Children in Franco's Spain, 1936–1945

Michael Richards

We cannot hide our bitter pain as we remember so many innocent children taken from their homes and carried off to far away lands, often with such dangers of apostasy and perversion: we yearn for nothing so ardently as to see them restored to the bosom of their families, where they will find once again the fervent and Christian love of their own.

Pope Pius XII, radio message to the Spanish faithful, April 1939

It is not possible, without taking precautions, to return to society, or to social circulation, harmful, perverted, politically and morally poisoned elements, because their incorporation into the free and normal community of Spaniards would represent a danger of corruption and of contagion for everyone.

General Franco, interview with Manuel Aznar, April 1939

The civil war of 1936–1939 has long been seen as the defining moment of contemporary Spanish history. The dictatorship of General Franco, lasting from 1939 until the dictator's death in 1975, was created as a result of the defeat of the democratic Second Republic in the great cataclysm of the war. The military rebellion against the elected left-liberal government of the Republic which triggered all-out armed conflict in mid-July 1936 was supported by the Catholic Church, the majority of middle-class Catholics and most of society's economic and political élite sectors. The liberal Republic was defended by masses of ordinary people, particularly society's lower classes. The military anti-Republican revolt thus provoked a widespread and violent social revolution in areas which put up resistance. A dramatic and emotive element of this revolution was the burning down of churches and the mass killing of priests. Some 7,000 clerics would be killed across the totality of the area under Republican control during the war and revolution.[1] After the war, this shocking proletarian violence against the Church and against the middle classes (along with other less violent elements of the revolution, such as militia-women dressed in blue overalls) became essential to the official

'Nationalist' (or 'Francoist') visualization of the enemy and of the revolutionary 'otherness' of the enemy. Within a month of the start of the war, therefore, the Catholic Church had begun to justify the conflict as a crusade to save religion and Spanish nationhood.[2] For want of a sociological analysis of the revolution, the perpetrators were portrayed as 'deranged' and 'psychopathic' and witnesses to the violence of the revolution were claimed to be traumatized. Thus, the revolution was explained through religious and medical discourses – often focused on the family – both concluding something similar: that a large section of society was in need of some kind of 'treatment', 'therapy', or segregation. During and after the war, children became central to these ideas and therefore to the political propaganda contest to define the nation.

The violence of the war was not limited to that perpetrated in the name of the Republic and of the revolution, however. It has been plausibly calculated that some 350,000 Spaniards met an untimely death during the period 1936–1939. A high proportion of these deaths did not result from battlefield engagement but as a result of repression on both sides of the divide. Probably more of these deaths occurred at the hands of the counter-revolutionary Francoists (or 'Nationalists'). Waves of mass executions were unleashed by the Francoist authorities in a repression legitimated by a belief in the need for national 're-consecration' and 'purification'. Vast numbers of the victims of this repression were not guilty of violent crimes against persons or property during the revolution, but merely of giving political support to the Republican project. As in other parts of Europe in 1918 and, later, in 1945, the scale of the human losses of war and its aftermath influenced post-war ideas of social engineering. In excess of a further 200,000 Spaniards died in the period 1940–42, as a result of hunger, and of hunger-related diseases, political repression and imprisonment.[3] This tale of misery forms an essential part of the context for state initiatives in what was called 'racial hygiene'. Though many of these ideas associated with 'racial hygiene' came to the fore in the context of the war, many of them in fact pre-dated 1936.[4] The war, and the need for national reconstruction, allowed them to gain a greater level of acceptability among the triumphalist authorities.

At the same time, the victorious Nationalists began quickly to institutionalize their militarized system of social order and gendered view of morality. This included the notion of 'the military home', an aspect of the totalitarian system they had advocated during the war and its aftermath. This reinforced traditional gender divisions, circumscribed private life, civil rights and citizenship, restricting access to the public sphere and basic freedoms. The Church, aided by the regime's single-state political organization, the Falange, took hold of the education system and welfare system, allowing Catholic doctrine and ethics to determine the nature of the socialization process. At the same time, there was a substantial ideological 'cross-over' between the doctrine of the Church and psychological and psychiatric theory and practice. Previously, eugenics in Spain had formed part of the liberal discourse of medical science and social reform. Conservative race hygiene in Spain was an offshoot of the Latin eugenics movement (including France, Italy and South America), influenced by Catholicism and Lamarckism. The socially 'progressive' elements of the eugenic thinking of liberals – birth control, female emancipation, etc – were excised from this conservative version. The conservative programme was also somewhat different, however, to the predominant strand of 'Nordic eugenics' in Britain and Germany which followed the more rigid Mendelian 'laws of inheritance'.[5] Though heredity still played a role, there would be no concrete 'negative' measures (such as sterilization) to restrict the fertility of 'moral imbeciles'. Such a 'negative' strategy would go against explicit Papal instructions and would also require a substantial infrastructure to set in train. Instead, the emphasis was on 'positive' eugenics – puericulture, a form of paediatrics combined with moral training – to encourage healthy births. Inevitably, even this 'softer' version of race hygiene involved directive propaganda aimed at women in particular.[6]

This chapter begins by setting the policies of Franco's regime toward the children of its Republican wartime enemies within the broad context of the war culture in Spain and the suppression of civil society.[7] Key themes related to children are the experience of war and consequent trauma, exile and displacement, psychological discourse and practice, the 'measuring of minds' and hierarchies of human value, and collective or social memory and inter-generational dialogue. In connection with the last of these, recently collected testimony suggests that some wartime and post-war children believed, because of indoctrination by the authorities, that their Republican parents had been in some way 'bad' – a reason, prompted by the state's discourse, not to speak about them. Psychologists in Barcelona in the 1940s found that up to 72 per cent of children 'disapproved' of the 'immoral lives' of their parents.[8] The silence of those who were stigmatized as being part of 'the defeated' passed on a sense of guilt, imposed by the punishment inflicted by the Francoist state, from generation to generation.[9]

In the early 1940s many of the children of executed, imprisoned or exiled opponents of the Francoist 'New State' were secretly taken after the civil war, renamed and given to families sympathetic to the new triumphant regime. Many of their parents were already caught up in the maelstrom of the post-war Francoist repression and many had found themselves trapped by the expanding network of Nazi concentration camps after being forcibly exiled in France.[10] Thousands of children were deprived of their families and never told the truth. In a similar episode to the 'disappearing' of Argentine children during the military regime from 1976–83, thousands of children whose parents were 'Reds' were either forcibly taken from their families or deliberately not reunited with them when the opportunity arose. In often appalling conditions, trainloads of uprooted and confused infants and youngsters traversed the country in an operation which removed them from their homes and their loved ones. Many infants died during the callous and inhumane process.

These events have become central to the vexed question of collective memories of Spain's civil war as the grandchildren of the victims have begun to ask questions about the brutality suffered by innocent civilians during and after the war. This tragic story of the human suffering of war came to light only during the year 2000 as the autonomous Catalan parliament voted to compensate those deprived of their liberty during the Franco years in recognition of their suffering. Other concurrent initiatives included the 1999 proposition of the Basque Parliament in favour of official recognition of the forced nature of the expatriation of war children in the besieged Republican zone during the civil war. Among those who came forward to give testimony were the elderly victims – mothers deprived of their children and children taken from their parents – who had carried the burden of memory in silence for decades. For the first time they were able actively to participate in the recovery of a central part of their identities.

One woman from Valencia, now in her seventies, was placed in an orphanage in Madrid during the civil war when she was 5. Her father was a captain in the Republican army who had been responsible for evacuating refugees. Although she had no way of knowing that he had stayed behind to do his duty and been executed by the Francoist state in 1940 as a result, she knew who he was – his name and identity – and held on to this simple fact throughout her long ordeal. But the nuns at the orphanage refused to acknowledge her own identity. She was renamed and offered for adoption:

> The head of the home would call me. 'Your parents have come. They were lost in the war but now they're here.' And I'd run through the corridors convinced I'd meet my father, but they were always strangers.[11]

Two sisters, now 72 and 70, had been sent by their parents to France during the war for safety – to avoid the bombing and the threat of occupation by Franco's forces, and to be sufficiently fed. In 1941, they were to be subjected to the great effort mounted by the Franco regime at the end of the war to repatriate such children. They were brought back, though their family could not be found, and they were separated and given for adoption. When each asked about her sister she was told that the other must have perished. The sisters were only able to become reunited 60 years later when one of them saw the other on television, showing photographs of her missing sibling.

Infants were also taken away at birth. Women were often imprisoned, for being politically active, for supporting the Republic, or because they came from a family which included political activists. One sister of a resistance fighter told how she had been deprived of her tiny son. 'They claimed they were taking him to be baptized, and it was the last I saw of him. It has always tormented me throughout my life, because I know I gave birth to him ... .'

It was the post-Franco generation growing up in the period since 1975, however, who had taken up the issues of recovering memory, who had broached the subject – in making a television documentary on the subject, helping to recuperate the history which has been kept from them.[12] This episode has been a part of an upsurge of interest in the post-civil war period in Spain, and many other stories have recently emerged of mass wartime graves, imprisonment and repression. These revelations, essential to the process of recovering memories which had been 'lost', have not, however, been accompanied by analysis of the ideological-religious-psychological context of attitudes to children as such in the wake of the civil war. This is the aim of the current chapter: to explain the brutality, through discussion of the prevalent ideas of the new regime born of the war. In essence, a series of stereotypes constructed over decades by social, medical and religious élites in Spain about the 'congenital' weaknesses of the lower orders were explicitly linked to the leftist political activism of these 'popular classes'. The status of political enemy, conferred by the reality of defeat in the war, was confirmed by the application of racial or eugenic categories, giving further legitimation to the intimate, bodily and emotional repression of Republicans.[13]

The remainder of this chapter will be structured in two sections: first, a summary of the political context is designed to show how formal political relations were shaped by conflicts of religion and by ideas associated with morality, moralism and gender. The Catholic Church's long-standing resistance to the laicization of society was based on defence of religious practice and customs in, for example, the rites of passage of children, their place in the family, and their education. Psychologists after the war blamed war children's 'inability to make value judgements' on the extent of co-education and secular teaching which were both seen as morally damaging.[14] Thus, the discourse of the leading Francoist psychiatrist linked his gendered analysis of the 'crisis' of the Spanish family to overtly political questions:

> The head of the family and the schoolteacher were, in the years before the civil war, the leaven which in certain social classes fermented hatred of the rich, the noble and the virtuous ... Democratic ideas have had the unhappy ability to inculcate in children the idea of certain rights, uprooting the principles of traditional morality and fomenting depravity, and opposing the notions of subordination and hierarchy.[15]

This kind of declaration bolstered the view that it was legitimate to aim methods of repression, such as imprisonment and even execution, at the families of Republicans as though the family, most essential 'cell' of the 'body' of the nation, had to be 'treated' to cure its 'defectiveness'.

Second, the processes and stories about 'disappeared children' exemplify the repressive ideas and practices within the overlapping communities of authority of Franco's Spain. These agencies consisted primarily of the charitable institutions of the Catholic Church and the welfare sections of the Franco state's political movement, the Falange. Their activities, however, were underpinned by the convergent and already existing ideas offered by religious doctrine and psychological and psychiatric theory and practice. Jesuit teachers, for example, had for some time been enthusiastically applying psychological methods and practices. The Consejo Superior de Profesores de Menores held regular courses in modern psychological techniques and all of the Jesuit schools were supposed, since 1925, to have psychological-pedagogic 'laboratories'.[16] Much later, after the civil war, Francoist ideologues and educationalists developed this link between Catholic doctrine, psychology and human typology into an ascetic struggle through such curious concepts as 'Thomist biology' and 'biological pedagogy'.[17]

Civil War: The Political Context of Pro-natalism

Post-war 'demobilization', through an unspoken social consensus on how to redeem wartime sacrifices, is problematic in post-civil war cultures. This problem is not unique to civil wars but is found in situations which are in some ways similar. Wherever continued latent conflict over 'collaboration' in recently occupied societies makes an effective process of 'demobilization' difficult, some ritualized method for channelling conflict is found. While recognition of the Nationalist sacrifice was facilitated with the aid of the state, in its sponsoring of commemoration rituals, for example, the Republican war effort and social revolution was depicted exclusively as a problem of public order and 'a crime' committed by so-called 'foreigners' (the 'anti-Spain'), and could only be redeemed through punishment. The gendered aspects of this repression are noteworthy since they suggest at least a 'subliminal' legitimation for depriving some mothers of their children. Rituals were often directed against individuals or groups who could be identified as transgressors against the ethics of the 'whole' community. Women tended to be idealized as performing a cathartic social role and if they transgressed this ideal they were prone to punishment. In many locations as they were being occupied by the Francoist forces, the heads of women who had supported the Republic were shaved. In this way they became scapegoats.[18] Thus, communities traumatized by war and revolution, turned on previously integrated members of the community in semi-ritualized displays of violence as an emotional outlet.[19] This stigmatization was encouraged in Spain during the civil war by the ideology of the wartime 'crusade' and 're-Christianization'. Shaved women would be paraded through the village – sometimes with babes in arms – and publicly vilified, becoming the target upon which the rest of the community projected its collective sense of guilt or shame.[20] Older people in Spain still remember the fate of these humiliated women who had done nothing wrong.

With the support of the Church, the Nationalists became highly censorious, ordering the destruction of works of literature likely to offend against the holy principles of religion and Christian morals. Co-education – considered a 'crime against decent women' and against the 'health' of the people – was suppressed within weeks of the rebellion.[21] Women teachers would only be permitted to teach in girls' schools. According to the nascent Francoist power, all the organizations of the Republic and its supporters (and their ideas) would fall outside of the law. The 'purging' of state officials and functionaries included schoolteachers, university professors, prison officers, medical doctors and nurses, leaving vacancies filled by ambitious new-comers who advocated programmes in accordance with the ideology of the 'New State'. This was an opening for highly conservative psychiatrists – some of them directly influenced by leading German Nazi doctors – who preached a doctrine of 'racial regeneration'.[22]

Civil marriages were declared null and void in the Nationalist zone, and the 1889 Civil Code, under which women were treated effectively as children before the law, was reintroduced. The Republican law which had permitted the right to divorce was abolished. Catholic doctrine was re-established as a distinct subject of instruction, and the cult of the Virgin Mary became compulsory in all Nationalist schools. A system of obligatory 'Social Service' for middle-class women, provided they could demonstrate their 'impeccable morality', was introduced in October 1937 to assist with the 'training' of working-class mothers in child-rearing duties, nutrition and morals. This was organized exclusively by the women's section of the Falange, the Sección Femenina. Advice and assistance with infants were accompanied by a level of indoctrination. The realization of national 'rebirth' (a significant metaphor) depended very specifically on the physical and moral health of mothers and children.[23]

Provisions for 'Family Subsidies' and for Nationalist widows and orphans were introduced in 1938 and 1939. The families of those who had died on the Republican side in the war were denied any financial assistance. Not for another year would attention turn toward the orphan children of Republicans. By 1941 there was widespread starvation in much of Spain. The authorities in Madrid were beginning to intern beggars en masse. Some 800 women and children were forced into a single barrack in one of the institutions for beggars in the city. More than half were to die during the following 12 months.[24] The great increment of the national infant-mortality rate to a position not seen since the influenza epidemic of 1918 (109 per 1000 births in 1940) only began slowly to decline toward the end of the 1940s (68 per 1000 in 1950), partly because of the social-welfare aspects of the state's programme of 'racial hygiene'.[25] Sección Femenina health visitors in particular were beginning to have some effect.

It was within this context that institutions such as the Casas de Maternidad, the Patronato de Protección de la Mujer and the Obra de Protección de Menores were given shared responsibility for women and children's moral re-education and vigilance. In January 1941 a 'Law for the protection of the birth rate' made the deliberate termination of pregnancy a crime against the state.[26] Marriage loans and prizes for multiple births were introduced shortly afterward. Laws against adultery and against infanticide followed in 1942, but the secular trend of a declining birth rate continued.

'Disappeared' Children

In the second section of this chapter, the pro-natalist strategies, moral and physical hygiene programmes and children's 're-education' forming the context for the process of 'disappearing children' are examined. There were four overlapping categories of detained civil-war children, according to these agencies in the immediate post-war years: (i) Minors classified as 'delinquent', often in Catholic charitable institutions. (ii) Those deemed to be 'morally abandoned', again, usually in similar institutions. (iii) The children of prisoners (particularly detained mothers). (iv) Children repatriated after exile to other countries. These putative 'types' will be reduced to just two groups for the purpose of discussion here: detained children and repatriated children.

There were two principal pre-war institutions which dealt with 'delinquent' children in Spain: the Provincial Committees (Juntas) for the Protection of Minors (first established in 1904), and the Tribunales Tutelares de Menores (1918) (the equivalent of the Juvenile Courts found in the US), established in Spanish cities from 1920. In Spain these institutions were built upon quite informal and variable charitable work directed through particular benefactors and the lay organs of the Catholic Church. They dealt with four broad areas: infant and child health and paediatric issues, social assistance, begging and moral tutelage, and legislation and jurisprudence. In the immediate post-civil war period these functions were amended by laws in December 1940 and July 1942. The 1942 law, as part of what was seen as a 'renaissance in the psychological study of children', introduced 'psycho-physical examinations' of children and codified the study of child personality. The Tribunales Tutelares had technical establishments, with psychiatrists, for observation and therapy and for special treatment of 'abnormal' children.[27]

Pro-natalist strategies, and children's 'hygiene' and 're-education' were influenced both by wartime population loss and by military psychiatrists' ideological claims about the revolution's perversion of children. Their Catholic discourse of 'positive' or 'moral' eugenics – as already mentioned, 'softer' than the 'harder' physiological intervention to be practiced in Germany – was designed to ensure 'healthy' marriages and guard against the hereditary transmission of mental and social 'defects'. These ideas shaped the practices and legal instruments of social categorization, segregation, and stigmatization in the 1940s. They were already being applied to adult political prisoners. In 1938/39, while the civil war was still in progress, programmes of psychological studies of Republican prisoners were begun, combining tests as used in psychiatric clinics, forensic examinations and racial anthropology. It was concluded that 'Marxism' had 'psycho-biological roots' and that women were particularly prone to this threatening 'bio-psychic' conditioning.[28] The leading Nationalist psychiatrist wrote in 1939: 'the segregation of these subjects from infancy (those from "Marxist" families) could free society of the most terrible plague'.[29]

In terms of the state's political project of building a 'resurgent Spain', medicalizing or pathologizing the causes of conflict helped 'absolve' the 'Spanish nation', thus 'resolving' contradictions in the regime's rhetoric of nationhood. Discourses of the 'Other' – the mental, racial, or sexual Other – intertwined to become an approved composite framework for 'understanding' the war. This framework had as a devastating side-effect the violent coercion of enemies. Political enemies were depicted as 'Russianized', 'Oriental', or 'Asiatic' – they were 'without God' and therefore of lesser value than 'the select' who had contributed to Spain's 'resuscitation' in 1939. Alien ideas were combated particularly through the persecution of women and children who did not 'fit' the new national ideal and who were considered as prime material for psychological testing.

Detained Children

Those Spanish families who had offered a sacrifice 'for God' in 'the national cause' (i.e. 'Nationalist' families) were favoured by the state in its 'permanent attitude of remembrance, affection and gratitude'. The others, who could not demonstrate loyalty by association with 'the Fallen', the war-wounded and the 'ex-combatants', fell within the broad and overlapping spheres of the state's justice and welfare strategies. The practical application of the Ministry of the Interior's decree of 30 November 1940 on 'the protection of orphans' is an illustration of this precarious situation.[30] Children who had lost families as a result of the conflict would be placed with persons disposed 'to ignite in them the fire of family affection' – suggesting that formerly, as the children of Republicans, they had not benefited from any such affection. Alternatively, children were placed with state social-welfare institutions, seen 'as militant organs of the idea of national brotherhood'. Often this was merely because parents had been imprisoned, or 'purged' for association with the Republic. Some had been volunteer militia-women who fought for the democratic government. Others, as exiles, had been swept up into the network of concentration and labour camps of the Nazi empire.[31] Taking children from such allegedly 'dangerous' parents was a strategy designed to sever the link with the past of families who were considered of dubious loyalty to the Francoist 'New State'.

Other families lost their legal rights over their children once they submitted them to the feeding stations and shelters of the Falange's social-welfare organization, *Auxilio Social* (Social Aid). There are documented cases of children in the early 1940s given up to prevent them starving. This was often a starkly rational decision made by desperate mothers. One woman whose husband was 'redeeming himself' through hard labour in a penal work detachment, gave up one child to the local Junta for the protection of minors and sold half of her own meagre food ration on the black market enabling her to buy enough of the staple necessities for her other children. She had come into contact with Social Aid – and its Central Department for the Protection of Mothers and Children – by eating daily at one of its public kitchens.[32] Many of these families were living in the urban shanty towns which grew vertiginously following Franco's victory. Other mothers were denied their children because of moral considerations. One woman was accused of being unfaithful to her husband who had fled to France and been billeted in a work battalion as labour by the Nazi occupiers in 1940. Though she had been released from her own prison term as a Republican, her children were kept by the state as it was legally permitted to do because of her 'immorality'.[33] More than 9,000 children of parents in prison were still interned in public state and religious institutions in 1942. By 1943 there were more than 12,000. Though it is not possible to say just how many of these children were the offspring of mothers who had been raped by their captors or had been executed as political enemies, some certainly were.[34] They were all, however, victims of the various misfortunes which had beset their parents because of the war and its political implications.

The welfare institutions relied on the income which children attracted from the state. The government would pay 4 pesetas a day for the upkeep of each child to institutions which maintained 'the most careful vigilance over (the children's) formative process' based on 'adhesion to the ideals and principles professed by the state'. The child's legal protection was under the jurisdiction of the highly moral and ideologically shaped local or provincial Juvenile Court (*Tribunal Tutelar*). Moreover, the task of finding 'irreproachable' families would be undertaken by Social Aid which would arrange for reports about the 'morality' and political leanings of the families concerned (Articles 2 [b] and [c], 8 of the November 1940 decree).

It was a proud boast of the authorities that the Spanish pro-natalist penal system allowed infants to remain with interned mothers. The reality of life in the regime's prisons was not shaped by innovation and modernity. Overcrowding, disease, hunger and death were the everyday accompaniment to political internment for men, women and children. At the end of 1940 there were still, officially, 240,916 prisoners in Spain, most in overcrowded concentration camps, of whom 7,762 had been sentenced to the death penalty.[35] The women's prison at Ventas, in Madrid, constructed to hold 500, had between 6,000 and 11,000 detainees at the beginning of 1940.[36] One of the penitenciaries proclaimed as a 'model' establishment was the Prison for Nursing Mothers in Madrid where, in reality, mothers were kept from their infants for virtually the whole day and many children died from disease and malnutrition.[37] In March 1940 a law was introduced which forcibly removed children more than three years old and placed them in orphanages.[38] Many were not seen by their mothers again. The institution established by the state to care for the children of prisoners claimed in its 1944 report to the government that 'thousands and thousands of children have been relieved of material and moral misery' as a direct result of these processes. In this year the cases of more than 30,000 children were expedited.[39] Well over 14,000 such children passed through the local Junta for child protection in Barcelona, for example, from 1939 to 1944.[40]

The more extreme plans for post-war 'Hispanization' depended on the family names of the offspring of Republican prisoners being renounced in order to leave no trace of them ever having existed.[41] Prison chaplains baptized new-born children with the names of the many and various popular invocations of the Virgin Mary.[42] Tests revealed to Spanish child psychologists that many evacuated children had forgotten their 'mother languages', had few memories of their parents nor any sense of 'feeling Spanish'. There was resentment among the authorities that many were unaware of their real names or had been renamed 'by foreigners'.[43] The Spanish authorities ensured that the family names of children could be changed in a law formulated in December 1941 to 'physically and spiritually reintegrate children into the Fatherland'.[44] Rapid reinscription in civil registries, with the new name, following an application to the juvenile court (*Tribunal Tutelar*), would facilitate adoption as the process of repatriating Spanish children sent away to other countries during the worst period of the war gathered pace.

Childhood Post-war Repatriation

During the civil war, the besieged Republic had implemented a strategy to evacuate children from its zone of authority in Northern Spain. Many were found shelter in Republican Catalonia to the east, and many more were sent by sea to other countries. By the end of 1938 some 40,000 Spanish refugees were in France; the majority of them were children, housed in 'colonies'. With the fall of France in 1940 hundreds of Spanish children would find themselves transported to French concentration camps, suffering unimaginable hardships. About 20,000 Basque children had been evacuated from the Bilbao region to escape the civil-war bombing and food shortages in the early spring of 1937.[45] The port of Bilbao was blockaded by the Nationalists and the calorific intake of the population was vastly below the basic minimum.[46] Some 100,000 refugees had crowded into the area from Guipúzcoa as this region had been occupied by the Francoist forces. By the spring of 1937, for lack of healthy housing space, Bilbao was suffering an epidemic of typhoid fever.[47] Most exiled children (approximately 17,500) remained in France throughout the period of the Spanish civil war, while others ended up in Belgium (5,130), the Soviet Union (estimates ranging from 3,000 to 5,000) or Britain (about 4,000).[48] It was claimed by the Francoist authorities that the most robust children were selected for the Soviet Union, as though Communism were attempting to suck the very lifeblood from Spain, though there is no evidence of such a selection process.[49] In total, some 500,000 Spaniards had fled into exile by the end of the civil war. Some 50 per cent of exiles were women and children, representing a dramatic displacement.[50] During the second half of 1940, German forces occupying France began handing over these so-called 'stateless enemies' to Spain for assessment and punishment. Adults went first to prison, and many of them were executed for wartime 'crimes' – their Republican political activism was reformulated by the Francoist judicial system as 'military rebellion'.[51]

The Nationalists depicted the expatriation of the children of Republican families in an ideological way, viewing the process as a 'communist' strategy resulting from the aims of 'the revolution' rather than a humanitarian requirement forced by the war.[52] The children's colonies established by the Republican authorities for refugees – mainly in Catalonia – were, according to the Nationalist-Francoist authorities, subjected to 'intense propaganda'. In an attempt to deflect responsibility for the harm done to children, it was also argued that the revolution, particularly its anti-clerical violence, 'damaged' children more than the effects of the war. The welfare institutions conducted psychological tests involving questionnaires to discover children's levels of patriotism, the state of their 'consciences', and their levels of intelligence and use of language. In general, the children of Republicans were 'shown' to be of markedly lower intelligence than average children.[53] In order to arrange the most suitable regime for individual cases, the children were also questioned about their attitudes to their parents, the moral lessons learned from the Republican defeat, and the extent of their repentance and willingness to reform themselves.[54]

A Nationalist Delegación Extraordinaria de Repatrición de Menores was instituted, later based in Paris, to 'recover' as many children as possible in what was seen as an ideological battle for young hearts and minds. It was claimed that Franco himself had intervened to ensure a regime of 'special guardianship' to 're-educate' children who had spent time in 'foreign environments'. The Nationalist 'Delegation' for repatriation would come under the auspices of the Franco state's political organization, the Falange (or '*Movimiento*'), in July 1941, through the party's foreign section, the Servicio Exterior.[55] The authorities would decide if any given family was 'fit to re-educate the repatriated child in the principles of the

Catholic religion and in the patriotic doctrinal postulates which informed the Glorious National Rising (of 18 July 1936)'.[56]

Almost as soon as the Basque Country was occupied by the Nationalist forces in June 1937 a Papal envoy, unofficially representing the Franco authorities, was dispatched to Britain, with letters from anxious parents, to urge repatriation and, indeed, by the end of 1938 some 1,300 children had been returned and more than 230 further claims were awaiting investigation.[57] As in other countries, a British 'Repatriation Committee' was formed by eminent British supporters of Franco to speed the process. Letters printed in *The Times* suggested, among other things, that innocent children were being turned into 'Christ-hating little Communists'.[58] The British Joint Committee for Spanish Relief determined, however, that no evacuee should be returned to Spain unless it could be established that a relative or official guardian was willing and capable of taking care of the child. The Committee was on its guard against political attempts in Spain to take charge of such children and 're-educate' them: 'Some had no homes to return to, others were orphans with relatives still untraced, others had a father or mother, sometimes both, in prison'.[59] The recent testimonies of victims show that such caution was indeed justified. One prominent member of the British Basque Children's Committee wrote in such terms to *The Times*:

> It would be a dishonorable breach of trust if they (the children) were returned to Bilbao where, in the absence of their parents, they would almost certainly be put into reformatories or other institutions, there to be – in the insurgent authorities' own phrase 're-educated', i.e. brought up to believe that the cause for which their parents are fighting and suffering is not merely misguided but wicked.[60]

According to the official records, most of the efforts at repatriation made by the Spanish state were not instigated at the prompting of the parents or families of exiled youngsters.[61] This claim was used to suggest that these families cared little for the future welfare of their children. In fact, these children had from the beginning been sent abroad for the sake of their safety and there is certainly anecdotal evidence to suggest that, however painful separation was, families believed they would be better off away from Francoist Spain. The claim of 'uncaring' Republican parents was used to give a spurious legitimacy to state intervention and of obscuring the state's own determination to socially engineer the process of 're-integration' of children into society. The offspring of 'Reds', sent away from Spain, were equated with other children already in welfare institutions of some kind, and for a variety of reasons. These institutionalized children had long been described as 'morally delinquent' or 'morally abandoned'. In the context of the civil war and its repressive aftermath, the children of Republicans would be categorized en masse in the same way. It was claimed by the Spanish authorities that '99 per cent' of those looking after Spanish children in exile refused to allow the youngsters to be returned voluntarily. Although, for many, the experience of exile was dreadful, repatriation to a repressed, often vengeful and half-starving Spanish society after 1939 was itself a deeply unpleasant prospect. Returning to Guernica in the Basque Country after exile for three years, the Ozamiz children were placed in a convent of stern nuns near Bilbao: 'They treated us like miniature monsters, the children of Reds'.

It was not just the Spanish children in France who were engulfed by the wider war beginning in 1940. With the German advance into Russia, the Spanish exiled children there found themselves removed from the front-line areas toward the Caucasus. Any youngsters who were caught by the Nazi invasion were returned to Spain through the offices of the Servicio Exterior of the Falange. Those whose families were deemed by local religious and civil authorities of the state to be 'irreproachable from the religious, ethical and national point of view' were supposed, officially, to be returned to their families but others were inducted into Auxilio Social. The officials of Auxilio Social would then make decisions about the children's future: what was good for them and what was harmful according to the normative moral-patriotic code of the Spanish 'New State'. From here they were shifted on to one of the provincial Juntas de Protección de Menores. These ideological-moral considerations were played down in official documents. According to the 1949 report of the Servicio Exterior:

> in cases where there is no claim for the child, and when the child can give no information about the whereabouts of its family [Auxilio Social], having done everything possible to locate the parents, even through press and radio announcements ... will hand the child over to the Junta de Protección. ...[62]

The Repatriation Delegation had considerable success in the early years until 1943. The majority of children in France (some 12,800) were located and brought back to Spain, and a large number were similarly returned from Belgium and Britain. By 1949 it was calculated that some 20,000 children in total had been returned from exile. Far fewer were recorded as returned from the Soviet Union in the 1940s; those who did return were considered negatively as 'sovietized' and there were fears that they would turn out to be dangerous 'sexual libertines' or 'communist agents'. The term 'desespañolizados' ('de-Spanishized') was used to describe the exiles in the Soviet Union whom it would be 'imprudent' to allow to return. According to the official discourse, they would need 'physical and moral disinfection' on arrival in Spain.[63] In fact, there are documented cases of children who made a reasonable life for themselves in the Soviet Union, some of them returning to Spain after decades. Many, of course, suffered the privations and hunger of war in the Soviet provinces from June 1941.[64]

Some Conclusions

Although the brutalization of children in wartime and post-war Europe was always only a part of a more generalized experience of suffering, in Spain the plight of war children has to be understood within a context of extreme social polarization. Spain's war was a civil war, not primarily an international war: it was a struggle to define what 'the nation' consisted of, ideologically, morally and bodily. The term 'war children' in Spain does not, therefore, refer to children born as a result of foreign occupation, but to those born to the 'internal enemy'. Many of the effects, however, as we have seen, were the same as in occupied Europe. Historical analysis therefore requires some account of the generalized context of division and physical and psychological violence. Indeed, as part of a definable process of repression, directed by one section of society against another, analysis of the brutal treatment of war children, and especially those who were 'disappeared', allows us to analyse in turn the nature of the Franco dictatorship itself. Hence, 'war children', as a category of analysis, does not become marginalized within a historiographical 'ghetto'. It has been argued here that the way in which certain Spanish war children were treated tells us a great deal about the ideological-religious-psychological make-up of the regime and the society produced by the Spanish civil war.

In defining 'the nation', those who were 'the defeated', including their children, became demonized as the 'anti-Spain' (or the potential, future, 'anti-Spain'). The Spanish nation which emerged from the war was officially an entity shaped around Catholic moralism. This code of ethics became an idealized guide to behaviour which Republican war children were always likely to find difficult to live up to because they were tarred with the brush of 'anti-Spanishness'. Next to this Catholic guide to 'Spanishness' there existed a well-articulated and documented psychopathology of the 'anti-Spain' – of delinquency and disorder. Therefore, the 'nationalization', 're-christianization', and 'treatment' of the enemy tended to be focused on the family as most essential cell of traditional authority and order. The bedrock of the family – though not the source of its authority – was the woman and mother, whose primary responsibility was to bear and educate children. Thus, in the on-going 'crusade', which seemed hardly to cease with the end of formal hostilities in April 1939, women and children, the future generation, became absolutely central.

Thus it was that children became potential targets of the repression – both institutional and capricious – which was such a prominent feature of the Francoist state and of society in the 1940s. The political and cultural conditions, as mentioned already, were combined with the terrible human losses of the war and in the disease-ridden aftermath. These losses affected the youngest children most.[65] A repressive programme combined with fears about population loss to produce a resurgence of programmes of racial and mental hygiene. Children were the central preoccupation of those who fretted about the 'life-blood' of the nation. For the children, the trauma of war and displacement were real enough. But the manner in which they were addressed was determined by the triumphant ideology of the war. The nature of Republican children's trauma was explained by reference to the 'defects' of Republicans as human beings – the problematic nature of their minds and bodies as inherited features.[66] The 'segregation' which was prescribed did not, however, entail the 'hard' eugenic intervention advocated in other parts of Europe. Rather, in Catholic Spain, it was more appropriate to segregate such children by use of cultural measures: institutions of re-education, control of schooling, withdrawal from parents as primary agents of socialization, and even the construction of new identities by depriving youngsters of positive political, social and familial memories.

There was no legal redress for the victims of Francoism, because it became more or less accepted that Republicans – and their families – had indeed been 'bad'. War children in general and not just those who were 'disappeared' by the regime therefore became the 'obedient generation' which was cowed into submission by the regime and by society's desire to forget the past. There was no war pension for disabled Republican soldiers, even those who had been conscripted, or for the widows of Republicans. Children, therefore, had to go and work rather than finish their schooling. Those who died fighting for the Republic could not be publicly remembered and mourned, and the treatment of their children was founded on the same essential discrimination and will to eradicate everything associated with the Republic. This also helped deflect criticism and a sense of collective shame about the enormous catastrophe of the civil war. The sense of 'original sin', frustration, guilt complexes, generational conflict and moral disinheritance mentioned in the testimonies of many Spaniards in talking about the effects of the war on children suggest the enormously negative influences of this repressive culture.[67]

War and dictatorship presented an opportunity for establishing the 'mental type' of the Spanish 'child delinquent' because there was plenty of captive material for analysis and few enforceable safeguards to protect individual rights. In common with other aspects of Francoist ideology, psychological theory and practice in the early post-war years shifted attention from the class origins of revolution and war toward mental typologies. At least rhetorically, Marxism was formulated as a 'sickness' and its 'treatment' lay in reinforcing cultural nationalism through Catholic doctrine reinforced by psychologists and psychiatrists.[68] The 'psycho-affective complexes' of the parents, it was argued, were vital in determining the nature of the child. The ideas, habits, customs and behaviour of parents were important to the construction of the 'military home', and, thus, to the militarized or highly ordered society, because of the threat posed by the 'imitative instincts of children':

When the familial environment is strictly moral, similar moral qualities, the purest ethical ideals, and exemplary social conduct are habitually obvious in descendants.[69]

In November 2002, the Spanish Congress finally (and unanimously) approved a motion condemning the coup d'état of July 1936 which had begun the civil war. This effectively rehabilitated, in moral terms, those who had defended the Republic and suffered as a consequence. Recuperating the memories of the Spanish war children, especially those who were wrenched from their families, is a part of this rehabilitation. This is a positive spin-off of the globally popular culture of remembrance which has been produced by generational change, the collapse of the Eastern bloc in 1989 and the resultant end of the 'long post-World War II' era, and the downgrading of political ideology. This movement, with an impetus essentially 'from below', has imposed an imperative to remember and the necessary public space for remembrance to occur. The subject is not merely about memory, however. The full implications of the theories and responses to political and social conflict and the manner in which children became used to further political, national and scientific purposes have yet to be realized. Rather than mere moral condemnation, it is the broad historical context that allows for such a realization.

Notes

1. See for example José Sanabre Sanromá, *Martirológio de la Iglesia en la diócesis de Barcelona durante la persecución religiosa, 1936–1939* (Barcelona, 1943).
2. Report of the Cardinal Primate, Isidro Gomá, to the Holy See, 13 August 1936: José Andrés-Gallego and Anton M. Pazos (eds), *Archivo Gomá. Documentos de la guerra civil*, 1 (Madrid, 2001), pp. 80–9.
3. Juan Díez Nicolás, 'La mortalidad en la guerra civil española', *Boletín de demografía histórica* 3(1), March 1985.
4. Michael Richards, 'Spanish psychiatry *c.*1900–1945: constitutional theory, eugenics, and the nation', *Bulletin of Spanish Studies* 81(6), November 2004, pp. 137–62.
5. See for example Nancy Leys Stepan, '*The Hour of Eugenics*': *Race, Gender, and Nation in Latin America* (Cornell University Press, 1991), esp. pp. 189–92. A 'Catalan Eugenics Society' associated itself with the Latin International Federation of Eugenics Societies which held its first Congress in Paris in 1937, p. 189.
6. On Catholicism's doctrinal anti-eugenicism, see the Papal Encyclical *Casti Connubi* (December 1930). Also Richards, 'Spanish psychiatry *c.*1900–1945'.
7. See Michael Richards, 'From War Culture to Civil Society: Francoism, Social

Change and Memories of the Spanish Civil War' *History and Memory* 14(1/2), Fall, 2002, pp. 93–120.

8. José Piquer y Jover, *El niño abandonado y delincuente: Consideración etiológica y estadística* (Madrid, 1946), p. 76.

9. Richards, 'From War Culture to Civil Society', *passim*; Ángela Cenarro, 'Memory Beyond the Public Sphere', *History and Memory* 14(1/2), Fall, 2002, pp. 174–5; Consuelo García, *Las cárceles de Soledad Real: una vida* (Madrid, 1982), p. 127.

10. See for example Montserrat Roig, *Noche y niebla: Los catalanes en los campos nazis* (Barcelona, 1978).

11. *El Mundo*, 18 August 2002.

12. The documentary, *Els nens perduts del franquisme*, was shown by Catalan television (TV-3) and attracted a large audience. See also Ricard Vinyes et al., *Los niños perdidos del franquismo* (Barcelona, 2002).

13. For an extended discussion, see also Michael Richards, 'Morality and Biology in the Spanish Civil War: Psychiatrists, Revolution and Women Prisoners in Málaga', *Contemporary European History* 10(3), 2001, pp. 395–421.

14. Piquer, *El niño abandonado y delincuente*, p. 41.

15. Antonio Vallejo Nágera, *Niños y jóvenes anormales* (Madrid, 1941), p. 62.

16. The Dean of the Jesuit Upper School of San Ignacio in Sarriá, Barcelona, in 1940, for example, was a psychologist. Piquer, *El niño abandonado*, pp. 1–6. Also the professional journal *Revista de la Obra de Protección de Menores*. Other religious orders were also involved in such projects.

17. See for example Vallejo Nágera, *Niños y jóvenes anormales*, p. 9, pp. 17–20. See, in a similar vein, Isidro Gomá, Archbishop of Tarazona, *La familia según el derecho natural y cristiano* (2nd edn, Barcelona, 1931), p. 9; Alfonso Iniesta, *Garra marxista en la infancia* (Burgos, 1939), pp. 263–7; Víctor García Hoz, *Pedagogía de la lucha ascética* (Madrid, 1941).

18. Jordi Roca i Girona, *De la pureza a la maternidad: La construcción del género femenino en la postguerra española* (Madrid, 1996), p. 30; Gabriel Jackson, *The Spanish Republic and the Civil War* (Princeton, 1965), p. 377; Shirley Mangini, *Memories of Resistance: Women's Voices From the Spanish Civil War* (New Haven, 1995), pp. 106–7; Francisco Moreno Gómez, *Córdoba en la posguerra* (Córdoba, 1987), p. 304; Giuliana Di Febo, *Resistencia y movimiento de mujeres en España, 1936–1976* (Barcelona, 1979), pp. 96–7. See also Chapters 7 and 8 in this volume on the Netherlands and France, by Monika Diderichs and Fabrice Virgili respectively.

19. René Girard, *Violence and the Sacred* (London, 1988).

20. See for example Vinyes et al., *Niños perdidos*, pp. 90–1.

21. María Teresa Gallego Méndez, *Mujer, Falange y franquismo* (Madrid, 1983), p. 154.

22. See for example Antonio Vallejo Nágera, *Eugenesia de la hispanidad y regeneración de la raza* (Burgos, 1937).

23. See for example Mary Nash, 'Pronatalism and Motherhood in Franco's Spain', in Gisela Bock and Pat Thane (eds), *Maternity and Gender Policies: Women and the Rise of the European Welfare States, 1880s-1950s* (London, 1994), pp. 160–77.

24. Antonio Cazorla Sánchez, *Las políticas de la victoria* (Madrid, 2000), p. 93.

25. Amando de Miguel, *40 millones de españoles 40 años después* (Barcelona, 1976), p. 37.

26. Geraldine Scanlon, *La polémica feminista en la España contemporánea, 1868–1974* (Madrid, 1986), p. 322.

27. Vallejo Nágera, *Niños y jóvenes anormales*, *passim*.

28. See Richards, 'Morality and Biology in the Spanish Civil War'.

29. Antonio Vallejo Nágera, *La locura y la guerra: psicopatalogía de la guerra española* (Valladolid, 1939), p. 52.

30. *Boletín del Estado*, 1 December 1940.

31. Piquer, *Niño abandonado y delincuente*, pp. 217–18.

32. Ibid., pp. 231–2.

33. Ibid., p. 232.

34. Mirta Núñez Díez Balart and Antonio Rojas Friend, 'Víctimas del franquismo en Madrid: Los fusilamientos en el cementerio del este (1939–1945)', in Javier Tusell et al., *El régimen de Franco, I* (Madrid, 1993), pp. 286–7; Di Febo, *Resistencia y movimiento de mujeres en España*, pp. 22, 30.

35. 5 November 1940, Documentos inéditos de la Fundación Nacional Francisco Franco (FNFF), Vol. 2, pp. 386–7. Also 8 May 1940, FNFF, Vol. 2, pp. 176–7.

36. Mercedes Núñez, *Carcel de Ventas* (Paris, 1967); Fernanda Romeu Alfaro, *El silencio roto. Mujeres contra el franquismo* (Madrid, 1994), p. 41.

37. Juana Doña, *Desde la noche y la niebla: mujeres en las cárceles franquistas* (Madrid, 1978), pp. 131–60.

38. *Boletín del Estado*, 6 April 1940.

39. Patronato Central de Nuestra Señora de la Merced para la Redención de Penas por el Trabajo, *Memoria que eleva al Caudillo de España y a su gobierno* (Madrid, 1944), p. 202.

40. Piquer, *Niño abandonado y delincuente*, pp. 21–3.

41. Vallejo Nágera, *Divagaciones intrascendentes* (Valladolid, 1938), p. 105.

42. See for example *Redención* 7, 13 May 1939, 5, 'Niños perdidos', p. 52.

43. Piquer, *Niño abandonado y delincuente*, pp. 83, 91.

44. The state had already decreed in May 1938 that the new-born would 'not be given abstract or tendentious names, or, for Catholics, others which do not appear in the Roman Calendar of Saints'.

45. Adrian Bell, *Only For Three Months: The Basque Children in Exile* (Norwich,

1996); Dorothy Legarreta, *The Guernica Generation: Basque Refugee Children of the Spanish Civil War* (Reno, 1985).

46. José Luis Aldecoa y Juaristi, 'Contribución al estudio de la lactancia maternal (Experiencias de la guerra en Bilbao)', *Revista de Sanidad e Higiene Pública* 13(4), July–August 1938, pp. 243–4.

47. Ángel Uruñuela, 'Organización de los servicios sanitarios en la provincia de Vizcaya a partir de su liberación', *Revista de Sanidad e Higiene Pública* 13(1), January–February 1938, pp. 56–63. On refugees, see Manuel González Portilla and José María Garmendia, *La guerra civil en el País Vasco* (Madrid, 1988), pp. 94–5.

48. Smaller numbers went to Mexico, North Africa, Switzerland and Denmark.

49. In fact, even those wounded in the Spanish war were accepted in the Soviet Union. The Soviet authorities were concerned about importing disease, as the process of cleansing, delousing and shaving of Spanish children at the Leningrad quay in 1937 suggests. Teresa Pàmies, *Los niños de la guerra* (Barcelona, 1977), pp. 116, 119.

50. José Luis Abellán (ed.), *El exilio español de 1939*, 6 vols (Madrid, 1976).

51. The most well-known cases of those executed were the Catalan nationalist leader Lluis Companys in September 1940 and the leading Socialist Julián Zugazagoitia.

52. See for example *La Vanguardia Española*, 11 March 1939; 2 June 1939.

53. Piquer, *Niño abandonado y delincuente*, p. 59.

54. Ibid., pp. 75–80.

55. Informe sobre la labor desarrollada hasta la fecha para la repatriación de menores españoles expatriados, Servicio Exterior, FET y de las JONS, 1949, SGM, AGA.

56. Letter, Consejo Superior de Protección de Menores, 20 July 1943; letter of President of Junta Provincial de Protección de Menores de Barcelona, 14 July 1944; Piquer, *Niño abandonado y delincuente*, pp. 256–7, 262.

57. Isidro Gríful, 'La tragedia de los niños vascos en el extranjero', *Razón y Fe* 113, 1938, pp. 385–409; Enrique Gábana, *Mi campaña en Inglaterra* (Barcelona, 1939). By 1939 some 3,000 Basque children had been repatriated and by 1941 only some 400 remained in Britain. *Report of the Work of the National Joint Committee for Spanish Relief* (Essex, 1939), p. 6.

58. 'The Children They Sent Away', *Lookout Magazine*, September 1983.

59. Report. *National Joint Committee for Spanish Relief* (London, 1941), p. 9.

60. 7 February 1938. See Bell, *Only For Three Months*, pp. 103–4. Also pp. 97–111.

61. Fewer than 25 per cent of expatriated children were claimed by families, according to the official reports. Informe menores españoles.

62. See for example *La Vanguardia Española*, 21 March 1939.

63. *La Vanguardia Española*, 7 December 1939.
64. See for example Pàmies, *Los niños de la guerra*, pp. 114–24.
65. See for example Jesús J. Alonso Carballes, 'La integración de los niños vascos exiliados durante la guerra civil en la sociedad franquista de posguerra', in José Manuel Trujillano Sánchez and José María Gago González (eds), *Historia y memoria del franquismo*, 1936–1978 (Ávila, 1997), pp. 173–84.
66. See Richards, 'Morality and Biology', *passim*.
67. See for example Rafael Borràs Betriu, *Los que no hicimos la guerra* (Barcelona, 1971), pp. 192, 197, 232–2, 541, etc.
68. Director of the state asylum in Valencia, Francisco Marco Merenciano, 'Nuevas orientaciones sobre higiene mental', originally 1942, reprinted in *Ensayos médicos y literarios: antología* (Madrid, 1958), pp. 98–9.
69. Vallejo Nágera, *Niños y jóvenes anormales*, pp. 47–8.

References

Abellán, J.L. (ed.), *El exilio español de 1939*, 6 vols, Madrid: Taurus, 1976.

Aldecoa y Juaristi, J.L., 'Contribución al estudio de la lactancia maternal. (Experiencias de la guerra en Bilbao)', *Revista de Sanidad e Higiene Pública* 13(4) (July–August 1938).

Alonso Carballes, J.J., 'La integración de los niños vascos exiliados durante la guerra civil en la sociedad franquista de posguerra', in J.M. Trujillano Sánchez, J.M. Gago González (eds), *Historia y memoria del franquismo, 1936–1978*, Ávila: Fundación Cultural Santa Teresa, 1997.

Andrés-Gallego, J. and Pazos, A.M. (eds), *Archivo Gomá: Documentos de la guerra civil*, 1, Madrid: Consejo Superior de Investigaciones Científicas, 2001.

Bell, A., *Only For Three Months: The Basque Children in Exile*, Norwich: Mousehold Press, 1996.

Borràs Betriu, R., *Los que no hicimos la guerra*, Barcelona: Ediciones Nauta, 1971.

Cazorla Sánchez, A., *Las políticas de la victoria*, Madrid: Marcial Pons, 2000.

Cenarro, A., 'Memory Beyond the Public Sphere', *History and Memory* 14(1/2), Fall (2002).

Díez Nicolás, J., 'La mortalidad en la guerra civil española', *Boletín de demografía histórica* 3(1) (March 1985).

Doña, J., *Desde la noche y la niebla: mujeres en las cárceles franquistas*, Madrid: Ediciones de la Torre, 1978.

Febo, G. Di, *Resistencia y movimiento de mujeres en España, 1936–1976*, Barcelona: Icaria, 1979.

Gábana, E., *Mi campaña en Inglaterra*, Barcelona: np, 1939.

Gallego Méndez, T., *Mujer, Falange y franquismo*, Madrid: Taurus, 1983.

García, C., *Las cárceles de Soledad Real: Una vida*, Madrid: Alfaguara, 1982.

García Hoz, V., *Pedagogía de la lucha ascética*, Madrid: Consejo Superior de Investigaciones Científicas, 1941.

Girard, R., *Violence and the Sacred*, London: Athlone, 1988.

Gomá, I., *La familia según el derecho natural y cristiano*, 2nd edn, Barcelona: Librería Litúrgica, 1931.

González Portilla, M. and Garmendia, J.M., *La guerra civil en el País Vasco*, Madrid: Siglo Veintiuno, 1988.

Gríful, I., 'La tragedia de los niños vascos en el extranjero', *Razón y Fe* 113 (1938).

Iniesta, A., *Garra marxista en la infancia*, Burgos: np, 1939.

Jackson, G., *The Spanish Republic and the Civil War*, Princeton, NJ: Princeton University Press, 1965.

Legarreta, D., *The Guernica Generation: Basque Refugee Children of the Spanish Civil War*, Reno: University of Nevada Press, 1985.

Leys Stepan, N., *'The Hour of Eugenics': Race, Gender, and Nation in Latin America*, Ithaca NY: Cornell University Press, 1991.

Mangini, S., *Memories of Resistance: Women's Voices From the Spanish Civil War*, New Haven: Yale University Press, 1995.

Marco Merenciano, F., 'Nuevas orientaciones sobre higiene mental', originally, 1942, reprinted in *Ensayos médicos y literarios: antología*, Madrid: Ediciones Cultura Hispánica, 1958.

Miguel, A. de, *40 millones de españoles 40 años después*, Barcelona: Grijalbo, 1976.

Moreno Gómez, F., *Córdoba en la posguerra*, Córdoba: Francisco Baena, 1987.

Nash, M., 'Pronatalism and Motherhood in Franco's Spain', in G. Bock and P. Thane (eds), *Maternity and Gender Policies: Women and the Rise of the European Welfare States, 1880s-1950s*, London: Routledge, 1994.

Núñez, M., *Carcel de Ventas*, Paris: Editions de la Librairie du Globe, 1967.

Núñez Díez Balart, M. and Rojas Friend, A., 'Víctimas del franquismo en Madrid: Los fusilamientos en el cementerio del este (1939–1945)', in J. Tusell et al., *El régimen de Franco*, I, Madrid: UNED, 1993.

Pàmies, T., *Los niños de la guerra*, Barcelona: Bruguera, 1977.

Piquer y Jover, J., *El niño abandonado y delincuente: Consideración etiológica y estadística*, Madrid: Consejo Superior de Investigaciones Científicas, 1946.

Richards, M., 'Morality and Biology in the Spanish Civil War: Psychiatrists, Revolution and Women Prisoners in Málaga', *Contemporary European History* 10(3) (2001).

Richards, M., 'From War Culture to Civil Society: Francoism, Social Change and Memories of the Spanish Civil War', *History and Memory* 14(1/2), Fall (2002).

Richards, M., 'Spanish Psychiatry c.1900–1945: Constitutional Theory, Eugenics, and the Nation', *Bulletin of Spanish Studies* 81(6) (November 2004).

Roca i Girona, J., *De la pureza a la maternidad: La construcción del género femenino en la postguerra española*, Madrid: Ministerio de Educación y Cultura, 1996.

Roig, M., *Noche y niebla: Los catalanes en los campos nazis*, Barcelona: Ediciones Península, 1978.

Romeu Alfaro, F., *El silencio roto. Mujeres contra el franquismo*, Madrid: np, 1994.

Sanabre Sanromá, J., *Martirológio de la Iglesia en la Diócesis de Barcelona durante la persecución religiosa, 1936–1939*, Barcelona: Editorial Librería Religiosa, 1943.

Scanlon, G., *La polémica feminista en la España contemporánea, 1868–1974*, Madrid: Akal, 1986.

'The Children They Sent Away', *Lookout Magazine* (September 1983).

Uruñuela, A., 'Organización de los servicios sanitarios en la provincia de Vizcaya a partir de su liberación', *Revista de Sanidad e Higiene Pública* 13(1) (January–February 1938).

Vallejo Nágera, A., *Eugenesia de la hispanidad y regeneración de la raza*, Burgos: Editorial Española, 1937.

Vallejo Nágera, *Divagaciones intrascendentes*, Valladolid: np, 1938.

Vallejo Nágera, A., *La locura y la guerra: psicopatología de la guerra española*, Valladolid: Librería Santarén, 1939.

Vallejo Nágera, A., *Niños y jóvenes anormales*, Madrid: Sociedad de Educación 'Atenas', 1941.

Vinyes, R. et al., *Los niños perdidos del franquismo*, Barcelona: Plaza Janés, 2002.

–7–

Enfants de Boches:
The War Children of France

Fabrice Virgili

Translated by Paula Schwartz

In July 1941, the Secretary of State for Health and Family of the Vichy government, Jacques Chevalier, alerted by his own services, approached Admiral Darlan,
then Vice-President du Conseil, about calling a special meeting of the cabinet ministers on the subject of prisoner-of-war wives. Since June 1940 and the fall of
France, nearly 1.6 million men were prisoners in Germany. Half were married, and
their wives, who were left behind in France, had to manage their family and home
as best they could. After the Armistice, France was divided under several different
authorities. In the East, Alsace-Moselle was annexed by the Third Reich; near the
border with Belgium, Nord Pas-de-Calais was under German command from
Brussels; in the Alps very small territories were annexed by Italy. But the main part
of France was divided by the demarcation line. The North and Atlantic coast was
the Occupied zone. The South was 'la Zone libre'. The collaborating Regime of
Marshal Pétain was established in Vichy, a small spa city in the centre of France.
After the American landing in North Africa in November 1942, the whole of
France was occupied by German forces. However, from October 1940 and the
Montoire meetings of Marshal Pétain and Adolf Hitler, the new regime was
engaged in a state collaboration. The Vichy government continued to manage the
administration even under the German pressure.

So in this defeated and divided country, the Secretary of State described the dis-
astrous situation in which many women found themselves: 'the prisoner of war's
family is condemned through very severe privations to looking for non-existent
resources. Family allowances are so low that we see a significant development of
prostitution on the part of women and minors in the countryside as well as in the
city, in addition to numerous births or expected births, in the occupied and even
unoccupied zones, of children fathered by Germans'.[1] Thus, barely a year after the
defeat and the start of the occupation, Vichy authorities were worrying about the
numerous children born of French women and German soldiers. Since pregnancy

lasts for nine months even in wartime, the speed at which intimate relations had taken place between occupied and occupier is striking.

Flirt with the Enemy

This phenomenon should be understood in the more general context of the relations between the victors and the defeated population. While the memory of 'German atrocities' of summer 1914 remained particularly strong, the German command took great pains to avoid the rumors resulting from such practices through propaganda aimed at the French population and through control of the German troops. One of the first posters exhorted the 'abandoned' population to 'have confidence in the German solder!' In a defeated France where eight million people found themselves fleeing the invaders (the phenomenon known as 'the exodus'), the slogan made sense in more ways than one. It spoke to people who found themselves far from home and separated from their families as a result of the war. It also suggested that the French had been abandoned by their own political leaders and army, that they had no choice but to place their faith in the victors. Depicted on the poster was a soldier with no weapon, his helmet hanging discreetly from his belt, carrying in his left arm a smiling little boy, happily munching a slice of bread and jam. His right arm is around two little girls who appear to be reassured by his protective gesture. The victorious soldier is here portrayed as a fatherly protector.

The horrors inflicted on the civilian populations of Belgium and northern France in 1914 contributed to anti-German sentiment, which had been fuelled by rumours of children whose hands had been cut off by the Germans. In 1940, despite the bombing of civilian targets, the executions of African soldiers after they had already surrendered or the rape and pillage committed by German soldiers which appeared to have been sanctioned by German military authorities, there was a widely held notion that the invaders of 1940 were 'correct', or polite and proper. In a defeated France, it seemed that the German soldier was there to stay; he was the victor and had considerable buying power. However, if the Wehrmacht seemed to have won the battle for public opinion, the high command had not anticipated intimate relations between soldiers and French women. On the contrary, the fear of venereal disease which was typical of the military/nazi racist notions about a degenerate French population, had even prompted German commanders to prohibit sexual relations with the population aside from tightly controlled and officially sanctioned prostitution.[2] In fact, the living arrangements provided by the high command did not make frequent cohabitation and sexual relations impossible. Depending on the period, between 400,000 and 1 million men between 20 and 40 years of age were occupying a country with about 2 million of its own men in the same age bracket out of commission: POWs, deportees, voluntary or forced labourers, partisans in the Maquis, and so on.

The relationships which took place before the conception and subsequent birth of these children were various in nature; they could consist of one-time contacts or longer frequentations over time. Marriages between German soldiers and native women were forbidden in France. Nonetheless, special permission could be obtained. A certificate of 'prenuptial intent', a racial exam, and pro-German sentiments were required but not always sufficient unto themselves. Indeed, it appears that only the Waffen SS received such permission, directly from the Führer himself. Nonetheless, the prohibition of marriage between German occupiers and French women did not prevent the existence of lasting relationships which often ended by the soldiers' change of post or even reassignment to the eastern front. For others still, the liberation of France and the German retreat marked the end of the story, like the case of a German soldier who barely had the time to scribble a quick note saying goodbye to his French girlfriend:

> My dearest Jeanne, first we got orders that we were going to leave during the night, but we are still here today. But we will leave tonight. I can't forget you and the time we spent together. Jeanne, fierce fighting awaits us, but I go with the grace of God, who does wish for us to be apart ... and so I am leaving with you in my heart, and very distressed. A thousand, thousand kisses and do not forget your [signed, illegible].[3]

To be Pregnant

When these children of mixed German-French heritage were questioned several decades after the war, all of them attributed the circumstances of their birth to a love story between their parents. In that sense, they are not unlike the rest of the population; however, if such love stories indeed existed, they were rather the exception to the rule. In fact, the women often went through their pregnancies alone. Whether they were reproached for being unmarried single mothers, having sex outside marriage or being unfaithful to their husbands, all were accused of infidelity of one sort or another. In addition to this moral condemnation, the fact that these women had taken German lovers also made them traitors to the nation.

For all of these women, the situation was far from simple; but whether they were alone, ostracized or supported by friends or family, they had to decide whether or not to keep the child. Although it is impossible to know the exact numbers, some women had abortions, others gave up their children at birth and still others kept them.

Upon learning of an unforeseen pregnancy, women practiced the utmost discretion by trying to hide their condition for as long as possible. Together with the lack of contraceptives at the time, the unlikelihood that the soldiers used any means of birth control such as condoms meant that few if any of these pregnancies resulted from the joint decision to have a child. Some women sought abortions of their own volition; others acceded to pressures from family or partners to abort the fetus. When in August 1944 Madeleine announced to her partner Siegfried that she was expecting a child, he proposed that she seek an abortion since the German defeat and the ultimate separation were inevitable. Siegfried, who worked as a nurse in the Wehrmacht (German army), was posted to a military hospital in the south of France where it would have been possible to procure an abortion without significant medical or legal risks. Madeleine refused. Others like her, however, did not. But whether they employed home remedies or sought an abortionist ('angel maker' in French) or complicitous doctor, for both women and men the risks were enormous. Of the twenty-six abortions which Marie-Louise Giraud was accused of performing, several were for women who became pregnant by German soldiers. Condemned to death by the Section spéciale of Paris, she was guillotined on 12 July 1943.[4] Her case is unique, an example of the most extreme form of repression, but many other women were condemned to months or even years of prison for performing abortions.[5] When it was no longer possible to hide a pregnancy, many women moved to another city or 'went up' to Paris.

Births

There they stayed with friends or in institutions. Vichy enacted the law of 13 December 1941 which permitted women to give birth anonymously. The authorities did everything possible to see that there was no getting around this law. For example, in 1943 the directors of hospitals and maternity wards received a circular entitled 'Birth records: professional confidentiality applies to children born of adulterous wives of prisoners of war'. The document was circulated to protect the identities of children whose mothers had to furnish the official card which enabled them to obtain food (*cartes d'alimentation*). The Director of the Assistance publique (public hospital for the needy) notes 'the grave consequences which the violation of confidentiality can have under the present circumstances in the case of children born of adulterous prisoner-of-war wives' and that 'pregnant women admitted to the maternity ward who ask that their identities remain secret are not required to surrender their personal food cards' (which bore the identity of the holder), 'but only food coupons' (to which no names were affixed).[6] After they were born, such infants were placed in child care or foster homes until adoption. From that time on, nothing in their file makes it possible to trace their birth mothers. Nor is it possible now to know exactly how many children were in this situation at the time.

Of course, not all women who became pregnant by Germans gave birth anonymously. Once removed from their family environment, they could keep their child or place it with a foster mother in order to be able to work. At the time it was easy to find a job with the German authorities, either in France or in Germany. In any event, the situation was common enough for there to be maternity wards or hospitals specifically intended for these women and their children. In the case of Corrèze, the prefect noted in a monthly report dated October 1941 the creation of 'a secret maternity hospital for pregnant prisoner-of-war wives', estimating that there were approximately three hundred such women in his region.[7] The goal was to help these women, as discreetly as possible, often in the interest of their husbands. The following record is one of many just like it kept by different public or private institutions which took in these women.

> Number 2039. Boy, born in April 1944 in Paris.
> Mother: 25-year-old waitress in a hotel occupied by the German army.
> Father: unknown, 37 years old, soldier in the German army. Spent three days in Paris. Must leave for the Russian front.
> Reason [for giving up the child]: Madame is married, her husband has been a prisoner of war since 1940 and is now working in Germany. His wife does not want to break up her marriage.

Upon the birth of the child, the situation was rarely easy. A woman had either to continue to hide or tell her family, even her husband, the truth. She also had to arrange material support: work, childcare, housing. Finally, she had to decide whether to await the hypothetical return of the German father, hope to find another man who was prepared to marry and legitimate her child, or rear the child alone, with all the reprobation that would entail.

French or German?

The first children to result from such relations surprised and worried the authorities at Vichy as well as in Berlin. From the perspective of the new 'French State' which had replaced the Republic, these relations undermined the principles set forth in the National Revolution. The fact that many of these women were prisoner-of-war wives revealed the glaring failure of Vichy's programme. Indeed, not only had the politics of collaboration from October 1940 on failed to bring the prisoners back home, Vichy was also incapable of providing decent living conditions for prisoners' families. And despite increased social control and mounting repression, the authorities were unable to guarantee the faithfulness of their wives. The reality of the family as lived by many diverged from the idealized version which Vichy had placed at the centre of its motto: Travail – Famille – Patrie. Separation, extraconjugal relations and adultery were the antithesis of the family the National Revolution sought to foster. However, by way of parapolitical associations such as the Secours national or the Famille du Prisonnier de guerre, Vichy remained concerned about the fate of these children, who were the cause of a particular kind of attention. Various German documents indicate a reticence vis-à-vis these children on the whole, but a particular interest in those who corresponded to the racial ideals of the Nazis. Children whose mothers came from Normandy in the north of France were deemed acceptable and could be brought to Germany if necessary. The demographic obsession on both sides of the Rhine ensured that the fate of these children became an increasingly significant issue. Born in France and therefore French according to Vichy, fathered by German soldiers and therefore German for Berlin, they received guarded attention from both countries. A letter of May 1942 addressed to Reichsfuhrer Himmler by Leonardo Conti proclaims:

> *Reichsfuhrer!* French women have given birth to approximately fifty thousand children. In my estimation, these children are not bad, in most cases no worse than those pro-created by Norwegian women in Norway. At the moment, Madame Huntzinger, the widow of the general who was killed in an accident, is very interested in these children. They will therefore be lost to Germany. Even if, as has already been the case, a German in a childless marriage would take care of the child, Madame Huntzinger's organization would make that impossible. I propose that the Lebensborn take an active interest in these children as well.[8]

Madame Huntzinger was the widow of one of the most important members of the Vichy government who died on 12 November 1941. His position helped her to found 'La Famille du Prisonnier', a relief association for prisoner-of-war families with a relative autonomy from the French government. Even Leonardo Conti exaggerated her action, the fact that Madame Huntzinger was easily in contact with the head of Vichy Regime seems a sufficient cause for Germans to renounce taking care of these children.

Throughout the Occupation the authorities of both countries seem to have kept an eye on these children without ever having made any significant provisions for them. In September 1944, the Paris préfecture de police [Commissariat of police] undertook 'a general overview of the organization and activities of various German administrative offices in Paris, in particular those of the German Embassy, for the period of the occupation, from 1940 to 1944'. The office of social affairs headed by Doctor Martha Unger was evidently assigned responsibility for these children: 'It seems that she has undertaken to bring all the French women who have had children with German soldiers to Germany, and has brought them to a château in Chantilly while they await transport to Germany. It is reported that she did this in order to keep them from Madame la Générale Huntzinger, who wanted to take these women in. The château in Chantilly is guarded by the SS'.[9] A *Lebensborn* called Westwald was eventually created in France at Lamorlaye. Having opened late, in early 1944, it probably housed only a few dozen children, together with their mothers, en route to Germany. This is a negligible group given the total number of children of Franco-German origin.

How many Children?

For their number was not insignificant. Unfortunately it is impossible at this time to know how many of them there were; nonetheless a certain number of indicators and documents suggest that this was a massive phenomenon. We have seen that in May 1942 Leonardo Conti mentioned some fifty thousand children. Other reports cite from fifty thousand to seventy thousand births as of autumn 1942, or eighty thousand by spring 1943. These figures are impressive because they do not include the southern zone, which was invaded in November 1942. Moreover, different cases which have come to light show that the births do not stop in 1943. Not only were children being born nine months after the end of the Occupation, but later still, because such relations were either ongoing or initiated with German prisoners of war. All the figures came from the German side; unfortunately, we don't know how they had recorded them. But if the number of births is correct, from April 1941 (nine months after the beginning of the Occupation of France) to October 1942, it puts 8 to 12 per cent of the births in the Occupied zone. A projection for the entire territory (northern and southern zones) and for the entire period could be as high as 120,000–200,000.

From a statistical standpoint we can also observe that the number of illegitimate births rises considerably in the years from 1943 to 1946: 10 per cent of children born alive during this time were illegitimate, as opposed to 7 per cent outside this timeframe. At the same time, the number of children recognized by their fathers was on the wane – fewer than 10 per cent as compared to 15 per cent at other times. In Paris, where the main maternity hospitals are located, there was a veritable explosion of illegitimate births. In the Montparnasse area, they constituted more than 50 per cent of all births for 1944.[10] Of course the paternity of these children cannot necessarily be attributed to a member of the occupying troops, but despite the imposed rule of secrecy, a few remarks from hospital staff reveal part of the secret: 'we discreetly question them about the father in order to find him and have him accept responsibility; in the end they relieve their tortured conscience, in so many words … "he's a soldier, he is gone," [they say] and we understand'.[11]

At War's End

At the end of the war numerous strictures which had weighed against women who had kept their children were lifted. For those who awaited the return of their German partners in anticipation of a hoped-for or promised wedding, the end of the war was sometimes a time of disillusionment. Months or even years later they received news of the death of the German soldier, who in many cases had died on the eastern front. In other instances, there was a soldier's refusal to renew a relationship which had ended with the occupation, or an unremitting silence leading to the erasure of a soldier's memory. Some soldiers were either married or engaged in Germany; others had embarked upon a new life. Some French women later met other men who accepted more or less enthusiastically to legitimize the child of another. Finally, some married women managed to have their husbands forgive them and not refuse to acknowledge paternity of another man's child. This was essential if the child born of an adulterous relationship was to be recognized de facto as that of the woman's husband. In fact, the authorities encouraged couples to take this route; the Ministry of deportees and refugees published a brochure to this effect intended for 'pregnant wives of absent men' which recommends that 'when it is expected that the prisoner-of-war husband will be noble enough to accept the child, his wife, who is in the best position to choose the right time, will tell him about the child at an opportune moment and in her own way. Such a family should be supported in every way possible, materially as well as morally'.[12]

Finally, and once again without being able to quantify the phenomenon, some Franco-German couples reunited when the soldiers were taken prisoner at the end of the war; they then decided whether to settle in France or to move to Germany. In March 1945, before the war was even over, the Minister of War was asked to rule on the requests for French women and German prisoners of war to enter into marriage. In his answer to the ICRC he concluded, 'this practice would create an inadmissible situation, all the more so because in public opinion it would seem contrary to national values and evidence of a weakening of authority, and justifiably so ... the Minister of War ... considers it inappropriate to authorize marriages under the present circumstancess'.[13] It was not until after March 1947 that such couples were permitted to regularize existing unions, some of which had been long-standing.

A Punishment for Women

The particular status of a given relationship, however, had no bearing on public reactions of various sorts. Because these French women had entertained relations with the occupiers, and sometimes worked for them or even enlisted, all of them had reason to be worried about the purge at the time of the Liberation. A conspicuous practice emblematic of the purge was the shaving of women's heads, but this did not happen to all of these women. Of the 20,000 women whose heads were shaved at the Liberation, only half had had sexual relations with the enemy; the others were accused, like their male counterparts, of collaboration, denunciation, working for the Germans or being a member of a collaborationist organization which espoused pro-Nazi beliefs. The shaving of women's heads was not punishment for sexual collaboration; rather, it was a gender-specific form of punishment meted out to women accused of collaboration. The photograph taken by Robert Capa at the liberation of Chartres has become one of the most famous images of the purge. We can attribute this not only to the photographer's talent, but also to his subject: a woman whose head has been shaved holds in her arms a child fathered by a German. But this 'virgin with child' is exceptional; such an image does not appear in any other photograph of shorn women of the Liberation. At the very moment when French society as a whole is condemning sexual relations with the enemy, the child of the enemy remains in the shadows. Moreover, women who were tried before purge courts made every effort to conceal the German nationality of the father of their children. Said one young woman from Béziers during her interrogation: 'I am about four months pregnant as a result of intimate relations with a certain Roger, a refugee from Strasbourg who says he is in the Maquis. I formally declare that I am not pregnant by a German serviceman'.[14] Another in the Oise declared: 'I admit having worked for the Germans but I deny having had any intimate relations with them. As for the father of my child, that is no one's business but my own'.[15]

The same holds true for the new civil authorities. Once the republic was reestablished, documents show that these children were not lost from sight. The new Minister of the Family conducted an investigation of the regional health authorities. Each was directed to supply figures for *pupilles de la nation*, children who had been declared wards of the state on account of having suffered German atrocities, and figures for 'the number of abandoned children who resulted from relations between German soldiers and French women'. In his response to the minister's request, the Health Director for the Aube region replies, 'it is impossible to give a precise number. We may indeed presume that there is a certain number [of such children] among the abandoned children admitted to our service since 1941. But nothing indicates with any certainty their German origins'.[16]

They were French ...

A debate over the status of children resulting from rape by a German soldier took place among the Ministry of Health, the Ministry of Prisoners of War, and several associations. Such cases were numerous enough at the time of the German retreat to attract the attention of the authorities. One proposal aimed to grant them the status of *pupilles de la nation* (wards of the state); however there were two arguments against doing so and the proposal was dropped. For one, a *pupille de la nation* whose parents are listed as 'unknown' might readily guess the dramatic circumstances of his birth. Moreover, 'the distinction between births resulting from rape and others is difficult to make and many guilty, undeserving mothers would not hesitate to claim the right to state benefits'. Other exchanges concern the case of children born in Germany to German mothers and French fathers who were either prisoners of war or voluntary or forced labourers at the time. The overall tone of these exchanges reveals a concern which explains the follow-up of many such cases, but there is also the overwhelming sentiment that there was no reason for these children to be anything but French. The *jus soli* explains this, but it is particularly because of the capacity of French society to integrate. Despite the beginning of the baby boom, the natalist obsession of the authorities had yet to abate. It predated the Vichy period, was exacerbated by the National Revolution, and continued after the war. At one point, the adoption of little German orphans by French families was even envisioned: 'The Bidault government decided over the course of last summer that France would welcome several thousand German children without families who were refugees in Denmark, with the aim of caring for them, educating them, and ultimately making them French citizens'.[17]

There appears to have been no policy of discrimination or ostracism of children fathered by German soldiers on the part of the authorities. But this was anything but the case in the child's social or familial environment. It is important, however, to distinguish among different types of public and private reactions: some family members or members of the community were unaware of the origins of such children in their midst; others were aware of their origins and rejected such children as a result; still others knew but made every attempt to shroud those origins in secrecy.

... but Guilty for having been Born

Children who, like those around them, knew that they had been fathered by German soldiers, suffered poor treatment at the hands of others. They were called 'fritzouille' and 'boche', for example. Grandparents, stepfathers, aunts and uncles could have some vague idea of the child's paternal origins. Worse yet was the fate of those children who were the living proof of their mothers' guilt. They were considered the burden a guilty mother had to bear, living punishment for her acts. Although individual children had different sorts of experiences, physical or psychological violence, suicide attempts or depression were not uncommon. External reprobation was quickly internalized by many of them: [I was] 'guilty for being born', as a certain Françoise stated in an interview. Such children carried the weight of German guilt on their tiny shoulders: '[the teacher] really emphasized the brutality of the Germans, the monstrousness of these barbarians, and she kept reiterating it throughout the entire lesson, so that I felt she was speaking to me, singling me out'.[18] When children born during World War II were growing up, they were surrounded by grown-ups like their grandparents who had lived through World War II. The veteran of 1914 had trouble swallowing the fact that his grandchild was the offspring of 'the *boche*'. This had already been the case in northern France after World War I, where children of the enemy had also been rejected. So what happened after World War II was not new.

Sixty Years Later

Another category consists of children who learned the true facts of their origins later in life. What 'later in life' means varies from case to case; more than a mere revelation, this knowledge is accompanied by a long process of self-questioning, self-doubt, and denial until the 'child' allows himself to ask questions or to seek information. Sometimes there are clues that suggest the secret of his origins. A photograph, a letter, an awkward comment can create doubt. Such was the case with Hervé, who at sixteen heard his grandparents say, 'he is as tall and handsome as his father', although he already towered over the man he called 'Papa'.[19] His uncertainty lasted twenty years, when he found a photograph of his mother on the arm of an officer in the Luftwaffe. After he'd made several attempts at learning the truth, his mother finally told him that the man in the photo was his biological father. The belated discovery of an inconsistency in the official birth records could also beg the question, like finding a date of birth when the only father one knew had not been around nine months before. Sometimes it took very little, and in the troubled period of adolescence, not looking like one's siblings could also create doubt: the little blue-eyed blond stands out in the family portrait. Nonetheless, all these clues are meaningless as long as a person refuses to see them. The reason for maintaining the silence surrounding one's origins, for not daring to ask questions can be stated in one word: respect. All of these children say that they refrained from asking questions out of respect for their mothers or adoptive fathers. Only at the death, imminent death or illness of a parent is the secret revealed. Sixty years later, it seems as if the time has come to investigate one's true origins. These men and women, now age sixty, can finally seek the answers to questions they always wondered about but were unable to formulate. Their adoptive father or mother is no longer living.

But grandchildren do not have the same reluctance to probe family secrets. At sixty comes retirement, when having free time allows one to do some research. This time also lends itself to thoughtful consideration of one's past. The study of genealogy has become a hobby for many older people. They scan the regional archives hoping to find the trace of this ancestor or that, always going farther back in time. For Franco-German children who have now grown old, the search does not extend to earlier centuries, and the search for forebears is for those of the father. A father about whom nothing is known, save the fact that he was the enemy. So one prays that he was a regular German who had no choice but to serve his country just like any Frenchman, not a SS officer or a Nazi. A father whose disappearance remains a mystery, who did not return after the war for either good or bad reasons which one tries to determine. Most of all, one hopes yet dreads that one's father is still alive.

The study of genealogy is also a search for the living and for a possible family on the other side of the Rhine. Whether one has always known one's origins or has only recently discovered them, the six decades elapsed seem to constitute a necessary waiting time. With the deaths of those who erred in the preceding generation and the coming of age of a new one, the generation of 'children of the enemy' can live with their origins more easily. This can take the form of learning more about their past, of talking about their stories to family members, of going to Germany when the search has uncovered the existence of a place, a gravesite, a family.

These tens of thousands of children are now adults. Whether or not they know their origins, their story belongs to the story of post-war French society, of its ability to remember or to forget the so-called betrayal of their mothers. Although French society has for the most part assimilated these children, for the children themselves the break remains. From their stories, it is clear that their wounds have not healed. Fathered by the enemy and lacking any personal memory of the war, sixty years later they are still the children of war.

Notes

1. Letter from Jacques Chevalier to François Darlan, Vice-Président du Conseil, 10 July 1941, National Archives, F60/558.
2. Insa Meinen, *Wehrmacht und Prostitution im besetzten Frankreich* (Edition Temmen, 2000).
3. Purge Committee File, Béziers, 11 September 1944, Departemental Archives, Hérault, 506W317.
4. Michèle Bordeaux, *La Victoire de la famille dans la France défaite: Vichy 1940–1944* (Flammarion, 2002), p. 237.
5. Before the war fewer than 500 persons were sentenced for abortion. In 1943, there were 4,055 sentenced, for the first time more than 4,000. But in the French post-war society the number sentenced was the highest: 5,151 in 1946 and 4,602 in 1947. B. Aubusson de Cavarlay et al., 'La justice pénale en France: Résultats statistiques (1934–1954)', *Les Cahiers de l'IHTP*, no. 23 April 1993, p. 139.
6. 18 March 1943, 'Archives de l'Assistance publique et des hôpitaux de Paris, RAC 1943', p. 64.
7. Prefect of Corrèze Report, 31 October 1941, Departemental Archives of Corrèze, 185W1/49.
8. Letter from L. Conti to H. Himmler, 29 May 1942. *Bundesarchiv* NS 048/000030

9. Police Department of Paris Report, 28 September 1944, Préfecture de Police Archives, 25 341 H.
10. *Atlas statistique de la ville de Paris*, 1946.
11. Marie-Gabrielle Dervan, *Le drame des filles mères* (Éditions familiales de France, 1952), p. 127.
12. Ministère des prisonniers déportés et réfugiés, *Conseils aux femmes d'absent qui vont être mère*, Paris, 1945. Health Ministry Archives, 1976/0175, art. 124.
13. Letter from the French War minister to ICRC Representives in France, 21 March 1945, ICRC Archives, G25/38.
14. Purge Committee File, 11 September 1944, Departemental Archives of Hérault, 506W323.
15. Purge Committee File, 26 December 1944, Departemental Archives of Oise, 34W8468–1.
16. Letter from 'Directeur régional de la Santé et de l'Assistance à Châlons-sur-Marne to Ministre de la Santé publique', 2 May 1945, Health Ministry Archives, 1976/0175, art. 124.
17. 'Direction générale des affaires administratives et sociales', 24 February 1947, Foreign Affairs Ministry Archives, Europe 1944–1966, Allemagne, vol. 110.
18. Elisabeth's interview, 15 September 2002.
19. Hervé's interview, 12 September 2002.

References

Aubusson de Cavarlay, B., Huré, M.-S. and Pottier, M.-L., 'La justice pénale en France: Résultats statistiques (1934–1954)', *Les Cahiers de l'IHTP*23 (April 1993).

Bordeaux, M., *La Victoire de la famille dans la France défaite: Vichy 1940–1944*, Paris: Flammarion, 2002.

Dervan, M.-G., *Le drame des filles mères*, Paris: Éditions familiales de France, 1952.

Meinen, I., *Wehrmacht und Prostitution im besetzten Frankreich*, Bremen: Edition Temmen, 2002.

–8–

Stigma and Silence: Dutch Women, German Soldiers and their Children

Monika Diederichs

Individual Stories: Stereotyped Opinions

Three years after the end of World War II, Mrs Schild married the son of the family who had taken her into their home as an unmarried pregnant woman in 1943.

> His acknowledgement of paternity was very important to me. I had two more sons, my marriage drifted hopelessly toward the reef; I remarried, became a widow, and then found happiness with the man I now share my life with. I never told my dead husband or my present partner about my past. I buried it deep down. And as far as I know my two other sons know nothing about it either.[1]

Mrs Schild is one of fifty-five women who have been interviewed as part of the research project on which this chapter is based. The interviews were conducted between 1995 and 1998. All fifty-five women have one thing in common: they consorted with German troops between 1940 and 1945.[2] Apart from that, the personal experiences were very diverse, but most of them were dramatic. Manuscripts and printed sources used in the study reveal a different picture of these women.[3] In contrast to the diverse personal experiences of the women, the public opinion of them was quite stereotyped. *Moffenhoeren* was the general term applied to them, especially if they had children from the relationship. The term *moffenhoeren* or *moffenmeiden* is a striking stereotype connecting dislike of the enemy with a form of behaviour heavily stigmatized socially: that is, prostitution. There was also often an implicit or explicit reference to a low social status, insinuating that as they originated from the lower socio-economic milieus, they were principally out to make financial gain. Many a strait-laced patriot believed that the *moffenmeiden* unscrupulously played off one German soldier against another in order to achieve their goal. It was assumed that they knew no solidarity or sense of honour and their actions were solely directed at satisfying their self-interest and greed.[4]

This chapter seeks to show the ways and means by which the children, and their mothers who had had relationships with German soldiers, were pointed out and treated as both a national and a social threat to Dutch society. The stigma and enforced silence inflicted by these policies upon both the women and their children distorted their lives up to the present time.

Prostitution as Degeneration

As in other occupied countries, for example Norway, Dutch girls having relations with German soldiers, the *moffenhoeren,* were described within a eugenic paradigm and a diagnostic system favoured by the psychiatric profession at the time. Within this approach, socially deviant behaviours such as prostitution, crime or vagabondage were perceived as criteria of individual intellectual and moral inferiority.

As early as July 1940 the contacts of the female part of the population of the Netherlands with the occupying forces were described as a phenomenon confined to prostitutes.[5] A month earlier a well-known professor at the University of Leiden described girls who had contact with the occupying forces as backstreet girls.[6] An inquiry into youth crime in the Netherlands during the Occupation, published in December 1945, singles out the contacts between Dutch girls and the occupying forces as the most abject symptom of the degeneration of young people during the Occupation.[7] It is interesting to note that the women who had relations with Germans were divided into categories of immorality in this inquiry. It distinguished the wanton girl, the fallen girl and the girl 'who is seriously socially disturbed and psychopathic'. The sexual behaviour of these girls is characterized as that of a prostitute, while the road leading to contacts with the occupying forces was paved by visits to bars, the use of alcohol and sexual intercourse.[8] The increasing professionalization of the social and psychological sciences and notions of 'good' and 'bad' during the Occupation ensured that in the years after the Occupation too, the emphasis was still placed on the unpatriotic behaviour of the *moffenmeiden*. 'Alarming' reports from places where garrisons were located reinforced the belief that girls who sought contact with German soldiers were or behaved as prostitutes. For instance, it was alleged that Dutch girls who were out for sexual contact with the occupying forces were supplied by the wagonload to one village situated in the centre of the country.[9]

The Uncertain Number of War Children

No exact statistics are available on the number of girls and women in the Netherlands who had a German friend during the Occupation, but there are signs that many Dutch girls, particularly in the garrison towns, did choose a German soldier as a boyfriend. No statistics are available on the exact number of children born in the Netherlands of a German father, although a number of scattered figures are given by the Nationalsozialistische Volkswohlfahrt (NSV), a German organization in the Netherlands caring for the children of German troops. On the basis of these statistics, the number of children can be estimated to be somewhere between eight and ten thousand, the equivalent of almost half of all illegitimate births in the period 1940–1945.[10]

As the figures given by the NSV are only based on the number of children who were cared for by its institutions, we are bound to assume that the actual number of children of German soldiers serving in the Netherlands was considerably higher. Both the written sources and the interviews indicate that the vast majority of the unmarried girls and women who gave birth to children fathered by a German did not contact the German care organization for unmarried mothers. They awaited childbirth in a Dutch home for unmarried mothers or in one of the general hospitals established in the cities. Little is known about the number of German-sired children who were born there, although the Federation for Institutions for Unmarried Mothers stressed in 1941 that the 22 per cent increase in the number of illegitimate births could be attributed to the births of the children of German troops. This trend continued in the following years. In 1943, there were 648 illegitimate children born in the institutions of the organization. According to the FIOM, 194 of these children were of German parentage. In the same year 355 unmarried women gave birth in a private clinic in The Hague. Almost 34 per cent of these children had German fathers.

Unmarried Mothers and Maternal Care in Pre-war Holland

The first homes for unmarried mothers in the Netherlands were opened at the end of the nineteenth century and developed against the background of a political campaign for the regulation of prostitution and against sexual hypocrisy. From 1930 onward, the Federation of Institutions for Unmarried Mothers was the coordinating centre and organization representing private homes for unmarried mothers. In the previous year an attempt to put care for unmarried mothers on the political agenda had failed because a Protestant and Roman Catholic morality lobby opposed an unmarried pregnant woman's entitlement to sick benefit. This lobby regarded care for unmarried mothers through a compulsory insurance scheme as an attack on the sacred state of marriage and the Christian character of family life. The reluctance of the government to contribute to the expense of childbirth by unmarried mothers and care for their children meant that care for unmarried mothers became the responsibility of subsidized religious and private institutions.[11]

The regime in the homes for unmarried mothers was austere and the regulations with which the girls had to comply were very strict. For instance, they were forbidden to leave the premises, they were not allowed contact with married women, and they had to observe a strict daily routine in which domestic work had to be done all day long.[12]

The Need for German Intervention

Mrs West had a boyfriend who was a pilot in the German Luftwaffe. When she became pregnant she received several anonymous letters. The first was at the start of the Occupation. It read: 'Who is a mattress for Jerry?' She recalls 'And when I was visibly pregnant I didn't dare go out of doors at all. Then I received a letter saying "Expectant mother of viper's brood". And just after peace had been declared I received another saying "What a shame, no German officer to screw any more!"'.[13]

The stigmatizing of Dutch girls and women who became pregnant by German soldiers was a reason for the Generalkommissar 'zur besonderen Verwendung' Schmidt to instruct the Nationalsozialistische Volkswohlfahrt (NSV) in March 1941 to provide special childbirth clinics for these unmarried mothers. In December 1941 Schmidt sent a circular to all of the divisions of the NSV in the Netherlands to inform them that girls whose children were not officially acknowledged by a German soldier could still be cared for in childbirth clinics. To meet the growing demand for care, a former girls' home in Amsterdam was set up in January 1941 as a home for unmarried mothers.

The first Mütter und Sauglingsheim in the Netherlands was opened in Amsterdam in February 1942. This was a well-equipped childbirth clinic and home for infants, functioning in addition to the NSV homes in Rotterdam and The Hague. The NSV homes in Valkenburg, Velp and the former Hoog-Holten hotel in Friesland were smaller and were also intended to provide shelter for pregnant German women who had been made homeless as a result of bombardments.[14] Care for the children of German soldiers and Dutch girls in special clinics originated in a Führer Erlass of 28 July 1942 which stated that 'for the preservation and promotion of the racially valuable Germanic stock in the occupied Norwegian and Dutch territories, the Reichskommissar must take measures to guarantee special care and attention, at the request of the Norwegian or Netherlandish mothers, for their children parented by members of the Wehrmacht'.[15]

The living expenses of the mother and child during the period before and after the birth were covered by an allowance, to enable mothers and their children to develop optimally. The mother also received assistance for the childbirth itself. If the mother approved, her child could be taken into a children's home connected to the childbirth clinic.

Moreover, special wartime tribunals of the army, air force and navy were set up in Norway and the Netherlands to simplify the paternity procedures connected with children who were born in the institutions of the NSV or Lebensborn and to speed up the handling of applications from the unmarried mothers.[16] Hitler abruptly turned down the proposal by the Oberkommando of the Wehrmacht to include Belgium, France and the British Channel Islands in the provisions 'We want to protect and care for illegitimate Germanic children, but in terms of racial policy we are not interested in the French'.[17] German authorities attributed a special status to the Dutch children of members of the Wehrmacht. The children who were born in the Mütter- und Sauglingsheimen in the Netherlands after 1 March 1943 had to be registered with the German civic registries that were established in the Netherlands in 1941. Duplicates of these notifications were sent on to Standesambt I in Berlin.[18]

The birth policy of the German government served not only racial but also demographic ends, namely the prevention of abortion. In order to encourage unmarried pregnant women not to terminate their pregnancy, the women who were cared for in NSV clinics were treated remarkably well. The pregnancy was kept secret by taking the mother in at a very early stage. The Lebensborn organization, competing with the NSV in Holland, operated homes with a separate civic registration and settled questions of guardianship by themselves. (For further information on the relation between NSV and Lebensborn, see Chapter 1 by Olsen in the present volume). The births of illegitimate children of German soldiers in the Mütter-und Sauglingsheimen in the Netherlands were reported to the German civic registry. Moreover, from 1943 the NSV was involved in the guardianship of the children who were born in the homes run by this organization. Himmler advocated the homes because of their obligation to treat information confidentially: 'In the homes of the NS Volkswohlfahrt and the Lebensborn the opportunity is provided to bear and give birth to the child in calm and security thanks to the extremely necessary and desirable confidentiality'.[19]

Maintenance allowances were paid to 4,000 Dutch women up to September 1942 to care for the children of Wehrmacht fathers. Little can be said with certainty about exactly how much was involved because the regulations kept on changing and there were many rulings on exceptional cases. At all events, it was a generous allowance. The maintenance allowance must have been an appreciable source of income for an unmarried mother who was aware of the facilities available.[20]

Mother and Child

We sat in a separate group and were treated as unmarried mothers. When my contractions began I was at work. The pain grew worse and I asked a sister what I should do. She said nothing and took me to a small, dark room. I was to press a button when the baby came. There was nobody there with me. I was all on my own. When I was giving birth a nurse came in. I wanted a bit of consolation and felt for her hand, but she pulled it back. I brought the baby into the world entirely on my own.[21]

This woman gave birth to a son in the spring of 1945 in a Roman Catholic institution in the south of the Netherlands which was affiliated to the Federation for Institutions for Unmarried Mothers (FIOM). Apart from this testimony, little is known of the personal experiences of mothers in maternity homes during the war.

There are few traces in the archives of the fates of children who were put into a Mütter-und Sauglingsheim. However, when politico-demographic interests were at stake, the NS Volkswohlfahrt was ready to take the law into its own hands. If it was convenient for the organization, it did not hesitate to take the mother's right to care for her child away from her and to assume guardianship of the child.[22]

In Amsterdam, the mothers could be taken into the children's home connected to the childbirth clinic in the first year after the birth if they wanted to, though it was not a very common practice. The care of the girls and women for their children proved in general to be very limited. Remarks such as 'the mother no longer takes an interest in her child' and 'we do not know the whereabouts of the child's mother' are more the rule than the exception in the guardianship dossiers.[23] An adoption procedure could take years because of the eugenic demands on the biological parents of the child and on the adoptive parents.[24] The long procedure and the massive bureaucracy involved in such adoptions make it more likely that the children who had been left in the German homes for unmarried mothers in the Netherlands ended up in an NSV children's home in the Netherlands or Germany (like the children who were left behind by their mothers to be cared for by the childbirth clinic).

Most of the children placed in the children's homes in West Germany returned to the Netherlands in children's transports between 1946 and 1948. Like the NSV adopted children who ended up in children's homes in the Netherlands, most of them grew up in homes because their mothers did not want to be confronted with an embarrassing past.[25]

Murderous Revenge and Sexual Punishment

When I was picked up by the OD (members of the former resistance movement) after the Liberation, my mother was carrying my daughter in her arms. The child did not understand what those men with rifles wanted and kept crying. One of them said to me: 'You'll never see your daughter again, kids of Germans all get gassed'.[26]

The extent of anti-German sentiment in the Netherlands, both during and shortly after World War II, can be gauged from a number of unsavoury incidents. During the war, babies of girls who had become pregnant by German soldiers in Zeeland were killed after birth by the girls' parents.[27] In the same period the baby of a German soldier was snatched from its cradle by a member of the resistance movement and dashed to the floor in North Holland.[28] It is not unlikely that anti-German sentiments toward children of German soldiers in other places in the Netherlands led to similar incidents.

> After the Liberation, Mrs van der Graaf and her sister, who also had a German boy friend, were picked up by four armed men and had their heads shaved in a public place. As Mrs van der Graaf walked through the village, she was led past a cheering crowd who shouted 'Shave their heads bare!' She herself said 'My sister and I walked on proudly with our noses in the air'.[29] A woman who had already had her head shaven said 'I felt terrible, but did not cry. I begrudged them that favour, the same as the pleasure of wearing a wig or a headscarf'.[30]

After the Occupation, Dutch women and girls who had consorted with the Germans were accused of treason. It was known before the war was over that they would be punished by having their heads shaved. The shaving of *moffenmeiden* was done all over the Netherlands. The date of the Liberation did not affect this. Women and girls who were suspected of having had contact with Germans were rounded up by members of the resistance movement and had their hair shaved off, in the places liberated in September 1944 and in those liberated in the spring of 1945.

Working-class girls and women were the main victims; women from the 'better' neighbourhoods were not usually rounded up to be shaved. The many photographs taken of this rough justice clearly show that those responsible came from all walks of Dutch society. The women would have been stripped of their hair by neighbours, groups of adolescent boys, adult men, the local hairdresser and men of the resistance movement.

In a number of places in the Netherlands, members of these groups had begun to keep lists of girls and women who consorted with German troops right from the beginning of the Occupation. These lists contained precise indications of how long the relationship had lasted, whether the girl had had contact with more than one soldier, and whether she was engaged or had marriage plans. In addition, the profession and political persuasion, if any, of the girl were recorded.[31]

The fact that in an appreciable number of places in the Netherlands the shaving of the heads of *moffenmeiden* was not a spontaneous event but had an organized character is clear to see on many of these photographs. For instance, in a small village in the west of the Netherlands, well-respected citizens cooperated with members of the resistance movement and the local police to prevent a general day of reckoning by having a number of known '*moffenmeiden*' shaved.

In one city in the south of the country, girls who were suspected of having consorted with the Germans were dragged by members of the resistance movement to a public place where their heads were shaved. In some places only one woman was shaved, but usually they were shaved in groups. A swastika was painted with tar or red lead on the woman's head while it was still bleeding. The spectacle concluded with their either walking or being driven on a wagon through the village or town. This followed a practice of rough justice which had been traditional in some places before the war. In the course of the procession, the women were often pelted with stones, and kicked and beaten by a cheering and screaming crowd. On their knees, or with their hands above their head, they were driven through the streets with a portrait of Hitler on their back.

There were also places where the *moffenmeiden* had to wear a headscarf with the words: 'Only for the Wehrmacht'.[32] Elsewhere the names of the girls and women suspected of collusion with the occupying troops were announced in the newspapers.[33]

Negotiable Nationality

'My German boyfriend acknowledged paternity of my son, and the boy was given my maiden name when he was born in Rotterdam in 1944. When I needed a birth certificate for him in 1946, it stated that he had no nationality. How can a child not have a nationality if he is acknowledged by his Dutch mother and German father?' says Mrs Braam as she looks inquiringly at me.[34]

After the liberation, feelings of revenge, anti-German sentiments and ideas that the child was the property of the nation caused difference of opinion between the Ministries of Justice and Domestic Affairs, and the FIOM, the umbrella organization for unmarried mothers in the Netherlands. The matter at stake was the nationality of children acknowledged as theirs by their German fathers. The dispute was provoked by the refusal of the Ministry of Justice to distinguish between a Dutch acknowledgement in which the name and nationality of the father were known and a German one which only guaranteed a monthly allowance to the mother. Both ministries considered a child who had been acknowledged by a German to be of German nationality. German legislation, however, did not recognize the children as German citizens. Thus children who had been acknowledged by their German fathers during the Occupation were de facto stateless. As German, these children could not be declared legitimate if the mother was to marry a Dutchman.

The FIOM defended the rights of the children and emphasized that a German acknowledgement of paternity did not have the same legal status as a Dutch one. In the view of this organization, the standpoint adopted by the Ministries of Justice and Domestic Affairs was morally unjustifiable and above all based on anti-German sentiments.[35]

In October 1948 the view defended by the FIOM received unexpected support from the Supreme Court of the Netherlands, which underlined the fact that the child of an unmarried mother, who had been acknowledged as his by a German, was entitled to Dutch nationality. At the instigation of the organization for unmarried mothers, the Ministry of Justice reluctantly accepted the verdict of the Supreme Court. In a pronouncement on 22 September 1948, the Rotterdam magistrate's court also adopted the standpoint that the child of an unmarried woman, who had been acknowledged during the Occupation by a German father, had Dutch nationality. All the same, in practice the Ministry of Justice still clung stubbornly to its own view.

On 4 November 1948 the Maastricht magistrate's court followed the Rotterdam pronouncement, and on 16 February 1949 the court in The Hague reached the same conclusion. Still, a request from the FIOM to the Ministry of Justice to reconsider its opinion received no reply, and in a letter to the mayor and aldermen of Leeuwarden in April 1949 on the nationality of the child of a German father in that district, the pronouncement of the Supreme Council was completely ignored by the Ministry of Justice. This prompted the FIOM once again to address an urgent request to the minister to reconsider his position. This request received no reply either. It was in fact not until November 1952 that the Ministry of Justice no longer interpreted a German acknowledgement of paternity as an acknowledgement in the sense of Dutch law and that the children of Dutch unmarried mothers who had been acknowledged by their German fathers received Dutch nationality.[36]

Two years later, in 1954, it was laid down by law that the registers of the German civic registry, where the German acknowledgment of paternity was entered, must be treated as civic registers in conformity with the terms of the Dutch Civil Code. On this occasion it was also laid down that extracts from the former register could only be issued in Dutch, though a photocopy of the birth certificate was provided in exceptional cases.

This conversion of these registers to the Dutch system implied ignoring the acknowledgement of German paternity and covering up the German fatherhood of the child. However, when a change in the German law in 1973 threatened to lead to children acknowledged by German fathers during the Occupation receiving German nationality after all, the Dutch authorities declared that it was not applicable to the children of German fathers. Eventually a change in the German law in 1993 stated that children recognized by a German parent would also receive the name and nationality of the father. This change in the law, however, had no legal consequences for the acknowledged children of German troops in the Netherlands because, in the meantime, they had become adults.[37]

Left on their Own

After 1954 the Dutch government no longer interfered with children who were born from relationships between Dutch girls and German soldiers. At best the mothers and the government tolerated them, while their paternity was glossed over as much as possible. Post-war Dutch society was dominated by thinking in terms of 'good' and 'bad' behaviour during the German Occupation. As a result, women who had consorted with Germans during the Occupation were regarded as collaborators and their children were spurned because their fathers were enemy soldiers. This stigmatization was the reason why many of the children were also rejected by their mother, while on the other hand there were also mothers who covered up the paternity of their child in order to protect him or her from the hostile environment. It was not uncommon for adoptive parents or relatives to be asked to raise the child, whose name and date of birth were altered. If the mother brought up her child herself, she usually moved home and adopted the name of the stepfather to shield the identity of the child.

The situation of the children of Germans who grew up in Dutch children's homes was no better. One of the women who cared for the children, who worked in 1947 in an institution which catered primarily for the children of German and Allied soldiers, wrote in 1995 'Thirty children, in the same classroom all day, drinking, playing and school. Little outdoors, the children were very active. They never received visits and were not eligible for adoption either. Because of their background! What has become of them? The young American children had a much better start and future. If they were abandoned, there was no shortage of adoptive parents. Their mothers, grandmothers and aunts came to seen them each week. They were given a cuddly toy and a feeling of being accepted.'[38]

To date no research has been carried out on the consequences of the anti-German sentiment in Dutch society for the lives of the children of German soldiers. A questionnaire conducted among a hundred of them in the autumn of 2000 indicated that many of them not only felt rejected by Dutch society and by their mother, but also suffered from feelings of guilt, shame and frustration about their paternity.[39]

Stigma and Silence Inflicted upon Mother and Child

'I still don't dare to talk about being pregnant from a German, I simply don't dare', she whispered during the interview, and then walked to the door to see if there was anybody behind it. What was remarkable about the interview with one of the women was that, fifty years after the Occupation, she still did not dare to say openly that she had given birth to the child of a German soldier.

This respondent was 24 years old when she met a German soldier in Dordrecht, where she worked as a servant. She fell in love with him and followed him to Arnhem, where she lived with him for eighteen months. She did not inform her parents. They assumed that their daughter was still in service in Dordrecht. When she returned after the liberation of Breda, she was three months pregnant. She did not dare to tell her parents, so she asked for a place in a home for unmarried mothers. The letter turning her request down was addressed to her parents, who thereby learnt the truth about her pregnancy. Their urgent request eventually led to a reconsideration of placement, and she was finally taken into the crowded home in November 1945.[40]

One respondent was stigmatized not only because she bore the child of a German father, but also because she had a baby without being married. She gave birth in a Roman Catholic institution for unmarried mothers in The Hague. The mother was called Mary Magdalene by the gynaecologist, while the nuns who nursed her told her that her difficult childbirth was a punishment from God because she had given birth to an illegitimate child.[41]

Half of the women interviewed had had a child by a German father. Six of them eventually married their male friend and moved to Germany after getting married. Another woman was given the cold shoulder by older and younger men after the Liberation. 'They didn't want me, if they had made an evening date they kept you waiting or didn't show up, that happened several times, that's why I've never married.'[42] Another woman emigrated to the USA to escape from her past: 'After the war I spent seven years in Germany, after that I returned to Holland, and a year later I left for America for good'.[43]

Conclusion

Dutch girls and women who consorted with German troops during World War II were stigmatized as prostitutes and *moffenmeiden*. It is noteworthy that this term was applied particularly to women from the lower socio-economic class. The women who gave birth to a child were doubly stigmatized: as unmarried mothers, and as the mothers of the children of fathers who were on the enemy side. The stigmatization was an important cause of the foundation of German clinics for unmarried mothers in the Netherlands. Another reason for opening the NSV Mütter und Sauglingsheimen was the fact that the German authorities had an interest motivated by racial politics in the children of Dutch mothers and German troops. The care for mothers and children in the German homes was remarkably good, while the women who took their children home with them received a monthly allowance. Children who could not be cared for by their mothers remained in the home for unmarried mothers, after which they were transferred to an NSV children's home in the Netherlands or Germany.

It was already common knowledge in the Netherlands during the Occupation that girls and women who went with Germans would be punished by having their head shaved. After the war was over, not only 'ordinary' citizens but also members of the resistance movement were involved in shaving the heads of women who had befriended the occupying forces. It is noteworthy that in a number of places the *moffenmeiden* were used as scapegoats to avoid a general day of reckoning.

The taboo on relationships between Dutch women and the occupying troops meant that the births of children from these relationships were often hushed up. The children were rejected by liberated Holland because their mothers were considered to be traitors. The conversion of the registers of the German civic registry to the Dutch system in 1954 was also the product of anti-German feeling. By concealing the name of the father on the certificates, the paternity of the child was denied. This was done so systematically that there are still many children of German fathers living in Holland who are not aware that their fathers were members of the German occupying forces in the period 1940–1945. Official Dutch policies toward war children bear many similarities to those of both the Danish and the German authorities. Whether the level of violence toward the Dutch women was higher in Holland than in Norway and Denmark is still open to question. The fact that the *moeffenhoren* were so easily accepted as the sacrificial lambs of the Dutch nation, however, underlines the general notion shared by occupied countries of women fraternizing with foreign soldiers as threatening the very survival of the nation.

Notes

1. Code 41 (30.3.1995) Letter from Mrs Schild.
2. Forty-four of these women lived in a large or medium-sized city at the time. The others grew up in a provincial town or in the countryside. Thirty-two of the fifty-five respondents came from a middle-class background, seventeen from a working-class background. Six came from very wealthy families.
3. This research will lead to a dissertation at the University of Amsterdam, which will go into much more detail and will range over more aspects of the results.
4. T. de Vries, *Het Wolfsgetij of een leven van liefde* (Pegasus, 1980).
5. Netherlands Institute for War Documentation (NIOD) Wartime newspapers (25 July 1940).
6. L. de Jong, *Het Koninkrijk der Nederlanden in de Tweede Wereldoorlog*, Vol. 5, Pt. 1 (Martinus Nijoff, 1972), p. 276.
7. J. Koekebakker, 'Onze kinderbescherming in oorlog en vrede', Study commissioned by the National Federation for Mental Health (Purmerend, 1945).
8. Ibid., pp. 29–31.

9. L. de Jong, *Het Koninkrijk der Nederlanden in de Tweede Wereldoorlog*, Vol. 7, Pt. 1 (Martinus Nijoff, 1976), p. 269.
10. L. de Jong, *Het Koninkrijk der Nederlanden in de Tweede Wereldoorlog*, Vol. 5, Pt. 1 (Martinus Nijoff, 1972), p. 246.
11. E. Hueting and R. Nej, *Ongehuwde Moederzorg in Nederland* (Naarden, 1990), p. 34.
12. Code 37 (4.7.1995) Mrs Ewoud, p. 30.
13. Code 14 (2.8.1995) Mrs West, p. 21.
14. These women were evacuated from Germany in connection with the continuous bombardments.
15. NIOD, Book of Regulations 1943; Gazette, Part 1, p. 102, published 22.2.1943; Regulation for the implementation of the regulation concerning care for the children of members of the German Wehrmacht in the occupied territories of 13 February 1943.
16. Ibid.
17. G. Lilienthal, *'Der Lebensborn e. V.: Ein Instrument nationalsozialistischer Rassenpolitik* (Fischer Taschenbuch Verlag, 1993), p. 163.
18. NIOD, Book of Regulations 13, 26.1.1943; Regulation to supplement the Regulation no. 39/1941, containing provisions on the civic registration of Germans in the occupied territories of the Netherlands.
19. NIOD, N.K.C.A. in 't Veld, De SS en Nederland (Nijhoff 1976) no. 450 circular Himmler.
20. NIOD, The archive of the National Sozialistische Demokratischer Arbeiterpartei (NSDAP) circular of the NSV 19.9.1942.
21. Ewoud, p. 30.
22. Lilienthal, *'Der Lebensborn e. V.*, p. 210.
23. NIOD, Vormundschaftsgericht box 13.
24. NIOD, Archive of the National Sozialistische Volkswohlfahrt (NSV) 18/19 I.
25. The children found in children's homes in East Germany usually grew up in these homes or were placed in German adoptive families.
26. Code 20 (2.5.1995) Mrs Joosten, pp. 26–7.
27. Code 45 (28.8.1995) Van Dijk, pp. 52–3.
28. Private archive of P. Ruigrok: camp diary of Petra Ruigrok born 1.2.1921.
29. Van der Graaf, p. 29.
30. Letter from Mrs van Nijmegen 13.3.1995.
31. L. de Jong, *Het Koninkrijk der Nederlanden in de Tweede Wereldoorlog*, Vol. 10 b, Pt. 2 (Martinus Nijoff, 1962), p. 1431.
32. K. Happe, 'Die Kollaboration mit der Deutschen Besatzung in den Niederlanden: Konsequenzen und Folgen nach dem Ende des Zweiten Weltkrieges' (unpublished master's thesis, Siegen, 1998), p. 4.
33. Ibid.

34. Code 4 (16.2.1994) Mrs Braam, p. 33.
35. International Information Centre and Archive for the Women's Movement (IIAV), Archive of the Union For Unmarried Mothers (UVOM), dossier 5, annual report FIOM 1947.
36. HAV, UVOM, dossier 5, annual report FIOM 1951.
37. 23.9.2003, telephone conversation with H. Plasschaert, former member of staff of the Amsterdam register, and specified in the records of the former German civic registry in the Dutch capital.
38. April 1995, letter to M.H. Diederichs.
39. The original questionnaire was developed in Norway by Stein Larsen. The questions were adapted for the Netherlands and sent to 100 children who were or are members of the Contact Group of Children of German Troops (CKDM).
40. Ewoud, p. 31.
41. Code 40 (25.7.1995) Mrs van Seeland, p. 6.
42. Code 34 (21.6.1995) Mrs van Seeland, p. 40.
43. Letter 4.4.1995.

References

Happer, K., 'Die Kollaboration mit der Deutschen Besatzung in den Niederlanden: Konsequenzen und Folgen nach dem Ender des Zweiten Weltkrieges'. Unpublished Master's thesis, Siegen, 1998.

Hueting, E. and Nej, R., *Ongehuwde Moederzorg in Nederland*, Naarden, 1990.

Jong, L. de, *Het Koninkrijk der Nederlanden in de Tweede Wereldoorlog*, Vol. 10b, Pt. 2, The Hague: Martinus Nijoff, 1962.

Jong, L. de, *Het Koninkrijk der Nederlanden in de Tweede Wereldoorlog*, Vol. 5, Pt. 1, The Hague: Martinus Nijoff, 1972, p. 246.

Jong, L. de, *Het Koninkrijk der Nederlanden in de Tweede Wereldoorlog*, Vol. 7, Pt. 1, The Hague: Martinus Nijoff, 1976.

Koekebakker, J. 'Onoe kinderbescherming in oorlog en vrede', Study commissioned by the National Federation for Mental Health (Purmerende 1945).

Lilienthal, G., *'Der Lebensborn e.V.: Ein Instrument nationalsozialistischer Rassenpolitik,* Frankfurt: Fischer Taschenbuch Verlag, 1993.

Vries, T. de, *Het Wolfsgetij of een leven van liefde*, Amsterdam: Pegasus, 1980.

Part III

East

Between Extermination and Germanization: Children of German Men in the 'Occupied Eastern Territories', 1942–1945

Regina Mühlhäuser

On 8 September 1942 the commander of the 2nd Armoured Division, General Rudolf Schmidt, submitted a report to Hitler in which he estimated the number of 'racially mixed children' (*Mischlingskinder*) expected in the 'occupied Eastern territories'[1] to be about 1.5 million per year. His extrapolation was based upon a rather simple arithmetic operation. He assumed that half of the six million German men stationed in 'the East' had sexual encounters with local women.[2] A pregnancy would be the natural consequence in half of the cases. To further simplify the matter, he arrived at the conclusion that 750,000 half-German girls and 750,000 half-German boys would be born each year.[3] One week later, at field headquarters on 16 September 1942, the Reich Commissioner for the Strengthening of Germandom (*Reichskommissar zur Festigung des deutschen Volkstums; RKF*), Heinrich Himmler, presented to commanders of the SS and police the figure of at least one million 'soldiers' children' (*Soldatenkinder*).[4] As soon as the Nazis started to register the children in 1943, however, these extremely high estimates proved to be false. Rather, they served the megalomaniac Nazi vision of a 'racial restructuring in the East' (*rassische Neuordnung im Osten*). Gigantic resettlement programmes, expulsions, 'racial inspections', and 'Germanization' programmes were meant to realize the policy of 'selection and extermination' (*Auslese und Ausmerze*).

The children of German fathers – of soldiers, members of the SS, the police, and the occupation authorities – were first and foremost considered a risk for the racial and societal order. In the theory of Nazi 'racial hygiene', 'racially mixed children' had been established as 'undesirable'.[5] They served as symbol and evidence for a lack of 'racial awareness' among Aryan men, and were generally perceived as a direct threat to the purity of the Aryan race and to national vitality. In order to prevent the birth of 'racially mixed children', sexual encounters[6] of German soldiers and women 'of alien races' (*artfremde Frauen*)[7] or 'ethnically alien' women (*fremdvölkische Frauen*) were subject to control and penalties.[8]

Despite such regulations, however, children of German fathers were born in the 'occupied Eastern territories', and various Nazi authorities felt the need to make them objects of their population policies in 'the East'. First of all, the Nazis feared that the 'Eastern peoples' (*Ostvölker*) would profit from the 'share of Aryan blood' of the German fathers. In order to prevent strengthening the enemy, they reasoned, the 'racially mixed children' needed to be claimed for the 'German *Volk* community' (*Deutsche Volksgemeinschaft*). Furthermore, the children of German fathers were seen as a human resource and in terms of their military and economic potential. Various Nazi officials harboured interests to 'render the children useful' (*nutzbar machen*), i.e. to balance the relatively low birth rate in the 'old Reich',[9] and strengthen future military campaigns.

The debates about the implementation of action in order to deal with the children and their parents reveal conflicting interests and practices within the German bureaucratic and military institutions. At any rate, the Nazis planned to locate, register and select the offspring of German men. The children designated as 'racially undesirable' were supposed to be left with their mothers to become objects of the extermination politics directed against 'ethnically alien people' in 'the East'. By contrast, the children designated as 'racially fit' were supposed to be 'inserted into the body of the German people' (*in den deutschen Volkskörper eingefügt*), and transferred to the Reich. They should become part of the Nazi 'Germanization' programme, and grow up in children's homes or foster families. Still, even the 'racially desirable' children posed a threat to the 'German *Volk* community' by transgressing racial boundaries and classifications. For the purpose of keeping them under control, the Nazi authorities thus began to discuss a range of measures and regulations regarding language skills, education, their names and the treatment of their mothers.

When the German army had to start its retreat after the defeat of Stalingrad at the beginning of 1943, however, few of these plans were realized in the occupied territories of the Soviet Union. The only measure actually implemented was the 'registration of extramarital children of Reich German fathers', and even this was not carried out in all occupied regions. Furthermore, the number of children registered by July 1944 was extraordinarily low. Even taken into account the unavailability of exact figures because of various problems during the process of registration, the results were extremely disappointing. Still, the fantasies about the impact of the children of German men remained vital until 1945.

The following analysis will explore the Nazi debates about the children of German men in the 'occupied Eastern territories' in the light of conflicting economic, military and racial aims. The first section will focus upon the 'soldiers' children' as human resource and military potential. How did the Nazis assess the 'racially mixed children' in the light of 'demographic and ethnic politics' (*Bevölkerungs- und Volkstumspolitik*)? The second part will turn to the Nazi debates about the children as a threat to the racial and societal order. Why and how did specific authorities oppose the promotion of the 'racially mixed children' in the 'occupied Eastern territories'? The third section will then outline the discussion of measures to 'render the children useful'. What kind of regulations did the different authorities anticipate, and which controversies arose? To conclude, the enormous difference between the figures initially estimated and the number of children actually registered will be reconsidered in order to highlight the ambiguity of National Socialist categories of 'race' and 'ethnicity' in the course of the war. An epilogue will briefly touch on further research perspectives regarding the children of German men in the 'occupied Eastern territories'.

Human Resource and Military Potential

When RKF Himmler introduced the figure of at least one million 'soldiers' children in the East' in September 1942, he clarified the significance of the matter:

> For the Russian people, who experience a great loss of blood today, these children would be an outrageous gain, in terms of quantity, and particularly regarding the quality of the race.[10]

The fear that the 'Eastern peoples' would profit from the influx of 'German blood' from the German fathers was also expressed by the Reich Minister for the Occupied Eastern Territories (*Reichsminister für die besetzten Ostgebiete*), Alfred Rosenberg:

> [A]s undesirable as it is in principle, if Germans engage in extramarital sexual relations with women of alien ethnicity, it must, however, be avoided that a German blood-flow reaches the foreign peoples of the East through children conceived in extramarital relations and, simultaneously, that the German people [*das deutsche Volkstum*; RM] loses valuable powers.[11]

This line of reasoning reveals the military distress and racial fear the Nazis harboured by the autumn of 1942. Consequently, not only were they eager to avoid strengthening the enemy, but they implemented different measures to acquire 'valuable blood' from 'other ethnic groups' (*anderen Volksgruppen*) and 'insert it into the German ethnic body'. Himmler illustrated these ethnic goals in September 1942:

> In all these peoples we are dealing with, anything in this hotchpotch – be they Pole, Ukranian, Belorussian etc. – anything of good blood in this giant organism, if I take the people [*das Volk*; RM] as an entire organism, each extracted drop of pure blood is going to be assimilated or, if it cannot be assimilated any longer, extinguished.[12]

Himmler used the category of blood as much metaphorically as biologically. In his line of reasoning, different 'streams of blood' could be detected within its carriers and isolated from each other. This logic contradicts the traditional 'racial hygiene', according to which the 'mixing of blood' would necessarily lead to infertility and the deterioration of the race. The delusional belief in the 'predominance of Germanic blood' (*Vorherrschaft germanischen Blutes*), however, outweighed the fear of a biological decay. Even the 'share of Aryan blood' in people designated as Jewish or 'of Jewish descent' was considered to be valuable. When Secretary of State Dr Wilhelm Stuckart opposed the deportation of 'Half-Jews' (*Halbjuden*) to 'the East' in March 1942, he argued that their 'share of German blood' would enable them to fight Germany in a particularly effective way, and thus strengthen the enemy:

> I have always thought it to be biologically extremely dangerous to supply the enemy with German blood. This blood is only suitable to produce personalities on the other side who will make use of the valuable characteristics they inherited through the German blood to benefit the other side against the German blood.[13]

The same logic is displayed in Himmler's plan for a 'substantial new blood-protection law after the war' (*umfassendes neues Blutschutzgesetz nach dem Kriege*). As Cornelia Essner has emphasized, Himmler intented to enhance the distinction between 'German blood' and 'Jewish blood'. In favour of the aims of 'Germanization politics', he planned to distinguish 'Germanizable persons or families' (*eindeutschbare Personen oder Sippen*) within the people 'of alien races'.[14]

In the light of these developments in 'racial politics', specific attention was directed to the 'racially fit' children of 'alien ethnicity' (*fremden Volkstums*). Younger children were considered to be especially valuable for the SS, for they could yet be formed and educated. Himmler had no doubts about the successful 'Germanization' of these children,

> for we still believe in this, our own blood, which has flown into an alien nationality due to the errors of German history, and we are convinced that our world and our ideals will resonate within the racially kin soul of these children.[15]

The SS took 'racially fit' orphans from children's homes in Poland and the occupied territories of the Soviet Union and deported them to Germany; they also abducted children from their families and declared them orphans afterwards.[16] In addition, the SS deported 'racially fit' children of alleged partisans who had been murdered or interned. They were then transported to children's homes and families in the Reich.[17] All children who passed the 'racial inspection' were expected to strengthen the 'German *Volk* community' and assure the 'future of the German people'.[18]

In this context, the 'soldiers' children' played an eminent role. Due to the fact that they were direct descendants of German men, their 'racial value' was expected to be comparatively high. Thus the idea emerged that the children designated as 'racially fit' in the 'occupied Eastern territories' could be put into use in order to balance the extremely low birthrate in the 'old Reich'.[19] But soon different voices cast doubt on the estimated figure of one to one and a half million 'soldiers' children'. In February 1943, Rosenberg informed the Reich Minister and Head of the Reichskanzlei, Hans Heinrich Lammers, that he expected the number of extramarital children of German men to be substantial, but not nearly as high as anticipated.[20] Six months later, in August 1943, the 4th Army started to register the 'racially mixed children'. From now on, the monthly reports of the district-headquarters were supplemented with 'attachment 2', titled 'registration of extramarital children of Reich Germans'. In most areas the attachment solely read 'negative report' (*Fehlanzeige*) or 'no incidents' (*keine Vorkommnisse*), sometimes it listed one or two births.[21] The highest number – thirteen children, born between February and August 1943 – was established in Smolensk City.[22]

In the light of such low figures, the Reich Ministry estimated the total number of children in the occupied territories of Belorussia, the Ukraine, Estonia, Latvia and Lithuania between 10,000 and 12,000. On 17 November 1943, the head of the SS-Main Leadership Office (*SS-Führungsamt*), Obergruppenführer Gottlob Berger, asserted,

> that the findings in the General Commissariat for Belorussia [*Generalkommissariat Weissruthenien*; RM] established only a very small number of cases. The number of 4000 extramarital children which had been assumed at the beginning has turned out to be far too high. ... According to the reports of my office in the Reich Commissariat Ukraine, even a figure of 10000 children for Ukraine ... for the time between occupation and the end of this year is already a very high estimate.
>
> The proportion of extramarital children of Reich Germans for the general districts Estonia, Latvia and Lithuania should, according to the data of the Reich Commissioner for the Ostland, amount to between 1000 and 2000, but it is not impossible that this number will rise after a thoroughly organized survey.[23]

The greatest factor of uncertainty appeared to be the process of registration. Various obstacles rendered an exact count of the children impossible. First, local women did not necessarily want anybody to know that the father of their child was German. Often, they feared to be designated as 'whores of the enemy', traitors or collaborators. This could lead to social exclusion, severe punishment and even death. For instance, when the German Army was successful in reoccupying Charkow (Ukraine) for a short time in the spring of 1943, they found that the Soviet People's Commissariat for Internal Affairs (NKVD) had killed 4,000 local inhabitants on account of alleged collaboration. Among these were women who had had sexual relations with German soldiers; some of them had been pregnant.[24] Secondly, the danger for the individual women was not met by any protection or balanced by benefits. While the majority of pregnant women in Norway could expect material and social support by the German authorities after their registration,[25] no similar incentives existed in the 'occupied Eastern territories'.[26] Thirdly, many married women whose husbands were absent as soldiers, forced labourers, etc. might have tried to have an abortion or kill the infant directly after birth. The local occupation authorities explicitly emphasized they wanted to prevent 'trouble and political unrest in the ethnically alien families' to be expected after the births of an extramarital child of a German.[27]

But the Nazi authorities not only suspected a potentially large number of unreported children: they feared as well a secret infiltration of 'racially undesirable infants'. The enemy, according to this assumption, would declare children 'of low quality' falsely as 'half-German' to deceive the 'German *Volk* community' and weaken the German (military) power. In Latvia and Estonia, mothers of children born out of wedlock were not obliged to name the father of their child. Therefore, the German occupation authorities in the Reich Commissariat Ostland (*Reichskomissariat Ostland*; i.e. the occupied territories of Estonia, Latvia and Lithuania) discussed in 1943/44 whether the local registrar should be requested to supply the identities of the German fathers.[28] However, by the middle of 1944, Himmler made a point of stating that

> ordering the registrars in the local administration to name German fathers would probably only lead to the registration of children by inferior parents whom the Estonians and Latvians do not want. In addition, efforts have already been made to look after the orphans and extramaritally born children since the Latvians and Estonians begin to realize the impact of their low birth rate. If the fact that the German soldiers want to win children for Germandom should become public in a clumsy manner, a clandestine or open counter-organization [*Gegenorganization*; RM] by the Latvians and Estonians is to be expected.[29]

Himmler acted on the assumption that the 'Eastern peoples' would naturally share the National Socialist categories of 'valuable and invaluable human material'. The absoluteness of Nazi ideology displayed here seems striking, all the more because the politics of exclusion in the 'occupied Eastern territories' were ambivalent on constructing the very same categories. The identification of 'racial affiliation' (*rassische Zugehörigkeit*) was highly ambiguous and contested.[30] In addition, paternity could not yet be established through biological tests. Consequently, the definition of the biological descent of the children became a field and method of (racial) warfare. Himmler's term 'counter-organization' reveals the extent of worries about racial competition and espionage.

But despite these anxieties, the difficult process of registration and the unavailability of exact figures on the number of children of German men in the 'occupied Eastern territories', Nazi fantasies about them remained vital. Indeed, the persistent ideas about the transport of 'soldiers' children' to the 'old Reich' at a time when the German army faced military defeat suggests that the 'racially mixed' infants provided a fantasmatic vision of a loophole, a back door to the 'final victory' (*Endsieg*).

A Threat for the Racial and Societal Order

Not everybody, however, saw the children as a resource and a potential. 'Racially mixed children' also posed a problem to military discipline. If a soldier became seriously attached and distracted by personal matters, it would most likely affect his military performance.[31] Particularly the Wehrmacht leadership was interested in disciplining the individual soldier and preventing the birth of 'racially mixed children'. Different rules and regulations were written to prevent 'undesirable intercourse'.[32]

A strict ban on sexual relations, however, was not in the interest of the army. Hitler himself had emphasized the soldier's need for regular (hetero)sexual acts in order to improve their military performance.[33] Similarly, the medical corps of the Wehrmacht had coined the term 'sexual desperation' (*Sexualnot*) in order to explain the inability to gain complete control over the desire of individual soldiers.[34] As the Supreme Commander of the Army (*Oberbefehlshaber des Heeres*) Walther von Brauchitsch had emphasized in July 1940, the military command would not be able to prevent sexual 'tensions and necessities … here and there'. In his opinion, a general ban of sexual relations with local women would lead to a higher frequency of rape and to an increase of homosexual contacts between the soldiers.[35] In order to deal with such anxieties, the Wehrmacht had already established military brothels or organized controlled access to local brothels in occupied France and Poland.[36] Accordingly, in September 1942, the head of the Wehrmacht High Command (OKW), Field Marshal Wilhelm Keitel, suggested establishing brothels in the 'occupied Eastern territories' in order to ensure military discipline, and to prevent sexually transmitted diseases and the 'siring of racially mixed bastards that are of no interest for Germany'.[37] The fact that most of the women working in these brothels were not what the Nazis themselves would have considered 'Aryan' was at least tolerated. Himmler had explicitly approved of this kind of 'racial mixing' (*Rassenmischung*) in 1942, for it was allegedly outside the context of personal attachment and reproduction.[38] Obviously, military ideas about the soldiers' need to fulfill their sexual drives in order to fight strongly contradicted racialized measures to control sexuality.

At any rate, sexual regulations and bans did not necessarily have the anticipated effect. A considerable number of German men chose women 'of alien ethnicity' as the objects of their desire.[39] Accordingly, the picture of the female enemy spy was conjured up in order to raise the soldiers' vigilance and willingness to murder women.[40] Furthermore, the civil authorities in the 'occupied Eastern territories' began to worry about the 'mastery of the Aryan race'. Among other things, they advised the military leadership to provide training sessions for the individual soldier to be instructed about relationships with women 'of alien ethnicity'.[41] As Field Marshal Keitel anticipated in September 1942, all kinds of relations between German men and local women were likely to intensify the longer the occupation lasted.[42]

The contingent implementation and ambivalent significance of Nazi racial ideology in everyday life became all too clear. Accordingly, 'racially mixed children' symbolized the lack of 'racial awareness' of men who were categorized 'Aryan'. On account of this, the siring and births of these children should be prevented. In November 1942 Reich Health Leader (*Reichsgesundheitsführer*) Leonardo Conti turned to the issue:

> Reich Leader Bormann has informed me that the Führer wishes that instant measures be taken in the occupied territories
> 1. in order to prevent German military and civilian personnel from siring children with women of alien ethnicity,
> 2. in order to restrict any further spread of sexually transmitted diseases, and
> 3. in order to reduce the number of children of the local population itself.[43]

It becomes clear that these measures addressed German men as well as the local population. Conti suggested the distribution of condoms to German men in the occupied territories of the Soviet Union. Since the war-related shortage of rubber products posed a problem, the local population should be supplied with chemical contraceptives.[44] Furthermore, abortion was viewed as a solution of the military problem. At least some military men declared abortion to be 'a question directly related to the Wehrmacht'.[45]

Summed up, especially the military leadership suggested that the siring of children should not be promoted. However, the existing offspring should be put to use for the 'German *Volk* community'.

Measures and Policies

For the purpose of employing the children for their goals, but keeping them under control at the same time, the Nazi authorities discussed a range of measures and regulations. Only a few days after Schmidt's initial estimate of one and a half million 'racially mixed children in the East', Himmler met the head of the SS Race and Settlement Office (*Rasse- und Siedlungshauptamt; RuSHA*), Otto Hoffmann, and the leader of the National Socialist People's Welfare Organization (*National-sozialistische Volkswohlfahrt; NSV*), Erich Hilgenfeldt, to discuss the first measures to be taken.[46] After further consultation with Hitler, a plan was quickly drafted. The children should be located and registered, and should undergo a 'racial inspection'.[47]

The children designated as 'racially undesirable' were supposed to be left in the 'occupied Eastern territories' even though Himmler feared that their 'share of Aryan blood' would strengthen the enemy:

> [E]ven the child originating from a liasion of a German with a Russian woman of poor race is an improvement for the Russians; for we don't know what will result from this blood in the third, fourth, fifth, sixth, and even later generations if it is combined once again with a share of blood of equal value.[48]

The temporal dimension in which the value of the children was assessed becomes particularly clear when Himmler refers to future generations at a time when the children themselves are still infants or not even born yet. Since no resources existed to keep track of the children, however, leaving them behind seemed to be the only possible option. In contrast, the 'children of good blood' (*Kinder guten Blutes*) were supposed to be transferred to the Reich. The NSV should take care of their further support and education.[49]

Soon, however, the practicability of this plan was called into question. Negotiations between Himmler and Hilgenfeldt had arrived at the conclusion that the NSV was lacking children's homes and nursery staff necessary to care for the children. Furthermore, the 'racial inspections' had to be delayed. As Rosenberg remarked in a letter to the Reich Minister and Head of the Reich Chancellory, Hans Heinrich Lammers, on 19 February 1943, an immediate 'racial evaluation' programme would be impossible due to the very young age of the objects of examination. They had not yet, Rosenberg argued, developed significant characteristics.[50]

Still, on 11 October 1943 the higher authorities of the Reich were notified about a secret 'Decree of the Führer on the care of illegitimate children of Germans in the occupied Eastern territories'.[51] The general idea was based on a similar decree that Hitler had issued in July 1942 to ensure the support of children of German fathers in Norway and the Netherlands.[52] From now on, the regular registration of the 'racially mixed children' should be officially organized in all occupied regions; the lists were then supposed to be distributed to the Reich Commissioner for the Strengthening of Germandom (RKF), Heinrich Himmler.

Directly following this decree was a discussion of the related 'rules of procedure'. Involved in these discussions were not only the men who had devised the first draft of the plan, Himmler, Hoffmann and Hilgenfeldt. As well, military and civil institutions – the Wehrmacht High Command, the SS Main Leadership

Office, the Reich Ministry, the Reich Ministry for the Occupied Eastern Territories, various District Commissioners (*Gebietskommissare*) and the Nazi Party (*Nationalsozialistische Deutsche Arbeiterpartei*: NSDAP) – commented on the rules of procedure. In addition, the Reich Minister of Justice and the Reich Minister of Internal Affairs expressed their desire to take an active part in the determination of proceedings. As soon as the children arrived within the borders of the 'old Reich', they argued, the issue would also be under their responsibility.[53]

The issues tackled in these discussions were the registration of the 'racially mixed children', the identification of their biological fathers, 'racial inspections' of the children and their families, the treatment of their mothers and child support, i.e. the care for and education of the children. Furthermore, the question of the national identity of the children played an important role, as is illustrated in the discussion of whether the children should be given the surnames of their fathers or their mothers.

In the course of these negotiations, conflicting interests were revealed. This became particularly clear during the discussion about the determination of paternity. Himmler as RKF made a strong point of stating that the biological fathers of the children should be determined beyond any doubt. The authorities of the Reich should be reserved the right to hold the biological father to financial support if necessary. In contrast, the Wehrmacht High Command (OKW) intended to spare their soldiers any obligation in order to prevent any kind of irritation touching their civilian lives.[54] In Norway, some soldiers had committed suicide after being confronted with an illegitimate child.[55] Correspondingly, the Reich Minister of the Occupied Eastern Territories agreed that the process of determination of paternity needed to be conducted in a very sensible manner. However, his motivation resulted from the wish to prevent 'trouble and political unrest in the ethnically alien families'.[56]

The financial aspects of the whole, rather bold venture were remarkably neglected. For the measures which some of the officials wanted to take – such as examining the children, their parents and their families every other month until the age of sixteen – the material costs would have been horrendous. Even if the economy had not been shaped by the war effort, it would have been impossible to implement these measures. In this, too, a fantasy of redemption can be detected.

The actual transport of 'soldiers' children' was tackled only in singular cases. For instance, the military administration department of the Army Group Central (*Heeresgruppe Mitte*) negotiated with the Repatriation Office for Ethnic Germans (*Volksdeutsche Mittelstelle*: VOMI) in March 1944 in order to enable 70 'soldiers' children' and their mothers to travel westward towards Łódź on a transport of 'ethnic Germans' (*Volksdeutsche*).[57] Such efforts, however, were not implemented on a larger scale, and little by little the issue turned out to be politically marginal.

Ambiguous Categories

On 4 July 1944 Himmler recorded that the extramarital offspring of German men registered in Estonia, Lithuania, Latvia and Belorussia added up to no more than 500 children. He expected less than one-third of these, approximately 150 children, to be evaluated as 'racially fit'. These figures did not include the registration of children in Ukraine, Russia and other countries. However, the figures initially estimated at one to one and a half million children for the 'occupied Eastern territories' as a whole had definitely proven to be a phantasmatic illusion.

> The alleged numbers about the extramarital children are vastly exaggerated. For instance, it was claimed that 2000 extramarital children of Germans were born in Estonia in the year 1943. According to a rather detailed statistic, however, there were actually only 2500 children (marital and extramarital together) born in this year in Estonia.[58]

Even though the issue turned out to be politically marginal, Himmler did not abandon his attempts to 'render the children useful for the German *Volk* community'. He intended, rather, to tighten the obligation to report 'racially mixed children' for military personnel and members of the civil administration. In order to establish a more realistic figure on the number of 'soldiers' children', he furthermore suggested that the NSV should offer incentives to the mothers upon their registration. They should receive material support, in particular linen and cribs, and – in some cases – jobs at the offices of the German occupation authorities.[59] Similar measures had proven to be fruitful in Norway before.[60] Given the fact that the German army suffered constant military defeat and had difficulties organizing its retreat by mid-1944, however, registration incentives for 'ethnically alien' women seem to be rather out of time and place.

Still, Himmler was not the only one whose fantasies regarding the children remained vital. Only six weeks earlier, the Deputy Chief of the General Staff (*Oberquartiermeister*) of the Army Group Central, colonel Georg von Unold, had suggested:

> Over the course of the war, circa 500 000 children of 50% German descent have been born in the occupied Eastern territories. From the perspective of 'biological warfare', the question arises if and when these children are to be relocated to Germany. O.Qu. [*Oberquartiermeister*; R.M.] suggests to transport the Russian children [*Russenkinder*; R.M.] under 10 years of age into the Reich and to start with a transport of 10–20 000 children of 8–10 years of age.[61]

The number of 'racially mixed children' registered by then amounted to about 500; yet von Unold acted on the assumption of half a million children. Even though he could assume, in all likelihood, the existence of more than the registered children, the question arises as to how von Unold expected to be able to recognize and locate them. In addition, the transport of 500,000 children would have presented a major military, logistic and financial problem. The fact that von Unold suggested this plan – despite the increasingly hopeless military situation – depicts the fantasies of power and potency harboured by the Nazis even as they faced defeat.

The Nazi ideas and debates about the 'soldiers' children' also present an example of how demographic aims shape ideologies during times of war. The general idea of the deterioration of race and civilization as a result of 'racial mixing' had not been created during National Socialism. Rather, the 'bastard' as a hybrid formation had been a constitutive element of racial hygienic discourses in the Weimar Republic and before. Already then, scientists had endeavoured to proclaim racial forms clearly distinguishable from one another.[62] Nazi ideology radicalized these ideas in a specific way. When the demographic goals changed over the course of the war, however, the allegedly fixed and stable presuppositions of racial hygiene were stirred up and modified. In accordance with the idea of a 'racial restructuring of the East', 'racially mixed children' who had initially been established as 'undesireable bastards' became interesting and valuable for various Nazi officials.

Whereas the children suddenly represented a chance, they still posed a threat. The degree to which the details of control over the children were discussed on the one hand, and the almost complete neglect of financial aspects to realize the imagined measures on the other hand, illustrate how much the Nazis feared the 'racially mixed children'. Considering these ambivalent ideas about the 'soldiers' children', it is not surprising how inconsistent the Nazis were regarding their number, their race, their 'share of Aryan blood', the question of paternity and the treatment of the children and their mothers. Nazi desire to exercise control in this situation of insecurity prompted their plans about the fate of the children lying between extermination and 'Germanization'.

Epilogue

The precise number of children of German men born in the 'occupied Eastern territories' can never be established. Since the official registration of 'half-German' children presented – as outlined above – a great risk for their mothers, the number of unreported cases will probably be comparatively high. Current research in archives in the Baltic States, Ukraine and Belorussia, however, might enable us to produce a more substantial estimation. The files of local authorities, specifically records of the local registration offices and hospitals, could also indicate how the local administration treated the children and their mothers, and if and in what ways they cooperated with the occupation regime.

Further research should reveal whether any of the last-minute plans to transport the children to Germany at the end of 1944 were actually carried out, i.e. whether any of the children or their mothers actually stayed in Germany after the war. In addition, the files on reparation claims in the *Bundesarchiv* (Federal Archives) in Koblenz will need to be consulted in order to establish whether any reparation claims regarding the 'racially mixed children' have been lodged.

The lives of the children themselves have not yet been subject to in-depth research. The TV documentary *Liebe im Vernichtungskrieg* (Love in the War of Annihilation) displays short clips of four interviews with descendants of local women and German men.[63] Their narratives indicate that mothers of 'racially mixed children' frequently concealed the origins of their offspring while the children grew up with secrets or lies about their biological fathers. At the end of the war and directly afterward, the Soviet People's Commissariat for Internal Affairs (NKVD) persecuted individual women for alleged collaboration. There are, however, no indications of widespread punishment of women by the local population as known from countries in Northern and Western Europe.[64] A thorough research and in-depth interviews with the descendants of German men, their mothers and other contemporary witnesses could establish more detailed information on the fate of the children and their mothers after the war, their societal and material situation, their biographies and their psychological background.

Since the area the Nazis called 'occupied Eastern territories' included a number of different countries, i.e. a variety of conflicts, memory cultures and historiographic traditions, a comparison between the post-war treatment of the children in the different countries could also provide us with important insights on national politics of remembrance and similarities and differences in the ways to master the past after 1945.[65]

Notes

1. This Nazi term refers to the German occupied territories of the former Soviet Union. For an introduction into the German administration in these different countries see R. Hilberg, *Die Vernichtung der europäischen Juden*, Vol. 2, 21 edn (Fischer TB, 1994), pp. 362 ff.
2. Different sources indicate that German women, too, had sexual encounters with local men. Apparently, the Nazi officials treated these in a distinctly different way. However, corresponding policies, the number of these women, their biographies, the places of their deployment etc. have thus far not been subject to research. On the deployment of women in general see E. Harvey, *Women and the Nazi East: Agents and Witnesses of Germanization* (Yale University Press, 2003); G. Schwarz, 'Frauen in der SS: Sippenverband und Frauenkorps', in K. Heinsohn, B. Vogel and U. Weckel (eds), *Zwischen*

Karriere und Verfolgung: Handlungsräume von Frauen im nationalsozialistischen Deutschland (Campus, 1997).

3. Schmidt's report is among others mentioned in Persönliche Handakte Major Hans von Payr zu Enn und Caldiff, Oberkommando der Wehrmacht/ Wehrwirtschafts- und Rüstungsamt (OKW), Notiz, 18.9.1942, Betrifft: Vorsorgliche Erfassung von zusätzlichen Arbeitskräften, Bundesarchiv-Militärarchiv Freiburg im Breisgau [BA-MA] RW 19/473. See also B. Beck, *Wehrmacht und sexuelle Gewalt. Sexualverbrechen vor deutschen Militärgerichten 1939–1945* (Schöningh, 2004), p. 212; I. Heinemann, '*Rasse, Siedlung, deutsches Blut': Das Rasse- und Siedlungshauptamt der SS und die rassenpolitische Neuordnung Europas* (Wallstein, 2003), p. 528; Christian Gerlach, *Kalkulierte Morde: Die deutsche Wirtschafts- und Vernichtungspolitik in Weißrußland 1941 bis 1944* (Hamburger edn, 1999), p. 1080; Barbara Johr and Helke Sander (eds), *Befreier und Befreite, Krieg, Vergewaltigungen, Kinder* (Fischer TB, 1995), p. 69. It is interesting that Schmidt assumed half of all German men in 'the East' would have had intimate relations. Which cultural codes led to this presupposition? For a discussion of the dominant beliefs about military masculinity and sexual needs see R. Seifert, 'War and Rape: A Preliminary Analysis', in A. Stiglmayer (ed.), *Mass Rape: The War against Women in Bosnia-Herzegovina* (University of Nebraska Press, 1994).

4. Rede Himmlers am 16.09.1942 auf der SS- und Polizeiführer-Tagung in der Feldkommandostelle in Hegewald bei Shitomir, Bundesarchiv Berlin Lichterfelde [BA] NS 19/4009, 78–127, 88. See also *Der Dienstkalender Heinrich Himmlers 1941/42*, edited, commented on and introduced by P. Witte, M. Wildt, M. Voigt, D. Pohl, P. Klein, C. Gerlach, C. Dieckmann and A. Angrick (Christians, 1999), p. 548; Bericht über Himmlers Rede vom 16.09.1942 vor den Polizeiführern, enthalten in 'Besichtigungsfahrt nach der Ukraine (Rußland-Süd)', BA NS 2/82, 221.

5. In *Mein Kampf*, Hitler had established in 1925 that the 'mixing of blood' would lead to infertility and the deterioration of the race (Adolf Hitler, *Mein Kampf*, 2 vols in 1 edn, 573–577 edn, Munich 1940: 311 ff.).

6. The term 'sexual encounter' denotes various forms of contacts between occupiers and occupied, ranging from sex-based violence, military and civil prostitution, instrumental relations (in order to receive protection, etc.) to sexual affairs and romantic relationships.

7. Women classified as Jewish or 'of Jewish descent'.

8. R.-D. Müller, 'Liebe im Vernichtungskrieg: Geschlechtergeschichtliche Aspekte des Einsatzes deutscher Soldaten im Rußlandkrieg 1941–1944', in F. Becker et al. (eds), *Politische Gewalt in der Moderne: Festschrift für Hans-Ulrich Thamer* (Aschendorff, 2003); Beck, *Wehrmacht und sexuelle Gewalt*. For a discussion of the research on sexuality, race and reproduction

see E. D. Heineman, 'Sexuality and Nazism: The Doubly Unspeakable?', *Journal of the History of Sexuality* 11(1/2) (2002). On racialized sexual regulation within the borders of the 'old Reich' see G. Bock, *Zwangssterilisation im Nationalsozialismus: Studien zur Rassenpolitik und Frauenpolitik* (Westdeutscher Verlag, 1986); G. Czarnowski, *Das kontrollierte Paar: Ehe- und Sexualpolitik im Nationalsozialismus* (Deutscher Studienverlag, 1991); A. F. Timm, 'The Ambivalent Outsider: Prostitution, Promiscuity, and VD Control in Nazi Berlin', in R. Gellately and N. Stoltzfus (eds), *Social Outsiders in Nazi Germany* (Princeton UP, 2001). On Nazi politics regarding relations between Germans and forced labourers 'of alien ethnicity' see G. Czarnowski, 'Zwischen Germanisierung und Vernichtung: Verbotene polnisch-deutsche Liebesbeziehungen und die Re-Konstruktion des Volkskörpers im Zweiten Weltkrieg', in H. Kramer (ed.), *Die Gegenwart der NS-Vergangenheit* (Philo, 2000). On the treatment of the 'racially mixed children' resulting from such liasions see B. Vögel, ' "Rassisch unerwünscht". Sowjetische und polnische Zwangsarbeiterinnen und ihre Kinder', *Beiträge zur Geschichte der nationalsozialistischen Verfolgung in Norddeutschland*, 8 (2004); Heinemann, *'Rasse, Siedlung, deutsches Blut'*: pp. 499 ff.; G. Schwarze, *Kinder, die nicht zählten: Ostarbeiterinnen und ihre Kinder im Zweiten Weltkrieg* (Klartext, 1997).

9. Germany in its borders of 1937.

10. Rede Himmlers am 16.09.1942 auf der SS- und Polizeiführer-Tagung in der Feldkommandostelle in Hegewald bei Shitomir, BA NS 19/4009, 78–127, 88.

11. Reichsminister für die besetzten Ostgebiete [RmfbO], Rosenberg, an den Reichskommissar für das Ostland [RKO], Betrifft: Behandlung der von den deutschen Staatsangehörigen in den besetzten Ostgebieten mit einheimischen Frauen erzeugten unehelichen Kinder, 9.10.1942, BA R 90/380.

12. Rede Himmlers am 16.09.1942 auf der SS- und Polizeiführer-Tagung in der Feldkommandostelle in Hegewald bei Shitomir, BA NS 19/4009, 78–127, 90. See also Georg Lilienthal, *Der 'Lebensborn e.V.': Ein Instrument nationalsozialistischer Rassenpolitik* (Fischer TB, 2003), p. 220.

13. Cited in C. Essner, *Die 'Nürnberger Gesetze' oder Die Verwaltung des Rassenwahns 1933–1945* (Ferdinand Schöningh, 2002), p. 420.

14. Ibid., p. 421.

15. Denkschrift über die Behandlung der Fremdvölkischen im Osten, 28.05.1940, cited in H. Krausnick, 'Denkschrift Himmlers über die Behandlung der Fremdvölkischen im Osten (Mai 1940)', in *Vierteljahreshefte für Zeitgeschichte*, 5 (1957), p. 198.

16. Heineman, *'Rasse, Siedlung, deutsches Blut'*, pp. 508 ff.; Lilienthal, *Der 'Lebensborn e.V.'*, pp. 200 ff.; H.-C. Harten, *De-Kulturation und Germanisierung: Die nationalsozialistische Rassen- und Erziehungspolitik in Polen*

(Campus, 1996), pp. 299 ff.; Georg Lilienthal, 'Kinder als Beute des Rassenkriegs. Der 'Lebensborn e.V.' und die Eindeutschung von Kindern aus Polen, der Tschechoslowakei und Jugoslawien', *Dachauer Hefte*, 9 (1993), pp. 181–96; Gerlach, *Kalkulierte Morde*, pp. 1082 ff.; R. Hrabar et al., *Kinder im Krieg – Krieg gegen Kinder: Die Geschichte der polnischen Kinder 1939–1945* (Rowohlt TB, 1981); K. Sosnowski, *The Tragedy of Children under Nazi Rule*, 2nd edn (Howard Fertig, 1983).

17. Heineman, '*Rasse, Siedlung, deutsches Blut*', p. 515; Lilienthal, *Der 'Lebensborn e.V.'*, pp. 216 ff.

18. Krausnick, 'Denkschrift Himmlers über die Behandlung der Fremdvölkischen im Osten (Mai 1940)'. The fear to be 'overrun by the Asian masses' due to the low birthrate in the 'old Reich' is subject to talks of high-ranking Nazi officials until late 1944 (see among others Martin Bormann, Vermerk zu Gespräch mit dem Führer, Betrifft: Sicherung der Zukunft des deutschen Volkes, Führerhauptquartier, 29.11.1944, BA NS 19/3289, 2–11, 2 f.).

19. Persönliche Handakte Major Hans von Payr zu Enn und Caldiff, Oberkommando der Wehrmacht/Wehrwirtschafts- und Rüstungsamt (OKW), Notiz, 18.9.1942, Betrifft: Vorsorgliche Erfassung von zusätzlichen Arbeitskräften, BA-MA RW 19/473.

20. RmfbO, Rosenberg, an den Reichsminister und Chef der Reichskanzlei, Betrifft: Entwurf eines Führererlasses über die Betreuung der unehelichen Kinder von Reichsdeutschen in den besetzten Ostgebieten, 19.2.1943, BA R6/383, 2.

21. Anlagen zu den Lageberichten, BA-MA RH 23/155, 58, 71, 80, 91, 104, 111, 122, copies on microfilm BA-MA WF 03/14396, 1115, 1129, 1141, 1150, 1161, 1174, 1181, 1194, 1205, 1218.

22. Anlage Nr. 2 zum Lagebericht für Smolensk-Stadt für die Zeit vom 19.7.–15.8.1943, Betrifft: Erfassung unehelicher Kinder von Reichsdeutschen, BA-MA RH 23/155, 33, 49.

23. RmfbO (gez. Berger) an den Reichsminister und Chef der Reichskanzlei, Betrifft: Uneheliche Kinder von Reichsdeutschen in den besetzten Ostgebieten, 17.11.1943, BA R6/383, 41, copy on microfilm BA-MA FPF-01/7840. See also Gerlach, *Kalkulierte Morde*, p. 1081.

24. Fremde Heere Ost, Dienststelle Braun, Stimmungsbericht über 'Charkow', 17.4.1943, BA-MA RW 4/v. 309a. See also Müller, 'Liebe im Vernichtungskrieg', 263 ff.; H. Kaminski, *Liebe im Vernichtungskrieg. Die Frauen im Osten und die deutsche Besatzungsmacht*, TV Documentary, broadcast on Arte, 20.5.2002.

25. Kåre Olsen, *Vater: Deutscher. Das Schicksal der norwegischen Lebensbornkinder und ihrer Mütter von 1940 bis heute* (Campus, 2002), pp. 72 ff.; Lilienthal, *Der 'Lebensborn e.V.'*, pp. 60 ff.

26. For instance, the RmdbO asserted that the admittance of local women into the maternity homes of the NSV could only be the absolute exception (RmfbO (gez. Berger) an den RKO, Betrifft: Entwurf des Führererlasses über die Betreuung der unehelichen Kinder von Reichsdeutschen in den besetzten Ostgebieten, 17.11.1943, BA R6/383, 42).

27. RmfbO (gez. von Allwörden) an den Reichsführer-SS, Betrifft: Durchführung des Führererlasses über die Betreuung der unehelichen Kinder von Deutschen in den besetzten Ostgebieten, 20.11.1943, BA R6/383, 43–45, 44.

28. Korrespondenz innerhalb des Führungsstabes Politik, Februar 1944, BA R6/383, 72 f., 112, 115.

29. RKF, Himmler, Geheimer Vermerk, Betrifft: Erfassung von unehelichen Kindern in den besetzten Ostgebieten, 4.7.1944, Abschrift, BA R6/383, 127–8, 127.

30. Heineman, 'Sexuality and Nazism: The Doubly Unspeakable?', pp. 44 f.; D. Bergen, 'Sex, Blood, and Vulnerability: Women Outsiders in German Occupied Europe', in R. Gellately and N. Stoltzfus (eds), *Social Outsiders in Nazi Germany* (Princeton UP, 2001).

31. This had already proved to be a problem in Norway (Olsen, *Vater: Deutscher*, pp. 133 ff.).

32. Several of these are mentioned in Müller, 'Liebe im Vernichtungskrieg'; Beck, *Wehrmacht und sexuelle Gewalt* and I. Meinen, *Wehrmacht und Prostitution im besetzten Frankreich* (Edition Temmen, 2002). However, a thorough analysis of the various regulations in different regions at changing stages of the war has not been published yet.

33. Gespräch vom 23.04.1942, Wolfsschanze, cited in H. Picker, *Hitlers Tischgespräche im Führerhauptquartier: Entstehung, Struktur, Folgen des Nationalsozialismus* (Propyläen TB, 1997), p. 332.

34. Geheimer Vortragsvermerk für Generaloberstabsarzt Prof. Dr Hanloser, 4.11.1942, BA-MA H 20/479. As Birgit Beck has shown in detail, the alleged sexual drives of a soldier often led to a mitigation of punishment in rape trials (Beck, *Wehrmacht und sexuelle Gewalt*, pp. 272 ff.).

35. Oberkommando des Heeres [OKH], von Brauchitsch, 31.7.1940, BA-MA RH 53–7/v. 233a/167.

36. Meinen, *Wehrmacht und Prostitution im besetzten Frankreich*; Beck, *Wehrmacht und sexuelle Gewalt*, pp. 107 ff.

37. Oberkommando der Wehrmacht [OKW], Keitel, Betrifft: Verkehr des deutschen Soldaten mit der Zivilbevölkerung in den besetzten Ostgebieten, 12.9.1942, Abschrift, BA-MA RH 26–6/67. About the establishment of brothels in Poland and the 'occupied Eastern territories' see also Beck, *Wehrmacht und sexuelle Gewalt*, pp. 106 ff. On 'undesirable intercourse' see F. Ni Aolain, 'Sex-based Violence and the Holocaust: A Reevaluation of

Harms and Rights in International Law', *Yale Journal of Law and Feminism*, 12 (2000), pp. 43–85.

38. He refered to brothels in the General Government (RKF, Himmler, an SS-Obergruppenführer Friedrich Wilhelm Krüger, Betrifft: Geschlechtsverkehr von Angehörigen der SS und Polizei mit Frauen einer andersrassigen Bevölkerung, 30.6.1942, BA NS 19/1913, 3–4, 4, printed in H. Heiber (ed.), *Reichsführer! Briefe an und von Himmler* (dtv, 1970), pp. 156 f., Doc. 120; see also B. Beck, 'Sexuelle Gewalt und Krieg: Geschlecht, Rasse und der nationalsozialistische Vernichtungsfeldzug gegen die Sowjetunion, 1941–1945', in V. Aegerter et al. (eds), *Geschlecht hat Methode: Ansätze und Perspektiven in der Frauen- und Geschlechtergeschichte* (Chronos, 1999), p. 229). However, the establishment of brothels in the Reich Commissariats Ostland and Ukraine suggest a similar attitude.

39. Müller, 'Liebe im Vernichtungskrieg'; Kaminski, *Liebe im Vernichtungskrieg*; Beck, *Wehrmacht und sexuelle Gewalt*.

40. Omer Bartov, *Hitlers Wehrmacht* (Rowohlt, 1995), pp. 145 f.

41. Auszugsweise Abschrift aus dem Lagebericht des Generalkommissars in Riga, 29.4.1944, BA R6/383, 113–14. See also Korrespondenz zwischen RmdbO und RKO, 24.11.1941 und 3.1942, Abschrift, BA R 90/460; Wehrmachtsbefehlshaber Ukraine, Merkblatt für den deutschen Soldaten über die Behandlung der ukrainischen Bevölkerung, 18.8.1942, BA R6/36, 104–8, pp. 107 f. See also Müller, 'Liebe im Vernichtungskrieg', pp. 246 ff.

42. OKW, Keitel, Betrifft: Verkehr des deutschen Soldaten mit der Zivilbevölkerung in den besetzten Ostgebieten, 12.9.1942, Abschrift, BA-MA RH 26–6/67.

43. Reichsgesundheitsführer, Conti, an den Reichsführer-SS, 9.11.1942, Geheim, BA NS 19/1886, 1–3, 1; see also BA NS 19/0288. About the problem of venereal disease see Beck, *Wehrmacht und sexuelle Gewalt*, pp. 209 f. About the distribution of contraceptives to the local population see also A. Dallin, *Deutsche Herrschaft in Rußland 1941–1945: Eine Studie über Besatzungspolitik* (Droste, 1958), 469 ff.

44. Reichsgesundheitsführer, Conti, an den Reichsführer-SS, 9.11.1942, Geheim, BA NS 19/1886, 1–3, pp. 1 f.

45. Berück Mitte, Quartiermeister, Tätigkeitsbericht Juli, 4.8.1942, BA-MA FPF 01/7840, 235. Hitler and Himmler agreed that abortions of local women should not be prevented, even if the women were designated 'racially fit' (Rede Himmlers am 16.09.1942 auf der SS- und Polizeiführer-Tagung in der Feldkommandostelle in Hegewald bei Shitomir, BA NS 19/4009, 78–127, 81; Dallin, *Deutsche Herrschaft in Rußland 1941–1945*, p. 470).

46. These talks took place on 13 and 14 September 1942 in Himmler's field-headquarters in the Ukraine close to Winniza (*Der Dienstkalender Heinrich*

Himmlers, pp. 548–50). See also Heinemann, *'Rasse, Siedlung, deutsches Blut'*, p. 529.

47. Rede Himmlers am 16.09.1942 auf der SS- und Polizeiführer-Tagung in der Feldkommandostelle in Hegewald bei Shitomir, BA NS 19/4009, 78–127, 89; see also his handwritten notes titled 'Vortrag beim Führer', 22.9.1942, BA NS 19/1447, 78–88, 86; Lilienthal, *Der 'Lebensborn e.V.'*, p. 204. Hoffmann summarized the results of the talks and emphasized that he and Hilgenfeldt had been assigned to enforce the selection of the children (Der Chef des RuSHA, Hoffmann, an das RSHA, III, Betrifft: Die Betreuung von Kindern deutscher Wehrmachtsangehöriger in den besetzten Gebieten, 23.10.1942, BA NS 2/71, 24–5).

48. Rede Himmlers am 16.09.1942 auf der SS- und Polizeiführer-Tagung in der Feldkommandostelle in Hegewald bei Shitomir, BA NS 19/4009, 78–127, 89.

49. Der Leiter des Hauptamts für Volkswohlfahrt, Hilgenfeld, an den Leiter der Parteikanzlei, 16.9.1942, BA NS 19/2427, 3–4; Der Chef des RuSHA, Hoffmann, an das RSHA, III, Betrifft: Die Betreuung von Kindern deutscher Wehrmachtsangehöriger in den besetzten Gebieten, 23.10.1942, BA NS 2/71, 24–5. About the dispute between Lebensborn e.V. and NSV concerning competence and authority see Lilienthal, *Der 'Lebensborn e.V.'*, pp. 204 ff.

50. RmfbO, Rosenberg, an den Reichsminister und Chef der Reichskanzlei, Betrifft: Entwurf eines Führererlasses über die Betreuung der unehelichen Kinder von Reichsdeutschen in den besetzten Ostgebieten, 19.2.1943, BA R6/383, 2.

51. Erlass des Führers über die Betreuung der unehelichen Kinder von Deutschen in den besetzten Ostgebieten vom 11. Oktober 1943, Beglaubigte Abschrift, BA R6/383, 32, 80, copy on microfilm BA-MA FPF 01/7840, 209. The first draft had been composed in December 1942 (RmfbO (gez. A. Meyer), Betrifft: Betreuung von unehelichen Kindern von Reichsdeutschen in den besetzten Ostgebieten, 29.12.1942, cited in Gerlach, *Kalkulierte Morde*, p. 1081). Other versions are archived in BA R6/383.

52. Verordnung über die Betreuung von Kindern deutscher Wehrmachtsangehöriger in den besetzten Gebieten, 28.7.1942, Reichsgesetzblatt I 1942, 488. See also Verordnung zur Durchführung der Verordnung über die Betreuung von Kindern deutscher Wehrmachtsangehöriger in den besetzten Gebieten, 13.2.1943, Reichsgesetzblatt I 1943, 102–4.

53. Reichsminister der Justiz (gez. Rothenberger) an RmfbO, Betrifft: Betreuung der unehelichen Kinder von Deutschen in den besetzten Ostgebieten, 6.12.1943, BA R6/383, 55; Reichsminister des Innern an RmfbO, Betrifft: Betreuung der unehelichen Kinder von Deutschen in den besetzten Ostgebieten, 18.1.1944, BA R6/383, 63.

54. OKW (ohne Signatur) an RmfbO, Betrifft: Betreuung der unehelichen Kinder von Deutschen in den besetzten Ostgebieten, 22.5.1944, BA R6/386, 95–8,
55. Olsen, *Vater: Deutscher*, p. 123.
56. RmfbO (gez. von Allwörden) an den Reichsführer-SS, Betrifft: Durchführung des Führererlasses über die Betreuung der unehelichen Kinder von Deutschen in den besetzten Ostgebieten, 20.11.1943, BA R6/383, 43–5, 44.
57. Oberkommando Heeresgruppe Mitte, O.Qu./Qu.2/VII (Mil.-Verw), 3.1944, BA R6/281, 136. For a similar attempt to transport 'extramarital children of Germans' from the Ostland into the Reich see Fernschreiben Dr Wilhelmi an RmfbO, Kinkelin, 15.8.1944, BA R6/383, 124.
58. RKF, Himmler, Geheimer Vermerk, Betrifft: Erfassung von unehelichen Kindern in den besetzten Ostgebieten, 4.7.1944, Abschrift, BA R6/383, 127–8.
59. Ibid.
60. Olsen, *Vater: Deutscher*, pp. 72 ff.
61. Chef WiStab Ost, Reisebericht über die Dienstreise Chef WiStab Ost 17.–21.5., 24.5.1944, BA MA F 43390, 624, also cited in Gerlach, *Kalkulierte Morde*, p. 1081.
62. F. Axter, *Die Angst vor dem Verkaffern. Rassenreinheit und Identität im deutschen Kolonialismus* (University of Hamburg, 2002); K. Bayertz et al. (eds), *Rasse, Blut und Gene: Geschichte der Eugenik und Rassenhygiene in Deutschland* (Suhrkamp, 1996); A. Grossmann, *Reforming Sex: The German Movement for Birth Control and Abortion Reform* (Oxford University Press, 1995).
63. Kaminski, *Liebe im Vernichtungskrieg*; Müller, 'Liebe im Vernichtungskrieg'.
64. Anette Warring, *National Bodies: Fraternisation, Gender and Sexuality in Occupied Europe 1940–45*, Lecture at the University of Hamburg, 29.10.2003; Fabrice Virgili, *Shorn Women: Gender and Punishment in Liberation France* (Berg, 2003); C. Duchen, 'Crime and Punishment in Liberated France: The Case of *les femmes tondues*,' in C. Duchen and I. Bandhauer-Schoeffmann (eds), *When the War was Over: Women, War and Peace, 1940–1956* (Leicester University Press, 2000); Ebba Drolshagen, *Nicht ungeschoren davonkommen: Die Geliebten der Wehrmachtssoldaten im besetzten Europa* (Propyläen TB, 2000).
65. Special Thanks to Christine Achinger, Carsten Gericke, Steve Giles, Michaela Hampf, Birthe Kundrus, Klaus Naumann, Therese Roth and Gaby Zipfel!

References

Axster, F., *Die Angst vor dem Verkaffern: Rassenreinheit und Identität im deutschen Kolonialismus*, Unpublished Thesis, University of Hamburg, 2002.
Bartov, Omer, *Hitlers Wehrmacht*, Reinbek bei Hamburg: Rowohlt, 1995.

Bayertz, K., Kroll, J. and Weingart, P. (eds), *Rasse, Blut und Gene: Geschichte der Eugenik und Rassenhygiene in Deutschland*, Frankfurt: Suhrkamp, 1996.

Beck, B., 'Sexuelle Gewalt und Krieg: Geschlecht, Rasse und der nationalsozialistische Vernichtungsfeldzug gegen die Sowjetunion, 1941–1945', in V. Aegerter et al. (eds), *Geschlecht hat Methode: Ansätze und Perspektiven in der Frauen- und Geschlechtergeschichte*, Zurich: Chronos, 1999.

Beck, B., *Wehrmacht und sexuelle Gewalt: Sexualverbrechen vor deutschen Militärgerichten 1939–1945*, Paderborn, Munich, Vienna and Zurich: Schöningh, 2004.

Bergen, D., 'Sex, Blood, and Vulnerability: Women Outsiders in German Occupied Europe', in R. Gellately and N. Stoltzfus (eds), *Social Outsiders in Nazi Germany*, Princeton: Princeton University Press, 2001.

Bock, G., *Zwangssterilisation im Nationalsozialismus: Studien zur Rassenpolitik und Frauenpolitik*, Opladen: Westdeutscher Verlag, 1986.

Czarnowski, G., *Das kontrollierte Paar: Ehe- und Sexualpolitik im Nationalsozialismus*, Weinheim: Deutscher Studienverlag, 1991.

Czarnowski, G., 'Zwischen Germanisierung und Vernichtung: Verbotene polnisch-deutsche Liebesbeziehungen und die Re-Konstruktion des Volkskörpers im Zweiten Weltkrieg', in H. Kramer (ed.), *Die Gegenwart der NS-Vergangenheit*, Berlin and Vienna: Philo, 2000.

Dallin, A., *Deutsche Herrschaft in Rußland 1941–1945: Eine Studie über Besatzungspolitik*, Düsseldorf: Droste, 1958.

Der Dienstkalender Heinrich Himmlers 1941/42, edited, commented on and introduced by P. Witte, M. Wildt, M. Voigt, D. Pohl, P. Klein, C. Gerlach, C. Dieckmann and A. Angrick, Hamburg: Christians, 1999.

Drolshagen, E., *Nicht ungeschoren davonkommen: Die Geliebten der Wehrmachtssoldaten im besetzten Europa*, Munich: Propyläen TB, 2000.

Duchen, C., 'Crime and Punishment in Liberated France: The Case of *les femmes tondues*', in C. Duchen and I. Bandhauer-Schoeffmann (eds), *When the War was Over: Women, War and Peace, 1940–1956*, London and New York: Leicester University Press, 2000.

Essner, C., *Die 'Nürnberger Gesetze' oder Die Verwaltung des Rassenwahns 1933–1945*, Paderborn, Munich, Vienna and Zurich: Ferdinand Schöningh, 2002.

Gerlach, C., *Kalkulierte Morde: Die deutsche Wirtschafts- und Vernichtungspolitik in Weißrußland 1941 bis 1944*, Hamburg: Hamburger Edition, 1999.

Grossmann, A., *Reforming Sex: The German Movement for Birth Control and Abortion Reform*, New York: Oxford University Press, 1995.

Harten, H.-C., *De-Kulturation und Germanisierung: Die nationalsozialistische Rassen- und Erziehungspolitik in Polen*, Frankfurt and New York: Campus, 1996.

Harvey, E., *Women and the Nazi East: Agents and Witnesses of Germanization*, New Haven and London: Yale University Press, 2003.

Heiber, H. (ed.), *Reichsführer! Briefe an und von Himmler*, Munich: dtv, 1970.

Heineman, E., 'Sexuality and Nazism: The Doubly Unspeakable?', *Journal of the History of Sexuality* 11(1/2) (2002).

Heinemann, I., *'Rasse, Siedlung, deutsches Blut': Das Rasse- und Siedlungshauptamt der SS und die rassenpolitische Neuordnung Europas*, Göttingen: Wallstein, 2003.

Hilberg, R., *Die Vernichtung der europäischen Juden*, 3 vols, 21 edn [first published in 1961], Frankfurt am Main: Fischer TB, 1994.

Hitler, A., *Mein Kampf*, 2 vols in 1 edn, 573–577 edn, Munich, 1940.

Hrabar, R., Tokarz, Z. and Wilczur, J.E., *Kinder im Krieg – Krieg gegen Kinder: Die Geschichte der polnischen Kinder 1939–1945*, Reinbek bei Hamburg: Rowohlt TB, 1981.

Johr, B. and Sander, H. (eds), *Befreier und Befreite, Krieg, Vergewaltigungen, Kinder*, Frankfurt am Main: Fischer TB, 1995.

Kaminski, H., *Liebe im Vernichtungskrieg. Die Frauen im Osten und die deutsche Besatzungsmacht*, TV Documentary, broadcast on Arte, 20.5.2002.

Krausnick, H., 'Denkschrift Himmlers über die Behandlung der Fremdvölkischen im Osten (Mai 1940),' in *Vierteljahreshefte für Zeitgeschichte* 5 (1957).

Lilienthal, G., 'Kinder als Beute des Rassenkriegs. Der 'Lebensborn e.V.' und die Eindeutschung von Kindern aus Polen, der Tschechoslowakei und Jugoslawien', *Dachauer Hefte* 9 (1993).

Lilienthal, G., *Der 'Lebensborn e.V.': Ein Instrument nationalsozialistischer Rassenpolitik*, 3 edn, Frankfurt am Main: Fischer TB, 2003.

Meinen, I., *Wehrmacht und Prostitution im besetzten Frankreich*, Bremen: Edition Temmen, 2002.

Müller, R.-D., 'Liebe im Vernichtungskrieg: Geschlechtergeschichtliche Aspekte des Einsatzes deutscher Soldaten im Rußlandkrieg 1941–1944', in F. Becker et al. (eds), *Politische Gewalt in der Moderne: Festschrift für Hans-Ulrich Thamer*, Münster: Aschendorff, 2003.

Ni Aolain, F., 'Sex-based Violence and the Holocaust: A Reevaluation of Harms and Rights in International Law', *Yale Journal of Law and Feminism* 12 (2000).

Olsen, K., *Vater: Deutscher. Das Schicksal der norwegischen Lebensbornkinder und ihrer Mütter von 1940 bis heute*, Frankfurt and New York: Campus, 2002.

Picker, H., *Hitlers Tischgespräche im Führerhauptquartier: Entstehung, Struktur, Folgen des Nationalsozialismus*, 2nd edn [first published in 1951], Berlin: Propyläen TB, 1997.

Schwarz, G., 'Frauen in der SS: Sippenverband und Frauenkorps', in K. Heinsohn, B. Vogel and U. Weckel (eds), *Zwischen Karriere und Verfolgung: Handlungsräume von Frauen im nationalsozialistischen Deutschland*, Frankfurt and New

York: Campus, 1997.

Schwarze, G., *Kinder, die nicht zählten: Ostarbeiterinnen und ihre Kinder im Zweiten Weltkrieg*, Essen: Klartext, 1997.

Seifert, R., 'War and Rape: A Preliminary Analysis', in A. Stiglmayer (ed.), *Mass Rape: The War against Women in Bosnia-Herzegovina*, Lincoln, NE and London: University of Nebraska Press, 1994.

Sosnowski, K., *The Tragedy of Children under Nazi Rule*, 2nd edn [first published in Poland in 1962], New York: Howard Fertig, 1983.

Timm, A.F., 'The Ambivalent Outsider: Prostitution, Promiscuity, and VD Control in Nazi Berlin', in R. Gellately and N. Stoltzfus (eds), *Social Outsiders in Nazi Germany*, Princeton: Princeton University Press, 2001.

Virgili, F., *Shorn Women: Gender and Punishment in Liberation France*, Oxford and New York: Berg, 2003.

Vögel, B., ' "Rassisch unerwünscht". Sowjetische und polnische Zwangs- arbeiterinnen und ihre Kinder', *Beiträge zur Geschichte der nationalsozialistis- chen Verfolgung in Norddeutschland* 8 (2004).

Warring, A., *National Bodies: Fraternisation, Gender and Sexuality in Occupied Europe 1940–45*, Lecture at the University of Hamburg, 29.10.2003.

Young, R., *Colonial Desire: Hibridity in Theory, Culture and Race*, London and New York: Routledge, 1995.

–10–

Race, Heredity and Nationality:
Children in Bohemia and Moravia, 1939–1945

Michal Šimůnek

Introduction

The hopes and expectations of applying knowledge on hereditary (genetic) mechanisms in man on a large scale in order to improve the so-called population quality were stated by the founder of the eugenic movement, Francis Galton, in 1869.

> I conclude that each generation has enormous power over the natural gifts of those that follow, and maintain that it is a duty that we owe to humanity to investigate the range of that power, and to exercise it in a way that, without being unwise towards ourselves, shall be most advantageous to future inhabitans of the earth.[1]

The main aim of this chapter is to explore how this hereditary fatalism of science in the early 1930s, coupled with state-supported systematic racism in mother- and childcare, came to influence the fate of the generation of children born during the existence of the Protectorate of Bohemia and Moravia between 1939–1945. The chapter will also focus on the application of the Nazi concepts of hereditary and racial hygiene (*Erb- und Rassenhygiene*) and the literally lethal measures of the so-called racial care (*Rassenpflege*) and heredity health care (*Erbgesundheitspflege*). Both racial care and heredity health care will be discussed within the broader context of a eugenic rationalization of population policy.[2] The chapter will mainly describe the goals and objectives of the Nazi decision-makers and planners. However, the fate of the victims will also be considered. Children born during this period of time to nationally mixed families in the Czech *Lands* were deeply affected by the Nazi policies. There are unique aspects to the fate of these children; however, parallels may also be found to the fate of war children in other occupied European countries during World War II.

Childcare as Eugenic Measure

At the beginning of the 20th century there was a strong hope in Europe and the US that by developing and implementing coherent programmes for the protection of motherhood and children, high levels of child mortality were to be reduced. The first decades of the twentieth century saw a major expansion of government activities in the supply of childcare: 'one of the most remarkable social transformations of the twentieth-century world'.[3] Between the two World Wars most politically advanced European nations had or were about to introduce some state-sponsored welfare measures. At the beginning of the1930s welfare policies took a new and different direction, at least in continental Europe. This new direction was partly a consequence of the Great Depression. More comprehensive welfare services were introduced, and the welfare policies and services became increasingly politicized. In Germany, where the Nazis were in power from 1933, welfare policies were a core issue of the new national socialistic state. The doctrine of the racial inequality of men was prominent in the political programme of the Nazi party. In accordance with this programme, the thesis of the *völkisch Rassenkunde* and population and medical genetical research, expressed in biological and medical terms, were combined.[4] Under the control of the German state and the Nazi party, this combination of racial doctrines and biologistic science was to lead and determine the practical social and racial policy of the Nazis in the years to come.

Since the beginning of the twentieth century, theoretical and practical biomedical science had developed at great speed. This process went on parallel to the growth of the modern welfare state.[5] Improvement in hygiene and nutrition, and the eradication of several pernicious diseases and epidemics, led to decreasing mortality levels in all age groups, above all in children. Reduced mortality levels were considered to have economic, political and national implications. If the quality of all these children was not properly controlled, the future existence of peoples and states might be endangered, according to Nazi views.

Since the 1930s science, scientific experts and infrastructure had gained an unprecedented importance and prestige. One may speak of a general rationalization trend. Both European dictatorships – Germany under Hitler and Russia under Stalin – played a crucial role in this process. In the middle of the war (1942) the science chief editor of the *New York Times* Waldemar Kaempffert described the stages precisely:

Back of the ideologies of the dictators, back of the professional pliancy, is something more than political expediency, something more than blind obedience ... To say that the dictators emerged because science and technology had taken possession of society and stamped it with a pattern utterly different from that which the égalitarians of the eighteenth century knew is an over-simpflification. There are psychic factors that cannot be ignored – inner drives, national traditions, habits of life. Yet if the dictators are to be overthrown, if democracy is to be preserved, the part that science and technology played in the rise of democracy cannot be ignored. Research produces not only change within the science itself but social change. The democratic method is to adapt social change to technological change. The dictators are trying to do the contrary.[6]

The most important manifestation in family- and childcare of these efforts to bring about social change through scientific means was the broad acceptance of practical eugenic measures in Germany. Eugenics at that time was the result of more than forty years of passionate debates and disscussions. Ideas of hereditary (genetic) determination of human behaviour, combined with a strong conviction that the knowledge of how to change (manipulate) man's hereditary constitution was within reach, made eugenics part and parcel of contemporary intellectual and scientific discourse.

Historical and Political Determinants

For centuries, the Czech *Lands* (Bohemia, Moravia and Silesia) have been areas with a long tradition of mixed ethnicities. The two most important groups within the local population (and since the second half of the nineteenth century also the greatest rivals) were Czechs and local Germans, who since the first decade of the twentieth century used the term Sudeten-Germans (Sudetendeutsche). Apart from these two, however, there were also large Jewish and limited numbers of Polish and Roma communities.

Mutual cohabitation proved to be a crucial factor in the modern history in this part of Central Europe.[7] Since the second half of the nineteenth century, extreme nationalism, which was reflected in all dimensions of life during the twentieth century, influenced most political decisions, including population and family policy, as well as routine family care.

The geographical distribution of various ethnic groups changed over time. Basically there were homogenous Sudeten-German areas along the borders facing Germany and Austria. Gradually inland areas changed into more mixed Czech-German districts on the borders with Czech settlements and finally into genuinely Czech settlements. Nevertheless, there were special 'ethnic islands' even within these genuinely Czech areas, such as the greater cities of Praha (Prague), České Budějovice (Budweis), Jihlava (Iglau), Brno (Brünn) and Olomouc (Olmütz).

The international crisis provoked by the Nazi government in 1938–1939 led first to the establishment of an independent territory called Reich District Sudetenland (*Reichsgau Sudetenland*), which was attached directly to the German Reich.[8] Following the military action of 15 March 1939, after the separation of Slovakia, the rest of the Czech *Lands* was occupied by German armed forces and became – as a Protectorate of Bohemia and Moravia (*Protektorat Böhmen und Mähren*) – a

part of the Nazi Greater German Reich.[9] It included the remaining (inland) territory of Bohemia and Moravia with about 7,700,000 inhabitants and a few inland
German 'ethnic islands'. This pseudo-state may have had a guaranteed autonomy,
but it was occupied by the German army and was subordinated to the supreme
power of the Reich. In the course of time, its autonomy became more and more
illusory.

The following six years saw a deliberate attempt to incorporate and integrate the
population of the 'old heartlands of the Reich', repeatedly named Bohemia and
Moravia in official Nazi propaganda, into the rising Nazi German empire.
Integration was pursued by all sorts of means and measures. In the opinion of the
Nazi establishment in both Berlin and Prague, strategies of Germanization
(*Eindeutschung*) should be employed toward the non-German part of the population living in the Protectorate. The main goal was to create ethnically 'clean areas',
by Nazi terms. The adopted strategies and the subsequent events of World War II
brought with them a redefinition of inter-ethnic relations in a most absurd and up
to that moment unconceivable manner, very far from the Nazi policies in the
western parts of occupied Europe:

> It is ... no exaggeration to say that the Czechs, as a nation, are fighting quite literally
> for their lives. It is a different sort of war from that between Englishmen and Germans.
> There is less bloodshed and fewer deaths. The heroism which is demanded is less direct
> and immediate, less spectacular, and the price paid is lower in terms of the bereavement
> of families and the sheer irreplaceability of the killed. But it is also a life-and-death
> struggle, and, if possible, the stakes are even higher. There will always be an England,
> but there might not ever again be a Czechoslovakia. There will always be Englishmen,
> Scotsmen, Welshmen and Irishmen, and whatever happens to them, there will always
> be Canadians, Australians, New Zealanders and South Africans, but there may not
> always be Czechs and Slovaks ... If Germany keeps her hold on Czechoslovakia, by the
> time this century turns both branches of the Czechoslovak nation may be remembered
> only by their pottery and their needlework, their dances and their songs.[10]

The crucial event which directly or indirectly affected all circumstances of life
was, of course war. War influenced nearly all decisions. War started the unprecedented extermination and annihilation programmes (forced sterilizations,
'euthanasia', S.H.O.A.H.) that should create the very foundations of the Nazi
'New Europe'.

Social Selection and Strenghtening of Germanhood

The leading principles of the official population policy were based on a perverted
biologistic logic. In accordance with this logic, so-called social selection
(*Sozialauslese*) was the essential political and social strategy developed by the

Nazis in the Protectorate. In practice this strategy meant discrimination, segregation and in many cases also physical extermination of people, all in the name of 'race'.[11] These policies aimed at regulating everyday interpersonal relations, marriages and the birth of children. The SS were the leading exponents of these policies. Consider an illustrative example from the top political level of the Protectorate, a quotation from the speech of the deputy Reichsprotektor in Bohemia and Moravia and SS-Obergruppenführer Reinhard Heydrich to German officials on 2 October 1942, concerning the plan of 'Germanizing People and Space'

> And now, gentlemen, a few thoughts on the final solution, which I beg you to keep to yourselves, but which you should know about, so that no mistakes are made when you go about your next assignment. Gentlemen, the final solution [of the 'Czech question'] will mean 1) that these areas once and for all become German. This land is the very core, the 'heartland' of the Reich and we must never tolerate – as the history of Germany clearly shows, that the Reich again may experience a lethal stab from this land. For the final German possession and colonizing of these areas I will be frank; that by traditional methods we will try to Germanize this Czech mob, as we are already secretly doing.[12]

Implementing the politics of Germanisation (*Eindeutschung*) in everyday life was a complex task. Several interconnected steps were involved, such as personal identification, selection, segregation and potentially also physical elimination of people, based on expert judgements of the racial, hereditary, political and social status of individuals. For so-called practical reasons, the totality of this political agenda was divided into mutually reinforcing strategies, which were implemented both by state authorities and by Nazi party institutions or bodies. The total approach included the racial policy (*Rassenpolitik*) with nationality policy as a part of it, social policy (*Sozialpolitik*) and last but not least also health policy (*Gesundheitspolitik*) with hereditary health care (*Erbgesundheitspflege*) as one of its pillars. The Office of the Reich Protector served as the highest authority.[13]

Special institutions were created during the time of occupation in order to promote politics of population and racial planning. Two such institutions turned out to be of crucial importance. The first one was the regional office of the Racial and Settlement Main Office (*Rassen- und Siedlungshauptamt*). The second was the regional office of the Commissar for the Strenghtening of the Germanhood (*Kommissar für die Festigung des deutschen Volkstum*).[14] Both were not only anchored in the SS, but were also integrated into the state institutions, first of all the Office of the Reichsprotektor (*Amt des Reichsprotektors*).

Locally, there was an accepted tradition of mixed, inter-ethnic marriages. Under these new circumstances, mixed marriages acquired a strong political aspect and a new dimension. Getting married ceased to be mainly a private matter, and turned into a collective issue with fateful consequences. The family was regarded as the fundament of the state and of national existence. Based on perverted racial hygienical premises, state authorities claimed the right to intervene into the most private areas of people's lives:

> Today every German takes an interest in the incontestable determination of his descent, his blood. His position as citizen, his skills, as civil servant, as an officer, as heir to a farm, to be a party member and other rights may depend on that. The court, or the national family stock department [*das Reichssippenamt*], which are to decide disputable cases, apply heredity – and racially based investigations. Everyone is obliged to go through these examinations.[15]

In the territory of the Protectorate, there were, from an official point of view, two kinds of Czech-German marriages. On one side there were marriages between Czech and Sudeten-German partners. On the other side there were mixed marriages between Czech and Reich-German partners (Germans who came to the Protectorate after 15 March 1939 and were not former Czechoslovak citizens). Apart from these two categories, there were a number of other ethnic groups, such as prisoners of war who were sent mostly to the Sudeten-German District as forced labour between 1939 and 1945. These prisoners became objects of the official racial policy not only in the Sudeten-German District but partially also in the Protectorate.[16]

At the beginning of the war, nationally (ethnically) mixed marriages were no exception in the Czech *Lands*. They were customary, although gradually becoming more problematic in times of growing nationalistic sentiments. Still, the number of marriages between Czechs and Germans actually increased during the occupation. In 1938, about 56,000 people married a partner with a different (Czech or German) nationality.[17] A year later, this number grew by nearly 30 per cent to about 78,000. In 1942 the number of such people still exceeded the pre-war numbers.[18]

For a number of reasons children of mixed Czech and Sudeten-German couples were regarded as a major and acute problem by the Nazi authorities. Basically, their existence made a clear division between the two ethnic communities impossible, as these children continued to represent an interlayer (*Zwischenschicht*). In the long run their existence threatened the Nazi national political aim of complete Germanization of the population of the Protectorate. Apart from that, the issue had an important social aspect. Mixed families were seen as less socially adaptable in the local national community. As a result, the children of these mixed marriages became the focal point of the official national policy (*Volkstumspolitik*).

From the very beginning this national policy was based on an unambiguous and preferably permanent classification of every single inhabitant of Bohemia and Moravia as a member belonging to a specific ethnic category. These categories were labelled in bizarre ways such as Czechhood (*Tschechentum*), Germanhood (*Deutschtum*) or Jewry (*Judentum*). Being classified in this way had dangerous and far-reaching implications for every individual. The classification system determined the approach of state authorities to whole groups of Protectorate inhabitants, and motivated specific social policies toward mixed families and their children. At the same time, the implementation of the classification system was watched closely from the Czech side. Any leaning toward the adversary's side in the times of the German occupation was not perceived as a decision of a sovereign individual, but was interpreted in collective terms as a weakening of Czech national positions.

German or Czech?

The first measure of the Nazi strategy in the field of social policy was targeted at married couples, or potential parents. Social, political and economic pressure was exerted by the government on the non-German partners to make them declare themselves of German nationality even before the child was born. The child could then be automatically counted as ethnically German.[19] Many Czechs in the Protectorate used this opportunity, as it facilitated access not only to better-paid jobs, but also to better social security for the family. Administratively, this implied acquiring new citizenship, which in the Protectorate could be either Reich-German or Protectorate.

Shortly after the establishment of the Protectorate and the occupant authorities, a major problem emerged. The protectorate Citizenship Act of 1939 ruled that the nationality of a child was to be determined by the nationality of the head of the family – that is, of the father.[20] However, this legal provision was not in accordance with the practical situation. The mother, who raised the children and spent most time with them, usually defined their nationality and formed their national identity, culturally if not legally.

In order to resolve this problem, a special regulation was issued in 1940, allowing German women who married Czech men to keep their German citizenship unless provided otherwise by a political administration authority. This measure had several goals, but one was to facilitate access of Czech partners to Reich-German citizenship. It was important to ensure that the children of these couples were to be educated in German schools. The result of this provision was an increase in German families, in both the cultural and the legal sense. German mothers in the Protectorate not only could preserve their own state citizenship and nationality, but also were given the chance to determine the state citizenship – and thus the nationality – of their children.

In early 1941 at the latest, a massive state-organized selection programme of Czech partners was launched, using a set of criteria. The most important norms or standards were race and health condition. If the potential German female partner happened to be a member of the Nazi party or one of its many organizations, a recommendation from the local party official was also required. The non-German partner was required not only to declare in writing his positive attitude to the 'German cause', but also to confirm that the children would receive only German upbringing and education.[21]

In other words, a process of Germanization had started, a process expected to be successfully completed within the lifespan of two generations. The German female partner was thus playing the role of a 'missionary' of the 'German cause' in practice, and her children had favourable and totally different opportunities from those of children born to Czech couples. After receiving full citizenship of the Greater German Reich, the Germanizable (*eindeutschungsfähige*) were preferred in the Protectorate, where they were granted many special privileges.[22] They had access to superior social and health care, as well as to high-quality education. They also had substantially better prospects for the future. However, if their German mother neglected the 'German upbringing', the children could be taken away from her and offered for adoption. These and other measures confirmed and deepened the trend introduced at the very beginning of the war – i.e., discriminatory re-definition of ethnically mixed couples by means of organized social selection.

A different approach was applied in the case of children who had already been born, and whose non-German parent refused to adopt German nationality. If all forms of pressure failed, the attention of German governmental and partisan authorities focused on winning over the child – if not the whole family – for the German cause.[23] The child was to be intensely socialized and integrated in a German environment (*Umwelt*). Material and social benefits played a key role in this process as well, as government and partisan bodies actively worked together.

Accepting German nationality usually provoked strongly negative and disapproving reactions among both the close and distant Czech family, and also in the Czech community at large. This hostility took on different forms – from disapproval, to contempt, to outright exclusion. We should not forget that German citizens were also targets of Czech social and economic boycott. The national conflict strongly affected children born in mixed marriages, who from their earliest age became subjects of nationalistically motivated hatred. They were placed in an almost schizophrenic position: being someone 'in between', burdened with the absurdity of a collective identity.

The second, and substantially different group of mixed Czech-German couples were the result of voluntary marriages of Czech Protectorate citizens (mostly women) and Reich-German citizens, who came or were sent to the Protectorate as part of their duties in the civil or military occupying administration after the 1939 occupation of the Czech *Lands*. In general they would work as civil servants or military staff. The frequent private encounters between Czech girls and women and these Reich-German citizens soon became a public secret. Their encounters were seemingly not limited to brief adventures, though we can always consider the pecuniary motives of the Czech partners. Some relations ended in marriages. These marriages, however, were a thorn in the eye of Nazi administration. The German partners were accused of impetuous sexual affairs resulting in marriages with Czech women, undermining the official policy and tarnishing the 'German honour'.[24] According to the opinions of German officials, the German partners far too often accepted a submissive role in the relationship. Interestingly, local Czech Germans usually criticized such couples with the greatest vigour. To many local Czech Germans, mixed marriages of this kind subverted their own struggle to strengthen the German element in Bohemia and Moravia.

According to the twisted Nazi logic, children of such mixed marriages – or rather the Czech upbringing they received from their mothers – sabotaged the Nazi efforts. In the early period of occupation, this situation was symptomatically described by the Nazi party official and 'racial policy practitioner' Erwin Künzel, head of the Sudeten District Border Authority [*Sudetendeutsches Gaugrenzlandamt*], in this manner:

> Today, we are standing here and we can see that the number of mixed marriages has grown ominously. Reich German officials meet a Czech girl for the first time and marry her without a single thought, even though these women come from racially inferior regions. Over 30 per cent of mixed marriages concern German civil servants coming from the Reich, for they lack all feelings towards national interests. Children of Czech mothers will always follow their mothers, making these marriages an explosive charge within the German nation. Mostly soldiers and civil servants marry girls from the nation's margins. [Czech nation's – auth.][25]

The exact number of children born to these ethnically mixed couples is unknown, but can be estimated at a few thousand.

Apart from these long-term systematic and cynically planned actions, many ad hoc acts of repression also occurred. These were usually carried out by various units of the German Security police [*Sicherheitspolizei*] and concerned mostly the activities of the Czech resistance movement. Victims of such repressions were usually condemned to death as traitors. If the condemned had children in formative years who were seen as Germanizable, they were generally taken away from their relatives or guardians. The children were placed in appropriate institutions according to the Nazi ideology, and raised there. It may be assumed that the originally positive eugenical institutions of Lebensborn, e. V. were mostly used for such purposes.[26] This was also the fate of the children of Lidice (Liditz), whose fathers were killed and whose mothers were sent to concentration camps after the assasination of Reinhard Heydrich in June 1942, while most of their children were selected by the officials of the RuSHA and then most probably killed in General Gouvernement.[27]

Between 'Protection' and 'Treatment'

In the Protectorate the official Nazi nationality policy was closely coordinated with the population policy (*Bevölkerungspolitik*), which was guided by the official racial doctrine.[28] This is the reason why the the concept of hereditary health care occupied such an important place.[29] Through hereditary health care, the official Nazi planners and authorities expected fundamental and long-term changes in the reproductive trends in the Protectorate, changes which would 'improve the quality' of the population. Compared to circumstances during the Austrian-Hungarian monarchy and Czechoslovak republic, a qualitatively new dimension to the existing Czech-German and German-Czech relations was introduced by the Nazi regime through the policies of racial hygiene and the strategies of Germanization. The main aim was a systematic change and replacement of hereditary traits within a given population. In the Nazi jargon, treated (*behandelt*) principally meant eliminated or exterminated. The final goal was to be the complete elimination (*gänzliche Ausschaltung*) of all carriers of hereditary illness (*Erbkrankheit*) or hereditary disease (*Erbbelastung*), and the healing of the body of the nation (*Heilen des Volkskörpers*).[30] Expressed in the words of the authors of a significant synthesis of contemporary population genetics, the Hereditary Maths (*Erbmathematik*) from 1938, elimination meant when

> the hereditary disposition of one part of the population is not apparent, either because they die or are made infertile by it, or are being sterilized ... By natural selection 'the taking out' is a result of ontogenese, but planned selection is dependent on the appearance or phenotype.[31]

In the view of the Nazi experts on hereditary and racial hygiene and psychiatry, the most complicated cases of hereditary disease were patients suffering from mental diseases such as schizophrenia, Huntington Chorea, etc. Later the so-called anti-socials (*Asozialen*) such as alcoholics, prostitutes, prisoners, etc. were also included among the complicated cases.

In the Protectorate the Institute for Hereditary and Racial Hygiene (*Institut für Erb- und Rassenhygiene*, abbreviation IERH) was established in April 1940 at the Faculty of Medicine of the German Charles-University in Prague (*Medizinische Fakultät der Deutschen Karls-Universität in Prag*).[32] This institution was extremely important both for the planning of the perverted system of 'hereditary and racial welfare', and for the identification and selection of the potential victims. The IERH was managed by a former student of Ernst Rüdin, who was a highly respected psychiatrist of worlwide renown. After 1943, the manager of the institute was a full professor of hereditary and racial hygiene, the Viennese-born Karl (Johannes) Thums.[33] Two sections, Central Authority for the Hereditary-Biological Registration in the Protectorate of Bohemia and Moravia (*Zentrallstelle für die erbbiologische Bestandaufnahme im Protektorat Böhmen und Mähren*) and Marital Counselling Bureau of the State-operated Sanitary Office in Prague (*Eheberatungstelle des Deutschen Gesundheitamtes in Prag*), were integral parts of the IERH. Between 1940 and 1945 the institute was responsible for the practical implementation of the hereditary health care and racial care agenda, and also for research initiated by the institute.[34] In coordination with the Reinhard-Heydrich-Foundation and later also with the German Research Fund (*Deutsche Forschungsgemeinschaft*), Thums together with the Professor of sociology and social anthropology Karl (Valentin) Müller (1896–1963) developed the special research project of the so-called German hereditary lines in the Czech population.[35] Their main goal was to use the increasing number of mass registration of the mostly Czech-German and German-Czech mixed couples and their children to identify the level of Germanhood (*Deutschtum*) in the youngest generation of the Czech children. The research was meant to help the practical application of racial policies. Because the original records are lacking, the exact number of persons or couples registered remains unknown.

The perverted logic of the highly selective hereditary health care led to the Nazi top-secret program of 'euthanasia' ('*Euthanasie*': *Gnadentod*) launched in the summer of 1939.[36] According to our contemporary knowledge, the so-called 'child-euthanasia' (*Kindereuthanasie*) programme began and continued through the war in parallel with the organized killing of adult patients. Up to September 1941 these killings were organized in special centres. After 1941 the murders took place in a number of other sanatora. The target group was mostly mentally or physically disabled children between birth and puberty. Any child who showed symptomps of handicaps was to be registered by authorized midwives and doctors. The decision on whether the child was to live or to die was then made by three medical 'experts' solely on the basis of a questionnaire from the midwives or doctors. No examination of the child took place. Each expert placed a plus mark or a minus mark under the term treatment (*Behandlung*) on a special form. A red plus mark meant a decision to kill the child, a blue minus mark meant a decision against killing. Three plus signs resulted in the transfer of the child to the Children's Special Department (*Kinderfachabteilung*), where they were mostly killed by injection or gradual starvation.

The two academics appointed by the Berlin T4 headquarters to handle treatment of babies born in mixed marriages in the Protectorate after September 1942 were Carl Gottlieb Bennholdt-Thomsen (1901–1976) and Wilfried Wokurek.[37] Bennholdt-Thomsen was the head of both united Paediatrics Clinics (*Kinderklinik*) at the Faculty of Medicine of the German Charles-University in Prague. Wokurek was full professor and head of the Children's Hospital (*Kinderspital*) in Brno. Both were at the same time also physicians in the Hitler Youth (*Hitlerjugend*) organization.[38] Another Children's Special Department was probably in the lunatic asylum in Dobřany (Wiesengrund). As research into these matters is still in progress, the exact number of child victims is unknown.

Toward the 'Exchange of Populations'

After the defeat and collapse of Nazi Germany in May 1945, many children born between 1939 and 1945 of mixed Czech-German marriages were still considered a problem, but now in a different context. The new context was the planned 'transfer of populations' in which the Sudeten-Germans from re-established Czechoslovakia should be 'transferred' to Germany (both West and East) or Austria.[39] In an atmosphere influenced by mass psychosis and hatred immediately after the end of the war, also aggravated by sabotage actions of Nazi guerrillas, the attitude toward mixed families became extremely hostile. Undoubtedly, communists and their radical followers played a major role in this situation.

All mixed families with a Nazi follower among them (especially in cases of Nazi administrative and coercive staff) were treated harshly. Their wives were considered true 'traitors of the nation' or 'the enemy's hirelings' and their children were seen as 'renegades'.

Those who did not manage to escape before the capitulation of Nazi Germany and stayed in the Protectorate were subjected to mass psychosis and public revenge as soon as the war ended. Some were accused of collaboration with the enemy and of undermining the 'national cohesion'. Some were tried before ad hoc and extraordinary so-called people's tribunal (*lidový soud*). When parents were sentenced, their children were handed over to their Czech relatives or to state institutions. However, Czechoslovak authorities took a special interest in Czech wives of mixed families and their children. Wives who decided to follow their husbands in the transfer were put under pressure by state authorities to stay on. By making the mothers stay in Czechoslovakia, the children would remain in the country. But the women who decided not to follow their husbands suffered from very poor economic and social conditions. Their property was confiscated, and they had severe difficulties in securing a job or a decent social position.

Mixed families and marriages became the motive behind frequent Czech criticism of the drastic methods of the so-called wild transfer in which many Sudeten-Germans lost their lives.[40] Eventually, however, demographic and rational arguments prevailed over extreme nationalism, and former German mothers with their children were allowed to stay in Czechoslovakia.[41] They were nevertheless required to apply for Czechoslovak citizenship within a given period, which meant that state security and police authorities were examining their 'political and national reliability', often subjecting them to humiliating procedures.[42]

According to archives studies to date, no special plan was adopted by the Czech or the Czechoslovak authorities or experts after 1945 to test, for example, the intellectual capability of parents of these children. This does not mean however, that no attempts were made to evaluate the 'biological' quality of the children. Karel Klaus (1896–1969), professor of gynaecology at the Medical Faculty of the re-established Czech Charles University in Prague, for instance, expressed this position in June 1945 uncompromisingly:

> The Germans must leave our country, all of them. There were no righteous and good Germans: some murdered, others cheered and the rest was silent. Not one single German university professor did raise his voice when our schools were closed down, our students and professors were executed, or imprisoned and tortured in concentration camps. In order to meet the challenge of populating regions once Czech but long since Germanized, we need a strong and healthy nation, not only biologically sound, but also spiritually strong, which would subject all its action to a moral judgment.[43]

Conclusion

German occupation of Czech *Lands* substantially changed the child's position in society, childcare and the meaning of children. The Nazi ideology based on the assumption of natural inequality of people, their hereditary determination and the war of races (*Rassenkrieg*) became a major point of departure for the official population policy in the Czech *Lands* and resulted in specific social and health-care measures which had concrete impacts on everyday life, including family relations.

The biological trends in politics acknowledged governmental demands to interfere with traditionally private and intimate affairs of individuals and families through its normative politics. The main objective of these intrusions was to develop a comprehensive system of political and social control. Children and youth played a key part in these efforts, based on Nazi racist and racial-hygiene ideology and doctrine. This perspective defined children as the 'property of the nation'. When these racial criteria were being applied in an ethnically mixed population, relations between national and social groups were changed radically, resulting in a policy of revenge after the war. The position of children was turbulent and turned up side down. The formerly 'preferred'children under the Nazi rule became 'unpreferred' and 'undesirable' after the war.

Answering the introductory question of the effect of the brutal Nazi politics on the progenies who survived both the war and the post-war period, it may be said that they made a major, even crucial impact. Nazi policies created a society in which a bizarre combination of fear, incomprehension, stigma, human intolerance and destruction of personality became the leading motives of the official policy toward the most defenceless members of this society. The true dangerous and absurd character and the long-lasting effects of this modern totalitarian regime are revealed in the way these children were treated.

Notes

1. Francis Galton, *Hereditary Genius: An Inquiry Into Its Laws and Consequences* (MacMillan, 1989), p. 1.
2. See for example Daniel Kevles, *In the Name of Eugenics: Genetics and the Uses of Human Heredity* (Knopf, 1985), Mark B. Adams (ed.), *The Wellborn Science: Eugenics in Germany, France, Brazil, and Russia* (Oxford University Press, 1990), or Diane Paul, *Controlling Human Heredity: 1865 to the Present* (Humanities Press International, 1995).
3. Christopher Pierson, *The Modern State* (Routledge, 1996), p. 100.
4. Michael Burleigh and Wolfgang Wippermann, *The Racial State: Germany 1939–1945* (Cambridge University Press, 1991), and further also Michael Burleigh, *Die Zeit des Nationalsozialismus: Eine Gesamtdarstellung* (Fischer Verlag, 2000), pp. 397–441, and Karl Saller, *Die Rassenlehre des National- sozialismus in Wissenschaft und Propaganda* (Progress, 1961).
5. For this context in Germany see Paul J. Weindling, *Race, health and German politics between National Unification and Nazism 1870–1945* (Cambridge University Press, 1989).
6. Waldemar Kaempffert, 'Science in the Totalitarian State', *Foreign Policy*, 19 No. 2 (1941), S. 438–9.
7. See first of all Jan Křen, *Konfliktní společenství: Češi a Němci 1780–1918* [Conflict Fellowship: Czechs and Germans 1780–1918] (Academia, 1990) and further also Jiří Kořalka, *Češi v habsburské říši a v Evropě 1815–1914: Sociálněhistorické souvislosti vytváření novodobého národa a národnostní otázky v českých zemích* [Czechs in the Habsburg Empire and in Europe 1815–1914: Social and Historical Aspects of the Nation Building and the Nationality Question in Czech Lands] (ARGO, 1996).
8. See first of all Václav Kural and Zdeněk Radvanovský, *Sudety pod hákovým křížem* [Sudetenland under the Swastika] (Albis International, 2002) and Volker Zimmermann, *Die Sudetendeutschen im NS-Staat: Politik und Stimmung der Bevölkerung im Reichsgau Sudetenland (1938–1945)* (Klartext, 1999).
9. Detlef Brandes, *Češi pod německým protektorátem: Okupační politika, kolaborace a odboj 1939–1945* [The Czechs under the German Protectorate: Occupation Policy, Collaboration and Resistance 1939–1945] (Prostor, 1999); further Pavel Maršálek, *Protektorát Čechy a Morava: Státoprávní a politické aspekty nacistického okupačního režimu v českých zemích 1939–1945* [Protectorate Bohemia and Moravia: Aspects under Public Law and Political Aspects of the Nazi Occupational Regime in the Czech Lands 1939–1945] (Karolinum, 2002); and Jan Gebhart and Jan Kuklík, *Dramatické i v?ední dny protektorátu* [Dramatic and Normal Days of the Protectorate] (Themis, 1996).

10. Shiela G. Duff, *A German Protectorate: The Czechs Under the Nazi Rule* (Macmillan 1942), pp. 205–6.

11. Isabel Heinemann, '*Rasse, Siedlung, deutsches Blut': Dass Rasse- und Siedlungshauptamt der SS und die rassenpolitische Neuordnung Europas* (Wallstein, 2003), pp. 127–86.

12. Miroslav Kárný and Jaroslava Milotová and Margita Kárná, *Protektorátní politika Reinharda Heydricha* [The Politics of Reinhard Heydrich in the Protectorate] (TEPS, 1991), p. 109.

13. Oldřich Sládek, *Od 'ochrany' ke 'konečnému řešení': Nacistický teror v českých zemích v letech 1939–1945* [From the 'protection' to the 'final solution': The Nazi Terror in the Czech *Lands* during the Period 1939–1945] (ČSPB, 1983).

14. Miroslav Kárný, 'Hlavní rysy okupační politiky Reinharda Heydricha' [The General Outlines of the Politics of Reinhard Heydrich in the Protectorate], in Kárný et al., *Protektorátní politika Reinharda Heydricha* ... , pp. 5–84 and also Heinemann, '*Rasse, Siedlung, deutsches Blut'*, pp. 127–86.

15. Otmar von Verschuer, *Leitfaden der Rassenhygiene* (Verlag Georg Thieme, 1943), p. 230.

16. See for example Kural and Radvanovský, *Sudety pod hákovým křížem*, pp. 260–82.

17. Chad Bryant, 'Občanství, národnost a každodenní život: Příspěvek k dějinám česko-německých smíšených manželství v letech 1939–1946' [Citizenship, Nationality and Everyday Life: Contribution to the History of the Mixed Czech-German Marriages, 1939–1945], *Kuděj* 4 (2002), pp. 43–54, here pp. 44–5.

18. Ibid.

19. Ibid., pp. 47–52.

20. Ibid.

21. Ibid.; and also Jiří Doležal, *Česká kultura za Protektorátu: Školství, písemnictví, kinematografie* [Czech Culture during the Protectorate: Educational System, Literature, Cinematography] (Národní filmový archiv, 1996), pp. 33–85.

22. Doležal, *Česká kultura*.

23. Bryant, 'Občanství, národnost a každodenní život', pp. 47–52.

24. As it is known from other parts of occupied Europe.

25. The quotation is taken from Bryant, 'Občanství, národnost a každodenní život', pp. 47–52.

26. Jolana Macková and Ivan Ulrych, *Fates of the Children of Lidice – Memories, Testimonies, Documents: Based on the Narrations and Memories of Lidice Women and Children* (Vega-L, 2004) and Eduard Stehlík, *Lidice: Příběh české vsi* [Lidice: The Story of a Czech Village] (Památník Lidice, 2004).

27. Also in both Macková/Ulrych and Stehlík. General Gouvernement (*Das Generalgouvernement 1939–1944*) was the official German term for that part of German-occupied Poland not directly incorporated into Germany. In accordance with Nazi power politics, the very concept of Poland was to be extinguished. The General Gouvernement was intended to function as a kind of reservation for Poles and an economic colony for Germany.

28. Heinemann, '*Rasse, Siedlung, deutsches Blut*', pp. 127–86.

29. Michal Šimůnek, 'Ein neues Fach: Die Erb- und Rassenhygiene an der Medizinischen Fakultät der Deutschen Karls-Universität Prag 1939–1945', in Antonín Kostlán (ed.), *Kapitoly z dějin vědy Studies in the History of Sciences and Humanities* (Wissenschaft in den böhmischen Ländern in den Jahren 1939–1945), 9 (2004), pp. 203–340.

30. Winfried Süß, *Der 'Volkskörper' im Krieg: Gesundheitspolitik, Gesundheitsverhältnisse und Krankenmord im nationalsozialistischen Deutschland 1939–1945* (R. Oldenbourg Verlag, 2003).

31. Harald Geppert and Siegfried Koller, *Erbmathematik: Theorie der Vererbung in Bevölkerung und Sippe* (Verlag von Quelle & Meyer, 1938), p. 68.

32. Šimůnek, 'Ein neues Fach', pp. 203–340.

33. Ibid.

34. Ibid.

35. Karl Thums, 'Volks- und rassenbiologische Untersuchungen in gemischtvölkischen Ehen: Deutsche-Tschechen-Ehen in verschieden Bezirken Böhmens und Mährens – Antrag für das Jahr 1942/1943, 15. August 1942', in: BA Koblenz, R73/15195.

36. See for example Ernst Klee, *'Euthanasie' im NS-Staat: Die 'Vernichtung lebensunwerten Lebens'* (Fischer Verlag, 1983); Michael Burleigh, *Death and Deliverance. 'Euthanasia' in Germany 1900–1945* (Cambridge University Press, 1995) or Henry Friedlander, *The Origins of Nazi Genocide: From Euthanasia to the Final Solution* (University of North Carolina Press, 1995).

37. See Dietmar Schulze, '"Euthanasie" im Reichsgau Sudetenland und im Protektorat Böhmen und Mähren: Ein Forschungsbericht', in: *Beiträge zur NS-'Euthanasie'-Forschung 2002: Fachtagungen vom 24. bis 26. Mai 2002 in Linz und Hartheim/Alkoven und vom 15. bis 17. November 2002 in Potsdam, Berichte des Arbeitskreises zur Erforschung der nationalsozialistischen 'Euthanasie' und Zwangssterilization* (Verlag Klemm & Oelschläger, 2002), pp. 147–168 and also Michal Šimůnek, 'Getarnt-verwischt-vergessen: Die Tätigkeit von em. Univ.-Prof. MUDr Franz Xaver Lucksch (1872–1952) und Univ.-Prof. Dr med. Carl Gottlieb Bennholdt-Thomsen (1903–1971) im Kontext der NS-'Euthanasie' auf dem Gebiet des Protektorates Böhmen und Mähren', in Karen Bayer, Frank Sparing and Wolfgang Woelk, *Universitäten und Hochschulen im Nationalsozialismus und in der frühen Nachkriegszeit*

(Franz Steiner Verlag, 2004), pp. 125–45, here pp. 136–45.
38. Ibid.
39. See the recent monography written by Detlef Brandes, *Der Weg zur Vertreibung 1938–1945: Pläne und Entscheidungen zum 'Transfer' der Deutschen aus der Tschechoslowakei und aus Polen* (Oldenbourg, 2000); also Karel Jech (ed.), *Die Deutschen und Magyaren in den Dekreten des Präsidenten der Republik: Studien und Dokumente 1940–1945* (ÚSD, 2003).
40. Brandes, *Der Weg zur Vertreibung 1938–1945*, pp. 331–51 and also Bryant, 'Občanství, národnost a každodenní život', p. 52.
41. Bryant, p. 53.
42. Ibid.
43. Karel Klaus, 'Za války ve všeobecné nemocnici: Úvodní slovo ke studentům při zahajovací přednášce 11. června 1945' [During the War in the Public Hospital: Introduction Lecture on 11 June 1945], in: *ČLČ* 84 No. 24 (1945), pp. 846–49, here p. 848.

References

Adams, M. (ed.), *The Wellborn Science: Eugenics in Germany, France, Brazil, and Russia*, Oxford: Oxford University Press, 1990.

Brandes, D., *Der Weg zur Vertreibung 1938–1945: Pläne und Entscheidungen zum 'Transfer' der Deutschen aus der Tschechoslowakei und aus Polen*, Munich: Oldenbourg, 2000.

Bryant, C., 'Občanství, národnost a každodenní život: Příspěvek k dějinám česko-německých smíšených manželství v letech 1939–1946' (Citizenship, Nationality and Everyday Life: Contribution to the History of Mixed Czech-German Marriages, 1939–1945), *Kuděj* 4 (2002).

Brandes, D., *Češi pod německým protektorátem: Okupační politika, kolaborace a odboj 1939–1945* (The Czechs under the German Protectorate: Occupation Policy, Collaboration and Resistance 1939–1945), Prague: Prostor, 1999.

Burleigh, M., *Death and Deliverance: 'Euthanasia' in Germany 1900–1945*, Cambridge: Cambridge University Press, 1995.

Burleigh, M., *Die Zeit des Nationalsozialismus: Eine Gesamtdarstellung*, Frankfurt am Main: Fischer Verlag, 2000.

Burleigh, M. and Wippermann, W., *The Racial State: Germany 1939–1945*, Cambridge: Cambridge University Press, 1991.

Doležal, J., *Česká kultura za Protektorátu: Školství, písemnictví, kinematografie* (Czech Culture during the Protectorate: Educational System, Literature, Cinematography), Prague: Národní filmový archiv, 1996.

Duff, S., *A German Protectorate: The Czechs Under the Nazi Rule*, London: Macmillan, 1942.

Friedlander, H., *The Origins of Nazi Genocide: From Euthanasia to the Final Solution*, Chapel Hill, NC: University of North Carolina Press, 1995.

Galton, F., *Hereditary Genius: An Inquiry Into Its Laws and Consequences*, London: Macmillan, 1869.

Gebhart, J. and Kuklík, J., *Dramatické i všední dny protektorátu* [Dramatic and Normal Days of the Protectorate], Prague: Themis, 1996.

Geppert, H. and Koller, S., *Erbmathematik: Theorie der Vererbung in Bevölkerung und Sippe*, Leipzig: Verlag von Quelle & Meyer, 1938.

Heinemann, I., *'Rasse, Siedlung, deutsches Blut': Dass Rasse- und Siedlungshauptamt der SS und die rassenpolitische Neuordnung Europas*, Göttingen: Wallstein, 2003.

Jech, K. (ed.), *Die Deutschen und Magyaren in den Dekreten des Präsidenten der Republik: Studien und Dokumente 1940–1945*, Prague: ÚSD, 2003.

Kaempffert, W., 'Science in the Totalitarian State', *Foreign Policy* 19(2) (1941).

Kárný, M., 'Hlavní rysy okupační politiky Reinharda Heydricha' (The General Outlines of the Politics of Reinhard Heydrich in the Protectorate), in M. Kárný, J. Milotová and M. Kárná, *Protektorátní politika Reinharda Heydricha* [The Politics of Reinhard Heydrich in the Protectorate), Prague: TEPS, 1991.

Kárný, M., Milotová, J. and Kárná, M., *Protektorátní politika Reinharda Heydricha* (The Politics of Reinhard Heydrich in the Protectorate), Prague: TEPS, 1991.

Kevles, D., *In the Name of Eugenics: Genetics and the Uses of Human Heredity*, New York: Knopf, 1985.

Klaus, K., 'Za války ve všeobecné nemocnici: Úvodní slovo ke studentům při zahajovací přednášce 11. června 1945' (During the War in the Public Hospital: Introduction Lecture on 11 June 1945), *ČLČ* 84(24) (1945).

Klee, E., *'Euthanasie' im NS-Staat: Die 'Vernichtung lebensunwerten Lebens'*, Frankfurt am Main: Fischer Verlag, 1983.

Kořalka, J., *Češi v habsburské říši a v Evropě 1815–1914: Sociálněhistorické souvislosti vytváření novodobého národa a národnostní otázky v českých zemích* (Czechs in the Habsburg Empire and in Europe 1815–1914: Social and Historical Aspects of the Nation Building and the Nationality Question in Czech Lands), Prague: ARGO, 1996.

Křen, J., *Konfliktní společenství: Češi a Němci 1780–1918* (Conflict Fellowship: Czechs and Germans 1780–1918), Prague: Academia, 1990.

Kural, V. and Radvanovský, Z. (eds), *Sudety pod hákovým křížem* (Sudetenland under the Swastika), Unstí nad Labem: Albis International, 2002.

Macková, J. and Ulrych, I., *Fates of the Children of Lidice – Memories, Testimonies, Documents: Based on the Narrations and Memories of Lidice Women and Children*, Nymburk: Vega-L, 2004.

Maršálek, P., *Protektorát Čechy a Morava: Státoprávní a politické aspekty nacistického okupačního režimu v českých zemích 1939–1945* (Protectorate Bohemia and Moravia: Aspects under Public Law and Political Aspects of the Nazi Occupational Regime in the Czech *Lands* 1939–1945), Prague: Karolinum, 2002.

Paul, D., *Controlling Human Heredity: 1865 to the Present*, Atlantic Highlands, NJ: Humanities Press International, 1995.

Pierson, C., *The Modern State*, London: Routledge 1996.

Saller, K., *Die Rassenlehre des Nationalsozialismus in Wissenschaft und Propaganda*, Darmstadt: Progress, 1961.

Schulze, D., '"Euthanasie" im Reichsgau Sudetenland und im Protektorat Böhmen und Mähren: Ein Forschungsbericht', in *Beiträge zur NS-'Euthanasie'-Forschung 2002: Fachtagungen vom 24. bis 26. Mai 2002 in Linz und Hartheim/ Alkoven und vom 15. bis 17. November 2002 in Potsdam, Berichte des Arbeitskreises zur Erforschung der nationalsozialistischen 'Euthanasie' und Zwangssterilization*, Ulm: Verlag Klemm & Oelschläger, 2002.

Šimůnek, M., 'Ein neues Fach: Die Erb- und Rassenhygiene an der Medizinischen Fakultät der Deutschen Karls-Universität Prag 1939–1945', in A. Kostlán (ed.), *Kapitoly z dějin vědy-Studies in the History of Sciences and Humanities (Wissenschaft in den böhmischen Ländern in den Jahren 1939–1945)* 9 (2004).

Šimůnek, M., 'Getarnt-verwischt-vergessen: Die Tätigkeit von em. Univ.-Prof. MUDr Franz Xaver Lucksch (1872–1952) und Univ.-Prof. Dr med. Carl Gottlieb Bennholdt-Thomsen (1903–1971) im Kontext der NS-'Euthanasie' auf dem Gebiet des Protektorates Böhmen und Mähren', in K. Bayer, F. Sparing and W. Woelk, *Universitäten und Hochschulen im Nationalsozialismus und in der frühen Nachkriegszeit*, Stuttgart: Franz Steiner Verlag, 2004.

Sládek, O., *Od 'ochrany' ke 'konečnému řešení': Nacistický teror v českých zemích v letech 1939–1945* (From the 'protection' to the 'final solution': The Nazi Terror in the Czech Lands during the Period 1939–1945), Prague: ČSPB, 1983.

Stehlík, E., *Lidice: Příběh české vsi* (Lidice: The Story of a Czech Village), Prague: Památník Lidice, 2004.

Süß, W., *Der 'Volkskörper' im Krieg: Gesundheitspolitik, Gesundheitsverhältnisse und Krankenmord im nationalsozialistischen Deutschland 1939–1945*, Munich: R. Oldenbourg Verlag, 2003.

Thums, K., 'Volks- und rassenbiologische Untersuchungen in gemischtvölkischen Ehen: Deutsche-Tschechen-Ehen in verschieden Bezirken Böhmens und Mährens – Antrag für das Jahr 1942/1943, 15. August 1942', in *BA Koblenz*, R73/15195.

von Verschuer, O., *Leitfaden der Rassenhygiene*, Leipzig: Verlag Georg Thieme, 1943.

Weindling, P., *Race, Health and German Politics Between National Unification*

and Nazism 1870–1945, Cambridge: Cambridge University Press, 1989.
Zimmermann, V., *Die Sudetendeutschen im NS-Staat: Politik und Stimmung der Bevölkerung im Reichsgau Sudetenland (1938–1945)*, Essen: Klartext, 1999.

Part IV

Germany

–11–

A Topic for Life: Children of German Lebensborn Homes

Dorothee Schmitz-Köster

Taboo and Blind Spot

It took almost 50 years for the men and women born or accommodated in a German home of the SS organization Lebensborn to make their story public. They needed this length of time to develop enough self-confidence and courage to speak about their lives and the consequences that being a Lebensborn child had and still has for them. It took almost as long for the German public to be able to deal with this topic in a thoughtful manner. Meanwhile the false image of Lebensborn homes as 'stud farms', in which selected men and women were brought together solely for the purpose of procreating, has increasingly been corrected. Today there are frequent newspaper and magazine articles, and radio and television broadcasts about the Lebensborn children. In addition exhibitions, congresses and a first auto-biography are reaching a wider audience.[1] However, the topic is still neglected by social science, psychology and historical research. The only essay concerning the issue was published in 1970 by Theodor Hellbrügge.[2] Apart from its immediate significance, the results of such research might contribute to ongoing debates in Germany, for example discussions about anonymous birth ('*Babyklappe*'), pre-natal diagnosis and the desire for a perfect child.

The aim of this chapter is also to contribute to the increasing interest by Germans in revealing and discussing the Nazi past of Germany.

Lebensborn e.V.

The SS organization 'Lebensborn' was founded in 1935 and ran nine homes in Germany between 1936 and 1944.[3] These homes offered mainly unmarried preg-nant women the chance to give birth in a quiet place and to accommodate the baby there for a while. But also married women – nearly half of the Lebensborn mothers – came to the homes. They used them as quiet and comfortable maternity clinics, to which they could also bring their older children. In addition there was a political reason: many of them were married to a member of the SS or another NS organization and felt in their proper place within a Lebensborn institution.[4]

Above all the mothers could keep the birth and the name of the father secret. To this end the Lebensborn administration registered the birth only in a separate register of births and did not pass the data on to the authorities. If so desired, the name of the father could be omitted, even though it was known to Lebensborn.

As an initial impression this programme could be seen as a social-welfare programme aiming to protect single mothers, above all, against social discrimination. But the real background was the racial policy of the Nazis. Lebensborn and its leading patron, 'Reichsführer SS' Heinrich Himmler, wanted to increase the number of children who were 'Aryan', healthy and free of hereditary diseases – a pool from which the future elite would be recruited. For this reason only women who could prove that they were 'Aryan', healthy and free of hereditary diseases were taken into the homes. In addition they had to declare the name of the father, who had to fulfil the same criteria. And Lebensborn went a step further in its racial selection. It also examined the children who were born in the homes. Seriously ill or handicapped babies had to leave the homes. In the worst case Lebensborn sent them to a euthanasia clinic, in which the handicapped or seriously ill were killed.

The image of Lebensborn as a 'stud farm' does not correspond to reality. There are no documents which prove this, as Georg Lilienthal's research shows. My own research and the interviews I conducted with Lebensborn mothers and employees also contradict this assumption.

Children in German Lebensborn Homes

About 6,000 boys and girls were born in one of the German Lebensborn homes. The exact number cannot be ascertained because the documents of some homes are incomplete or completely missing.[5] Besides the children who were born in the homes, children of the employees also lived there. In addition babies and small children who fulfilled the selection criteria and whose parents had left them for adoption were sometimes brought to the homes too. Lebensborn was their guardian and tried to find foster or adoptive families for them.

At the beginning of World War II two new groups of children were added. Between 1939 and 1945 about 250 children kidnapped from Eastern European countries were brought to German Lebensborn homes. Because their appearance promised 'Aryan blood', which Himmler had ordered to be collected in the conquered and occupied countries of Eastern Europe,[6] they were snatched from the places where they lived and had to undergo a racial examination. Those who were considered worthy to become Germans (*eindeutschungsfähig*) were taken to homes of the *Nationalsozialistische Volkswohlfahrt* ('National Socialist People's

Welfare') or camps of the *Volksdeutsche Mittelstelle* ('Ethnic German Exchange Centre'). There they were forcibly re-educated and then taken over by Lebensborn, which tried to find foster or adoptive families for them.[7] The second group of children came from Norway. Between 1943 and 1945, about 200 to 250 children of Norwegian mothers and German fathers were brought to German Lebensborn homes. Most of the girls and boys were born in a Norwegian Lebensborn home and given away for adoption by their mothers, who did not know that they would be transferred to Germany. This measure was also based on the racial ideas of the Nazis who idealized the 'Nordic type', and on Himmler's policy of collecting 'Aryan blood' with the aim of improving German racial potential.

Objectives of the Study

During my research on the Lebensborn home *Heim Friesland*, its mothers and employees, I made the acquaintance of some former Lebensborn children.[8] Most of them contacted me directly, told me their stories, asked questions and looked for support in their investigations for their biological parents. Others, after visiting their place of birth and the local registry office, had left their names and addresses to make contact possible. Finally I met some at the meetings of the former Lebensborn children in Germany. The women and men whose acquaintance I have made so far constitute a very small minority of the 6,000 Lebensborn children. To this day the majority of them are not known. No doubt many of them have informed their husbands, wives and children, perhaps even friends and colleagues too, about the circumstances under which they were born. However, we have to assume that some have kept it a secret all these years, and that some may not even know they were born in a Lebensborn home.

For a further study of the SS organization I interviewed 47 Lebensborn children about the circumstances of their birth and its effects on their later life. The objective of these interviews was to picture the family background in which the children were conceived, under what conditions they grew up, the social situation in which they are living today and finally how they handle the topic of Lebensborn. The interviews are the basis for the following considerations.

Starting Life

The majority of my interviewees were born into difficult social circumstances. Their mothers were unmarried when they became pregnant[9] – and German society did not accept illegitimate birth at that time. 'My parents would have thrown me out if they had got to know about my pregnancy', a former Lebensborn mother told me. Another mentioned that her fiancé left her when she told him that he was going to become a father. Very often the fathers were married men who did not want to tell their wives and walked out on their lovers. Unmarried civil servants were dismissed when they became pregnant. Even Nazi organizations such as 'BDM' ('League of German Girls'), 'NS-Frauenschaft' ('National Socialist Women's League') and the general-welfare organization 'NSV' dismissed unmarried officials in the event of pregnancy. This was despite the fact that the Nazis tried to change the Christian middle-class morality in which parenthood and marriage were inextricably linked. Heinrich Himmler and Rudolf Hess, Hitler's deputy, even made propaganda in favour of illegitimate birth. At the same time, the law against abortion was tightened up, but public opinion could not be changed as fast as Himmler and Hess wanted.

Some of the later Lebensborn mothers wanted an abortion but found no one to help them. Others welcomed the child, but did not know how to handle the situation. They therefore hid the pregnancy for as long as possible or hoped in spite of everything for the support of their parents, but were disappointed when the good name of the family was seen as more important than the problems of the daughters. In cases like this admission to a Lebensborn home was a way out. However, all the support offered there – a quiet place to stay far away from home, concealment, the possibility of guardianship, support vis-à-vis the authorities, the child's father and employers – could not answer the fundamental question: what should happen after the birth of the child?

As a precaution most unmarried mothers decided to keep the birth secret from their parents, their relatives and also from the authorities – to protect themselves and the (married) fathers.[10] The authorities of the women's home towns therefore received no information about the birth, as required by law. Furthermore the name of the father was not mentioned on the birth certificate. Only Lebensborn had knowledge of the father, his 'racial suitability' and family status. The organization insisted on authorized acknowledgement of the paternity and payment of alimony on the part of the father. In return for this the organization took care that his name did not appear in any official document or file.

Despite this secrecy, most of the (unmarried) mothers wanted to bring up the child themselves rather than having it adopted.[11] This involved first of all establishing the right conditions, for example finishing their education or apprenticeship, moving to a place where they were unknown, finding a job compatible with childcare. For the children this generally meant staying in Lebensborn homes, while the mothers left a few weeks or months after the birth. And this had negative effects.

Although the homes were well-equipped by the standards of the time, the children often fell ill, sometimes even seriously ill. Some cases show evidence of setbacks in the children's development, resulting from lack of social contacts and emotional care. 'Anne is less developed in her mental and physiological abilities than her peers ... The child is now able to sit upright but cannot walk yet.' This is an extract from the Lebensborn doctor's note which the foster parents received with Anne M. She was aged 14 months and had spent her entire life alone in various Lebensborn homes.

The Lebensborn organization believed that life in a home had no detrimental effects on babies, but considered it an inadequate solution for older children. After one year at the latest the organization insisted that the children left the homes to be taken either by the mother or into foster families. Very often neither was possible. Some children therefore had to spend more time in the Lebensborn homes, while others were passed from one foster family to another.

However, most of my interviewees were brought up by their mothers. One mother had finished her education, another had found a job in which she could arrange work and childcare, others achieved reconciliation with their parents and lived there with the child. In the meantime some women had married the child's father or another man who was willing to take in the child. In this case the secrecy was often ended.

But the experience of being left alone, not having a place where they belonged, and not being wanted by anyone had left traces in the children's psyche. Some of my interviewees mentioned that to this day they cannot be alone, while others suffer from strong fear of loss or a lack of self-confidence. They attribute these problems to their early childhood experiences, and they see rooted in this time their exaggerated desire for reliable relationships and trustworthy partners.

Mothers' Attitudes

The cohabitation of mother and child could not compensate for these mental injuries. On the contrary, many of my interviewees experienced new disappointments and insults when living with their mothers. Most of those I have met or heard about remained distant mothers – regardless of whether they were married or not when the baby was born. According to their children, the mothers kept them at an emotional and physical distance and favoured authoritarian methods of upbringing. Some still believed in the idea of their children belonging to the elite and made high demands on them.

But it was not only the educational philosophy and ideological blindness which made many mothers so cool and severe.[12] Sometimes unmarried mothers continued their early rejection of the child. Gisela Heidenreich, the author of the first Lebensborn-child autobiography, experienced her mother's dening the existence of her daughter in public even when Gisela had grown to be a teenager. She acted as if she had no child – even though mother and daughter lived together in one apartment. The mother of Siegfried S. maltreated her son continually. 'My mother tried to abort me retrospectively', Siegfried S. suggests in order to explain her actions. Others passed on to their child their frustration and bitterness at being rejected by their family or lover, and blamed the child for the situation. Such attitudes were emphasized by the difficult economic, social and moral status of single mothers in the post-war period, regardless of the fact that many families were incomplete because men were killed in the war.

Finally, the fact of having given birth in a Lebensborn home proved to be another difficulty. During the National Socialist regime this meant that the mother was special, and had proved to be 'racially superior' and healthy, but after the war this judgement became a stigma. Thus most of the mothers – with only a few exceptions – did not talk about Lebensborn, even to their children. Evasive answers were given to the questions which inevitably arose when children realized that their birthplace was not their place of residence. Instead the children were told that the Lebensborn home had been a maternity hospital in the countryside, quieter and safer than German towns during the bombing raids. When asked who the father was, most mothers lied, telling that he had been killed in action.

With these answers the women undoubtedly wanted to protect their children from harassment and teasing. Another motivation was to protect themselves, whether they were married or not. A minority of them feared prosecution, especially those who were employees of the organization.[13] Most mothers were afraid that the image of Lebensborn, that of a stud farm, would damage their reputation. For decades everybody 'knew' that women in the Lebensborn homes had been made pregnant by unknown SS men. Books and films persistently spread this image although it was not based on facts. The only protection against this seemed to be to preserve secrecy.

During my research I have met only very few mothers who had talked to their children about their origin from the beginning. It is surely no coincidence that one of them was still a believing Nazi who regretted the lost opportunities her son would have had in the NS regime.

Most mothers broke their silence once the child reached maturity, left home or got married. Yet even then they provided little information. Paul D. received a letter from his mother, telling him the name of his biological father and a few basic facts about the Lebensborn project. He knew that he was not the natural child of his stepfather but had never heard of the Lebensborn homes before. Iris D. received only fragmentary information which did not help her at all: the first name of her father, his birthplace and the fact that he was an SS officer. Only when Hedda W. became seriously ill did her mother break her silence and provide the name of the father. Herta K. never succeeded in persuading her mother to talk, and the old lady died without revealing the name of the father. This obstinate silence had terrible consequences. Due to the complete secrecy of Lebensborn, and the fact that the files containing the names of the fathers and their acknowledgement of paternity disappeared at the end of the war, the children had and have no chance of ever finding out their fathers' names.

However, it should be borne in mind that not every Lebensborn mother acted in this way. Married women normally took their children home once they left the

Lebensborn home after giving birth. Some single women did the same. Some mothers, whose children had a long stay in the Lebensborn home, tried to overcome the neglect and establish a close relationship. There were mothers who told their children very early about their origin. Some illegitimate children were in contact with their fathers from the very beginning. These fathers openly accepted their paternity and also partially acted as fathers. Their attitude made it easier for the mothers to speak freely to the child. But such fathers were rare.

Children's Responses

All interviewees remember a vague feeling of something being wrong in their early childhood. They did not understand the implications – they only understood that they were different. They asked again and again, but after a while they stopped asking because they received only evasive answers. Instead of continuous questioning they started their search without even knowing exactly what they were looking for. They rummaged through drawers and closets, looked desperately into documents and photographs, eavesdropped on adults' discussions – without any result. The longer the situation lasted, the more insecure the children felt. They did not realize that it was the grown-ups who were both deceitful and false: on the contrary, these children started to feel guilty and responsible themselves for the way they were treated. There was only one answer: the strange behaviour of the others must be based on their own character or behaviour, so it was their own fault that they were treated like this. 'I have always felt an outsider,' Rita G. remembers. 'I was not only different than the others, but I was of less worth.'

Most of my interviewees tried to compensate for being 'different' by conformity. They were always obedient to their mother's wishes and hoped for attention, affection and love in return. It was impossible for most of them to express any contradiction or opposition. If they did so, they risked losing their mother's interest. Only a few dared to oppose. Ortwin S. for example argued and fought with his mother, disregarded her wishes and met his father against her will. But he had received so much attention, caring and love that he was strong enough to take the risk. Even as adults many of my interviewees never managed to tackle their mothers. Some preferred to leave home. Hans B. went to sea when he was 17, Paul D. joined the armed forces to escape from his mother's influence. Brigitte K. also chose the same strategy of a drastic good-bye: 30 years ago she cut off all contact with her mother, and they never have talked to each other again since. 'It is useless,' Brigitte K. says, 'I can do without all the pain that mother has caused me.'

A break in relations like this is rare. Most of my interviewees, among them many females, struggled for years to be accepted and loved by their mothers. They did everything possible, taking care of them even if it meant great sacrifices. Some were successful. 'When she became old, we got along well together,' Helga G.

says, 'She visited me frequently and I enjoyed her stays. All of a sudden we were close to each other.' In their later years some mothers were able to give up their distance and harshness and accept their 'child' as it was. 'Since my book turned out to be a success, my mother is proud of me', affirms Gisela Heidenreich, the author of the first autobiography by a Lebensborn child. When her mother realized that other people were interested in the topic, her attitude toward her daughter changed. Suddenly the old woman was able to reflect on herself and her involvement with Lebensborn, in which she had held an important position. In most cases a late change like this does not take place. Most of the old women are not able to modify their attitude. On the other hand the 'children' are not able to justify their right to be informed.

Reactions from Society

It is not known whether the Federal Republic of Germany treated Lebensborn children differently from the former German Democratic Republic (GDR). My interviewees (with one exception) grew up in the old Federal Republic. And there are only very few reports in the media about Lebensborn children in the GDR.

It took decades for Western German society to accept illegitimate children and regard them morally and legally as the equals of legitimate children. The illegitimate Lebensborn children, too, had to suffer from this general disapproval, even in their own families. 'My father did not shrink from calling my son a bastard and telling him again and again that he came from out of the gutter', an old Lebensborn mother told me. Helga G. as a young girl was warned by her concerned grandmother not to become like her mother – immoral and foolish in her attitude toward men. Outside the families there were teachers who outed Lebensborn children by telling the class that their fathers were not dead, but that they had no fathers at all. Other children teased the 'fatherless children' and told them the real facts. Adopted Lebensborn children, who hadn't been informed about the fact report similar experiences.

All these humiliations, the insults and pestering were mostly aimed at the illegitimate birth or adoption, not at the Lebensborn background. The 'conspiracy of silence' created by the SS organization, the mothers, the foster parents and adoptive parents was effective. Lebensborn children who were in the know supported this strategy. Rita G., informed by her mother about her birth in *Heim Harz*, told only her best friend when she was twelve. At the same time she asked for total secrecy and has not been disappointed to this day. Only those children who had been raised in an orphanage where the Lebensborn birth was known, or in foster or adoptive families who did not care for them lovingly, experienced discrimination. Sometimes they were called 'SS brats', which suggested they belonged to the SS by genes or 'blood' and laid a burden of crime and guilt on them.

Lebensborn was an issue for the authorities too. It was known to them that special Lebensborn registry offices (numbered registry office II) had existed and that births were documented in the *Geburtenhauptregister II*. But this knowledge was not passed on by the federal authorities to those concerned. Many of my interviewees only realized when they married that the authorities knew more about their origin than they did themselves. It then became a problem that their birth certificates were missing or incomplete. Sometimes their mothers tried to conceal the Lebensborn birth from the child once again. At Kerstin K.'s wedding, her mother and the registrar were engaged in negotiations behind her back about how to deal with the missing certificate. Kerstin K. soon noticed something was wrong but was told nothing. Yet she felt ashamed and guilty. Other mothers realized that it was finally time to tell their child when he or she was about to get married. Some registrars felt the urge to inform unsuspecting persons about their Lebensborn birth. With other federal authorities Lebensborn children experienced clumsiness, lack of information and sensitivity, and in consequence an absurd, literal application of the law. Oskar D. was 49 when he found out that he was not a foundling (as he had been told by his foster parents and the authorities for years) but instead the child of a Norwegian mother and a German father. He learned that his mother had brought him to Lebensborn, which took him to Germany. With this information a bureaucratic struggle began. Being the child of a Norwegian mother he was a Norwegian citizen himself. Immediately he lost his German citizenship and thus his status as a civil servant. Thanks to the vigorous intervention of a well-known politician he was re-naturalized and reinstated in his former position.[14]

In the GDR the national security authorities ('Stasi') also observed German Lebensborn children who grew up in foster or adoptive families of the GDR. The story of Hans-Ullrich Wesch is well-known. For years the Stasi collected information about his behaviour in school, during his apprenticeship, in the army and at work. Hans-Ullrich Wesch was a suspect simply because he was a Lebensborn child who was imputed to have a 'selected SS member' as father. When he started to gather information about his mother, the 'Stasi' summoned him. He was told that nothing was known about his mother and father and that it would be in his own interest to stop his investigations immediately. After the reunification of the two German states in 1989, Hans-Ullrich Wesch studied his Stasi files and discovered the name of his mother, which the Stasi had known along.[15]

Lebensborn Children as Adults

Today most of my interviewees live an unexceptional middle-class life. Many of them, especially the women, work in social welfare as nurses, doctors' assistants, teachers or therapists. Beyond this the whole range of professions are represented: technical assistants and management consultants, bookkeepers and officers in the armed forces, wholesalers and journalists, artists and scientists. Some lead successful professional lives, while some women live happily as housewives. Though none of them have failed in life, only a very few achieved the positions of leadership Lebensborn had intended for them, ironically enough.

In their political opinions all my interviewees show a distinctly different orientation than that expected by the SS organization. A majority of them believe in liberal, social democratic or socialist ideas, dissociate themselves from the so-called 'brown' fascist ideology of their parents and warn about the development of a neo-Nazi movement. Some interviewees have reflected intensely on the guilt of their fathers as members of the SS. Others, like Adele S., are concerned with the occupations their mothers held during the Third Reich. For six years her mother worked as a midwife in various Lebensborn homes. During Nazi rule the midwives (and not only those connected with the Lebensborn homes) were the ones who had to report to the health administration if a disabled child was born. This information was the first step to being sent to a euthanasia clinic. Even though she never loved her mother, Adele S. cannot bear the thought that her mother might have known about the planned killing and was probably involved in it.

The private lives of most of my interviewees are distinctively different from these of their parents. 'For me it was always important to have a real family', Rita G. declared. As a child she always lived alone with her mother. Her (married) father only showed up from time to time. After this experience, Rita G. married and had children – like the majority of my interviewees. Many report that they need the safety of a relationship, the warmth and strength of their partners. Some even have difficulties being alone. 'I always need someone near me', Hans B. – married for years and father of two children – told me. Once his wife leaves the house, he is bound to leave some minutes later, just to stroll around to be among people.

Partners play an important role in the lives of Lebensborn children. They are often the ones who give the impulse to start investigations. And they not only participate in the searches but also support their partners in digesting the facts which come to light in this process. In the long run this works more often in relationships where the man was born in Lebensborn; the women often have painful experiences of partnerships which have broken down, and they are divorced and living on their own. Many of them report missing the support and affection of a partner which they need as counterbalance to the wounds of their childhood.

Only a few interviewees live completely by themselves without partners or children, and sometimes even without any relatives. 'I do as my mother did, who always lived on her own', Herta K. proudly explains, 'forgetting' that her mother lived with her. The reason for her emphasized independence seems to be the protection she gains from living on her own. Someone who lives alone cannot be hurt.

Searching for Father and Mother

In their childhood and youth the Lebensborn children kept asking who their fathers were, why they were born far away from home and why they had lived in a home for some time. Their mothers' constant refusal to answer silenced them. At the age of 25, 35, 45 other things – profession, marriage, children – became more important. Ten years later, with the 'family phase'coming to an end, the old questions reappear. At this period every single Lebensborn child I interviewed was investigating his or her origin, some for the first time, others resuming their search. The cause for this might be that now one had more time to deal with one's own interests and needs. This might also be the effect of a more tolerant society in which illegitimate births are accepted and the false image of Lebensborn is increasingly being corrected. Furthermore this is a current topic in the media, and it is becoming more difficult to deny one's own origin. Yet another reason cannot be ignored: the generation of Lebensborn mothers and fathers is dying. 'It is my last chance,' believes Irene S., whose mother had never talked about the Lebensborn. 'If I don't ask now, I will never get an answer. Maybe my mother feels the same way and will finally tell me the whole truth.' For those who are still looking for their father or mother, the chance of discovering that their parents are dead eases the search, reduces insecurity and fear of an encounter – as paradoxical as this may seem. 'You never know whom you will find,' Anne M. tries to explain the ambivalent feelings which for a long time kept her from searching. 'You cannot be sure whether or not you will take a liking to the person you find, whether or not you want to give him or her the place of a father or mother.'

For many years Anne was not willing to think about her biological parents. She had known for a long time that she was a Lebensborn child and was adopted. After the death of her adoptive parents she found the names of her biological father and mother in the documents left behind. As her adoptive parents had always spoken disrespectfully about them, Anne was sure that she never wanted to meet them. Why should she look for people who had shown no interest in her? After watching a TV documentary about Lebensborn some years ago, Anne suddenly felt the urge to know everything – everything about Lebensborn, everything about her biological parents. Some information about her father she was able to gather quickly, because he had been registered in a military archive. Yet she was not able to meet him in person as he had died years before. To find the mother was not that easy: she had married a few years after the birth of her daughter and had changed her name. Anne called everyone with her mother's maiden name – without success. She went to cemeteries, searched the graves and interrogated the grave attendants. Again she received only negative answers. Fruitless searches in archives followed. Then chance came to her aid when she met a historian who had her mother's maiden name. By chance his family owned a personal archive which contained the name and address of her mother's sister. Sadly, that woman had to tell her that her mother had died half a year earlier. Nevertheless she was able to meet her half-brothers and -sisters. They told Anne that they had known of an elder half-sister and that their mother had always regretted having given away her first child. This reconciled Anne with her mother.

This woman's search is symptomatic of the investigations done by Lebensborn children. From my interviewees I heard a lot about the ambiguous need for true answers and information, the chance impulse (for example, as a result of a TV documentary) to start the search, the exhausting investigations in archives which requires energy and imagination, the stamina and the strength to continue through various setbacks, and finally the result – and there is no search without any result. When starting their search some women and men are tormented, while others seem to have a mainly historical interest. For some the motive is the question of the possible guilt of their mother, or the contrary, proof of her innocence. 'I started my research,' Rita G. explains, 'because I feel insulted when my mother is spoken of as "Nazi whore" who was available for insemination – as the old story of the Lebensborn goes.' But most of the Lebensborn children are mainly interested in who their parents are, why their mother went into a Lebensborn home, whether they still have sisters or brothers and to which family they belong.

Sometimes Lebensborn children find a family which accepts the new member. Half-brothers and -sisters are excited and curious to encounter somebody unknown who belongs to the family. Old relatives are happy to break the promise of silence they once had given. Fathers enjoy the interest of a 'new' son or daughter and are able to give love and attention in return. But very often the Lebensborn children have to go through rejection and hurt once more. There are half-brothers and -sisters who are afraid of having to divide their legacy and refuse all contact. There are widows of their fathers who pretend to be uninterested in the old stories of their husbands and are not willing to hand out even a photograph. And there are mothers who deny their child once again. Bruno Z.'s mother, for example, welcomed her son with the words: 'I had hoped that you were dead!'

A Second Generation

Today the children of the Lebensborn children are between twenty and forty years old, an age at which they are mainly occupied with their own lives: busy finishing training or education, finding a job or a partner, starting a family and bringing up children. Lebensborn is not on the agenda of most of them. Nevertheless many interviewees report that one of their children took up the topic during their school or university time, and my own experience supports this. 'My grandmother was a midwife in Lebensborn', a young girl once told me after a lecture I had given about the topic. She mentioned a heated debate in class with her teacher who insisted calling Lebensborn a 'stud farm', whereas for her it had been very important to correct this image. Many of my interviewees have noticed exactly the same interest in one of their children, who senses the stain on their mother or father and try to erase it.

Some go further. Paul K., brought up by foster parents, was urged by his son to find out who his biological parents were. Only when he had made a serious start was his son satisfied. Hedda W.'s first son started to show interest in the concentration camp 'Dachau' when he was twelve. After some time he continued his studies on the Holocaust and finally he began to study history. With his interest, his concentration and seriousness this son started to tackle a question his mother had refused to take on, even though in his opinion she had every reason to do so. Hedda W. was not only born in a Lebensborn home. Some years later her mother married a high National Socialist official who adopted Hedda W. After the end of the war, that man was found guilty, and after some years in prison he was executed. Neither his wife nor his daughter ever disavowed him. 'He was my father and a loving one', explains Hedda W. This was a contradiction which the grandson could not live with. Finally he broke with his mother. The story of another interviewee, Oskar D., and his daughters shows that the second generation not only deals with the problems their parents should have dealt with but sometimes actually inherit them.[16] Both young women repeated the situation into which their father had been born and became pregnant without being married. The first committed suicide just before giving birth, the younger one gave birth to the child but neglected it, disappeared one day and left the child with its grandparents.

A Topic for Life

To this day my interviewees are trying to shed light on the dark corners of their past. Only very few are still searching for their father and/or mother – most of them succeeded in finding out the names and the real persons. Today most of them are gathering widely dispersed documents and trying to find explanations for some remaining questions. But even the solution to their life-puzzle cannot heal early wounds. The fact is that many of them are hurt and damaged – because they have been unwanted, left alone and pushed from place to place, because mothers lied to them and kept them at an emotional distance, because their fathers vanished and did not care, because they were called 'bastard' or 'SS brats' and felt guilty and ashamed of their birth under the sign of the SS. Even if much of it has been put into perspective or partially overcome, a feeling of loss and shortcoming still exists for many of the Lebensborn children. For them, it will never be normal and accepted to be a 'Lebensborn child'. Maybe these feelings can be soothed through the planned association of German Lebensborn children. Rita G. puts it like this: 'When we Lebensborn children meet, it is almost like coming home.'

Notes

1. See Georg Lilienthal, *Der Lebensborn e.V.* (Fischer, 1993). Christiane Ehrhardt: *Brand-Zeichen: Kinder aus dem Lebensborn,* Bayrischer und Mitteldeutscher Rundfunk 1993. Dorothee Schmitz-Köster, *Deutsche Mutter, bist du bereit. Alltag im Lebensborn (*Aufbau Tb, 1997, 2002). Georg Mascolo and Hajo Schumacher, 'Kinder für Führer und Stasi', *Der Spiegel,* No. 25, 16.6.1997. *Deutsche Mutter, bist du bereit: Alltag im Lebensborn.* An exhibition in Delmenhorst, Bernburg and Wernigerode (there under the title: *Lebensborn: Vom Gerücht zur Legende*) 2001, 2002, 2003. Gisela Heidenreich, *Das endlose Jahr. Die langsame Entdeckung der eigenen Biografie – ein Lebensbornschicksal* (Scherz, 2002).
2. Hellbrügge examined 70 young men and women aged between 17 and 23 who lived in Lebensborn homes at the end of World War II and grew up later in foster families or in orphanages. Compared to other children they suffered from depressions, neurotic fears, low educational standards, difficulties in social contacts, lack of emotion and a low intelligence quotient. Hellbrügge does not mention if the 70 young people originally came from foreign countries or had German parents. See Theodor Hellbrügge, 'Das Deprivations-Syndrom in Prognose, Diagnose und Therapie', *Bericht der Arbeitstagung vom 15. bis 17. Mai 1968 für Heimärzte und Heimleiter an Säuglings- und Kinderheimen* (Frankfurt am Main, 1970), pp. 42–59.
3. In Germany there were nine Lebensborn homes, but births only took place in seven of them. *Heim Sonnenwiese* (Kohren Sahlis near Leipzig) was a children's home; *Heim Franken* (Ansbach) seemed to have been a home for mothers, children and employees who were evacuated from other homes at the end of World War II.
4. See Schmitz-Köster, *Deutsche Mutter, bist du bereit* , pp. 43–4, pp. 137–68.
5. Complete files concerning registration, birth, death and marriage in the Lebensborn homes exist from *Heim Friesland* (near Bremen), *Heim Harz* (Wernigerode) and *Heim Hochland* (Steinhöring near Munich). The files from *Heim Taunus* (Wiesbaden), *Heim Kurmark* (Klosterheide near Berlin) and *Heim Schwarzwald* (Nordrach) are incomplete because employees hid them, destroyed them or did not fill in all birth data as correctly as they did during the last weeks of World War II. The files of *Heim Franken* (Ansbach), *Heim Sonnenwiese* (Kohren Sahlis near Leipzig) and *Heim Pommern* (Bad Polzin, now in Połczin-Zdrój) have vanished and could not be found until quite recently.
6. See Heinrich Himmler: 'Rede vor Reichs- und Gauleitern in Posen', 6.10.1943, in B.F. Smith and A.F. Peterson, *Heinrich Himmler. Geheimreden 1933–1945 und andere Ansprachen* (Propyläen, 1974).

7. See Lilienthal, *Der Lebensborn e.V.,* pp. 194–221.

8. See Schmitz-Köster, *Deutsche Mutter, bist du bereit* , pp. 254–64.

9. Statistics for 1940 from Lebensborn administration show that 53.4 per cent of the women were unmarried; in 1941/42 the percentage was 64.3. See Schmitz-Köster *Deutsche Mutter, bist du bereit,* p. 51. In my sample most of the mothers were unmarried when the baby was born.

10. For *Heim Schwarzwald* the following figures exist: 88 births from married women and 157 births from single mothers. Of the latter, 34 fathers had acknowledged paternity by name and 60 without name, and 63 birth registrations there is no hint about fathers at all.

11. As can be seen in files from *Heim Schwarzwald* and *Heim Friesland* very few children were adopted, often by their own mother or her later husband. In the beginning Lebensborn had not expected such a low rate of adoption, later on the organization idealized the fact that the mothers kept the children and regarded it as a sign of their 'racial worth'. See Schmitz-Köster, *Deutsche Mutter, bist du bereit,* p. 44.

12. Contemporary views of a proper mother-child relationship were introduced to Germany some years after the war. During the 'Third Reich' the following educational guidelines dominated: strict rules, suppression of the child's own ideas and the lack of emotions. See J. Haarer: *Die deutsche Mutter und ihr erstes Kind* (Carl Gerber, 1938).

13. After the end of the war former Lebensborn employees living in West Germany were denazified and mostly classified as followers. It is not known whether the East German government regarded the former employees as perpetrators of crimes. The Nuremberg court which ruled on the Lebensborn project judged it to be a welfare organization. The four accused members of the leadership were declared not guilty with regard to their work for the project. Nevertheless three of them were pledged guilty for their membership in the SS as criminal organization. See *The RuSHA case. Military Tribunal No. 1, Case VIII.* In Trials of War Criminals before the Nuremberg Military Tribunals under Control Council Law No. 10, Nuremberg 1946–April 1949, Vol. IV, pp. 597–1185, Vol. V, pp. 1–177

14. See Lilienthal, *Der Lebensborn e.V.,* pp. 259–60

15. See Antje-Maria Lochthofen, 'Der Makel Lebensborn: Hans-Ullrich Wesch aus Altenburg wurde jahrelang in falschem Glauben gelassen', *Thüringer Allgemeine,* 28.7.2001.

16. See Dan Bar-On, *Die Last des Schweigens. Gespräche mit Kindern von Nazi-Tätern* (Rowohlt, 1996); also Harald Welzer et al., *Opa war kein Nazi. Nationalsozialismus und Familiengedächtnis* (Fischer, 2002).

References

Bar-On, D., *Die Last des Schweigens. Gespräche mit Kindern von Nazi-Tätern,* Frankfurt am Main: Rowohlt, 1996.

Ehrhardt, C., *Brand-Zeichen: Kinder aus dem Lebensborn,* Bayrischer und Mitteldeutscher Rundfunk, 1993.

Haarer, J., *Die deutsche Mutter und ihr erstes Kind,* Munich: Carl Gerber Verlag, 1938.

Heidenreich, G., *Das endlose Jahr. Die langsame Entdeckung der eigenen Biografie – ein Lebensbornschicksal,* Munich: Scherz Verlag, 2002.

Hellbrügge, T., 'Das Deprivations-Syndrom in Prognose, Diagnose und Therapie', *Bericht der Arbeitstagung vom 15. bis 17. Mai 1968 für Heimärzte und Heimleiter an Säuglings- und Kinderheimen,* Frankfurt am Main, 1970.

Himmler, H., 'Rede vor Reichs- und Gauleitern in Posen', 6.10.1943, in B.F. Smith and A.F. Peterson, *Heinrich Himmler. Geheimreden 1933 – 1945 und andere Ansprachen,* Frankfurt am Main: Propyläen, 1974.

Lilienthal, G., *Der Lebensborn e.V.,* Frankfurt am Main: Fischer, 1993.

Lochthofen, A-M., 'Der Makel Lebensborn: Hans-Ullrich Wesch aus Altenburg wurde jahrelang in falschem Glauben gelassen', *Thüringer Allgemeine,* 28.7.2001.

Mascolo, G. and Schumacher, H., 'Kinder für Führer und Stasi', *Der Spiegel,* No. 25 (16 June 1997).

Schmitz-Köster, D., *Deutsche Mutter, bist du bereit. Alltag im Lebensborn,* Berlin: Aufbau Tb, 1997, 2002.

Welzer, H., Moller, S. and Tschuggnall, K., *Opa war kein Nazi. National-sozialismus und Familiengedächtnis,* Frankfurt am Main: Fischer, 2002.

–12–

Besatzungskinder and Wehrmachtskinder: Germany's War Children

Ebba D. Drolshagen

In Search of the Proper Words

A thorough analysis of the semantics of seemingly innocuous and randomly coined terms can reveal underlying social mechanisms which are far from innocuous and random. Frequently, the individual and social consciousness about something (or someone) depends on an existing term which denotes the fact or the person in question. Relevant here are terms for human beings who are grouped together because they are perceived as having something in common. Societies consider only some of all possible groups as relevant enough to create a word for them; examples are the Norwegian word *krigsbarn* (war child) and the German word *Besatzungskind* (child of occupation). Both denote groups with comparable definitions, the most important being that the fathers of the children are foreign occupation soldiers. In both countries, the members of these groups were and are also called abusive names alluding to their fathers' national background.

The question of who is singled out for a name – and why! – is important. It can tell us much about who is regarded as 'one of us' (and thus does not need a separate label) and who is set apart (not only) verbally.

A possible reason for the lack of a term is the existence of a taboo around an issue. Another and more common reason is that only some groups are considered relevant enough to 'deserve' a word. This criterion of 'relevance' means that semantic holes in a language – i.e. words which do not exist where a word might be created – can be very telling. Examples here would be a single expression for the children of a country's own soldiers and foreign women (for example a German word for the offspring of German Wehrmacht soldiers in the occupied European countries, or a Norwegian word for the children of Norwegian soldiers in Germany).

In this chapter, the existence, and *non-existence*, of terms to denote children of native women and occupant soldiers during World War II and its aftermath will be my point of departure for the exploration of two questions: (a) what does the

German public know about Germans whose fathers were soldiers in the allied forces, and (b) what do they know about the descendants of Wehrmacht soldiers in Europe in general and in Norway in particular? I will also give an overview of the media coverage and the research done on both topics. Through answering these (ostensibly) simple questions, I may also identify patterns of visibility and invisibility surrounding these children, as seen from Germany.

First, I want to look at some German terms used, often interchangeably, in literature, the media and research as well as in informal settings about children born in times of war and occupation. These terms are: *Kriegskinder* (children of war), *Besatzungskinder* (children of occupation), and *Wehrmachtskinder* (children of the Wehrmacht).

A fourth term which occasionally comes up in this context is *Soldatenkinder* (children of soldiers or soldier-children). It is used to describe at least three different groups: children who are soldiers, the offspring of soldiers in general, and sometimes, though rarely, the offspring of occupation soldiers. Since I find *Soldatenkinder* too general to be of any use as a definition here, I shall restrict myself to the first three terms, discussing each of them in turn and suggesting a definition for each one.

Kriegskinder

Kriegskinder is a broad term for children everywhere and at all times who live through a war and consequently suffer various degrees of trauma. In recent years, however, the word has come to denote two clearly defined groups of people. The members of one group are Germans; the members of the other Norwegians.

In 2000, a German conference which originally dealt with war children in Bosnia and other recent war zones led to the foundation of a German organization named *Kriegskinder* – meaning the approximately 12 million Germans who were children during World War II in Germany.

Now aged 60–75 years old, they never spoke in public about their experiences, memories or traumata. Harald Welzer, head of the Research Group 'Interdisciplinary Memory Research', suggests that the book *Der Brand* by Jörg Friedrich might be at least partly responsible for the fact that this silence is ending.[1] Friedrich's book, published in 2002, discusses the bombing of German cities by the Allied forces and describes the sufferings of German civilians. Never before had this aspect of World War II been told in such detail. Friedrich's book triggered intense debates. Welzer conjectures that a whole generation of Germans recognized themselves in Friedrich's book. This allowed them to interpret their haunting memories not as a personal and individual burden but as a fate they share with many others. As a consequence, some organized themselves into a group and in doing so, they appropriated the term *Kriegskinder* in order to make themselves visible as a group.[2] And once all those with shared experiences and memories had publicly been defined as a *group*, the new term offered a new interpretational frame for the biographies of many others.

In April 2003, the first (privately organized) conference was held: 'Kriegs-kinder: Eine unauffällige Generation und ihre vergessene Trauer' (Children of War: An Inconspicuous Generation and its Forgotten Sorrow). There were 50 participants expected, but in fact 200 came. This resulted in the foundation of an organization (*Verein*) named *kriegskind.de* in November 2003.[3] The organization seems to be growing. And as can be expected, the first autobiographical books written by German Kriegskinder have already been published.

This development strongly resembles the foundation of the Norwegian *krigs-barn* organization in 1985. There is, however, one very important difference: while the word *Kriegskinder* has always been quite neutral in German, the Norwegian word *krigsbarn* already denoted a clearly defined group *and* the word carried a negative connotation.

Over the last few years, *Kriegskinder* has increasingly been used for these *krigs-barn*: the Norwegian children of Norwegian women and German men who were stationed in Norway as soldiers of the German Wehrmacht between 1940 and 1945.[4] The term has become quite common since the German media (during the years 2000 to 2002) reported extensively about a lawsuit which several Norwegian *krigsbarn* filed against the government in an attempt to obtain compensation. In these articles, *Kriegskinder* is always used in the combination *norwegische Kriegskinder* (Norwegian war children).

Kriegskinder is the literal German translation of the Norwegian word *krigsbarn*. *Krigsbarn*, however, has very strong connotations. In Norway, *krigen* (the war) is always understood as referring to the five years of the German occupation, years which to this day have an extremely important function for the Norwegian self-image. For most Norwegians, the word *krig* conjures up a wealth of associations; one Norwegian social anthropologist even wrote that 'the myth about the war is like a creation myth for the modern Norway'.[5] As a consequence, *krigsbarn* has many connotations not carried over to the seemingly accurate German translation.

Although almost all German newspapers and magazines ran articles on the Norwegian children of war, the term *Kriegskinder* has never been extended to mean 'European (i.e., non-German) children of German Wehrmacht soldiers'. Only a proper context could possibly ensure that mentioning 'die französischen Kriegskinder' (the French children of war) would be interpreted as meaning 'Frenchmen with German-soldier father'. I will return to this point later in this chapter.

Besatzungskinder

A German word closer to the meaning of the Norwegian *krigsbarn* is *Besatzungskinder*, which, when literally translated, means 'children of occupation'. The connotations of the German word *Besatzung* are neutral with regard to the time and place of the occupation and does not carry the same strong connotations as the Norwegian word *krig*. Theoretically, *Besatzungskind* could describe any child born during a time of occupation anywhere. This, however, is not the case. The German usage is *very* specific: *Besatzungskinder* are children of Allied soldiers (American, Soviet, British and French, but also Norwegian) and German (or Austrian) women. These children were born in or after 1945/46, and most of them grew up in Germany or Austria. Frequently, the word denotes an even smaller subgroup: the children of Afro-American and Afro-French soldiers.

Reliable statistics on the total number of *Besatzungskinder* are hard to come by. Those available do not include the offspring of Russian soldiers born in the Russian Zone and the subsequent German Democratic Republic. The only available figures for West Germany were published by the *Statistische Bundesamt Wiesbaden* (Federal Bureau of Statistics) in 1956. They set the number of children with an 'allied' father at roughly 68,000 – of whom 37,261 had an American and 3,137 Soviet fathers. An additional figure specifies that 3,194 children were conceived as a result of rape.[6]

These figures, however, reflect *only* children of single mothers, since by German law at that time, *all* children of single mothers were under professional guardianship – *Jugendämter* (Youth Welfare Offices) and *Vormundschaftsgerichte* (Guardianship Courts) – and could thus be included in all kinds of statistics. A West German government hearing in March 1952 estimated a total of 94,000 *Besatzungskinder* in West Germany.[7]

Children of American Soldiers

The term Besatzungskinder is strongly associated with the children of American GIs – most notably of Afro-American GIs. The number of 'occupation babies' born peaked in 1946. They entered school in 1952, and started their vocational training in 1960. These transitions, as Lemke Muniz de Faria states in her doctoral thesis 'Zwischen Fürsorge und Ausgrenzung', were always accompanied by furious public debates.

In 1994, two German historians analysed four psychological and anthropological studies on Afro-German children. They were conducted between 1952 and 1960 and focused on the concepts of 'race' and 'difference' as criteria of this social minority.[8] The first research on the childhood of the offspring of Afro-American soldiers in Europe was done by the Austrian historian Ingrid Bauer. She presented the findings of her research in 1999 at a conference in Vienna.[9]

The studies show that both the mothers of Afro-German children and the children themselves were discriminated against (a fact which most people who lived in Germany at that time vividly remember). Some Germans and Austrians saw the mixed 'racial' ancestry of the children as proof that they were 'not one of us'. Interestingly, many Afro-Americans in the USA saw the children as 'one of us' and tried to help with money and adoptions. This was met with approval by many Germans, who wanted to send the children – for their own good, as they stressed – to Africa or to the USA for adoption by black couples.

Similar claims ('not one of us') and problem-solving strategies ('export the problem' by deporting the children) are well known from the Norwegian post-war debates on *krigsbarn*.

Children of British and French soldiers

I know of no German publication – be it in the mass media or in 'academia' – focusing on children of British or French soldiers. I suspect that the term *Besatzungskinder*, which from early on was strongly linked to children of GIs, might not even be associated with them any longer.

Children of Soviet Soldiers

It is widely know that in spring 1945, soldiers of the Red Army – while they were surging west and during and after the battle for Berlin – systematically raped women, most of them German. In 2002, the study *Berlin: The Downfall, 1945* by the British military historian Antony Beevor presented ostensibly new research on the mass rapes. His figures, however, had already been published in 1992 by the German team of Helke Sander and Barbara Johr.[10] Sander and Johr calculated the number of women in Berlin at the time and went through the medical files and other archive material of two large hospitals in Berlin (documents in other hospitals having already been destroyed). The two most important data were (a) the number of illegal, but openly performed abortions and (b) the mother's information about the father of children born between September 1945 and December 1946. Through complicated statistical and demographic evaluations, they arrive at the number of approximately two million women who were raped by Russian soldiers between the spring and autumn of 1945, 40 per cent of them more than once. In Berlin alone, over 110,000 girls and women suffered this fate. They furthermore conjecture that – in spite of mass abortions – about 1,100 children conceived as a result of rape were born in Berlin. If this is correct, 5 per cent of all children born in Berlin between the winter of 1945 and the summer of 1946 must have a Russian father. German does not have a separate word to denote these and only these children as a group, and it is my conjecture that no language does.

An unknown number of children of Soviet soldiers were born between 1946 and 1990 in the German Democratic Republic. Since these soldiers were forbidden any contact with German civilians, the sheer existence of these offspring was a strict taboo. There are only two known reports of Germans whose fathers belonged to the Red Army and who found their fathers.[11]

At the Children of War conference in Berlin in October 2002, a colonel (*Oberst*) of the Red Army told the audience of his secret love affair immediately after the war with a German woman who lived as his 'servant' in his house. The couple had a son. The Colonel was recalled to Moscow. When he returned to Berlin, his lover, their son and his lover's mother had been deported to Russia, where presumably they were killed.[12]

Children of Norwegian Soldiers

From 1947 to 1953, a total of 50,000 Norwegian Allied soldiers, the so-called *Tysklandsbrigade* (The Independent Norwegian Brigade Group), were stationed first in the German Harz area and later in Northern Germany. Only very few Germans outside the immediate geographical proximity of these former Norwegian garrisons know that Norwegian soldiers were part of the Allied forces.[13]

In the autumn of 2002, I contacted the mayor's assistant in Goslar, one of the early *Tysklandsbrigade* headquarters. *Tysklandsbrigade* veterans from Norway had held a reunion there just a few weeks earlier, and in preparation for this event, the mayor's assistant had done research into their history in Goslar. In our first conversation, he said that he had never heard of children with a Norwegian father. However, since he had not specifically looked for them, he checked the local birth registers from 1946 to 1948. He could not find a single entry with a Norwegian father.[14]

This seems odd. For one thing, the troops returning from Germany had a very high incidence of venereal diseases compared with that of the troops stationed in Norway.[15] In addition, several Norwegian veterans told me in personal conversations of numerous relationships between Norwegian soldiers and German women, some ending in marriage, most not. Not only the veterans today, but also official Norwegian reports on the *Tysklandbrigade* in the years 1947–1954 mentioned pregnancies resulting from these affairs. The children of unwed women led to enduring problems between German and Norwegian authorities regarding child alimony. The Norwegian historian Kåre Olsen mentions that by the spring of 1952, there had been 42 such cases brought to the attention of the Norwegian authorities.[16] As few in number as these children may be, it is still worth mentioning for the purpose of this chapter that the Norwegian language does not have a special term for them.

In all of Germany and in all Allied zones, however, *Besatzungskinder* were called names by their peers as well as by adults, names meant to hurt and to stigmatize them. They consisted of the (presumed) nationality of the father and an insulting word for an illegitimate child such as *Amibankert* and *Russenbalg*. On the one hand, such words symbolically deny a child its German citizenship by calling it 'American', 'Russian', 'French', etc.; on the other hand, they denounce the mother by alluding to her loose morals. Identically constructed words were given to the German lovers of the allied soldiers: the nationality of the lover was combined with an insulting word for a prostitute. Examples are *Amihure* or *Franzosen-flittchen*.[17]

Wehrmachtskinder

Between 1935 and 1945, there were 18 million men who served as soldiers in the German Wehrmacht. They were sent to Czechoslovakia, Poland, Norway, Denmark, the Netherlands, Belgium, Luxembourg, France, the Channel Islands,[18] Hungary, Bulgaria, Yugoslavia, Romania, Libya, Egypt, Greece, and the Soviet Union, as well as Finland and Italy.[19] Many soldiers had intercourse with women of the occupied territories. In some countries, especially in eastern and south-eastern Europe, rape was tolerated by the German Wehrmacht; in other countries, especially in northern and western Europe, it was not. But it is only fair to say that many women all over Europe actually fell in love with the German soldiers, enjoyed their company and wanted intimate contact with them. Many soldiers fathered a child. Some, of course, never learned about their 'foreign' child – in some cases because their contact with the mother was too short; in other cases, where the prospective parents did have a closer relationship, because the soldier was transferred or died before learning about the pregnancy.[20]

The total number of children born between 1940 and 1946 whose fathers were German soldiers of the Wehrmacht and whose mothers were citizens of one of the Nazi-occupied countries is completely unknown. Estimates range between 250,000 and the seemingly exaggerated total of 2 million. It is quite remarkable that in spite of this, the German language has no word for them as a group (nor did it have one during or directly after World War II).[21] This blank in the German lexicon is by no means arbitrary. On the contrary, it corresponds to the complete lack of awareness of their existence.[22] To denote them *and only them* as a separate group, I suggest the word *Wehrmachtskinder* – literally: 'children of the Wehrmacht'. The advantage of this term is that it clearly refers to Germany and a specific period of time in German history. The obvious drawback of the term, of course, is that terminologically it excludes all men who did not serve in the Wehrmacht but in the police force, the Security Service (*Sicherheitsdienst*), etc. However, the main function of the term may be to fill a 'semantic hole' in the German language and to raise public consciousness about the children it denotes.

The *Wehrmachtskinder* led very different lives depending on where they grew up. There must be tens of thousands of Germans (and Austrians) who are binational *Wehrmachtskinder* in the above-mentioned sense. They grew up in Germany (or Austria) with their biological parents who met during the war in one of the occupied countries, married and lived with their child or children in the soldier's home country. These 'binational German' *Wehrmachtskinder* have never been defined as a separate group – either by society or by themselves. This might be due partly to the fact that Germans, unlike Americans, show little interest in their ethnic heritage.

During the war, several hundred *Wehrmachtskinder* were brought from Norway to Germany after their mothers had given them up for adoption. All steps were efficiently arranged by Lebensborn.[23] Some of the children still live in Germany, other were brought back to Norway after the war.[24] Lebensborn was also involved in kidnapping countless children from their mothers or parents in eastern and southeastern Europe. Although little is known about the fate of these children, it can be assumed that many of them still live in Germany and are completely unaware of their backgrounds. It is likely, but not documented, that some of them were *Wehrmachtskinder*.

The majority of the *Wehrmachtskinder*, however, grew up in their mothers' countries, with or without their mothers (only rarely with their German fathers). The German public knows virtually nothing about these hundreds of thousands of *Wehrmachtskinder* who live all over Europe. Whenever I mention them in a conversation, the standard reaction is, 'It never occurred to me', an amazing comment when one considers the possible number of people involved.

The Wehrmachtskinder in the German Media

Norway

There are, however, some exceptions to the rule, some points of visibility: the Norwegian *Wehrmachtskinder* have indeed attracted a certain amount of publicity in Germany. They were first brought to the attention of the German public not by a historian, but by the famous Norwegian author Herbjørg Wassmo. Her novel *The House With the Blind Glass Windows* told the moving story of a Norwegian 'German child', Tora. It was published in Germany in 1984 and sold very well.[25]

In 1987, Lothar Kunst wrote a long article for the weekly *Die Zeit* with the title *Über das Schicksal norwegischer Kinder deutscher Soldaten* but the whole issue did not gather speed until 10 years later when *Der Spiegel* in June 1997 carried a sensational story about Norwegian Lebensborn-children in the German Democratic Republic, whose identities had been misused by the secret police Stasi as cover for their own secret agents.[26] The German media coverage of Norwegian *Wehrmachtskinder* peaked in 2000 and again in 2002, when seven of them filed a petition in an Oslo court to obtain compensation for the harsh treatment they claimed they had suffered from the Norwegian government during their childhood.

My personal archives, far from complete, include more than 30 magazine and newspaper articles on Norwegian *Wehrmachtskinder*, and more than ten TV programmes that dealing exclusively or in part with them. The headlines of the articles speak for themselves: *Ihr Verbrechen: das Kind eines Deutschen zu sein* (Their Crime: to be the Child of a German), *Verhaßte deutsche 'Bastard-Kinder'* (Hated German 'Bastards'); Die 'Kinder der Schande' (The 'Children of Shame', which was the title of several articles); *Verdammt, deutsch zu sein* (Damned to be German); *Gang durch die Hölle* (A Walk through Hell); *Das bittere Los der 'Deutschenkinder' Norwegens* (The Bitter Fate of Norway's 'German Children').

The tone of almost all of these articles is, at first glance, neutral. They repeat the stories and the claims of the plaintiffs. Some add interviews with Norwegian experts such as Kåre Olsen and others, but almost without exception they generalize from the cases at hand to all 8,000 to 12,000 *krigsbarn,* which results in a seriously skewed picture of the actual facts.

A subtlety completely lost on most journalists is that not all Norwegian *Wehrmachtskinder* were 'Lebensborn-children', i.e. children registered by Lebensborn. Moreover, some articles insinuate and some elaborate explicitly the old myth that Himmler's Lebensborn was an 'elite brothel'. An article in one of Germany's foremost national newspapers, *Die Süddeutsche Zeitung*, covering the Berlin exhibit of portraits of Norwegian *Wehrmachtskinder* by Einar Bangsund, is a typical (although quite drastic) example:

> Himmler believed that since the Norwegians were direct descendants of the Vikings, they had the perfect genes for his organization, Lebensborn, founded in 1935. This organization's aim was to breed a race of super Aryans from suitable human genetic material. The crossing of blond Norwegian Valkyries with valiant German soldiers would guarantee perfect Teutonic offspring.[27]

Although it is a fact that Lebensborn was established as an instrument to further Nazi racial policy, the idea of 'breeding' institutions is totally unfounded. However, such fantasies about the Nazi organization, Lebensborn e.V., are still believed by most Germans and, as in the extract above, repeated in connection with the Norwegian *Wehrmachtskinder*.

A 'fringe benefit' of the media coverage of the trials in Norway seems to be that it allows the contemporary German public to consider the guilt question in a new, almost consolatory light: many articles convey an implicit malicious joy over the

fact that Europe's star pupil, Norway, has been caught in a deed so obviously indecent and inhumane as well as relief that Germany, for once, is off the hook.

None of the journalists call the 'Norwegianness' of the problem into question.
This surfaces, for instance, in the fact that not one of them comments on the fact
that the German government and an overwhelming majority of the German fathers
could have tried to help the 'German children' in Norway, but chose *to this day* to
remain passive. Also unmentioned is the possible existence of *Wehrmachtskinder*
in other countries.

Soviet Union

There is much speculation and little knowledge about the number of
Wehrmachtskinder in the former Soviet Union and other eastern European countries which came under Nazi occupation. The few figures quoted by all post-war
publications are estimates from Nazi documents, which cannot be regarded as reliable. In a 1942 document, the *Oberkommando der Wehrmacht* (Armed Forces
High Command) talks of '750,000 German-Russian boys and the same number of
girls annually' in the Soviet Union alone.[28] It mentions a plan to force identical
middle names, Luise and Friedrich, on each child which would brand them as
'German' and make them recognizable after the war (an eerie parallel to the additional names Sarah and Israel enforced on all Jews).

Over the last 20 years, there have, to my knowledge, been three film documen-
taries about Russians with German fathers. The first was a documentary/book
project by the German authors Helke Sander and Barbara Johr, who combined
research on the mass rapes in Berlin at the end of the war by soldiers of the Red
Army with research into the offspring of German soldiers in Russia. At the time,
the film and book caused a scandal in Germany and were furiously debated. I will
return to this shortly.

The second documentary entitled *Liebe im Vernichtungskrieg* (Love in the War
of Extermination) was produced by Hartmut Kaminski for a German TV channel.
It focuses on relationships between Russian women and German soldiers and
includes some interviews with children born of such liaisons. Finally, in 1999, a
melodramatic TV documentary by Frank Berger (*Mein Vater war ein deutscher
Soldat* – My Father was a German Soldier) accompanied two Ukrainians in their
search for their German fathers.

The childhood memories of the interviewed 'children' in all three films include
discrimination and shame. In one case the nationality of the father was held secret
for fear that the mother might be arrested and deported by the Soviet authorities.
Sander and Johr tried unsuccessfully to find reliable data but speculate, as does
Kaminski, that the Nazi figure of one million *Wehrmachtskinder* in the former
Soviet Union might not be quite as unrealistic as it seems.

One million! It is impossible to confirm this figure although there can be no doubt about the existence of many thousands of *Wehrmachtskinder* in the former Soviet Union. The sheer fact of their existence has never been publicly discussed in either West or East Germany. As far as I know, only Sander and Johr have tried to search through the existing archives – which, of course, is also due to the fact that the former Soviet archives have not been open for research. At present, the German historian Regina Mühlhäuser is writing her doctoral thesis on the children of German men and local women in the Occupied Eastern Territories.[29]

It is my strong belief that the existence of the *Wehrmachtskinder* and particularly the *Wehrmachtskinder* in the Occupied Eastern Territories has been a taboo in both Germanys. The reason for this is not the existence of illegitimate children as such. The shocking fact which many Germans found (and maybe still find) politically intolerable and obscene is the combination of the war of extermination and German guilt with sexuality. A devastating review of Sander and Johr's documentary, for example, calls any speculation about 'acts of procreation and birth on a huge scale as a subtext to World War II macabre in view of the extermination and killing of millions'.[30]

Other Countries

I know of only one article published and one radio programme broadcast in Germany on French *Wehrmachtskinder*. The author was Raoul Hofmann, whose interviews with several French *Wehrmachtskinder* were obviously inspired by the publication of the excellent study *Les Tondues* by the French historian Alain Brossat.[31] The French *Wehrmachtskinder* whom Hofmann interviewed expressed experiences of shame and discrimination equivalent to those of the Norwegian and the Russian *Wehrmachtskinder*.[32]

In an ongoing research project, the French historian Fabrice Virgili estimates a total of up to 200,000 French *Wehrmachtskinder*. He stresses that, although they were stigmatized as *bébé boche*, they were never subject to governmental consideration or procedures of exclusion as their Norwegian counterparts had been.[33] His research has not been mentioned in the German media.[34]

Arne Øland in his recent research arrives at a possible total of 8,000 *Wehrmachtskinder* for Denmark. Figures for other European countries – all vague and without foundation in reliable contemporary archive sources – can be found in books such as Madeleine Bunting's on the Channel Islands or Arne Øland's on Denmark.[35] Neither Øland's nor Bunting's book has been published in Germany, because German publishers don't see a market for such 'foreign' subject matters.

At a conference on war children in Berlin in 2002,[36] the historian Michael Foedrowitz presented a paper on relationships between Polish women and Wehrmacht-soldiers. According to Foedrowitz, there must have been many such relationships and thus many Polish *Wehrmachtskinder*, but since no records were kept, their number cannot even be guessed. The same is true of the other countries which suffered under the Nazi occupation – and in all countries (with the exception of two or three) there is an eerie silence on the subject. Whether this silence is due to shame or to the fact that the *Wehrmachtskinder* lead normal, unspectacular lives is impossible to say.

I have not been able to confirm whether the eastern European descendants of soldiers of the Wehrmacht are categorized *as a group* by a similar word as are the descendents in northern and western Europe. It seems to be an established truth, though, that the *individual child as such* was verbally abused everywhere. The 'construction model' for these names is equivalent to those for the *Besatzungskinder*: the nationality of the father (German) plus an insulting word for an illegitimate child.

Summarizing Remarks

Unlike German, the languages of many if not all formerly occupied countries have both neutral and insulting terms for the offspring fathered by German occupying forces which officially *categorized them as a group*.

A possible explanation of these striking linguistic parallels could be that the naming of the children as a group hints at a perceived need to define them as 'others', as 'not belonging to us as nation and people'. Such an exclusion is linked to strict social rules about the proper sexual behaviour of women and about the men whom they may and may not accept as sexual partners. As long as a woman adheres to these rules, she and her legitimate children belong to the group – be it a family or a whole nation. If she breaks the rules, the woman and her child are perceived as having brought shame upon themselves and their families (the group). Often, not only the woman but also her child is ostracized. Even if they are not ostracized, their violation of the rules will not be forgotten, though it may become taboo to discuss it openly.[37]

In general, the rules for appropriate male sexual behaviour are much less strict (as long as the man doesn't marry). Their families and their nation are not interested in their illegitimate children; they are 'not one of us'. There is no need to actively ostracize them; they simply do not belong.

As a consequence, the 'illegitimate children of a nation' are given names identifing them as a group – but only in their mothers' countries: *krigsbarn* in Norway, *Besatzungskind* in Germany. Their fathers' countries have no names for them – they simply do not exist.

That the Norwegian children of war managed to make themselves heard in the German media is no counter-example. On the contrary. The journalists told an irresistible story about wronged children. They combined 'sex and crime' with the

Third Reich and the newly discovered disgrace of an impeccable nation: Norway. The kind of public attention devoted to the Norwegian *Wehrmachtskinder* in Germany is an excellent example of two very different issues: of the way in which a historical topic can be 'launched' with extensive media coverage, and of the fact that our fathers' (and grandfathers') illegitimate children 'do not belong to us' even if we talk and hear about them for months: they are *Norwegian* war children.

This chapter also examined the question of how well known these groups are in Germany and whether they have been the subject of any research and/or media coverage.

After a decade of heated debates about the *Besatzungskinder* between 1945 and 1955, the average German today has little to say about the topic. Their existence is known but they are not – or perhaps *no longer* – perceived as a problem, nor do they attract attention in any significant way. No doubt, many of them were discriminated against, although it is difficult to pin this discrimination on one single factor, i.e. the Allied father. Various other factors, especially the social status of an unwed mother, must also be taken into consideration.

The visible Afro-German *Besatzungskinder*, however, were perceived and treated as 'different from Germans' from the very start and were the object of much attention, often blatantly racist. Today, however, the interest in them seems to be virtually non-existent. The first historical study on the subject – Lemke Muniz de Faria's doctoral thesis – was all but neglected by the German media.

While at least some American citizens felt responsible for the Afro-German children of an American father, Germans have never felt – neither after the war nor in recent years – that any of the European *Wehrmachtskinder* 'belong to us'. The attention showered on the Norwegians by the German media did not extend to a greater awareness of the existence of other *Wehrmachtskinder* in numerous other European countries, nor was the question ever raised of why Germans know so little about their fathers' (and grandfathers') illegitimate war-offspring.

An unknown number of German men did pay alimony for their 'foreign' children. The German authorities (at least in West Germany) were cooperative when Norwegian authorities asked them for help in locating several hundred fathers who had acknowledged the fatherhood of a child,[38] and there are, of course, men who had contact with their children – some even wanted to bring them to Germany to be raised in their own families.

At present, the German public's knowledge of 'war children' is limited to two groups: The Afro-German *Besatzungskinder* and the Norwegian *krigsbarn*. Obviously, this is also due to the fact that both have been the subject of extensive media coverage. It is my conjecture that we presently can observe such a process 'in the making': A third group, the German *Kriegskinder*, is rapidly gaining attention. Part of this new 'fame' stems from the fact that the founders understand the crucial role of the media to get their message out. Given the large number of

Kriegskinder, their presence in German society and the fact that there is no shame attached to being one, it can be assumed that this group will become more prominent in the years to come.

Do we need a new term – *Wehrmachtskinder* – for a group of 'war children' we know little or nothing about? I see various good reasons: a name will help to make them more aware of themselves as a group with numerous members all over Europe who share a common fate; the shame and the taboo shrouding their origins, and which many of them remember (and still feel) might be eased when they understand that their experiences and grievances are not merely their own individual fate; the immense relief this might bring to each individual has been made obvious by the experiences of the Norwegian as well as the Danish *Wehrmachtskinder* who in 1996 followed the Norwegian example and founded an organization.

Only if the taboo surrounding their existence is removed in Germany as well as in their home countries will we have a chance to find out whether they do not speak out publicly because they are afraid or because they feel they have nothing to say.

Another reason for establishing a new name is to make the illegitimate children of the Wehrmacht soldiers more visible to us Germans – to throw light on this particular German 'blind spot'. Many *Wehrmachtskinder* have suffered all their lives because they did not know their fathers and were ignored by Germany. We must end the silence around them, which is rooted partly in indifference, partly in the suppression of the fact that German soldiers were not sexless beings, who did nothing but fight, kill and die.

We also need a name for them to allow us to see one of the very few good things that emerged from the horrors of World War II. Germans now have the closest of all possible ties, ties of kinship, with the rest of Europe; they have *real* brothers and sisters everywhere. The French journalist Jean-Paul Picaper, for example, guesses that at least one million French citizens – the *Wehrmachtskinder* and their children and grandchildren – have a German ancestor who was stationed as a Wehrmacht soldier in France.[39]

Notes

1. Harald Welzer, 'Im Gedächtniswohnzimmer', *ZeitLiteratur*, March 2004, pp. 43–6. According to Welzer, it can also be proven that the demand for psychotherapy has increased. See Jörg Friedrich, *Der Brand. Deutschland im Bombenkrieg 1940–1945* (Propyläen Verlag, 2002).
2. In colloquial German, the term is sometimes – mostly in jest – used to explain a certain type of behaviour due to having grown up during the hard times of World War II, for example when someone always finishes his or her plate although he/she is already full.

3. For further details, see www.kriegskinder.de.

4. Some might argue that the correct dates are 1940 until 1946 or even 1947, when the last German soldier left the country, but a clarification of this question is not important for this chapter. A high percentage of the soldiers in the Wehrmacht were by law German citizens, but in fact, some were nationals of Austria, Czechoslovakia, etc. Furthermore, 'soldiers of the German Wehrmacht' is meant to include 'all German men who came to Norway with the occupation force', including the police force, the 'Sicherheitsdienst', etc.

5. Anne Eriksen, *Det var noe annet under krigen: 2. verdenskrig i norsk kollektivtradisjon* (Pax Forlag, 1995).

6. Ute Scheub, 'Kriegsbeute: Kriegsbräute', *Die Tageszeitung*, 14 September 1995, p. 13. Also, Sander/Johr estimate an incredible total of 292,000 children fathered through rape by soldiers of all Allied troops. In Helke Sander and Barbara Johr, *BeFreier und Befreite: Krieg, Vergewaltigungen, Kinder* (Verlag Antje Kunstmann, 1992). An impressive contemporary contribution is the – presumably authentic – diary of an anonymous woman who describes in detail the horrible rapes that she and other women suffered between April 20 and June 22, 1945 in Berlin. It was first published in 1954 in the USA as *A Woman in Berlin* with subsequent translations into Swedish, Norwegian, Dutch, Danish, Italian, Japanese, Spanish, French and Finnish. The first German language edition wasn't published until 1959 (by a publisher in Geneva, Switzerland) and went virtually unnoticed. A new German edition, *Eine Frau in Berlin* (Eichborn Verlag, 2003), has become an overwhelming success.

7. Yara-Colette Lemke Muniz de Faria, *Zwischen Fürsorge und Ausgrenzung: Afrodeutsche 'Besatzungskinder' im Nachkriegsdeutschland* (Metropol Verlag, 2002).

8. Tina Campt and Pascal Grosse, ''Mischlingskinder' in Nachkriegsdeutschland: Zum Verhältnis von Psychologie, Anthropologie und Gesellschaftspolitik nach 1945', *Psychologie und Gesellschaft*, 6, Vol. 1/2, 1994, pp. 48–78.

9. Ingrid Bauer, *'Leiblicher Vater: Amerikaner (Neger)'. Schwarze Besatzungskinder im Nachkriegsösterreich* (Paper presented at Internationales Symposion der Österreichischen Gesellschaft für Literatur und des Instituts für Ethnologie, Kultur- und Sozialanthropologie: Afrika, Diaspora – Literatur und Migration, Vienna, 12–15 April 1999).

10. Sander and Johr, *BeFreier und Befreite*, p. 54f. Sander, who is both an author and a film-maker, also made a movie about this. The English title is *Liberators take Liberties*.

11. One (born in 1949) was the son of a high-ranking Russian officer. See: Jutta

Voigt, 'Russenliebe', *Wochenpost* No. 22, 24 May 1995. The other (born 1948) was the child of a secret relationship between a German who was imprisoned in a soviet camp in the German Democratic Republic and one of the Russian guards there. The Russian was sentenced to six years of forced labour. See Alexander Latotzky, *Kindheit hinter Stacheldraht: Mütter mit Kindern in sowjetischen Speziallagern und DDR-Haft* (Forum Verlag, 2001).

12. 7. Historikertreffen von Fantom e.V., Berlin, 28 October 2002.

13. Norwegian garrison towns were Bad Gandersheim, Braunschweig, Einbeck, Goslar, Göttingen, Holzminden, Höxter, Northeim, Seesen and Oerling-hausen.

14. He found, however, an unwed Norwegian mother who did not give the father's name.

15. Tore Berdal, 'Veneriske Sykdommer i de første fem tysklandsbrigader', *Tidsskrift for Den Norske lægeforening*, No. 7, 1 April 1950.

16. *Tysklandsbrigaden 1947–1953: Til Tyskland for freden.* Published by Tysklandsbrigaden Veteranforbund 1999. Also: Kåre Olsen, *Krigens barn: De norske krigsbarna og deres mødre* (Aschehoug, 1998), p. 425. German translation: *Vater: Deutscher. Das Schicksal der norwegischen Lebensbornkinder und ihrer Mütter von 1940 bis heute* (Campus Verlag, 2002), p. 358 f.

17. For a detailed discussion of these names see Ebba D. Drolshagen, *Nicht ungeschoren davonkommen. Das Schicksal der Frauen in den besetzten Ländern, die Wehrmachtssoldaten liebten* (Hoffmann und Campe, 1998), pp. 56–76.

18. The five-year occupation of the Channel Islands may be one of the best-kept secrets of the war. Not even the highly reputable *Meyer Grosses Taschenlexikon* (1987) mentions them as one of the occupied countries in the article 'Zweiter Weltkrieg 1939–1945'.

19. The rather unpretentious 'were sent' tries to account for the fact that the countries mentioned were partly invaded, partly bound to Germany by mutual treaties.

20. Since this chapter tries to give a very general overview of *Besatzungskinder* and *Wehrmachtskinder* in Germany, it does not distinguish between children conceived by consensual intercourse and those conceived by rape although this, of course, makes a dramatic difference for all involved.

21. The same is true for the offspring of German soldiers in World War I.

22. In a similar fashion, German had no word for the lovers of the soldiers – who in other European countries were (and are) called tyskertøs, moffenhoer, jer-rybag, femme à boche, etc. The German translation 'Deutschenmädchen' was introduced in Drolshagen, *Nicht ungeschoren davonkommen.*

23. Kåre Olsen, *Krigens barn,* pp. 201–11 (*Vater: Deutscher,* pp. 180–94). It is

important to note that the Norwegian mothers, even if they consented to give their children up for adoption, were not informed that their children might be sent to Germany.

24. Thirty of these children on their way to Norway were 'stranded' in Sweden where they were given up for adoption – presumably, as documented by Lars Borgersrud, with the knowledge of the Norwegian government and in conflict with several Norwegian laws. See: Lars Borgersrud, *Overlatt til svenske myndigheter: De norske krigsbarna som ble sendt til Sverige i 1945* (Televågkonferansen 2002: Born og krig).

25. Herbjørg Wassmo, *Huset med den blinde glassveranda* (Gyldendal, 1981). Four years later, Veslemøy Kjendsli's book *Skammens barn* (Metope, 1986), which caused a scandal in Norway because it was the first book about a Norwegian 'krigsbarn', was published in a German translation as *Kinder der Schande* (Verlag Dirk Nishen, 1988), but it went virtually unnoticed.

26. Lothar Kunst, '45 Jahre, kriegsbeschädigt. Über das Schicksal norwegischer Kinder deutscher Soldaten', *Die Zeit*, 11 September 1987. And: (Unknown author), 'Stasi Spione aus dem Nazi-Lebensborn: Von Hitler geraubt. Von der DDR missbraucht', *Der Spiegel*, No. 25, 16 June 1997.

27. Steffi Kammerer, 'Verdammt, deutsch zu sein', *Süddeutsche Zeitung*, 7–8 July 2001. The quote in German reads: 'Norweger, so glaubte Himmler, hätte als direkte Nachfahren der Wikinger perfekte Gene für seinen 1935 gegründeten Verein 'Lebensborn'. Dessen Ziel war es, mit geeignetem Menschenmaterial Super-Arier zu züchten. Die Kreuzung zwischen blonden norwegischen Walküren und wackeren deutschen Soldaten würde perfekte Teutonen garantieren.' (My translation)

28. 'Es wird dann gerechnet, dass bei 1½ Millionen russischer Mädchen dieser Verkehr nicht ohne Folgen bleibt. Der Vorschlag geht nun dahin, die dadurch jährlich anfallenden 750,000 deutsch-russischen Knaben und ebenso viele Mädchen zu erfassen "als wertvoller Ersatz für die kriegsbedingt ausgefallenen Geburten",' in Sander and Johr, *BeFreier und Befreite*, p. 69.

29. Regina Mühlhäuser, 'Kinder von deutschen Männern und "fremdvölkischen" Frauen in den "besetzten Ostgebieten" 1939–1945: Sexualität, "Rasse" und Nation' im Spiegel nationalsozialistischer Bio-Politik'. Hist. diss. in preparation).

30. Gertrud Koch, 'Blut, Sperma und Tränen', *Frauen und Film*, vol. 54–5; April 1994, p. 3–14 (My translation). It is my impression that in the ten years since this was published the taboo has 'softened'. It is quite likely that changed moral values of society as well as a changed atmosphere in German historical writing, and the new wave of novels and biographies describing the lives of individual soldiers, will end the taboo.

31. Alain Brossat, *Les Tondues. Un carnaval moche* (Édition Manya, 1992).
32. *Bayrischer Rundfunk* (1997) and *Frankfurter Rundschau* (1998), respectively.
33. Fabrice Virgili, *Enfants nés de couples franco-allemands pendant la guerre* (Institut d'histoire du temps présent – CNRS) http://www.ihtp.cnrs.fr/ recherche/enfants_franco_allemands.html
34. A recent exception is Ebba D. Drolshagen, 'Schattendasein der Feindeskinder. Die Nachkommen der Wehrmachtssoldaten in den ehemals besetzten Ländern', *Neue Zürcher Zeitung,* 17–18 January 2004, p. 75. It is worth noting that the paper which published this article is not German but Swiss.
35. On the recent research: Øland, personal communication. See also Madeleine Bunting, *The Model Occupation: The Channel Islands under German Rule, 1940–1945* (HarperCollins, 1995); and Arne Øland, *Horeunger og helligdage – tyskerbørns beretninger* (Det Schønbergske Forlag, 2001).
36. 7. Historikertreffen des Vereins Fantom e.V., Berlin, 28 and 29 October 2002.
37. For further discussion see Anette Warring, *Tyskerpiger – under besættelse og retsopgør* (Gyldendal, 1994); and Drolshagen, *Nicht ungeschoren davonkommen.*
38. cf. Kåre Olsen, *Krigens barn,* pp. 195–200 and 412–32 (*Vater: Deutscher,* pp. 116–32, pp. 349–62).
39. Jean-Paul Picaper, 'Besatzungskinder', *Airbag,* 3/2003. http://www.glacis. org/Num_01_02–D/Num_3_D/S12–N3/s12–n3.html Also Jean-Paul Picaper and Ludwig Norz, *Enfants maudits* (Éditions des Syrtes, 2004).

References

Bauer, I., *'Leiblicher Vater: Amerikaner (Neger)'. Schwarze Besatzungskinder im Nachkriegsösterreich* (Paper presented at Internationales Symposion der Österreichischen Gesellschaft für Literatur und des Instituts für Ethnologie, Kultur- und Sozialanthropologie: Afrika, Diaspora – Literatur und Migration, Vienna, 12–15 April 1999).

Berdal, T., 'Veneriske Sykdommer i de første fem tysklandsbrigader', *Tidsskrift for Den Norske lægeforening* 7 (1 April 1950).

Borgersrud, L., *Overlatt til svenske myndigheter: De norske krigsbarna som ble sendt til Sverige i 1945,* Televågkonferansen 2002: Born og krig.

Brossat, A., *Les Tondues: Un carnaval moche,* Paris: Édition Manya, 1992.

Bunting, M., *The Model Occupation: The Channel Islands under German Rule, 1940–1945,* London: HarperCollins, 1995.

Campt, T. and Grosse, P., ' "Mischlingskinder" in Nachkriegsdeutschland: Zum Verhältnis von Psychologie, Anthropologie und Gesellschaftspolitik nach 1945', *Psychologie und Geschichte* 6(1/2) (1994).

Drolshagen, E., *Nicht ungeschoren davonkommen: Das Schicksal der Frauen in den besetzten Ländern, die Wehrmachtssoldaten liebten*, Hamburg: Hoffmann und Campe, 1998.

Drolshagen, E., *Wehrmachtskinder. Auf der Suche nach dem nie gekannten Vater*, Munich: Droemer Verlag, 2005.

Eine Frau in Berlin, Frankfurt am Main: Eichborn, 2003.

Eriksen, A., *Det var noe annet under krigen: 2. Verdenskrig i norsk kollektivtradisjon*, Oslo: Pax Forlag, 1995.

Friedrich, J., *Der Brand. Deutschland im Bombenkrieg 1940–1945*, Munich: Propyläen Verlag, 2002.

Kammerer, S., 'Verdammt, deutsch zu sein', *Süddeutsche Zeitung*, 7–8 July, 2001.

Kjendsli, V., *Skammens barn*, Oslo: Metope, 1986. German: *Kinder der Schande*, Berlin: Verlag Dirk Nishen, 1988

Koch, G., 'Blut, Sperma und Tränen', *Frauen und Film* 54–5 (April 1994).

Kunst L., '45 Jahre, kriegsbeschädigt: Über das Schicksal norwegischer Kinder deutscher Soldaten', *Die Zeit*, 11 September 1987.

Latotzky, A., *Kindheit hinter Stacheldraht. Mütter mit Kindern in sowjetischen Speziallagern und DDR-Haft*, Leipzig: Forum Verlag, 2001.

Lemke Muniz de Faria, Y.-C., *Zwischen Fürsorge und Ausgrenzung, Afrodeutsche 'Besatzungskinder' im Nachkriegsdeutschland*, Berlin: Metropol Verlag, 2002.

Mühlhäuser, R., 'Kinder von deutschen Männern und "fremdvölkischen" Frauen in den "besetzten Ostgebieten", 1939–1945: Sexualität, "Rasse" und Nation', Spiegel nationalsozialistischer Bio-Politik, Hist. diss. in preparation.

Øland, A., *Horeunger og helligdage: tyskerbørns beretninger*, Aarhus: Det Schønbergske Forlag, 2001.

Olsen, K., *Krigens barn. De norske krigsbarna og deres mødre*, Oslo: Aschehoug, 1998. German translation: *Vater:Deutscher. Das Schicksal der norwegischen Lebensbornkinder und ihrer Mütter von 1940 bis heute*, Frankfurt/New York: Campus, 2002.

Picaper, J.P., 'Besatzungskinder', *Airbag* (3/2003): http://www.glacis.org/ Num_01_02–D/Num_3_D/S12–N3/s12–n3.html

Picaper, J.-P. and Norz, L., *Enfants maudits*, Paris: Éditions des Syrtes, 2004.

Sander, H. and Johr, B., *BeFreier und Befreite. Krieg, Vergewaltigungen, Kinder*, Munich: Verlag Antje Kunstmann, 1992.

Scheub, U., 'Kriegsbeute: Kriegsbräute', *Die Tageszeitung*, 14 September 1995.

'Stasi Spione aus dem Nazi-Lebensborn: Von Hitler geraubt. Von der DDR missbraucht', *Der Spiegel*, No. 25 (16 June 1997).

Tysklandsbrigaden Veteranforbund, *Tysklandsbrigaden 1947–1953: Til Tyskland for freden*, Oslo: Tysklandsbrigaden Veteranforbund, 1999.

Virgili, F., *Enfants nés de couples franco-allemands pendant la guerre*, Paris: Institut d'histoire du temps présent – CNRS. http://www.ihtp. cnrs.fr/recherche/ enfants_franco_allemands.html

Voigt, J., 'Russenliebe', *Wochenpost*, No. 22 (24 May 1995).

Warring, A., *Tyskerpiger: under besættelse og retsopgør*, Copenhagen: Gyldendal, 1994.

Wassmo, H., *Huset med den blinde glassveranda*, Oslo: Gyldendal, 1981.

Welzer, H., 'Im Gedächtniswohnzimmer', *ZeitLiteratur*, March 2004.

Black German 'Occupation' Children: Objects of Study in the Continuity of German Race Anthropology

Yara-Colette Lemke Muniz de Faria

Between 1945 and 1955, approximately 68,000 children of Allied occupation troops were born in the three occupied west zones and West Berlin (later the Federal Republic of Germany). What these children shared was that they were born the children of Allied soldiers and German women. Furthermore, according to German law they shared the citizenship of their German mothers. Finally, due to their illegitimate birth all but a few were placed either under the supervision of the state or in the care of an officially appointed guardian.

The particular attention of German officials from public and private youth-welfare organizations, in political circles, Churches and religious organizations, scientists and academics, as well as private parties, focused from the outset on a specific sub-group of these children – the so-called *Negermischlinge* or mixed-race black children. From 1946 (the earliest birth year of this cohort) through their entry into professional life in 1960, mixed-race black children in Germany were considered a special case – one that prompted caregivers, educators, scientists and politicians to create specific social and political guidelines and programmes to deal with their situation in German society.

The Black German children born after 1945 were neither the first German-born occupation children, nor the first group of mixed-race occupation children. During the Rhineland occupation about 500 children were born of German women and African soldiers used in the French occupation from Morocco, Algeria, Tunisia, Madagascar and Senegal following World War I.[1] The use of African troops in the post-World War I occupation had been viewed as a particular humiliation in Germany, one virulent expression of which was the polemic and openly racist propaganda campaign waged against the 'Black Shame on the Rhine' (*Schwarze Schmach am Rhein*) which lasted several years.[2]

Neither the existence of these children born immediately following World War I, nor the discussion and measures created for dealing with them in the 1920s, nor the fate of these children during National Socialism is mentioned in the research regarding Black Germans born after 1945. The one exception to this is the attention given to Afro-German children in the early 1950s, when this group of children became the object of scientific research in the field of social anthropology. These anthropological studies made detailed reference to earlier work on racial mixture conducted in the 1930s. The central concern of the studies from the 1950s was an engagement with the concepts of race and difference as criteria for defining this new social group. The studies demonstrate conclusively that German post-war anthropology referred almost exclusively to the biologist social model developed before the war, and are evidence of a direct continuity in their application of research on Black German children. The discussion in this chapter undertakes a detailed analysis of two of these anthropological studies, pursuing a close reading of their analysis, research methodology and the conclusions and prognoses drawn on the basis of this research.

Looking Back: Early Anthropological Studies of Racial Mixture, 1912–1945

Studies of racial mixture served the dual purpose of methodological entry into questions of the hereditary properties of physical and mental human characteristics and an investigation of social problems. The initial question posed regarding racial mixing was to what degree the basis of human social and cultural development changed as a result of what was assumed to be forced racial mixing arising as a result of modern colonialism, migration and acculturation. The studies proposed that such biological change influenced the intellectual capabilities and mental constitution of a given social group and, therefore, required practical social strategies and responses. Here theories of heredity and racial anthropology combined to form a biologist model of society bringing together pseudo-objective scientific methods and socio-political assumptions. While it is true that theories of racial mixture did not necessarily posit the deterioration of productivity for an entire group, according to Grosse and Campt, a review of anthropological and genetic interpretations from the first half of the century shows that the social and mental 'inferiority of racially mixed people' came to be taken for granted as the result of genetic deficiencies assumed to result from racial mixture.[3]

The first large-scale study of racial mixture was conducted in 1908 by the Freiburg anthropologist Eugen Fischer.[4] Fischer studied the local population of Rehoboth, in what was at the time the German colony of Southwest Africa. The results of Fischer's study were published in 1913 under the title 'The Rehoboth Bastards and the Problem of Bastardization Among Humans: Anthropological and Ethnographic Studies of the Rehoboth Bastard Population in German Southwest Africa'.[5] The group in question consisted of descendants of white Boers and black women who had migrated from the Cape colony around 1870. Fischer's approach tested the applicability of Mendel's laws to humans. His methodology consisted of anthropometrics combined with the reconstruction of genealogical trees using ethnological sources. His study led him to the conclusion that Mendel's laws did, in fact, apply to human heredity. After demonstrating that racial mixture between Boers and Hottentots did not result in any physical disadvantage, Fischer concluded in an appendix of his study titled 'The Political Significance of the Bastard' that racially mixed persons were mentally and culturally inferior to whites nonetheless, because 'a mixture between a superior and an inferior race necessarily resulted in a race located between the two extremes'.[6] In addition to his empirical research on this group's biological characteristics – research he declared to be purely scientific – Fischer was also interested in the emotional and mental characteristics of these individuals. Lacking any empirical basis, Fischer declared with regard to the psychology of the 'bastards': 'Surely, many of the bastards are equal in intelligence to the Boers … however, I maintain that they are culturally, in regard to mental capacity, inferior to pure whites … This racial characteristic, therefore, makes our bastards greatly inferior to Europeans, like all bastards … They will fail to achieve independent cultural progress and thus they will remain in need of white leadership.'[7]

This example reveals a pattern characteristic of the the dominant logic of much of this research: precise scientific observation on the one hand, coupled with statements based on preconceived notions on the other. The publication of his study in 1913 elevated Fischer to the status of the leading representative of scientifically based racial anthropology and established his hypothesis of racial characteristics as hereditary traits.[8] Against assertions of the alleged cultural and mental inferiority of 'coloured people', Fischer warned of the fundamental harmfulness of racial mixture, though nowhere in his work did he provide empirical proof for this claim.[9] From this point forward, virtually all research on mixed populations conducted in the 1920s and 1930s relied on Fischer's basic framework of anthropometrics and family reconstruction, while at the same time expanding it by adding psychological and sociological indicators, examples of which being intelligence, personality and scholastic achievement tests, third-party evaluations and examinations of parents.[10]

The eugenic movement had its greatest international impact in the late 1920s. The worldwide social, economic and political upheaval during and in the aftermath of World War I initiated a period of crisis arising from growing problems related among other factors to refugees, migration, nationality problems and population surplus. This unstable social and political landscape contributed to the eugenic movement's desire to place the category 'race' at the centre of social inquiry, in such a way that social processes and change were analysed and interpreted on the basis of biology. Yet race was not only an anthropological category –

it also became the 'quintessence of heredity.'[11] The linking of a qualitative assessment of races to theories of biological heredity led to the establishment of what in the German-speaking context came to be known as *Sozialanthropologie* or social anthropology. Social anthropology seeks to compare biological systems of constructed collectives to their productive capabilities in order to assess their capacity for social success in a communal system. In this framework of analysis, biological inferiority or superiority simultaneously implies a social categorization.

In relation to the effects of colonialism and migration, the racial hygienist Ernst Rodenwaldt[12] offered the clearest formulation of the relevance of his research as a contribution to social anthropology: 'What was of particular interest was the question of the mental life of the mestizo – whether, and if so, to what degree he differs from the European and the Native, and, most importantly, how his mental capacity translates into performance.'[13] Rodenwaldt's work did not foreground a reduction of biology to the body, but focused instead on the question of hereditary mental properties. His phrase '*seelische Eigenschaften*' referred to emotional life and in particular, intellectual ability. In an essay published in 1934, Rodenwaldt pursued an alternate psychologizing approach in examining the mental consequences of racial mixture, in this case, changing the definition of the social problem of racial mixture. His approach hypothesized that through confrontation with the environment, individuals were 'imprinted' in a way which must be considered '*gemeinschaftsschädigend*' ('detrimental to the community'): 'Racial mixture is a biological problem because the environment transforms inherited mental capacity into the specific phenotype of the racially-mixed individual. This, however, presents us with a social problem. Once he becomes conscious of his difference during the most sensitive, impressionable state of childhood he suffers a trauma that is virtually incurable. His conscious life as a member of society begins with the heavy burden of this mental "mortgage", or, to use a modern expression, with an inferiority complex, or, simply put, the feeling of being a pariah. Racial mixture is a risk for every human community, from the family to the nation-state – a risk that severely affects the coming generation.'[14] What had previously been seen as social inferiority due to limited inherited qualities was now reinterpreted by Rodenwaldt as a threat to social peace in an homogenous imagined community. The 'racially inferior' became 'social troublemakers'.[15] In later debates on the aptitude of children of Black American GIs these arguments resurfaced and were revived once again.

Further studies of racial mixture were also conducted in the 1930s. As early as nine weeks after the Nazi seizure of power, the head of the Interior Ministry (*Reichskommissar für das Innenministerium*), Hermann Göring, commissioned a statistical survey of the so-called 'Rhineland Bastards'. In addition to determining their exact number, Göring ordered that racial anthropological studies be conducted on some of the racially mixed children. Eugen Fischer was entrusted with the project on the basis of his established reputation as a specialist in the field of racial mixture since the publication of his study on the 'Rehoboth Bastards'. Due to his duties as rector and director of the Kaiser-Wilhelm Institute for Anthropology, Human Genetics and Eugenics (KWI) from 1933 to 1934, he was unable to conduct the research on this project personally. Fischer assigned this task to his assistant, Dr Wolfgang Abel,[16] who began his work in 1933. Abel was destined for this assignment in at least two respects: not only was he without question an ideologically committed and reliable veteran of the NS movement; in 1933, he was also Fischer's only student at the Institute who had (like Fischer himself) intensively engaged the problem of *Rassenkreuzung* (race crossing). This request for anthropological support for an action classified as secret in 1933 was one of the first incidents when the NS regime directly sought the scientific potential and technical know-how of the KWI for anthropology, to bestow the appearance of respectability on a research project directly serving racial and ideological purposes.[17]

Abel had considerable difficulty locating the children. He was finally able to account for 27 of the 'Morrocan bastards' ('*Marokkaner-Bastarde*') between the ages of five and eleven. After photographing and measuring the children, Abel examined their physical features, such as the pigmentation of their skin, eye colour, hair colour and hair structure. In addition, he studied the shape of their noses, lips, eyes and heads. As criteria for their state of health, Abel used health questionnaires provided by the local municipal school doctor in Wiesbaden. Abel described the physical health of the children, particularly the 'Moroccan Bastards', as extremely poor. Abel diagnosed the children as having a high rate of tuberculosis, deformations of the chest, deformed legs, high palates, bad teeth, swollen glands, bad posture due to weak muscle structure, bent necks, buckled feet and flat feet, as well as a number of early psychoses including night crying, nail biting, eye twitches and speech impediments. For each of these ailments, Abel attributed responsibility to the father's genetic material.[18]

In order to test the mental aptitude of mixed-race children in comparison with that of other children, Abel ordered an evaluation of all the report cards of children who had shared classes with his objects of research. After evaluating 1,500 report cards from 993 individual students, Abel found that only 86.9 per cent of the racially mixed children in question had achieved average results, and that they were seven to eight times more likely to repeat a grade than the other students in Wiesbaden. Abel argued that the children of Moroccan soldiers were prone to 'disobedience, slovenliness, excitability, and irascibility, as well as a preference for street life'. In conclusion, Abel emphasized the allegedly 'clear evidence of the bastard nature of the children and the racial origins of the fathers'. The children were recognizable by the strong pigmentation in their skin, hair and eyes. What was found to be both new and noteworthy were the noticeable physical and mental deficiencies among the children. These disorders were due not only to unfavourable social status and poor maternal genes, but also to 'the mixing of europoid, negroid, and mongoloid races'.[19]

Although Abel suggested no explicit solutions to the 'bastard problem', his research became the basis for further discussions and decisions regarding the treatment of the 'Rhineland Bastards'. In his 1934 article, 'Bastards at the Rhine', which appeared in the February edition of *Neues Volk*, a periodical published by the *Rassenpolitisches Amt* (Agency for Racial Politics), Abel left no doubt with regard to his own position. His call to readers to prevent continued or increased suffering among the population did not go unanswered for long.[20] The measures implemented during the NS regime against the mixed-race children of the occupation were in large part based on these insights.[21]

Despite the fact that Abel conducted his research in 1933, his results were not published until 1937. In the spring of the same year the Gestapo created *Sonderkommission 3* (Special Commission 3), a group commissioned to undertake the inconspicuous sterilization of the 'Rhineland Bastards'. The Interior Ministry provided detailed documentation on each child. Three commissions had been formed to adjudicate these sterilizations on a case-by-case basis. The commissions included anthropological experts who certified the children's racial affiliation, two of whom were Wolfgang Abel and Eugen Fischer.[22]

Anthropological Studies of the 1950s

When a new generation of black occupation children was born in Germany following World War II, scientists began once again to examine and interpret the allegedly 'problematic' situation of these children using the analytic framework of social anthropology. Walter Kirchner's 1951 dissertation conducted at the *Institut für Natur- und Geisteswissenschaftliche Anthropologie* in Berlin-Dahlem was the first of two post-war anthropological studies commissioned with the approval of the acting mayor of Berlin and in cooperation with the Berlin Children's Services Agency and the State Health Services Agency.[23] The research was supervised by Professor Dr Hermann Muckermann[24] and the results of the study were published in 1952 in a report titled: 'Analysis of Somatic and Mental Development of European-Negro Half-Castes of Preschool Age with Special Attention to Social Circumstances'.[25] Muckermann's supervision of the research and the assignment of this project to this particular institution illustrate links of continuity between the earlier Kaiser-Wilhelm-Institut for Anthropology, Heredity and Eugenic Research and its later incarnation, the *Institut für Natur- und Geisteswissenschaftliche Anthropologie* at the Free University of Berlin well beyond 1945.[26]

The second post-war study of Black German children was Rudolf Sieg's dissertation, 'Mixed-Race Children in West Germany: An Anthropological Study of

Coloured Children',[27] a study conducted at the *Institut für menschliche Stammesgeschichte und Biotypologien* of the *Johannes-Gutenberg-Universität* in Mainz between 1952 and 1954.[28] Kirchner's research evaluated data on fifty Black German orphans (24 boys and 26 girls) in Berlin between the ages of one and twenty, 43 of whom were children under five years of age. The first section of Kirchner's study focused on anthropometric data, while the second section undertook a psychological examination of the children. For the purposes of the study, Kirchner was given access to the children's complete case files, including health records, home and pre school reports, as well as psychological evaluations conducted by education counsellors. In addition, according to his own statements, Kirchner conducted extensive interviews with health- and family-care personnel.[29] As a normative control group, Kirchner cited data on white children in Berlin made available to him by the Department of Medical Statistics at the Robert Koch Institute. Due to the small number of children examined by Kirchner, and his use of sources primarily rendering the impressions of strangers about the children, Kircher's research is highly suspect. With regard to its inception and methodology, however, the study is extremely illuminating.

Kirchner's study is divided into the following four categories: physical[30] and emotional[31] development of the children, their state of health, their intelligence and their character. In his introduction Kirchner writes that 'from a eugenic standpoint, the examination of the physical health of racially mixed children is significantly more interesting than their purely morphological development'.[32] Of particular interest, he emphasized, were the mental and emotional characteristics of Afro-German children. Thus, Kirchner explicitly positioned himself in the tradition of Fritz Lenz and other racial anthropologists who, even after the war, maintained that mental and emotional 'racial traits' were more important than general morphological distinctions such as body or skull size, or skin colour.[33]

In his research Kirchner pursued two primary goals: one scientific and the other oriented toward youth welfare. His work on racial mixture among Europeans and Blacks purported to have the eugenic goal of demonstrating differences between the races and the resulting consequences of racial mixture.[34] The aim of his research was understanding the 'biological capacity of racially-mixed people', in other words, 'their ability to cope with a given situation.' Kirchner explained that he understood this as testing both their physical resilience and their social coping ability, each of which was primarily a function of emotional capacities.[35] In order to accurately judge the capabilities of mixed-race individuals, two preliminary questions had to be clarified. The first concerned 'milieu', understood as both geographically and socially defined. With respect to the latter, it was most important to account for responses from within the social environment in which individuals of racially mixed heritage lived. The community represented a significant influence on her/his emotional state, and thus had an indirect impact on their social coping abilities.[36]

With respect to the physical and emotional development of the mixed-race children evaluated in the study, Kirchner concluded that on average, these children were ahead of their peers by several months. This advantage, Kirchner speculated, remained until puberty; the onset of which he postulated as earlier for racially-mixed children than 'for us'. Based on other studies he hypothesized 'that the emotional development, and, in particular, the intellectual development of Negroes ended with the onset of puberty after which generally no further progress could be expected'.[37] Yet Kirchner saw as a strength the children's ability to imitate, their well-developed verbal memory, and their sensibility to rhythm and intonation.

Kirchner assessed the state of the children's health as generally good but, referring back to the results of earlier eugenic researchers such as Alfred Mjöen,[38] Fritz Lenz and Wolgang Abel, he traced the occurrence of respiratory illness back to a 'disharmony caused by racial mixture'. The pronounced enjoyment of physical exercise and a lively temperament were, according to Kirchner, characteristic of the children's behaviour. Furthermore, he argued that a certain lack of motivation which he had noted led to a certain arbitrariness in problem-solving and a lack of diligence.[39]

Along these lines, Kirchner concluded that, on average, female subjects were developmentally ahead of their peers by several months both physically and mentally. This was without a doubt a result of their 'negroid heritage'. Kirchner hypothesized that the developmental lead held by the racially mixed children would continue through puberty, if the attitude of the community where they lived did not change or complicate their continued emotional development. Kirchner feared that complications might occur upon entry into the school system. In particular, what he described as the '*Triebhaftigkeit*' (sexual instincts) of the children would most certainly have dangerous implications.[40]

On the topic of youth welfare, Kirchner wrote, the end results of the development process could not be judged with any degree of certainty. He did, however, view the situation as a 'practical opportunity to usefully influence the development of the children', insofar as there was reason to do so, if only to protect them from avoidable difficulties and to allow them to explore their abilities positively. For this reason, Kirchner hoped that his research would not only serve scientific interests but, beyond this, would provide answers to frequently asked questions regarding youth welfare.[41]

Kirchner concluded his study by emphasizing the problematic 'fact' that the health, character and physical and emotional development of the Afro-German children was genetically fixed because of their racial mixture and thereby not changeable. Although it was possible to alter these social circumstances within certain limits, he deplored the fact that genetic predisposition could be influenced only indirectly. Nevertheless, he argued for the existence of 'certain pedagogical approaches which might have a positive effect in bringing out the potential of the mixed race children, thereby avoiding their becoming "foreign bodies" (*Fremdkörper*) in our midsts'.[42]

Subsequent to his dissertation research, Kirchner published a later article entitled 'Coloured Occupation Children as a Pedagogical Problem'[43] in which he posed these arguments more assertively in the service of the enlightenment and improvement of the social situation of Afro-German children. In the article, Kirchner warned that the emotional characteristics of Afro-German children would manifest themselves to different degrees, similar to the physical characteristics. Yet this might lead to difficulties regarding an 'organic incorporation' of the child in question into a community, in particular a group of school children. Here Kirchner argued that the teacher who would bear the considerable responsibility of having a black child in his or her class would have to know, first and foremost, what the characteristics of the child were so that he or she might guide the child to a positive development of his or her individuality while, simultaneously, preventing that individuality from coming into conflict with the character of the group.[44]

Kirchner's main point was that Afro-German children represented a potential social problem because of the disharmony which could be expected as a result of their racial mixture. Kirchner saw a solution to the problem in intensive study of these children and familiarizing their teachers with their 'peculiar nature'. Kirchner's research and recommendations helped to establish the scientific discourse of race as a biologically defined concept setting the terms of a goal-oriented approach to racial diversity in the fields of education and pedagogy.

The second anthropological study conducted in the post-war period was Rudolf Sieg's dissertation entitled 'Mischlingskinder in Westdeutschland: Eine anthropologische Studie an farbigen Kindern' (Mixed-Race Children in West Germany. An Anthropological Study of Coloured Children').[45] Sieg conducted his research between 1952 and 1954 at the *Institut für menschliche Stammesgeschichte und Biotypologien* at the Johannes-Gutenberg-Universität in Mainz. The explicit goal of the study was formulated as a desire 'to contribute to the *biology* of mixed-race children' (emphasis added). Sieg studied 100 Afro-German children between the ages of three and six (48 boys and 52 girls), from 38 children's homes and orphanages in the Federal Republic.[46] His research methodology consisted quite literally of extensive measurement. For each child, sixteen body measurements[47] and eleven head measurements[48] were recorded; in addition, a total of 186 profile and frontal photographs were compiled. Three areas were prominent in Sieg's study: the state of health of the children, existing anomalies (disharmonies caused by racial mixing) and the pigmentation and hair structure of the children. Sieg focused particular attention on the alleged anomalies of the children, 'since the scientific literature repeatedly mentioned the increased disharmonies resulting from racial mixture'.[49]

In order to protect the Afro-German children from feeling singled out as objects of study, Sieg included white German children as a control group. Each Afro-German child was measured at the same time as a white child from the same group home. Sieg explained his procedure thus: 'The knowledge of having a different appearance is formed surprisingly early in coloured children. It is the ineptitude of adults which reminds them daily of their difference and their special situation.'[50] But it was precisely this 'difference' that each study sought to prove empirically and to 'interpret in a social and anthropological framework. Both studies attempted to approach the problem of racial mixture through a detailed scientific analysis of Black German children as compared to white children'.[51] In each case, however, the white children were taken as the norm. Any discrepancy posed by one or more Afro-German children in relation to the normative group of white children was interpreted by Sieg as 'negroid heredity'. One example he pointed to was the fact that a single Afro-German child in a children's home did not catch the measles. Here Sieg 'credited' this to the child's paternal heredity. He asserted that it was well-known from older American studies that American Negroes enjoyed a greater degree of immunity than whites against scarlet fever, measles and diphtheria.[52] Likewise, he attributed anomalies in the bite of Afro-German children to a 'trait inherited from the side of the Negroid father'. Here Sieg made explicit reference to Wolfgang Abel's 1932 study 'Morphological Examination of the Teeth of Bushmen, Hottentots, and Negroes'. Following a detailed presentation and explanation of more than seventy pages of measurements and photographs, Sieg concluded his comments with a single sentence: 'No evidence of unfavourable effects of bastardization was found among our racially-mixed children.'[53]

Although both Kirchner and Sieg claimed that their primary concern was for the improvement of the social situation of Afro-German children, their studies represented these children as isolated problems and failed to include or address their social environment in either analysis. Central to both studies was a conflict between the biologically-based definition of racial difference and its social factors; this, however, remain unexamined. The basic social problem of the children, prejudice, was thus projected back onto the children themselves. In this way, the scientific discourse mimicked the social construction of race more generally, insofar as the category of race was constructed in a way which meant that the 'stigma' of racial mixture was foregrounded and thereby transformed into a form of 'racial Otherness'.[54] Neither the fact that such studies existed nor their methodology or purpose was new or surprising. Significant, however, was the fact that anthropologists understood their research as contributing explicitly to the improvement of the social situation of the group in question. The uncritical use of their predecessors' research, particularly that of Wolfgang Abel and Eugen Fischer, demonstrates that neither the scientific interest in the effects of racial mixture nor the analytic lenses through which anthropologists viewed race had changed. What had in fact shifted was the political context, and hence the political aspirations motivating the studies.

The results of these studies and this anthropological research provoked great interest. The findings were published in the form of educational materials and, to this end, had been funded largely using public resources and in cooperation with public institutions, such as welfare agencies and health-service offices. The results were published in pedagogical journals and cited in numerous essays about the impending entry of the children into the school system. They were presented at pedagogical conferences, as well as before large professional audiences. As such, they undoubtedly became a significant part of popular social discourse on the status of Black German children at the time.

Moreover, the alleged empirical necessity of the negative effects of racial mixture on the temperament, character, intelligence and sexual behaviour of Afro-German children formed the basis for concrete political intervention in the field of education. The supposedly scientific character of the studies turned them into respectable references on which politicians and educators relied in the creation of pedagogical guidelines and policies. Regardless of their German citizenship, Black German 'occupation children' were classified as 'racially other' based on biological features assumed to differentiate them from white children of the occupation. The reductively racialized classification of Afro-German children led to their being seen as 'different' and 'Other' – a perception tantamount to a representation of them as 'not really German', displacing them instead to a homeland with a predominantly black population where they were assumed to 'really belong'. An unhappy future was forecast for these children in Germany, as it was anticipated that they would be handicapped by discrimination and unfavourable treatment. Frequently, these two perspectives combined such that, on the one hand, the race of the children was viewed as biologically fixed and unchangeable, while on the other hand, the negative reaction of society to their appearance was understood as the primary focus of conflict.

This ambivalent attitude led to the development of two diametrically opposed concepts regarding the treatment of Afro-German children. On the one hand, politicians, educators and private individuals pleaded for a complete separation of the children from their white German social contacts through adoption into foreign countries, or through their education in isolated institutions within Germany. On the other hand, other voices called for the complete social integration of the children, which was to be achieved by educating the *white* German population and through other governmental measures.[55]

Through the invocation of a scientific discourse of anthropological studies of Afro-German children as 'racially other' and reference to its empirical veracity, Walter Kirchner and Rudolf Sieg sought to establish the 'social construction of the concept of race while underwriting a biologistic attribution of Black German children according to race, even in a social context.[56] In so doing, these anthropological studies of the 1950s produced a notion of a 'moral stigma caused by racial mixture'.[57] However, a close reading of these studies reveals a far more complex picture of the scientists than of their objects of study.

Notes

1. Relatively little is known about the precise living conditions of these children. Through the work of Reiner von Pommerin it was established that some hundreds of them were sterilized by force by the Nazis or murdered in concentration camps. On the other hand, Tina Campt discovered that others among them grew up in Germany and lived, according to their own testimonies, in the Third Reich 'as any other German child'. See Reiner Pommerin, *Sterilisierung der Rheinlandbastarde. Das Schicksal einer farbigen deutschen Minderheit 1918–1937* (Droste, 1979); Tina Campt, *'Afro-German': The Convergence of Race, Sexuality and Gender in the Formation of a German Ethnic Identity, 1919–1960*, Dissertation (Cornell University, 1996).
2. The peace treaty of Versailles decreed in paragraph 428 that the German areas to the west of the river Rhein should stay occupied by Allied troops and associated powers for fifteen years after the armistice had come into force. During the war, Belgium, France and England had employed separate troops of black soldiers from their colonies. According to Pommerin's estimates, between 30,000 and 40,000 black soldiers participated in the army which occupied the Rhein area. The Germans considered this occupation by black soldiers a particular 'disgrace to the honour and worth of the German people and the white race'. In 1920 the German press started a hate campaign against the black soldiers stationed in the Rhein area. See also Pommerin, *Sterilisierung der Rheinlandbastarde*; Gisela Lebzelter, 'Die "Schwarze Schmach": Vorurteile – Propaganda – Mythos', *Geschichte und Gesellschaft* 11 (1985), pp. 37–58; Sally Marks, 'Black Watch on the Rhine: A Study in Propaganda, Prejudice and Prurience', *European Studies Review* 13 (1983), pp. 297–334; K. Nelson, '"The Black Horror on the Rhine": Race as a Factor in Post World War I Diplomacy', *Journal of Modern History* 42 (1970), pp. 606–27; Michael Burleigh and Wolfgang Wippermann, *The Racial State: Germany 1933–1945* (Cambridge University Press, 1991).
3. See Tina Campt and Pascal Grosse, 'Mischlingskinder in Nachkriegsdeutschland: Zum Verhältnis von Psychologie, Anthropologie und Gesellschaftspolitik nach 1945', *Psychologie und Geschichte* 6(1/2) (1994), pp. 48–78, here pp. 51–2.
4. Eugen Fischer (1874–1967) studied medicine, 1905 extraordinary professor of anatomy and anthropology in Freiburg, 1918 there extraordinary professor,

1927–1942 director of the Kaiser Wilhelm Institute of Anthropology, Science of Human Heredity and Eugenics in Berlin; in 1909 co-founder of the Freiburg section of the German Association of Racial Hygiene, 1929–1933 chairman of the German Association of Racial Hygiene.

5. Eugen Fischer, *Die Rehoboter Bastards und das Bastardisierungsproblem beim Menschen: Anthropologische und ethnographische Studien am Rehoboter Bastardvolk in Deutsch-Südwestafrika* (Jena, 1913).

6. See also Hans-Peter Kröner, *Von der Rassenhygiene zur Humangenetik: Das Kaiser-Wilhelm-Institut für Anthropologie, menschliche Erblehre und Eugenik nach dem Kriege* (Urban & Fischer, 1998), p. 272.

7. Fischer, *Die Rehoboter Bastards*, pp. 295ff.; Campt and Grosse, 'Mischlingskinder in Nachkriegsdeutschland', p. 53.

8. See also Peter Weingart et al., *Rasse, Blut und Gene, Geschichte der Eugenik und Rassenhygiene in Deutschland* (Suhrkamp, 1992), pp. 100ff.

9. Ibid., p. 102.

10. Campt and Grosse, 'Mischlingskinder in Nachkriegsdeutschland', p. 54.

11. Ibid., p. 56.

12. Ernst Rodenwaldt (1878–1965), studied medicine, 1910–1913 government physician in the German colony of Togo; 1921–1934 physician of tropical medicine in Dutch colonial service in Dutch India, 1935 – 1950 ordinary professor of hygiene in Heidelberg; from 1914 member of the German Association of Racial Hygiene.

13. Ernst Rodenwaldt, 'Vom Seelenkonflikt des Mischlings', *Zeitschrift für Morphologie und Anthropologie* 34 (1934), pp. 364–75, here pp. 368 and 374, italics in original.

14. Ibid, p. 57 (italics in original).

15. Campt and Grosse, 'Mischlingskinder in Nachkriegsdeutschland', p. 58.

16. Wolfgang Abel. From April 1931 assistant at the Kaiser Wilhelm Institute of Anthropology, Science of Human Heredity and Eugenics, 1934 senior lecturer of racial biology and science of human heredity in Berlin, 1940 extraordinary professor in Berlin, 1943 director of the Institute of Racial biology at the University of Berlin (successor of Fischer in his professorial chair). After 1945 painter living in private, co-signatory of the 'Heidelberg Manifestos' from 1980. Member of NSDAP (1932), SS and the NS Senior Lecturers' Association. See Niels C. Loesch, *Rasse als Konstrukt: Leben und Werk Eugen Fischers* (Peter Lang, 1997), p. 562.

17. Ibid., p. 345.

18. Pommerin, *Sterilisierung der Rheinlandbastarde*, pp. 78–84.

19. Wolfgang Abel, 'Über Europäer-Marokkaner und Europäer-Annamiten-Kreuzungen', *Zeitschrift für Morphologie und Anthropologie* 36 (1937), pp. 311–29, cited from Pommerin, *Sterilisierung der Rheinlandbastarde*, p. 48.

20. Ibid., p. 48.
21. Loesch, *Rasse als Konstrukt*, pp. 344ff.
22. Ibid., pp. 78–84.
23. Walter Kirchner, '*Eine anthropologische Studie an Mulattenkindern in Berlin unter Berücksichtigung der sozialen Verhältnisse*', Dissertation (FU Berlin, 1952).
24. Hermann Muckermann (1877–62) studied theology and zoology, 1927–1933 professor and leader of the Department of Eugenics at the Kaiser Wilhelm Institute of Anthropology, Science of Human Heredity and Eugenics in Berlin, 1948–54 ordinary professor of social ethics and applied anthropology, 1950 honorary professor of Freie Universität, Berlin, director of the Max Planck Institute of Natural Science and Psychological Anthropology, 1956–1962 editor of *Humanism and Technique*.
25. Also elaborated in Stefan Kühl, *Die Internationale der Rassisten* (Campus fachbuch, 1997), chapter 7.
26. Walter Kirchner, 'Untersuchung somatischer und psychischer Entwicklung bei Europäer-Neger-Mischlingen im Kleinkindesalter unter besonderer Berücksichtigung der sozialen Verhältnisse', in Hermann Muckermann (ed.), *Studien aus dem Institut für Natur- und Geisteswissenschaftliche Anthropologie* 11 (1952), pp. 29–36.
27. Rudolf Sieg, 'Mischlingskinder in Westdeutschland: Eine anthropologische Studie an farbigen Kindern', *Beiträge zur Anthropologie* 4 (1956), pp. 9–79.
28. The work was supervised by Egon Freiherr von Eickstedt (1892–1965), a student of Egon Fischer, who was the leader of the Institute in Mainz after 1945.
29. Kirchner, *Eine anthropologische Studie an Mulattenkindern*, p. 5.
30. To evaluate the level of bodily development, Kirchner used six relative body measurements and a series of somatic indicators: torso length, spinal length, shoulder breadth, pelvis breadth, circumference of chest and head. To evaluate the length growth and gain in body weight, Kirchner had at his disposal the measurements carried out four times a year by the infant and child services. As comparative material he used examinations of Berlin children of corresponding ages for the years 1946–1951, carried out by the Robert Koch Institute. See Ibid., p. 30.
31. To evaluate their psychological development, the children were given age-specific tasks. By this method, six mental faculties were differentiated: sensory reception, bodily control, social behaviour, learning, control of materials, creative production. See Ibid.
32. Ibid., p. 29.
33. Erwin Bauer et al., *Grundriß der menschlichen Erblichkeitslehre und Rassenhygiene, Vol. 11: Menschliche Erblichkeitslehre*, 4th edn (Munich,

1936), pp. 713–14, cited from Weingart et al., *Rasse, Blut und Gene*, p. 103.

34. Kirchner, *Eine anthropologische Studie an Mulattenkindern*, p. 3.
35. Ibid., p. 1.
36. Ibid., p. 2.
37. Walter Kirchner, 'Die farbigen Besatzungskinder als pädagogisches Problem', *Pädagogische Blätter* 17/18 (1953), pp. 387–90, here p. 388.
38. Alfred Mjøen, the leading racial hygienist of Norway (Mixed offspring of Lapps and Norwegians – Disharmony by racial mixing).
39. Kirchner, 'Die farbigen Besatzungskinder', p. 388.
40. Kirchner, *Eine anthropologische Studie an Mulattenkindern*, p. 36.
41. Ibid., p. 4.
42. Ibid., p. 29.
43. Kirchner, 'Die farbigen Besatzungskinder', pp. 387–90.
44. Ibid.
45. Sieg, 'Mischlingskinder in Westdeutschland', pp. 9–79.
46. Originally, Sieg did absolutely not want to concentrate only on examining children in institutions: 'The original intention not to examine children in institutions, but mixed children who lived with their mothers or relatives had to be abandoned after the first responses from several youth authorities. One feared great difficulties from guardians, and expected a flat refusal in most cases. It has been less difficult to carry out our examination in children's homes and orphanages in the German Federal Republic [in 38 institutions in Bremen/Bremerhaven, Heidelberg/Mannheim, Kaiserslautern, Mainz/ Wiesbaden, Nuremberg and Stuttgart, Y.L.] It should be pointed out, however, that only institutions run by Caritas and the home mission – that is, the free Youth Services (*Jugendhilfe*) – took part. It is assumed that state-owned children's homes would not give permission to an examination of this kind.'
47. Body height, skeletal height (*Akromionhöhe*), height over breast-bone (*Suprasternalhöhe*), Ileo-spinal height (*Iliospinalhöhe*), height of knee joint, height of ankle point, seat height, shoulder breadth, breadth of pelvis, chest circumference, length of arm from elbow to shoulder, length of arm from elbow to hand, foot length, foot breadth, hand length, hand breadth. Sieg, 'Mischlingskinder in Westdeutschland', pp. 12–13.
48. Head length, head breadth, brain breadth at the narrowest point, breath of cheek bone, breath of lower jaw angle, physiognomic face height, morphological face height, nose height, nose breadth, ear length, ear breadth. Ibid., pp. 12–13.
49. Counted as anomalies were cleft palate, pigmentation spots on the back or in the eyes, left-handedness, squinting, being club-footed, flat-footed, splay-footed, knock-kneed. Ibid., p. 28.
50. Ibid., p. 17.

51. Campt and Grosse, 'Mischlingskinder in Nachkriegsdeutschland', p. 63.
52. Sieg, 'Mischlingskinder in Westdeutschland', pp. 25–6.
53. Ibid., p. 79.
54. Campt and Grosse, 'Mischlingskinder in Nachkriegsdeutschland', p. 64.
55. About the different procedures in relation to Afro-German children, see Yara-Colette Lemke Muniz de Faria, *Zwischen Fürsorge und Ausgrenzung. Afrodeutsche 'Besatzungskinder' im Nachkriegsdeutschland* (Metropol Verlag, 2002).
56. Campt and Grosse, 'Mischlingskinder in Nachkriegsdeutschland', p. 64.
57. Ibid.

References

Abel, W., 'Über Europäer-Marokkaner und Europäer-Annamiten-Kreuzungen', *Zeitschrift für Morphologie und Anthropologie*, 36 (1937).

Bauer, E., Fischer, E. and Lenz, F., *Grundriß der menschlichen Erblichkeitslehre und Rassenhygiene, Bd. I: Menschliche Erblichkeitslehre*, 4. Aufl., Munich, 1936.

Burleigh, M. and Wippermann, W., *The Racial State: Germany 1933–1945*, Cambridge: Cambridge University Press, 1991.

Campt, T., ' "Afro-German": The Convergence of Race, Sexuality and Gender in the Formation of a German Ethnic Identity, 1919–1960', Dissertation, Cornell University, 1996.

Campt, T. and Grosse, P., ' "Mischlingskinder" in Nachkriegsdeutschland: Zum Verhältnis von Psychologie, Anthropologie und Gesellschaftspolitik nach 1945', *Psychologie und Geschichte* 6(1/2) (1994).

Fischer, E., *Die Rehoboter Bastards und das Bastardisierungsproblem beim Menschen. Anthropologische und ethnographische Studien am Rehoboter Bastardvolk in Deutsch-Südwestafrika*, Jena, 1913.

Kirchner, W., 'Eine anthropologische Studie an Mulattenkindern in Berlin unter Berücksichtigung der sozialen Verhältnisse', Dissertation, FU Berlin, 1952.

Kirchner, W., 'Untersuchung somatischer und psychischer Entwicklung bei Europäer-Neger-Mischlingen im Kleinkindesalter unter besonderer Berücksichtigung der sozialen Verhältnisse', in H. Muckermann (ed.), *Studien aus dem Institut für Natur- und Geisteswissenschaftliche Anthropologie* 11 (1952).

Kirchner, W., 'Die farbigen Besatzungskinder als pädagogisches Problem', *Pädagogische Blätter*, 17/18 (1953).

Kröner, H.-P., *Von der Rassenhygiene zur Humangenetik: Das Kaiser-Wilhelm-Institut für Anthropologie, menschliche Erblehre und Eugenik nach dem Kriege*, Stuttgart: Urban & Fischer Verlag, 1998.

Kühl, S., *Die Internationale der Rassisten*, Frankfurt am Main: Campus fachbuch, 1997.

Lebzelter, G., 'Die "Schwarze Schmach": Vorurteile – Propaganda – Mythos', *Geschichte und Gesellschaft* 11 (1985).

Lemke Muniz de Faria, Y.C., *Zwischen Fürsorge und Ausgrenzung: Afrodeutsche 'Besatzungskinder' im Nachkriegsdeutschland*, Berlin: Metropol Verlag, 2002.

Loesch, N., *Rasse als Konstrukt: Leben und Werk Eugen Fischers*, Frankfurt am Main: Peter Lang, 1997.

Marks, S., 'Black Watch on the Rhine: A Study in Propaganda, Prejudice and Prurience', *European Studies Review* 13 (1983).

Nelson, K., ' "The Black Horror on the Rhine": Race as a Factor in Post World War I Diplomacy', *Journal of Modern History* 42 (1970).

Pommerin, R., *Sterilisierung der Rheinlandbastarde. Das Schicksal einer farbigen deutschen Minderheit 1918–1937*, Düsseldorf: Droste, 1979.

Rodenwaldt, E., 'Vom Seelenkonflikt des Mischlings', *Zeitschrift für Morphologie und Anthropologie* 34 (1934).

Sieg, R., 'Mischlingskinder in Westdeutschland: Eine anthropologische Studie an farbigen Kindern', *Beiträge zur Anthropologie* 4 (1956).

Weingart, P., Kroll, J. and Bayertz, K., *Rasse, Blut und Gene: Geschichte der Eugenik und Rassenhygiene in Deutschland*, Frankfurt am Main: Suhrkamp, 1992.

Epilogue

–14–

Children in Danger: Dangerous Children

Eva Simonsen

The twentieth century was to be the 'Century of the Child', declared the Swedish author, educationalist and feminist Ellen Key in 1900. In 'the Century of the Child', the children of Europe had to live through two devastating wars. They were drawn into the maelstrom of warfare and politics, and were made pawns in ambitious projects planned and/or carried out by governments and other agencies. Humanitarian as well as strategic considerations motivated the actions taken and the words spoken: the wish to save the children from harm was intertwined with efforts to make them useful in processes of national and political construction. Both wars made an impact on how children were perceived. In the wake of World War II, the scientific and professional interest in children flourished, this upsurge reflecting not only concerns for the well-being of children but also concerns for the safety and stability of societies, and the strategic interests of nations.

New theories on developmental child psychology emerged, based on studies of the effects of mother-and-child separation during World War II, among these the studies by Anna Freud and Dorothy Burlingham.[1] New professions of the emerging welfare state advocated new approaches to child rearing and education, adapted to post-war needs. The new approaches emphasized the importance of bringing up children in the appropriate way, both for national political reasons and for the sake of humanity and its future. Theories on how the human mind is moulded rearranged existing boundaries between health and pathology, creating new categories of normality and deviance, followed by specific recommendations for therapeutic and educational handling of children.

The children who have been the subject of this book constitute a small minority of the millions and millions of children who were affected by the upheavals of war and peace. In the preceding chapters it has been demonstrated how the war children were made subjects of political, national and scientific interest, by the Nazi regime and in some instances also by the authorities of their native countries. Frequently the war children were made next to invisible after the war, and silence fell on the war-child issue, a silence which may also be interpreted as a national strategy. In this epilogue the broader picture will be sketched: the way the so-called war-handicapped children of Europe were conceptualized by authorities, relief organizations and professionals; what was planned for their future; and what was actually carried out. As is often the case, the ambitiousness of the plans was a far cry from their final implementation. In this broad picture, the war children of this book constitute merely a detail, but a dramatic and significant one. Additional light may be thrown, also on this detail, by examining the fate of war-handicapped children in general.

Exiled and Evacuated

Some of the practices employed during and after World War II in order to help children in need while simultaneously furthering political and national purposes may be traced to World War I and even further back. One example is the practice of evacuating or exiling children, temporarily or permanently. In Britain, private charity organizations such as Dr Barnardo's had operated for some time before the outbreak of World War I. They made an industry of searching out foundlings and poor children and shipping them off to the colonies, 'for a fresh start', as it was put.[2] The child emigration from Britain also served a eugenic purpose. By sending off British children the future white stock of the populations of the British Empire would be secured.[3] In Germany an extensive internal relocation programme for children was started, run by the German Red Cross. Hundreds of thousands of children were sent from cities to the countryside, in order to rescue them from the poverty, filth and sickness of the towns. From 1915 this programme included an adoption agency. The aim was to provide a better future for children whose fathers were missing or had been killed in the war, and for mothers working outside the home. The mothers were needed as labour: giving up their children was interpreted as a necessary sacrifice to be made by mothers in the interest of the nation. The children were said to benefit from being separated from their now single and 'free' mothers, whose influence was regarded as harmful. By separating mother and child, state authorities were protecting both the children and the future of the nation.[4] By the end of World War I, moving German and Austrian children abroad started. About half a million children were moved to countries such as Switzerland, Denmark, Sweden, Holland and Norway for shorter or more extended visits. The children were regarded as innocent and therefore worthy of help. Instead of receiving financial and material support in their home country, it was seen as important that the children were sent to the country which was helping them. The idea was that by visiting these countries the children would learn to be more thankful than if the help were to have been given at home. From the point of view of the country receiving the children, they might become useful contacts as adults for cultural, economical and political connections between the two countries.[5]

The Spanish Civil war represents the prologue to the extensive practice of moving children around, before, during and after the turmoil of World War II. Children were secretly transported to France and to the USSR in order to avoid the atrocities of war and the persecution of both them and their parents by the fascist nationalist regime. In 1939/1940, overseas evacuations from England to Australia was part of British wartime policy.[6] Overseas evacuation under these circumstances meant emigration. Children's Overseas Reception Board, organized by the government, received requests from Dominions such as Canada, Southern Rhodesia and Australia, all offering to receive evacuees. In the USA thousands of American families offered to adopt children. Some American families asked for children of 'Oxford and Cambridge dons', no less. More than 200,000 children were signed up for evacuation, but the Government hesitated: shipping off children in such great numbers might be interpreted as a signal of defeatism. In spite of the critical attitude of Prime Minister Winston Churchill, however, the scheme went ahead. According to Starns and Parsons, overseas evacuation during World War II was the 'useless mouths' policy, and children were in the category 'useless-mouths'.[7] The quality of the children who were to be sent off was an issue. The small evacuees ought to be carefully selected; intelligent, healthy and of sound hereditary background. They were to form the core part of the future population of the British Empire. In addition they were to 'tug at the heart strings' of other nations, through their mere existence persuading especially the American nation to join forces with the UK in the war.[8] Thousands of children were sent to sea on ships with a mixture of passengers, including soldiers, a fact making the ships valid targets for German submarine attacks.

Between 1939 and 1944 there were 70,000 Finnish children sent off to Sweden, with the blessing of the Finnish government. This grand-scale evacuation was part of both Finnish and Swedish foreign policy. Sweden as a neutral country needed to take part in the war in its own peaceful and humanitarian way. For fear of being regarded as ungrateful, the Finnish government banned all critique of the traffic from January 1942. Newspapers were censored. Even expressing worry about the well-being of the children was not allowed. Between 10,000 and 15,000 of the children never returned to Finland, but were adopted and taken care of in Sweden. From the Swedish side, however, it was said that the children were 'a precious loan, to be returned in an improved state'.[9]

When the war ended, the so-called war-handicapped children posed a national and political challenge to European governments, within both a preventive and a humanitarian perspective. Neutral countries such as Sweden and Switzerland were seen as suitable to receive children in need. Saving the children was conceived as a purely humanitarian task. At the same time national and international relief and charity organizations were on the outlook for adequate aims, preferably a cause with a preventive dimension in relation to peace and democracy. By taking care of the war-handicapped children of Europe, giving them shelter and food, and letting them undergo psycho-psychiatric examination followed by treatment and education, aid charities were contributing to a future democratic Europe.[10] Countries engaging in this kind of international relief work could portray themselves as humanitarian nations and vital contributors to the ongoing peace processes. Soon after the liberation in Europe, there began extensive transport of children for short-term or permanent stays in foreign countries, which was a continuation of previous practices.

Aid to Greek children from neighbouring countries after World War II is an example of how humanitarian and political arguments were competing to be the official motives for aid work in post-war Europe. The Greek Government told the world that children of communists were forced or kidnapped from their homes and transferred to neighbouring communist countries, to be brought up as future communists and threats to Greek society. A different opinion was voiced for instance by the two Norwegian journalists Lise Lindbæk and Mimi Sverdrup Lunden. Reporting from both Greece and Eastern Europe, they argued that the children had been moved due to the atrocities during and after the Civil War (1946–1949).[11] Disputes over unaccompanied children in DP (displaced persons) camps, and over hundreds of thousands of children who had been stolen from countries in Eastern Europe by the Nazis during the war, demonstrate the political significance of children in the (emerging) Cold War following World War II. How many of these children were returned to their parents and how many were sent overseas by the United Nations Relief and Rehabilitation Administration (UNRRA) in order to escape growing up in communist regimes is uncertain.[12]

In Norway, the brutal idea of sending thousands of children with German fathers and native mothers to Germany was voiced at liberation. The extensive and long-standing European practice of evacuating and exiling children, both for their own good and in the service of political and national strategies, makes it easier to understand why such a 'solution' to the war-child 'problem' was at all imaginable. In the Norwegian debate it was argued that the proposed exiling of the war children would not only 'clean' the country of the offspring of the enemy, but would also save the children from the hate and persecution which would be their certain fate if they were to grow up in Norway.

Separating Mother and Child

Should a child stay with its mother, even if the mother was in very difficult circumstances, for example being unwed and/or destitute? The answer to this question has varied, with time as well as place. Dominant opinions have shifted from one epoch to the next, and national traditions have differed.

According to the historian Linda A. Pollock abandonment of children was a distinctive element in early modern cultures in Europe.[13] As the Church was intent on preventing infanticide, a number of ways to handle the problem were introduced. Foundling homes were established and the placement of foundlings in foster homes and with wet-nurses was widely practised. Protection of the anonymity of parents became another feature in this system of prevention of infanticide.

The extent of abandonment of children was closely related to changing rates of poverty and the harshness of working conditions for women, according to Pollock.[14] During the first part of the nineteenth century, hundreds of thousands of children were abandoned each year. When the population question gained importance from about 1850 and beyond, saving the lives of these children became an urgent national issue. Fear of depopulation led to changes in abandonment policies in France. In order to force women to take care of their babies, mothers' rights to anonymity were restricted. Thus children's chances to live through infancy increased. Single-mother families were tolerated and even encouraged, in the best interest of the state. In Catholic countries, such as France, Portugal, Spain and Italy, and in cities like Brussels, foundling hospitals became the most important type of welfare for families from the eighteenth century onward, and in the nineteenth century public agencies (often working with the Church), became the supporting 'fathers' of the babies, prohibiting paternity searches, and leaving the biological fathers free of responsibility for their out-of-wedlock children (Code Napoleon).[15] Protestant countries such as England and some German states steered clear of child abandonment. Paternity searches were permitted in an attempt to fix responsibility for child support on the father, or next of kin, prior to having the community carry the burden.[16]

When population issues gained importance, the lives of infants, even those born in poor families and of unwed mothers, became more precious to the state. As a result, impoverished women were regarded with mounting suspicion. They were construed as 'dangerous mothers', liable to injure their children through neglect, harmful child-rearing practices and lack of hygiene.[17] Accordingly, they had to be controlled and assessed by state agencies to determine whether they were fit to keep their children. The question asked was no longer the simple one: should it be advocated that children, also children of poor and unwed mothers, stayed with their mothers? Now the question was more complicated: the answer depended on the quality of the mother.

The practice of separating children from mothers who were seen as unfit, long preceded World War II. In times of war and conflict, however, the conception of an 'unfit' mother might take on a highly political dimension. What happened in Finland in the aftermath of World War I is an example: after the end of the country's civil war in 1918, 20,000 children of Finnish socialists and revolutionaries were taken from their mothers and brought into the custody of child-welfare organizations and official authorities.[18] These children were seen to constitute a future threat to peace and democracy if they were to be brought up by their 'red' mothers, who were among the accused of being responsible for the atrocities of the civil war. Taking 'red' children from their families in order to place them in politically trustworthy families and giving them a new identity was a well institutionalized practice in Finland before World War II.[19]

From World War II and its aftermath, two examples demonstrating a parallel line of thinking have already been touched on in this book. One example is the politics of Norwegian authorities toward the mothers of war children in 1945. Women and mothers appeared as particularly dangerous if they were thought to be lacking in both their political and moral standards. The other example is that of Spanish women, presented by Michael Richards in Chapter 6 of this book. In the same way as for the mothers of German-Norwegian war children, Spanish revolutionary women were given IQ tests in order to prove their low moral quality. A majority of the Norwegian women were found to be 'mentally retarded', as were about half of the Spanish republican women tested. Norwegian psychiatrists argued for a biological link between Nazism and mental retardation, and Spanish Civil War studies postulated a connection between a bio-psychological personality constitutionally predisposed toward Marxism.[20] The 'red woman' was said to be unnaturally sexually active, with a 'psyche' comparable to that of a child or an animal. Caring for children of such parentage meant caring for the future of the country, be it Finland, Spain or Norway.

The question of whether mother and child were to stay together or be separated has been closely related to the population issue, with religious or psychological justification of the relevant answer. Another shift in mother and child policies came in the 1940s and 1950s as child psychologists argued for the psychological benefit of early separation of the unwed, destitute or otherwise unfit mother and her newborn baby. It was felt that separating the two immediately after birth would mean that no emotional bonds would be formed between mother and child. The child would not suffer from maternal deprivation, as it would be free to form attachments to a new mother. Underlying these assumptions one may also glimpse the increasing demand after World War II in affluent Western countries for children who could be freed for early adoption. This tendency was sustained by the steadily growing influence from child-developmental psychology and psycho-dynamic theory, as reported by the English psychiatrist John Bowlby to the World Health Organization (WHO) in 1951.[21] It was claimed by Norwegian medical doctors, for instance, that early weaning no longer represented a health threat to babies.[22]

War-handicapped Children of Europe: Wayward and Vagrant

By the end of the war about 13 million children in Europe were facing destitution, poverty and hunger. These were children whose parents had been killed, and who had been abandoned, kidnapped or deported. Now they were roaming the streets of the cities and the countryside all over Europe, homeless, hopeless, starving and stealing. Governments, national and international NGOs and the newly established United Nations were alarmed and soon took action. Efforts to solve the problem of the 'war-handicapped children' of Europe demonstrate how traditional values and practices merged with contemporary scientific, political and philanthropic interests and were translated into action. 'War-handicapped children' was the term applied by UNESCO and other relief organizations to the millions of destitute and abandoned children in post-war Europe.[23] The children were regarded as personally and socially handicapped as a result of the impact of the atrocities of war. These experiences ranged from separation from family, loss of home, deportation and living in concentration camps to being witnesses to killings and bombings, hunger, starvation and violence. As a consequence of their misfortunes the children represented a future threat to peace and democracy. Voiced by a hypothetical child in a *Letter to a grown up,* this was the message from the relief organizations:

> We have been cold and hungry, and lived in filthy conditions. We have witnessed violence and frequently we have been its victims. Thus in our idea of the world it has been necessary to lie, to cheat, to steal and to be cruel, just to live.[24]

Living mostly in groups, many were involved in the black market and many pilfered in order to live. Girls frequently had no other choice than to turn to prostitution. 'We certainly shall lose faith in that ideal for which you fought' was the logic of UNESCO, speaking on behalf of the abandoned children of Europe.[25] Warnings to both politicians and professionals were abundant: abandoning the children for a second time and failing to take care of and re-educate them would lead to disaster. If neglected, the children were in danger of turning to Nazi and fascist ideologies in the future.

Within this international framework governments throughout Europe designed their post-war politics toward children in general and war-handicapped children in particular. Post-war Europe faced numerous challenges in the problem of war-handicapped children. Deciding the 'true' nationality and thus the future home country of displaced children and children of mixed national origin was a key issue. Embedded in this matter were considerations of how repatriation could be dealt with in the best interests of both children and nations. Governments were eager to demonstrate their democratic and peace-loving approach in their plans for the future of war-handicapped children. Another topic was the contribution offered by science concerning the prospects of where and how the children should be repatriated and (re-)educated. The human sciences were potentially able to guide politics regarding war-handicapped children in general and children of enemy soldiers in particular, by assessing the biological and mental quality of the children. Thus the line between normality and deviance could be drawn, and the suitability of the child for society could be predicted.

Education for Democracy

Toward the end of World War II it had been recognized that one of the immediate measures in post-war times would be the education and re-education of children and young people, in order to safeguard a future democratic Europe. The long series of international conferences by professionals in aid of war children started off with a first principal meeting in Zurich in September 1945.[26] The conference lasted several weeks and was initiated and headed by a professor in special-needs education, Heinrich Hanselmann. A range of professionals such as medical doctors, lawyers, psychologists, psychiatrists, educators and social workers visited Swiss model reform and educational institutions for children and adolescents and discussed the future of the children. The theses presented by this first expert conference on the war-child issue were unanimous: children who had suffered from the war should be helped in all ways – materially, spiritually and psychologically. In principle all war children should be raised within their own families. If a family was missing, or unfit to raise the child, state authorities should take custody of the child. In search for foster or adoptive parents for a child, the suitability of the child for placement should be thoroughly examined – little or no mention of the suitability of the parents was made.

As a principle no child was to lose its nationality. All children were to be helped in the country where they were staying. Upbringing and education were the ultimate means of saving the children and securing peace in the future. Preceding all measures of education, all children who were victims of war were to be examined by an expert committee with child psychiatrists and experts in child psychology and education. Children who had been exposed to Nazi race theories were to be taken under specific moral and educational care. Five years later, in 1950, another UNESCO report on war-handicapped children summed up the experiences and needs of the child: Being separated from the mother was the most serious trauma of war, with the most negative prognosis for that child's future adult life.[27] Secondly, being separated from familiar surroundings was harmful. Witnessing acts of war, however, was considered far less damaging to the child than losing contact with his or her family.

Two contrasting views may be identified: on the one hand, there was a dawning psychological understanding of the importance of keeping mother and child together, as demonstrated by Anna Freud and Dorothy Burlingham; on the other hand, demands on the qualification of mothers and homes were expanded, so that in addition to giving love and care, they were also responsible for bringing up their children as future democratic and trustworthy citizens. Families and mothers considered unreliable were not to be trusted with the task of bringing up the citizens of tomorrow's peaceful world, as demonstrated in the Norwegian case in this book (see Borgersrud in Chapter 4, Ericsson and Ellingsen in Chapter 5 and Olsen in Chapter 1).

The quality of individuals and populations could be measured according to criteria of both biological and mental health. In 1946 the English biologist Julian Huxley, the first director of UNESCO, expressed a strong belief in taking eugenic measures to make minds safe for democracy:

> At the moment, it is probable that the indirect effect of civilization is dysgenic instead of eugenic; and in any case it seems likely that the dead weight of genetic stupidity, physical weakness, mental instability, and disease-proneness, which already exist in the human species, will prove too great a burden for real progress to be achieved.[28]

Despite the acknowledged atrocities performed by Nazi eugenic programmes Huxley advocated a strong future eugenics policy for UNESCO. He realized that any radical eugenic policy would be politically and psychologically impossible for many years, but his hope for the future was that policies unthinkable at the time 'may at least become thinkable'.[29] Whatever horrors the Nazis had been responsible for were 'unscientific' and thus irrelevant to future politics. Based on this knowledge and contribution from experts on science, it was clear that governments and relief organizations would have to take action. Huxley was met with opposition, however. His purely eugenic understanding of the social sciences was outdated among that of other scholars. Ideas from the mental-hygiene movement were interfering with the simple biological determinism voiced by Huxley. In most countries where measures to prevent the wayward and vagrant war child from turning into a juvenile delinquent were taken, a combined nature-and-nurture approach was adopted. In France, plans were made for a widespread system of child-guidance centres.[30] In Italy, reception and diagnosis centres were to follow. According to the English Children Act of 1948, assessment centres with psychosocial expert teams should be organized. In Prague, a multipurpose reception centre for classification of orphans was to be located at the Central institute for diagnosis of children. Those diagnosed as 'normal' were to be placed in families, the others in institutions. In Vienna, an Examination and Distribution Centre was to observe and diagnose children; in the Netherlands, child-guidance clinics were to take care of children in need.

Before any action could be taken by governments, however, there were both political and economical restraints to consider. The harsh realities such as economical ruin, general chaos and lack of food and shelter in post-war Europe effectively hindered most of the idealistic intentions and schemes of international relief organizations on dealing with war-handicapped children. During the years following 1945 hundreds of thousands of more or less homeless or orphaned children were transported across national borders. Numerous child communities or children's villages were established in several Europe countries. By means of 'self-government' or small democratic 'states' these villages were to fulfil their purpose; solving 'the problem of international understanding'.[31] 'Peace through schools' was an idea that had emerged during World War I, first in the USA and then in Europe. Paradoxically, a generation of particularly destitute, vulnerable and even menacing children were assigned the special duty of securing future peace and democracy. They were to be the primary target group for the new educational methods suited to prepare 'the children of the world for the responsibilities of freedom'.[32]

Into the Open – or Hidden Away?

War children such as *Soldatenkinder* or *Besatzungskinder* or war babies focused on in this book was just a minor group among the millions of children in Europe who were victims of the war. Singling out these children from other children who might be said to be victims of the war was not an obvious option to governments or experts on childcare.[33] These war-handicapped children of Europe rarely became the object of explicit governmental deliberations to any great extent. As stated above, silence may in some instances be interpreted as a deliberate national strategy. In two cases, however, this category of children gained particular governmental attention: in Norway in 1945 and West Germany around 1950. In these two countries the children were perceived and construed as definite social categories apart from the rest of the population, posing as both a national threat and as a threat to themselves, thus offering a double cause for action.

At the first European meeting for child relief and aid after the war, Norway was the only nation presenting the existence of children of German soldiers as a specific problem category and as objects of national and local hatred, contempt and suspicion.[34] While most other countries concentrated their efforts on war children in general, the Norwegian government immediately after the end of the war took action to solve their problem of the German-Norwegian children as a part of the political and national day of reckoning with traitors and collaborators. A specific law concerning the treatment of these children was prepared, but never carried out. Then, within half a year, as soon as the situation quieted down, alternative ideas either for deportation abroad or for special iniatives for assimilation in Norway were set aside. From then on the children and their mothers were left to fend for themselves with no particular assistance from either state or local authorities. The idea seems to have been that the problem would sort itself out in a natural way. After a while child-welfare authorities stated that the integration of war children in Norwegian society had been a success. The children either were adopted into new families, stayed with their mothers or their mothers' families, or were placed in temporary foster homes, orphanages or institutions for the mentally retarded.[35] On a national level the war children, the 'others', were assimilated and included in the national population.

The sudden loss in both public and official interest in the German-Norwegian war-child issue and the sudden silence that fell upon the question from about 1946 may be interpreted as the result of the unsuccessful plans for deporting the children abroad, either to Germany or to Sweden. It was assumed that under the care of close relatives and/or their mothers the children would blend in and soon become assimilated. Another element in explaining this loss of interest in the question of the war children lies in the interests and preoccupations of Norwegian private relief and welfare agencies. As early as September 1945, when the Children Relief group of the Red Cross arranged a Nordic meeting on child welfare, the war children were scarcely mentioned.[36] Along with their new top priority project on mental retardation, the organization, along with other child-welfare organizations across Europe, were soon deeply involved in the major task of relief work in the late 1940s: aid for the millions of children who were the victims of war in Europe, according to Norwegian media such as the journal of the Norwegian Red Cross.

In contrast to the apparently successful integration of the German-Norwegian war children, the difficult situation of the so-called African-German *Mischlingskinder* was reported in a Norwegian journal for child-welfare issues in 1953.[37] It was agreed that if the war children of Norway were accepted as Norwegians, their German descent had to be disguised. In both the Norwegian and the German case differing strategies for inclusion were argued for within each country. Based on the interests of the two nations, totally opposite iniatives in the best interest of the child were pleaded. In the Norwegian case, as in other European countries, full secrecy and erasure of the origin of the child was the suggested line in order to integrate the children into society. The paternity of the war children in Norway could remain anonymous, while the skin colour of the children of African-American soldiers revealed their origin. To German authorities concealing the existence of these war children thus was no option. Launching a public educational campaign on how to integrate these children in post-war Germany was a perfect way of demonstrating the anti-racial and democratic attitude of the 'new' Germany. According to Lemke Muniz de Faria, the exposure of the war children category in Germany, though well intended, contributed to the perception of them as strangers and thus led to further marginalization and social exclusion. Opitz and her colleagues in their book on the history of white racism toward Africans in Germany support this view.[38] To what extent the German line of action may be seen as more successful than, and preferable to, the non-intervention or laissez-faire policy of the Norwegian government is open to argument.

A Mixed Blessing?

In the aftermath of World War I children acquired a position on the political agenda in Britain. Deborah Dwork states how children were to be perceived as national property and an economical, political and military investment in the future.[39] As a precious future resource, children were to be looked after carefully. Removing the 'bad apples' or those in danger of turning out badly became an urgent task for professionals within psychology, psychiatry and social welfare. World War II seemingly led to an immediate enhanced interest in children, but this time not only in their potential quality as socially fit or unfit. The war added another dimension to the significance of children. Now the future peace and democracy of the world was seen to be reliant on children. This new increased political and scientific interest in the child made children in vulnerable positions such as war children and war-handicapped children easy targets for intervention by both politicians and professionals.

The increased interest in children in the wake of World War II may have been a mixed blessing to the children themselves. One may ask whether the perception of the child as a project with primary relevance for the future – as becoming, not as being – overshadowed the sensitivity to their immediate needs. Taking care of the children often meant planning for their future lives as young people or adults, and the education of future generations became a crucial issue in the struggle for peace and democracy, supporting the idea of children as investment projects for the future. Although a variety of child-educational agencies claimed that they were to be trusted with the risky assignment of bringing up the future generations, the children's immediate and urgent needs for food, love and protection did not receive an equal amount of attention.

Children of enemy or occupation soldiers were especially vulnerable to this lack of interest in the child as 'being'. When perceived as a national issue, with dire consequences for the future, governments took action to resolve their 'war-child problem', as was the case in Norway and Western Germany, and to some extent in Holland. When perceived as nothing but an ordinary social problem of poverty, illegitimacy and related issues, governments took little interest in the welfare of these children.

When public interest lacked or vanished, silence, shame and neglect fell upon the children. Growing up in families might mean a protective shield against hostile neighbourhoods and local communities. Still, many suffered within families, from deception by close relatives and as objects of hate and contempt. Children who were placed in the custody of child-welfare institutions in some ways suffered the same fate as foundlings of previous centuries. With mother and father unknown, they belonged to the state and were put up in orphanages and other institutions, suffering the hardship of the living conditions there.

In efforts to 'resolve' their 'war-child problem', some governments singled out and stigmatized the children. Others did their best to make the children invisible. Some, like the Norwegian government, did both. Through making the children invisible, the intention was that national and personal shame should disappear. As a consequence, on a national level most governments ignored the desperate situation and needs of the war children, as long as it carried no political weight. On the private level, the children along with the mothers were to be the carriers of both the nation's and the families' shameful secret of their origin.

In this concluding chapter, the attempt has been made to place the fate of the war children in the context of the millions of war-handicapped children left in the wake of World War II. The war-handicapped children of Europe reached the political and scientific agendas in the first post-war years. They were conceptualized as both endangered and dangerous; humanitarian appeals to help them were inextricably linked to the idea of the threat they might come to constitute to the social order, peace and democracy if they were not treated and educated properly. New psychological insights sometimes mixed with, and sometimes contested with, surviving eugenic doctrines in informing proposals on how war-handicapped children ought to be treated. Long-standing practices, such as moving children around within the state and also over national borders, acquired new justifications, or simply continued in the shadow of new doctrines stressing children's needs for stability and secure attachment.

The grand plans of governments, relief organizations and professionals more often than not faded or vanished in post-war chaos and destitution. This, however, did not mean that they were without effects. Some projects were implemented. Also, the perception of war-handicapped children as endangered and dangerous, lingered on. By the end of World War II, a general moral panic was spreading in several European countries. Juvenile delinquency was perceived as a serious threat to social stability and order. That confusion and disorder were results of abnormal wartime conditions was one explanation given. From a medical point of view, war was said to reveal the true biological and moral quality of people. In England a team of paediatricians and child psychiatrists was set up in order to deal with 'potentially' antisocial and insane children. According to David Winnicott, the psychiatrist of the team, the children were suffering from disorders not produced by the war, 'though evacuation made public the fact of their existence'.[40] Bed-wetting was the dominant criterion for mental disorders and deficiency, with theft, truancy from school and consorting with soldiers as other symptoms. Deprivation was given as explanation for outbreak of the symptom. A parallel explanation was given by a Finnish psychiatrist who in 1950 stated that juvenile delinquency was more frequent among the Finnish war children who had returned to Finland after their stay in Sweden than among other young Finns.[41] The idea of the war as both a catalyst and a producer of anti-social and criminal attitudes was shared by

Norwegian psychiatrists. These medical doctors claimed that the high number of Nazi party members in Norway was due to the lack of institutions and care for the mentally retarded. Within the current biological and eugenic paradigm it was logical to assume that children of women who had been intimate with German soldiers were biologically and morally defective.

The war children who have been the subject of this book seem to have been 'forgotten' by their respective governments shortly after the liberation. However, the conceptualization of these children as 'dangerous' may have lived on in their immediate surroundings, giving added motivation for fuelling harassment and abuse. That many of them were indeed endangered is confirmed by the research presented here.

Notes

1. A. Freud and D. Burlingham, *War and Children* (Greenwood, 1943/1973).
2. M. Humphreys, *Empty Cradles* (Corgi, 1995); B. Morrison, 'Lost and Found: The Forgotten Legacy of Dr Barnardo', *Independent on Sunday*, 11 June 1995.
3. B. Coldrey, 'A Charity which has Outlived its Usefulness: The Last Phase of Catholic Child Migration, 1947–56', *History of Education* 25(4) 1996, pp. 373–86.
4. M. Janfelt, *Stormakter i människokärlek: Svensk och dansk krigsbarnshjälp 1917–1924* (Superpowers of Philanthropy: Swedish and Danish Aid to War Children 1917–1924) (Åbo Academy University Press, 1998), pp. 23–41.
5. M. Janfelt, 'War children 1917–1925. State Interests and Ideas about Humanity in the Relocations after the First World War' (Paper *German-Norwegian War Children – An International Perspective*. Workshop Oslo, 15–17 November 2002).
6. M. Parsons, *Precious Commodities Overseas Evacuation: England's Future* (Paper War children conference Uleåborg, Finland, 13–15 June 2003).
7. P. Starns and M. Parsons, 'Against Their Will: The Use and Abuse of British Children during the Second World War', in J. Marten (ed.) *Children and War* (New York University Press, 2003), pp. 268–69.
8. Ibid., p. 269.
9. P. Kavén, *70,000 små öden* (70,000 small Destinies) (Sahlbergs, 2003), p. 122.
10. E. Thingstad, Report on *Semaines Internationales d'études pour l'enfance victime de la guerre* (S.E.p. E.G). Zurich, 10–29 September 1945.
11. M. Sverdrup Lunden, *Barnas århundre* (The Century of the Children) (H. Martinussens forlag, 1948); L. Lindbæk and M. Sverdrup Lunden, *Hellas i dag* (*Greece Today*) (Den norske Hellaskomiteen, 1949).
12. G. Sereny, *The German Trauma. Experiences and Reflections 1938–2001.*

(Penguin, 2001).
13. L. Pollock, 'Parent-child relations', in D. Kertzer and M. Barbagli (eds), *The History of the European Family. Volume One: Family life in Early Modern Times* (Yale University Press, 2001), pp. 191–220.
14. Ibid.
15. R. Fuchs, 'Charity and Welfare', in D. Kertzer and M. Barbagli (eds), *The History of the European Family. Volume Two. Family Life in the Long Nineteenth Century 1789–1913* (Yale University Press, 2002), pp. 155–94.
16. Ibid., p. 160.
17. C. Smart, 'Disruptive Bodies and Unruly Sex: the Regulation of Reproduction and Sexuality in the Nineteenth Century', in C. Smart (ed.), *Regulating Womanhood: Historical Essays on Marriage, Motherhood and Sexuality* (Routledge, 1992).
18. Janfelt, *Stormakter i människokärlek*.
19. Ibid.
20. M. Richards, 'Morality and Biology in the Spanish Civil War: Psychiatrists, Revolution and Women Prisoners in Málaga', *Contemporary European History* 10(3), 2001, pp. 395–421.
21. J. Bowlby, *Maternal Care and Mental Health* (WHO, 1951).
22. I. Haldorsen, 'Adopsjon: et ledd i vårt barnevern' (Adoption: an Element in Child Welfare), *Norges Barnevern*, 1948, pp. 71–3.
23. T. Brosse, *Report on the European Situation: War-handicapped Children* (UNESCO, 1950).
24. UNESCO, *Children of Europe* (UNESCO, 1949), p. 7.
25. Ibid., p. 12.
26. Thingstad, Report on *Semaines Internationales d'études pour l'enfance victime de la guerre*.
27. Brosse, *Report on the European Situation*.
28. J. Huxley, *Unesco: its Purpose and its Philosophy* (The Preparatory Commission of the United Nations Educational, Scientific and Cultural Organization, 1946), p. 21.
29. Ibid., p. 21.
30. Brosse, *Report on the European Situation*, p. 33.
31. J. Lindner, *Den svenska Tysklandshjälpen 1945–1954* (Aid to Germany 1945–1954) (University of Umeå, 1988).
32. T. Brosse, *Homeless Children: Report of the Proceedings of the Conference of Directors of Children's Communities, Trogen, Switzerland* (UNESCO, 1950), p. 49.
33. Huxley, *Unesco: its Purpose and its Philosophy*, p. 6.
34. Thingstad, Report on *Semaines Internationales d'études pour l'enfance victime de la guerre*.

35. O. Lyngstad, *Child Welfare in Norway 1936–1948* (Paper at the 6th Nordic Conference on Child Welfare, 5–8 August 1948) (Oslo, 1949), p. 63.
36. I. Carlsen, 'Barnevernet i Norge i dag. (Child Welfare in Norway Today). Foredrag ved Røde Kors Barnehjelpstevne på Modum Bad 4.-9. september 1945', *Norges Barnevern* 22(6) (October 1945), pp. 41–4.
37. K. Gilhus, 'Soldatbarn (Children of Soldiers/War Children)', *Norges Barnevern* 6, pp. 90–1.
38. M. Opitz et al., *Showing our colors: African-German Women Speak Out* (University of Massachusetts Press, 1992).
39. D. Dwork, *War is Good for Babies and Small Children* (Tavistock, 1987).
40. D. Winnicott, *Deprivation and Delinquency* (Tavistock, 1947/1984), p. 60.
41. Kavén, *70,000 små öden*, p. 167.

References

Bowlby, J., *Maternal Care and Mental Health*, Geneva: WHO, 1951.

Brosse, T., *Report on the European Situation: War-handicapped Children*, Paris: UNESCO, 1950.

Brosse, T., *Homeless Children: Report of the Proceedings of the Conference of Directors of Children's Communities, Trogen, Switzerland*, Paris: UNESCO, 1950.

Carlsen, I., 'Barnevernet i Norge i dag (Child Welfare in Norway Today). Foredrag ved Røde Kors Barnehjelpstevne på Modum Bad 4.-9. september 1945', *Norges Barnevern* 22(6) (October 1945).

Coldrey, B., 'A Charity which has Outlived its Usefulness. The Last Phase of Catholic Child Migration, 1947–56', *History of Education* 25(4) (1996).

Cooper, A., 'The Vanishing Point of Resemblance: Comparative Welfare as Philosophical Anthropology', in P. Chamnerlayne, J. Bornat and T. Wengraf (eds), *The Turn to Biographical Methods in Social Science*, London and New York: Routledge, 2000.

Dwork, D., *War is Good for Babies and Small Children*, London and New York: Tavistock, 1987.

Freud, A. and Burlingham, D., *War and Children*, Westport: Greenwood, 1943/1973.

Fuchs, R., 'Charity and Welfare', in D. Kertzer and M. Barbagli (eds), *The History of the European Family. Volume Two. Family Life in the Long Nineteenth Century 1789–1913*, New Haven and London: Yale University Press, 2002.

Gilhus, K., 'Soldatbarn' (Children of Soldiers/War Children), *Norges Barnevern* 6 (1954).

Haldorsen, I., 'Adopsjon: et ledd i vårt barnevern' (Adoption: an Element in Child Welfare), *Norges Barnevern*, no. 10 (1948).

Humphreys, M., *Empty Cradles,* London: Corgi, 1995.

Huxley, J., *Unesco: its Purpose and its Philosophy,* The Preparatory Commission of the United Nations Educational, Scientific and Cultural Organization, 1946.

Janfelt, M., *Stormakter i människokärlek: Svensk och dansk krigsbarnshjälp 1917–1924* (Superpowers of Philanthropy: Swedish and Danish Aid to War Children 1917–1924), Åbo Academy University Press, 1998.

Janfelt, M., 'War-children 1917–1925. State Interests and Ideas about Humanity in the Relocations after the First World War' (Paper at German-Norwegian War Children – An International Perspective Workshop, Oslo, 15–17 November 2002).

Kavén, P., *70,000 små öden* (70,000 Small Destinies), Stockholm: Sahlbergs, 2003.

Kertzer, D. and Barbagli, M. (eds), *The History of the European Family: Family Life in Early Modern Times*, New Haven and London: Yale University Press, 2002/2003.

Lindbæk, L. and Sverdrup Lunden, M., *Hellas i dag* (*Greece today*), Oslo: Den norske Hellaskomiteen, 1949.

Lindner, J., *Den svenska Tysklandshjälpen 1945–1954* (Aid to Germany 1945–1954), University of Umeå, 1988.

Lyngstad, O., *Child Welfare Work in Norway 1936–1948.* (Paper at the 6th Nordic Conference on Child Welfare, 5–8 August 1948), Oslo, 1949.

Morrison, B., 'Lost and Found: The Forgotten Legacy of Dr Barnardo', *Independent on Sunday,* 11 June 1995.

Opitz, M., Oguntoye, K. and Schultz, D., *Showing our Colors: African-German women Speak Out*, Amherst: University of Massachusetts Press, 1992.

Parsons, M., *Precious Commodities Overseas Evacuation: England's Future.* (Paper at War-children Conference, Uleåborg, Finland, 13–15 June 2003).

Pollock, L., 'Parent-child relations', in D. Kertzer and M. Barbagli (eds), *The History of the European Family. Volume One: Family life in Early Modern Times*, New Haven, London: Yale University Press, 2001.

Richards, M., 'Morality and Biology in the Spanish Civil War: Psychiatrists, Revolution and Women Prisoners in Málaga', *Contemporary European History* 10(3) (2001).

Sereny, G., *The German Trauma: Experiences and Reflections 1938–2001.* London: Penguin, 2001.

Smart, C., 'Disruptive Bodies and Unruly Sex: the Regulation of Reproduction and Sexuality in the Nineteenth Century', in C. Smart (ed.), *Regulating Womanhood: Historical Essays on Marriage, Motherhood and Sexuality*, London: Routledge, 1992.

Starns, P. and Parsons, M., 'Against Their Will: The Use and Abuse of British Children during the Second World War', in J. Marten (ed.), *Children and War*,

New York and London: New York University Press, 2003.

Sverdrup Lunden, M., *Barnas århundre* (The Century of the Children), Bergen: H. Martinussens forlag, 1948.

Thingstad, E., Report on *Semaines Internationales d'etudes pour l'énfance victime de la guerre* (S.E.P. E.G), Zürich, 10–29 September 1945.

Thom, D., 'Wishes, Anxieties, Play and Gestures: Child-guidance in Inter-war England', in R. Cooter (ed.), *In the Name of the Child. Health and Welfare, 1880–1940*, London and New York: Routledge, 1992.

UNESCO, *Children of Europe*, Paris: UNESCO, 1949.

Winnicott, D., *Deprivation and Delinquency*, London and New York: Tavistock, 1947/1984.

Index

abandonment of children 272–3
Abel, Dr Wolfgang 253–4, 256, 258
abortion 36, 122, 141, 233
   German policies 16, 155, 174, 216
adoption
   Afro-German children in USA 233
   Danish war children in Germany 62
   Dutch war children 156
   early twentieth-century German programmes 270
   French war children 141
   Lebensborn children 22, 214, 215, 220
   Norwegian war children 22, 28, 29, 30, 79, 84, 215, 236
Afro-German war children
   anthropological studies 232, 254–60
   from Allied occupation 1, 6, 10, 232, 233, 241, 249, 252, 279
   from Rhineland occupation 249–50, 252–4
Algeria 8, 249
alimony, see child maintenance
Allied nations 2, 36, 230
   German children of soldiers from 1, 230, 232–5, 249
Alsace-Lorraine 19
Alsace-Moselle region 138
Amsterdam 154, 156
anthropological studies
   early German work on race 10, 250–4
   German research in 1950s 232, 254–60
   see also racial anthropology
anti-fascism/anti-Nazism 2, 9
Argentine 'disappeared' children 117
'Aryan' blood
   children born in Eastern Europe 17, 168, 170, 175, 178, 214
   children born in regions of France 18–19
   Nazi ideas and policies 5, 15–16, 16, 54, 62, 167, 173, 214, 215
   Nordic race 16, 19, 215
Aube region, France 146
Australia
   evacuation of children from Britain to 75, 271
   interest in Norwegian children 27, 74, 86, 87
Austria 16, 201
Austrian children, relocation programmes after World War I 270

Austrian war children 232, 233, 236
autobiographies 213, 217, 231
Auxilio Social (Social Aid) 124, 128

Baltic States 171, 172, 177, 178
Bangsund, Einar 237
Barcelona 125
Basque Country 118, 125, 127, 128
Bauer, Ingrid 233
BDM (League of German Girls) 216
Beevor, Antony 233
Belgian war children 18, 155
Belgium 18, 20, 75, 126, 128, 235
Belorussia 171, 177, 178
Bennholdt-Thomsen, Carl Gottlieb 200
Bergen 20, 21
Berger, Frank 238
Berger, Gottlob 171
Berlin 31, 233–4, 238, 249, 254, 255
Besatzungskinder (children of occupation) 229, 230, 232–5, 240, 241, 278
Béziers 146
Bilbao 125
biological ideas
   assessments of war children 275–6
   German anthropological studies 10, 250, 252, 259–60
   and national identity 44, 94, 95
   in Nazi population policies 191, 202
   and trends in politics 202
biological identity
   debates on Eastern European war children 176
   war children's search for 53, 148–9, 215, 223–4, 225
Black German children, see Afro-German war children
body
   gender symbolism and national identities 43, 94
   as object of political history 2
   see also female body
Boers 250–1
Bohemia, see Protectorate of Bohemia and Moravia
Borgersrud, Lars 6, 7, 277
Bosnia 230
Bourdieu, Pierre 99–100

Bowlby, John 274
Brauchitsch, Walther von 173
Bremen, Norwegian war children at
  Lebensborn home 29–30, 79, 82
Britain
  brand of eugenics 117
  perception of children after World War I 280
  and repatriation of Spanish children 127,
    128
  sending of children to colonies 74, 270, 271
  see also Channel Islands; England; London
British military occupation authorities 76–7, 82
British soldiers, children of 233
Brittany 19
Brossat, Alain 239
Brünn 192
Brussels 273
Budweis 192
Bulgaria 235
Bundesarchiv (Federal Archive), Koblenz 179
Bunting, Madeleine 239
Burlingham, Dorothy 269, 276

Campt, T. 250
Canada 271
Capa, Robert 147
Capdevila, Luc 7
Carlsen, Ingvald 76, 77
Casas de Maternidad 122
Catalonia 118, 125, 126
Catholic Church in the Netherlands 156, 161
Catholic Church in Spain
  discourse of eugenics after Civil War 10,
    116–17, 122–3
  institutions for 'disappeared' children 120,
    122
  support of nationalists 115, 116, 121, 129
Channel Islands 155, 235, 239
Chantilly 143
charity organizations
  British practice of evacuating children
    270
  care for European war-handicapped children
    271–2
  Catholic Church in Spain 120, 122
Charkow, Ukraine 171–2
Chartres 147
Chevalier, Jacques 138
child maintenance
  allowances for Dutch war children 155
  Norwegian discussions and failure to
    enforce 85, 86, 89–90, 234
  policies in Denmark 55, 56, 59
child psychology, post-war theories 269, 274,
  281
child welfare
  early twentieth-century policies 191, 270
  and Norwegian deportation plans 74–5
Children's Overseas Reception Board 271
Christie, Johan K. 82, 82–3, 83
Church
  and problem of abandonment of children
    272–3, 273

see also Catholic Church; Clergy Committee
  (Norway)
Churchill, Winston 271
CICR (Comité international de la Croix-Rouge)
  145
citizenship
  of Black German 'occupation' children 249
  early regulations in Norway 72–3
  Norwegian women and war children
    deprived of 7, 26–7, 71–2, 81, 88, 89
  in Protectorate of Bohemia and Moravia
    196, 197
Clergy Committee (Norway) 75–6, 86
Cold War 31, 47, 88, 272
collaboration
  accusations in France 145–6
  accusations in Protectorate of Bohemia and
    Moravia 201
  in Denmark 35, 39, 40–1, 47, 49
  NKVD's punishment of Eastern Europeans
    172, 179
  perception of Dutch women who fraternized
    with Germans 160
  and post-war demobilization 120
collective/social memory, Spanish Civil War
  117, 118
communists 127, 272
compensation/reparation 102, 118, 179, 231,
  237
concentration camps
  Spanish political prisoners and children
    124–5, 125
  see also Nazi concentration camps
conferences/congresses
  in aid of war children 276
  recent events concerned with war children
    213, 231, 233, 239–40
Conti, Leonardo 143, 174
Copenhagen 61, 62, 84
Corrèze 142
cultural and national reproduction 44, 94, 95
Czech-German marriages 5, 195, 196–7,
  197–8
Czechoslovakia 201–2, 235
Czech territories 7
  see also Protectorate of Bohemia and
    Moravia

'dangerous mothers' 273, 274
Danish Red Cross 67
Danish soldiers, fathers of children in Finland
  85
Danish unmarried mothers 54–5, 57–8
  of war children 58–9
Danish War Child Association (DKBF) 53, 62,
  242
Danish war children
  attitudes and discrimination against 44, 48–9
  authorities' concealment of information
    from 53, 60, 68
  estimates of numbers 60–2, 62, 239
  paternity cases 56–8, 59–60
  personal testimonies 63–8

Danish women who fraternized with Germans
3, 36, 44–7, 48, 49, 94
  punishment and abuse of 4, 35, 36–7,
  38–40, 40–2
Darlan, Admiral 138
Debes, Inge 77, 78, 79, 84, 87, 88
Delegación Extraordinaria de Repatriación de
  Menores 126–7
democracy, and post-war concerns for children
272, 276, 278, 280
Denmark 4, 36, 147, 235, 270
  failure of Lebensborn 18, 20
  gendered national identity processes 42–4
  ideas of parenthood 53–5
  marriages between women and German
    soldiers 23, 140
  national community of memory 46, 47–9
  Nazi racial evaluation of population 5, 17,
    18, 20
  policies and concealment of paternities
    10–11, 53, 58–60, 60, 61, 62, 68
  pre-war policies on paternity 55–6
  treatment of women who fraternized with
    Germans 4, 35, 36–7, 38–40, 40–2
deportation
  aspects of history 72–4
  Norwegian plans for war children 71, 74–9,
    81–6, 87–90, 95, 233, 272
  of Norwegians by occupation authorities
    73–4
  SS abduction of 'racially fit' children 170–1
  story told by Soviet soldier 234
dictatorships 191–2
Diederichs, Monika 3, 4, 5–6
disabled children, Nazi euthanasia programme
  17, 200, 214, 222
'disappeared' children
  Argentina 117
  Spain 120, 130
DP (displaced persons) camps 272
Dr Barnardo's 270
Dr Holm's Hotel, Geilo 21
Drolshagen, Ebba D. 6
Dutch unmarried mothers 153–4, 154–5,
  160–1, 175
Dutch war children
  conflict over nationality 158–9
  estimate of numbers 153
  German intervention in care of 154–5, 175
  murder of 3, 156–7
  stigma and silence enforced on 152, 160–1
Dutch women who had relations with German
  soldiers
  punishment and humiliation 4, 157–8, 162
  stigma and silence enforced on 151–2, 154,
    160–1
  uncertain number 152–3
Dwork, Deborah 280

East German fathers of war children 90
East German, *see* German Democratic
  Republic (GDR)
Eastern Europe 3, 4, 179, 238, 272

Eastern European mothers of war children 5,
  171–2, 179
Eastern European war children
  estimates of numbers 167, 169, 177–8
  kidnapping of by Lebensborn 16, 170–1,
    214–15, 236
  Nazi control measures 174–6
  Nazis' thinking on mixed race 5, 17, 167–8,
    169, 173–4, 178
  registration of 171–3
  research 178–9, 239
education
  Catholic doctrine and policy in Spain
    116–17, 120, 121
  impact of German anthropological studies
    259
  new post-war approaches to children 269,
    276–8
Egypt 235
Eidsvold Constitution 72
Ellingsen, Dag 8, 105, 277
emigration 27, 74, 86, 87, 270, 271
England 73–4, 273, 277, 281
  see also Britain; London
Ericsson, Kjersti 8, 277
Eriksen, Anne 100–1
Erlander, Tage 84
Essner, Cornelia 170
Estonia, *see* Baltic States
ethnicity
  groups in Czech territories 192
  Nazi policies in Czech territories 193,
    195–6, 202
  Nazi selection of war children of Eastern
    Europe 168, 169–70
  relevance to paternity cases in Denmark 54
eugenics 44, 190, 192, 251–2, 281
  and child emigration from Britain 270
  Dutch ideas 152
  Julian Huxley's beliefs 277
  Kirchner's study of Black German children
    255
  Lebensborn scheme in Norway 21–2
  Nazi ideas 9–10, 277
  Norwegian attitudes 73, 76, 282
  in Spain 10, 117, 119, 122–3
euthanasia, Nazi programmes 17, 193, 200,
  214, 222
evacuation/exile of children 270–2
  from Spanish Civil War 125–6, 271

Faeroe Islands 59
Falange 116, 120, 121, 124, 126, 128
Famille du Prisonnier de guerre 142–3
family
  doctrine of Catholic Church in Spain 119
  Francoist policy after Civil War 7, 116, 121,
    124, 129
  Norwegian war children's reflections about
    97–9, 102–3, 104
  reactions attitudes towards French war
    children 147–8
  Vichy government's idea of 142

Fanon, Franz 8
fatherhood/fathers
    concealment of 53, 63, 104, 218
    of illegitimate children 176, 240, 241
    relevance to terms for war children 229
    see also paternity
Federal Republic of Germany 280
    children of Allied soldiers and German
        women 232, 249
    Dutch children in children's homes 156
    lack of information on foreign military
        paternities 60
    reactions to Lebensborn children 220–1
    Sieg's research on mixed-race children 257
    silence over Wehrmachtskinder in former
        Soviet Union 239
female body
    as combat zone 35, 37, 43
    punishment through hair-cutting 42
    significance for national identity 41, 44
female sexuality
    discourse on Norwegian mothers of war
        children 93, 94–5, 103
    national significance 2, 7, 37, 40, 41, 42–3
Finland 85, 235, 273–4, 274
Finnish children 271, 273–4, 281
Finnmark 73, 80
FIOM (Federation for Institutions of Unmarried
    Mothers) 153, 156, 158–9
Fischer, Eugen 250–1, 252–3, 254, 258
Flemings 18
Foedrowitz, Michael 60, 239–40
Foucault, Michel 100
foundling homes 273
France
    division into zones after Armistice 138
    imagery of imperialist conquest 8
    Lebensborn 19
    Nazis' racial evaluation of population 5, 17,
        18–19, 20, 143
    nineteenth-century policies on abandonment
        of children 273
    occupation of Rhineland 249
    post-war debates and policies on war
        children 144–5, 146–7
    post-war measures for child welfare 277
    relations with German occupiers 139–40
    Spanish Republicans exiles and children
        117, 118, 125, 126, 128, 271
    Wehrmacht soldiers 139, 173, 235, 242
Franco, General Francisco 115, 126
fraternization with the enemy 35
Fredrikstad, Norway 26
Free University of Berlin 254
French fathers of German war children 147,
    233
French mothers of war children 140–2, 144–6
French war children 6, 19, 231, 242
    births and adoptions 141
    estimates of numbers 144, 239
    media attention and research in Germany
        239
    personal testimonies 140, 147–9

post-war investigation by new authorities
    146
Vichy government concerns and policy
    138–9, 142–4
French women who had relations with German
    soldiers 35, 94, 140
prisoner-of-war wives 10, 138, 141, 142,
    145
shaving of heads for collaboration 145–6
Freud, Anna 269, 276
Friedrich, Jörg, Der Brand 230
Friesland, Hoog-Holten hotel 154
Frit Denmark 40
Frydenberg, Alf 77, 84, 87, 88

Galton, Francis 190
gender
    aspects of Francoist morality and family
        policy 116, 119, 120
    discourse on Norwegian mothers and war
        children 7, 93, 102–3
    and national identity in Denmark 35, 37,
        42–4, 46
genealogy 148–9
Gerhardsen, Einar 82
German Charles-University, Prague 199,
    200
German children
    relocation programmes after World War I
        270
    see also Afro-German war children; German
        Lebensborn children; German war
        children
German civilian refugees, Denmark 49
German Democratic Republic (GDR) 60
    children born of Soviet soldiers 232, 234
    German Lebensborn children 220, 221
    Norwegian Lebensborn children 237
    silence over Wehrmachtskinder in former
        Soviet Union 239
German Lebensborn children 11, 214–15
    birth and early life 215–17
    family relationships 217–20, 223
    publicizing of stories 213
    searching for origins 223–4, 225
    second generation 224–5
    today 221–4
German Red Cross 270
German Security Service (Sicherheitsdienst)
    236
German unmarried mothers 232
'German Volk community' 168, 170, 174, 177
German war children 147, 229–30, 249
    Besatzungskinder 229, 230, 232–5, 240–2
    Kriegskinder 230, 230–1, 241–2
    Wehrmachtskinder 235–40
    see also Afro-German war children; German
        Lebensborn children
Germanhood/Germanization programme 168,
    170
Protectorate of Bohemia and Moravia
    193–6, 197, 199, 200
Germany 3, 6, 7, 59, 62, 88, 117

attitude towards Afro-German children 233, 241, 259, 279
and care of Dutch unmarried mothers 154–5, 161
current issues surrounding war children 213, 230, 235–6, 240–2
early twentieth-century relocation of children 270
Lebensborn homes 16
media publicity about German war children 231, 236–40, 240–2
Nazi population policy 2, 15–16
nineteenth-century policy on paternity 273
Norwegian war children 28, 29, 30, 30–1, 104, 215, 221
plans to deport Norwegian war children to 71, 78, 81, 95, 272, 279
plans to transport Eastern European war children to 179
post-war Norwegian repatriation work 81–3
terms used for war/occupation children 6, 230–6, 242
transfer of Sudeten-Germans to 201
women who married Germans sent to 7, 27, 30–1
World War I atrocities in France and Belgium 139
see also Federal Republic of Germany; German Democratic Republic
Giraud, Marie-Louise 141
Godthaab orphanage, near Oslo 21, 28–9, 29, 87
Göring, Hermann 252–3
Goslar 234
Greece 235
Greek children, post-war aid 272
Greenland 59
Grosse, P. 250
Guernica 128
Guipúzcoa 126
gypsies, Norway 21

Hagelin, Nils 84
The Hague 154, 159, 161
hair-shearing of women 8, 41–2
  Denmark 36, 38–9, 40
  France 94, 145–6
  Netherlands 4, 157–8, 162
  Norway 25, 97
  Spain 120–1
Halden, Norway 26
Hambro, C.J. 78
Hanselmann, Heinrich 276
Hansteen, Kirsten 83
Harpøth, Otto 58–9
Haylen, Leslie 87
Heidenreich, Gisela 217
Heim Friesland 215
Heim Harz 220
Hellbrügge, Theodor 213
heredity, Nazi theories and health care policies 190, 194, 199–200, 250, 252, 258
Hess, Rudolf 216

'Hetaerer' (poem) 41
Heydrich, Reinhard 198
Hilgenfeldt, Erich 175
Himmler, Heinrich 16, 19, 143, 155, 216, 237
  and Eastern European war children 167, 169, 172, 174–5, 175–6, 177, 214
  notions of 'Aryan' blood 54, 169–70, 173, 214, 215
Hitler, Adolf 6–7, 23, 138, 155, 167, 173, 175, 191
Hitler Youth 200
Hoffmann, Otto 174–5, 175
Hofmann, Raoul 239
Holland, *see* Netherlands
Høsbjør (by Hamar) 21
human rights 48, 49
humanitarian perspectives, war-handicapped children 271–2, 281
Hungary 235
Huntzinger, Madame 143
Hurdal Verk, near Oslo 20

Iceland 59
Iglau 192
Institut für Natur- und Geisteswissenschaftliche Anthropologie, Berlin 254
Institute for Hereditary and Racial Hygiene (IERH) 199–200
Interdisciplinary Memory Research 230
international relief organizations 271–2, 275, 281
Italy 138, 235, 273, 277

Jews 4, 21, 72, 73, 170, 238
  in Czech territories 192, 196
Johannes-Gutenberg-Universität, Mainz 255, 257
Johr, Barbara 233, 238, 239

Kaempffert, Waldemar 191–2
Kaiser-Wilhelm Institute for Anthropology, Human Genetics and Eugenics (KWI) 253, 254
Kaminski, Hartmut 238
Keitel, Field Marshal Wilhelm 173, 174
Key, Ellen 269
Kirchner, Walter 254, 255–7, 258, 259–60
Klaus, Karel 202
Klekken maternity home, near Hønefoss 21, 22
Kriegskinder (children of war) 230, 230–1, 241–2
krigsbarn (Norwegian word for war child) 229, 231, 237, 240, 241
Kunst, Lothar 236
Künzel, Erwin 198
Kven (northern Norway) 73

Lagrou, Pierre 47
Lammers, Hans Heinrich 171, 175
Lamorlaye 143–4
language, *see* semantics
Latvia, *see* Baltic States

Lebensborn homes 16–17, 18, 19, 20–1, 28–9, 29, 59, 213–14, 215
  idea of as 'stud-farms' 16, 213, 214, 218, 225, 237
Lebensborn organization 15–17, 213–14
  archives 78, 79
  policy in Norway 5, 15, 19–24, 29, 74, 80, 215, 236
  role in Nazi racial policy 5, 18–19, 21–2, 198, 214, 237
  see also German Lebensborn children
Leeuwarden 159
Lenz, Fritz 255, 256
Libya 235
Liditz 198
Liebe im Vernichtungskrieg ('Love in the War of Annihilation') (TV documentary) 179, 238
Lilienthal, Georg 214
Lillehammer 75
Lindbaek, Lise 272
Lithuania, see Baltic States
Lofotposten 94
London, Norwegian authorities 25, 75, 76, 81
Lunden, Mimi Sverdrup 272
Luxembourg 235

Maastricht 159
Madagascar 249
Madrid 121, 125
marriages
  between German soldiers and French women 140, 145
  between Norwegian mothers and German fathers 7, 22–3, 26–7
  in Czech territories 5, 194–5, 196, 197–8, 201
  Hitler's sanctioning of 6–7
  of Norwegian war children interviewed 103, 106
Marxism, formulation of in Franco's Spain 123, 130, 274
media publicity
  Lebensborn children 213, 223
  war children 231, 236, 240
medical profession 2–3
  Norwegian discourse on war children and mothers 93, 101–2
  see also psychiatry/psychology
Mein Vater war ein deutscher Soldat (My Father was a German Soldier) (TV documentary) 238
Melby, Kari 2
memories
  German war children's publicizing of 230–1, 238
  Spanish war children's recuperation of 119, 131
  see also collective/social memory; national community of memory
men, roles and rules of behaviour 7, 43, 240
Mendel, Gregor 251
mental-hygiene movement 130, 277
Mischlinge/Mischlingskinder 10, 167, 279

Mjöen, Alfred 256
'moffenhoeren'/'moeffenmeiden' 8, 35, 151, 157–8, 161
Moldegaard orphanage, near Bergen 21, 28
Möller, Gustav 84
Montparnasse 144
Moravia, see Protectorate of Bohemia and Moravia
Moroccan (mixed-race) children 249, 253–4
Moss (Norway) 26
motherhood, in Denmark 43, 54–5
mothers of Afro-German children 233
mothers of children with German fathers 3, 8, 11, 20, 35, 45
mothers of Lebensborn children in Germany 214, 215–16, 217–19, 219–20
Muckermann, Dr Hermann 254
Mühlhäuser, Regina 5, 239
Müller, Karl 200
Muniz de Faria, Yara-Colette Lemke 6, 10, 232, 241, 279
Mütter und Saulingsheim (childbirth clinics), Netherlands 154, 155, 156, 161
Myrdal, Alva 84
Myrdal, Gunnar 84

Nadler, Dr (German staff judge) 59–60
names
  denoting children of native women and occupant soldiers 229–30
  derogatory words for war children 93, 101, 220, 225, 235, 239, 240
  derogatory words for women who had relations with Germans 8, 35, 40, 97, 151
Nansen, Fridtjof 83
national community of memory, Denmark 46, 47
national identity
  debates about Eastern European war children 176
  and gender discourse in Denmark 35, 37, 42–4, 46
  post-civil war building of Spain 123, 129–31
  status of Norwegian war children 71, 72
National Socialist People's Welfare Organization 175, 214–15
nationality
  conflict in Netherlands over war children 158–9
  and discourse on Norwegian war children 93, 94, 95
  German policy in Protectorate of Bohemia and Moravia 196–8, 199
  and handling of paternity cases in Denmark 54
  issues for children after war 275
  in Nazi population policy 5, 6–7
  Vichy concerns about war children 143
Nazi concentration camps 4, 73, 79, 117, 123, 198
Nazi extermination policies 167, 168, 193, 194, 199, 239
Nazi Party 18, 83, 176, 191, 282

Nazis 3–4
  anthropological studies by 252–4
  eugenics 9–10, 277
  ideas and selection policies for Eastern
    Europe 167, 168–9, 171–3, 174, 177, 178
  policies on population of Bohemia/Moravia
    193–201, 202
  racial population policies 2, 4–5, 15–16, 17,
    19, 44, 62, 121, 143, 190
neo-Nazi movement 222
Netherlands 3, 23, 235, 270, 277, 280
  anti-German sentiment 156–7, 158, 160, 162
  early care for unmarried mothers 153–4
  failure of Lebensborn 18, 20
  Nazis' racial evaluation of population 5, 17,
    20, 155
  NSV involvement with mothers and war
    children 5, 18, 154–5
  problems with nationality of war children 6,
    158–9
  shearing of hair of women 'traitors' at
    liberation 4, 157–8, 162
Neues Volk 254
New York Times 191–2
NKVD (Soviet People's Commissariat for
  Internal Affairs) 171–2, 179
Nord Pas-de-Calais region 138
Nordentoft, Lieutenant 67
'Nordic blood' 16, 19, 54, 215
Nordic Family Rights Convention (1931) 79
Normandy 5, 19, 143
Norway 4, 59, 235, 270
  attitudes to and treatment of war children
    and mothers 7, 15, 25–6, 29–30, 31, 35,
    79, 100, 101–2, 104, 237
  deportation policy during war 73–4
  descendants of Wehrmacht soldiers 230, 231
  early citizenship legislation 72–3
  ideas and opinions about war children 10,
    27–8, 278–9
  Lebensborn policy 5, 15, 19–24, 28, 215,
    236
  marriages between women and German
    soldiers 23, 26–7, 140
  Nazis' racial evaluation of population 5, 17,
    19
  plans to deport war children 6, 24–5, 71–2,
    74–9, 81–6, 87–90, 88, 95, 233, 272
  post-occupation policy towards war children
    and mothers 25–7, 28–31, 71–2, 87–90,
    274, 278–9, 280, 281
  questionnaires for poor-relief county
    councils 79–80
  Wehrmachtskinder 236–8, 241
Norwegian mothers of war children
  British occupation policy 76–7, 82
  discourse of sexuality 93, 94–5, 103
  experiences of exclusion 97–8
  Norwegian authorities' policy 79, 88, 89
  psychiatric examination of 27–8, 274
  strategies of silence 103–4
  as subject to symbolic violence 102–3
  supported by German authorities 172

Norwegian Red Cross 28, 30, 31, 84, 279
Norwegian soldiers 234
Norwegian war children
  British occupation policy 76–7
  constructed as social problem 6, 10, 93–5
  Lebensborn organization 19–24, 29, 215,
    237
  medical disourse 93, 101–2
  numbers 62, 71
  plans for deportation of 6, 24–5, 71–2, 74–9,
    81–6, 87–90, 95, 233, 272, 278–9
  post-occupation policy 8–9, 10, 27–8,
    28–31, 87–90
  post-war social burdens on 105–7
  recent issues and publicity in Germany 230,
    231, 236–8, 239, 240–1, 241, 242
  reflections of interviewees on life
    experiences 95–105, 107–9
  repatriated from Germany 30, 82
  support of by German authorities 175, 177
  use of word *krigsbarn* 229, 231, 240
Norwegian women who had relations with
  Germans 19, 24, 25–6, 72, 97
Norwegian women who married Germans 7,
  26–7, 77, 81, 88
NS-Frauenschaft (National Socialist Women's
  League) 216
NSV (Nationalsozialistische Volkswohlfahrt)
  17, 18, 19, 175, 177, 216
  Netherlands 5, 18, 153, 154, 155, 156
Nygaardsvold, Johan 76, 77

Obra de Protección de Menores 122
Ødegård, Ørnulf 27–8
Odense 38, 58
Oftedal, Sven 78–9, 84
Øland, Arne 10, 239
Olmütz 192
Olsen, Kåre 5, 62, 234, 237, 277
Opitz, M. 279
orphanages
  Norway 21, 28, 29, 30, 96–7, 279
  post-war plight of war children 280
  Spanish children of Republicans 118, 125
orphans
  Australia's interest in 87
  refugees entering Denmark from Germany
    67
  Spanish decree for 'protection' of 123–4
  transportation of in post-war Europe 277–8
Oslo 20, 21, 26, 27, 76, 80, 82, 87
Østfold 26
'the other'/'others' 3, 11–12, 123, 240, 259

Paris 19, 126, 141, 143
Parsons, M. 271
paternity
  cases in Norway 23, 88, 89–90, 154–5
  discussions on Eastern European war
    children 176
  Dutch war children 154–5, 159, 160, 162
  French war children 145
  Lebensborn secrecy 218

nineteenth-century policies of Catholic
  countries 273
policies in Denmark 54, 55–6, 59–60
problem of Afro-German war children 279
silence and secrecy around Danish war
  children 53, 61, 63, 68
Patronato de Protección de la Mujer 122
personal testimonies and stories 1, 3, 11
  Danish fraternizing women 36, 42, 46–7,
    48
  Danish war children 63–8
  Dutch women who had relations with
    Germans 151, 154, 155–6, 160–1
  French war children 147–9
  German Lebensborn children 213, 215–25
  victims of Spanish Civil War 118–19
Pétain, Marshal Philippe 138
Picaper, Jean-Paul 242
Pius XII, Pope 115
Poland 4, 16, 60, 66, 73, 170, 173, 235
Polish communities in Czech territories 192
Polish Wehrmachtskinder 239–40
political prisoners
  in Franco's Spain 124–5, 126
  Norwegians deported as 73
politics
  German anthropological studies 259
  and new interest in child after World War I
    280
  significance of marriage and family 6–7
  use of children of the twentieth century 2,
    269
Pollock, Linda A. 272–3
population
  and eugenics 190
  Nazi racial policies 178, 191, 193–6, 199
  nineteenth-century policies on abandonment
    of children 273
Portugal 273
Prague 192, 193, 277
prisoners of war
  French 10, 145, 147
  Norwegians deported as 73
  Spanish Republicans 123, 125
prisons/prison camps
  internment of Norwegian fraternizing
    women 26, 29, 97
  Norwegians deported to German-Polish area
    73
  woman detainee in Madrid 125
Protectorate of Bohemia and Moravia
  children born before occupation 197
  establishment as part of Reich 192–3
  hereditary health care and 'treatment'
    199–201
  Nazi ethnic policy on nationality 196–8
  social selection and Germanization 193–6
  suffering of mixed families 201–2
  war children born of mixed marriages 190,
    195, 197, 198, 200–1, 201, 202
psychiatry/psychology
  and Catholic doctrine after Spanish Civil
    War 116–17, 119, 120, 122

and German anthropological studies 232,
  252
ideas and strategies in Franco's Spain 121,
  122–3, 126, 130
Norwegian ideas and politics 8–9, 27–8, 73,
  86, 95, 274, 282
post-war projects and theories 276–7, 281–2
see also child psychology
publications
  breaking silence of German war children
    230–1
  on French Wehrmachtskinder 239
  Sander and Johr's work on war children 238
  see also autobiography

race
  German anthropological studies 10, 250–60
  Nazis' ambiguous categories 169, 172,
    177–8
Racial and Settlement Main Office 194
racial anthropology 255
  in Franco's Spain 123
  Nazi commissioning of studies 252–3
racial evaluation, Nazi policy 5, 17–19, 21–2,
  154, 175
racial hygiene
  initiatives in Spain 116, 117, 121, 130
  Nazi policy 167, 178, 190, 199–200, 202
  traditional discourses 170, 178
racial inspection, Nazi policy in Eastern Europe
  170–1, 175
racial policy
  application to political enemy in Spain
    119
  early Norwegian exclusion law 73
  Nazis 2, 4–5, 6–7, 44, 167, 168, 170–1,
    172–6, 178, 191, 194, 200, 202
  role of Lebensborn 5, 15–16, 16–17, 18–19,
    21–2, 198, 214, 237
racism
  attitudes towards Afro-German children 233,
    241, 259
  campaign against African soldiers in
    Rhineland 249
  in early German anthropological studies
    250
  of societies on Allied side 2
radio programme 239
rape
  French children born as result of 146–7
  of imprisoned 'immoral' Spanish women
    124
  Nazi attitudes towards 5, 235
  of women in Berlin by Red Army soldiers
    233, 238
Red Army 233, 234, 238
Red Cross, see CICR; Danish Red Cross;
  German Red Cross; Norwegian Red Cross
Rediess, Wilhelm 19, 74, 75
refugees 6, 25, 49, 66, 67, 125–6
Rehoboth, Fischer's study 250–1, 253
Reich District Sudetenland 192
reparation, see compensation/reparation

repatriation
  Norwegians brought home from Germany
    81–3
  Spanish children of Republican parents 6,
    118, 126–8
Republicans (Spain)
  deaths resulting from Francoist repression
    116
  evacuation of children from Northern Spain
    125–6
  fate of exiles in France 126
  medical, social and religious discourses 116,
    119
  post-war repression of 120–1, 126, 130
  see also Spanish women linked with
    Republicans
Resistance movement
  Danish 36, 39, 40, 41, 61
  Nazi atrocities against 4, 198
  reprisals against collaborators 48, 157
Rhineland occupation (1918) 249–50, 252–4
Richards, Michael 6, 274
Robert Koch Institute 255
Rodenwaldt, Ernst 252
Rogaland 80
Roma 192
Romania 235
Rosenberg, Alfred 169, 171, 175
Rotterdam 154, 158, 159
Rüdin, Ernst 199
Russia 128, 177
  see also Soviet Union
Russian war children with German fathers 238,
    239
Russian Zone of Germany 30, 31, 232
  see also German Democratic Republic
    (GDR)

Sami ethnic minority 21, 73
Sander, Helke 233, 238, 239
Sarpsborg, Norway 26
Save the Children 84
Scharffenberg, Johan 9
Schmidt, Generalkommissar 154
Schmidt, General Rudolf 167, 174
Schmitz-Koester, Dorothee 11
Secours national 142–3
semantics, terms for groups of human beings
    229
Senegal 249
separation of mother and child 272–4, 276
sex 2, 8
sexism 3, 58
sexual relationships
  with German soldiers 46, 139–40, 152
  regulations of German army 173–4
  and relations of dominance 100
sexuality
  and perspectives on German guilt 239
  role in conflicts and collective identity
    processes 35
  social rules 240
  see also female sexuality

Sieg, Rudolf 254–5, 257–9, 259–60
silence surrounding war children 1, 10, 11, 68,
    103–5, 109–10, 220, 223, 240, 269, 278
  breaking of 11–12, 108–9, 118, 230, 242
  concealment of fathers 53, 63, 104, 218
  and guilt 46–7, 117
  kept by mothers 10, 36, 46, 151, 160–1, 218
Silesia 192
Simonsen, Eva 9
Simunek, Michal 5, 7
Slovakia 192
Smolensk 171
social anthropology 250, 252
Social Work (Norway) 77
Soldatenkinder (children of soldiers or soldier-
    children) 230, 278
Sollmann, Max 20
Southern Rhodesia 271
Southwest Africa, see Rehoboth
Soviet soldiers 233–4
Soviet Union 4, 16, 48, 60, 235
  exiled Spanish children 126, 128, 271
  German occupied territories 168, 170, 174
  Wehrmachtskinder 238–9
  see also former Soviet Union; Red Army
Spain
  Catholic eugenics 10, 117
  foundling hospitals 273
  Francoist policies on family 7, 119
  political attitudes and mental pathology 9
  post-civil war building of social order and
    national identity 116–17, 123, 129–31
  post-war repression of Republicans 120–2
  recent condemnation of Nationalist coup
    131
  repatriation of refugee children 6, 118,
    126–8
  see also Catholic Church
Spanish Civil War 1, 8, 9, 115–16, 129
  collective memories 118, 130
  refugees from 125–6, 271
Spanish Civil war children of Republican
    parents 1, 11, 122
  eugenics in treatment of 10, 122–3
  evacuation of during Civil War 125–6, 271
  interned in Spain 124–5
  kidnapping/repatriation of 6, 117–19, 123–4,
    126–8
  psychiatric and political discourse 119, 120,
    129
  rehabilitation 131
Spanish women linked with Republicans 8, 9,
    118–19, 120–1, 274
Der Spiegel 236–7
SS (Schutzstaffel)
  and Lebensborn 5, 15–16, 17, 18, 19, 24,
    28–9, 74, 220, 222
  and policies on Eastern European war
    children 170, 174–5, 175–6
  policies in Protectorate of Bohemia and
    Moravia 194
Stalheim orphanage, Voss 21, 28
Stalin, Joseph 191

Stalingrad 168
Starns, P. 271
Stasi 221, 237
Statstidende 60, 62
Steincke, K.K. 57
sterilization 76, 193, 254
stigma/stigmatization 8, 11, 90, 107, 109,
   151–2, 160, 160–1, 281
Stockholm 74, 76, 78–9, 84
Stuckart, Dr Wilhelm 170
Die Süddeutsche Zeitung 237
Sudeten-Germans 192, 201
Sweden 23, 25, 59, 73, 270, 271, 281
   Norwegian war children moved from
      Bremen to 29–30, 82
   plans to deport Norwegian war children to
      78, 79, 84–5, 279
Switzerland 86, 270, 271
symbolic violence 99–100, 101, 102–3, 104,
   107

taboo 104–5, 229, 234, 239, 240, 242
Telavåg 73
television documentary films 119, 179, 238
Terboven, Josef 19, 20
Thingstad, Else Vogt 77, 78
Thums, Karl 199, 200
The Times 127
Topsøe-Jensen, Hans 56, 59
Tribunales Titulares (Juvenile Courts) 122, 124,
   125
Trondheim 20, 21
Tunisia 249
'tyskertøser' 8, 35, 40, 44, 47, 75, 81, 88
Tysklandsbrigade (Independent Norwegian
   Brigade group) 234

Ukraine 171, 177, 178
Ukrainian war children 238
UNESCO 9, 275, 276, 277
Unger, Martha 143
United Nations 272, 275
United States of America (USA) 73, 161, 233,
   241, 271, 278
Unold, Colonel Georg von 177–8
USSR, *see* Soviet Union

Valkenburg 154
Velp 154
venereal disease 37, 43, 139, 234
Ventas, Madrid, women's prison 125
Vichy regime 7, 10, 138–9, 141, 142–3
Vienna 233, 277
Virgili, Fabrice 6, 11, 94, 239
Volksdeutsche Mittelstelle (Ethnic German
   Exchange Centre) 215
Voss, *see* Stalheim orphanage

Walloons 18
war

and demographic ideas 178
effects on children of twentieth century
   269
effects on gender relations 7
and metaphor of sex 8
and Nazi extermination programmes
   193
and significance of female body 44
traumatic experiences and repercussions 1, 4
war children 1–3, 35, 48–9, 278
   Nazis' concern for 17–19
   post-war concerns and policies 269–70,
      276–8, 280–2
   stigmatization 8, 11, 107, 109, 281
   as term applied in Spain 129
   words created to denote 229–36
War Criminal and High Treason process,
   Norway 71–2
war-handicapped children 270, 271–2, 274–5,
   277–8, 278, 280, 281
Warring, Anette 3, 61–2, 94
Wassmo, Herbjørg 236
Wehrmacht 235
   concern over Eastern European war children
      173, 175–6, 176
   in Denmark 18, 37, 40, 61
   in France 139, 141, 242
   in Netherlands 154, 155
   in Norway 62, 74, 231
   relationships with women in Poland 239–40
Wehrmachtskinder (children of the Wehrmacht)
   6, 230, 235–6, 242
   recent attention in German media 236–40,
      241
Weimar Republic 178
welfare
   Catholic doctrine and policy in Spain
      116–17, 120
   European policies in 1930s 191
   institutions in Francoist Spain 124, 126
   see also child welfare
Welzer, Harald 230
Wesch, Hans-Ullrich 221
West Germany, *see* Federal Republic of
   Germany
Westwald (Lebensborn), Lamorlaye 143–4
Winnicott, David 281
Wokurek, Wilfried 200
women, *see* female body; female sexuality
women who had relations with German soldiers
   2, 8
women's movement, Norway 73, 81, 89
World Health Organization (WHO) 274
World War I 75, 139, 147–8, 249, 251, 273,
   278, 280

Yugoslavia 4, 235

Die Zeit 236
Zurich, conference on war children (1945) 276